The Official Dick Van Dyke Show Book

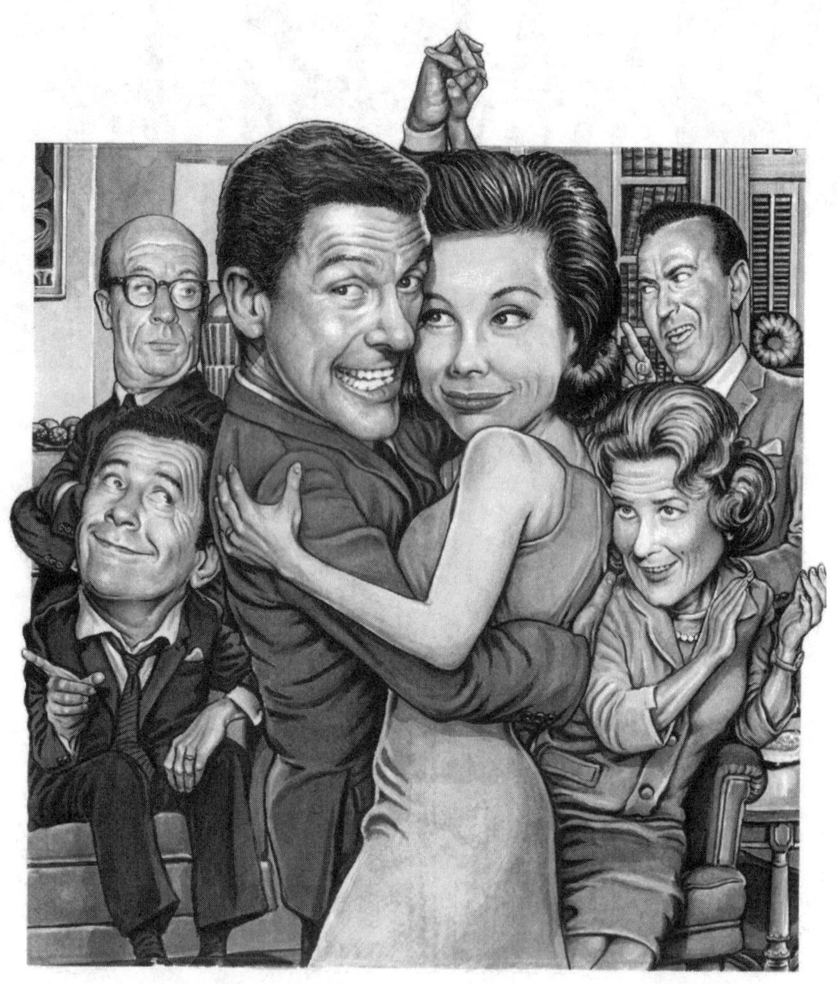

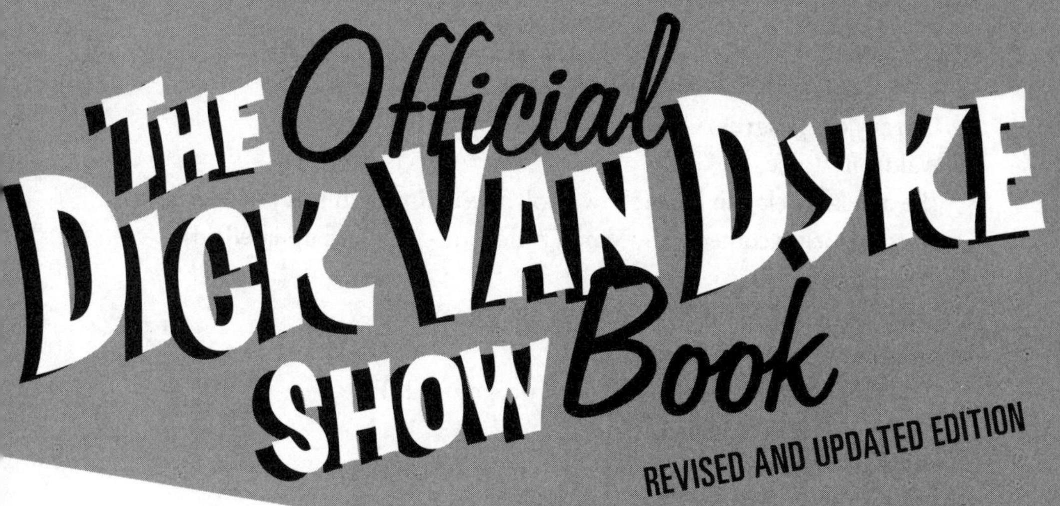

THE DEFINITIVE HISTORY OF TELEVISION'S MOST ENDURING COMEDY

VINCE WALDRON

An A Cappella Book

Library of Congress Cataloging-in-Publication Data
Waldron, Vince.
The official Dick Van Dyke show book : the definitive history of television's most enduring comedy / by Vince Waldron.—Rev. and updated ed.
p. cm.
Includes bibliographical references and index.
ISBN 978-1-56976-839-6 (pbk.)
1. Dick Van Dyke show (Television program) I. Title.
PN1992.77.D5W35 2011
791.45—dc22
2011016799

Cover and interior design: Visible Logic, Inc.

This comprehensively updated edition first published in 2011 by
Chicago Review Press, Incorporated
814 North Franklin Street
Chicago, Illinois 60610
ISBN 978-1-56976-839-6
Printed in the United States of America
5 4 3 2 1

ALSO BY VINCE WALDRON

Classic Sitcoms: A Celebration of the Best in Prime-Time Comedy

Be My Baby: How I Survived Mascara, Miniskirts, and Madness, or My Life as a Fabulous Ronette (with Ronnie Spector)

This book is dedicated to my brother, Robert, whose bright idea it was to write about *The Dick Van Dyke Show* in the first place.

CONTENTS

FOREWORD
By Dan Castellaneta

You may be asking yourself why they got the guy who plays Homer Simpson, maybe the dumbest dad in sitcom history, to write the foreword to a book about a show in which Dick Van Dyke played the smartest, best-dressed, coolest TV dad ever. The answer is simple: if it hadn't been for Dick Van Dyke and the show that brought him into your living room, there would never have been a Homer Simpson to make you wonder why they got the guy who plays him to write this foreword in the first place.

Allow me to explain. If there hadn't been a *Dick Van Dyke Show*, you would probably never have heard of Mary Tyler Moore, and James L. Brooks would never have produced a TV show for her in the seventies, in which case he probably wouldn't have hung around Hollywood long enough to hire Matt Groening to create *The Simpsons*, or me to act in it. So, in the same way a butterfly flapping its wings can create a tsunami, if it hadn't been for *The Dick Van Dyke Show*, I might be setting the type for this foreword instead of writing it, and my friend Vince Waldron would have to find some other sucker to write the opening for his book about a TV show that doesn't exist. And Bedford Falls would be called Pottersville. But only if Marty McFly had never been born. And . . . D'oh! I'm getting my butterfly effects all mixed up!

Luckily, *The Dick Van Dyke Show* does exist. I know this because I was about the same age as Ritchie Petrie when it went off the air in 1966—and even *then* I knew it was the best thing on TV. Months after the show disappeared from Wednesday nights, I'd stand in front of my parents' TV set and flip through all the channels, figuring that if I turned the dial long enough, I would eventually find a TV show good enough to make me forget Rob and Laura and Buddy and Sally—which I never did. Fortunately, I grew up in Chicago, where *The Dick Van Dyke Show* continues to be as popular as deep-dish pizza. So I was able to watch the show in reruns on Channel 9 almost every day of my life, or at least until I finally grew up and found my way to Second City, where I was determined to make other people laugh as hard as I'd laughed at *The Dick Van Dyke Show*.

At Second City, I discovered others who shared my passion for *The Dick Van Dyke Show*. One of them was Vince Waldron, who would one day write this book. Back then, Vince was, like me, a lowly member of Second City's touring company. Sometimes after a show, a bunch of us would gather at Vince's apartment, where we'd make little pizzas out of French bread, spaghetti sauce, and whatever kind of cheese we found in his refrigerator, and stay up till dawn watching grainy videos of all the great old sitcoms: *Leave It to Beaver*, *The Andy Griffith Show*, and everybody's favorite, *The Dick Van Dyke Show*.

Actually, I don't even think of *The Dick Van Dyke Show* as a single TV show but a bunch of great shows, all packed into one neat package. It was as good a sitcom as has ever been made, but it was also a great musical-variety show, a really funny sketch show—walnuts, anyone?—and a character comedy that could be surprisingly poignant. In a single half hour, *The Dick Van Dyke Show* managed to incorporate just about every style of entertainment that TV had to offer. And the common thread holding it all together was the extraordinary talent of Dick Van Dyke, who could act, sing, dance, and do a mean pratfall over an ottoman.

The Dick Van Dyke Show is still my all-time favorite sitcom. Only now when I watch it, I make sure I have a copy of this book nearby, and you should, too. Vince really brings the show, and the people who made it, to life. And his insights into what makes this show a classic are just as interesting today as when he and I used to stay up into the wee hours analyzing *The Dick Van Dyke Show* when we were both starting out back in Chicago.

Now, if Vince could just figure out how to include a slice of homemade French bread pizza with every copy, this book would be perfect.

Mmmm . . . !

INTRODUCTION
By Dick Van Dyke

It's a little hard to believe it's been half a century since we filmed the first episode of *The Dick Van Dyke Show*. After all these years, people still ask me what made our show so special—what was that secret ingredient in our success? I always answer that our show represented a perfect marriage of players and playwright. We had that great, great cast; and Carl Reiner understood exactly how to write to every one of our strengths.

Unlike a lot of writers, Carl never wrote a character and expected the actor to come in and play it as written. Carl is a student of human nature—before he'd write a script, he'd have his eye on us. He'd watch us on the set; he'd listen to us as we talked. Then he'd filter those observations through his own unique comic genius, and out would come one of those terrific scripts he wrote for the show. I think that's why, with Carl's scripts, the words always seemed to fit you so perfectly that you almost didn't have to memorize them. *That*'s good writing.

I don't suppose it hurt that we had actors like Morey Amsterdam, Rose Marie, and Mary Tyler Moore around to speak Carl's lines once he'd written them. None of us had ever met before that first day of rehearsal, but after Carl and Sheldon Leonard brought us all together for that very first show, it really was love at first sight. Gosh, they were just so good—all of them. Morey, who walked around with a Rolodex of jokes in his brain; Rosie, with her flawless sense of timing; and, of course, Mary, who had absolutely no background in comedy when she came to us—a serious young actress who was still in her early twenties. But boy did she learn fast! In no time at all, Mary was holding her own with old pros like Rosie and Morey and Richard Deacon.

And it didn't take me very long to figure out how good I had it on that series, either. After all, I wasn't a kid when we started—I'd already been knocking around the business for about fifteen years. So I was acutely aware, every minute that I was on that show, that it just didn't get any better than that. We had so much fun—we had so much latitude to be creative—that I knew even then that things would never get any better. And, as a matter of fact, they didn't!

I suppose the funniest part of it all is that if someone had walked onto our set in 1964 and told us that people would someday be writing entire books about our show, we would've had a good laugh. And then we would've very politely shown them the door! Who would have thought our show would still be around fifty years later? We all figured we had an entertaining series, but I can tell you, nobody thought in terms of posterity back then. We were so busy working every day for the five years our show was in production that I don't think any of us had any real idea of the impression we were making outside of that studio.

It reminds me of something that the great movie comedian Stan Laurel told me not long after I first came out to California. Stan must've been in his late sixties then, and I remember asking him what it had been like making all those classic Laurel and Hardy comedies. "But Dickie," he said—that's what he called me, Dickie—"we had no idea how successful those old films would be while we were making them." He and Ollie were so busy working in the confines of the studio every day, he told me, that they just lost touch with the outside world. It wasn't until much, much later that Laurel and Hardy realized what a deep and lasting effect their comedies had had on the entire world. And then Stan said something I'll never forget. "The nicest thing," he told me, "is knowing that you were part of something that has stood the test of time."

I guess, after fifty years of having people come up and tell me how much our show has meant to them, I think I finally understand what Stan meant. Looking back now on those five magical years I spent in the company of that wonderful group of people, I must say I agree with Stan completely. It is nice to know that you were a part of something that has stood the test of time.

Very nice.

Prologue

INAUGURATION DAY

By six o'clock on the evening of January 20, 1961, the line of people waiting outside Hollywood's Desilu Cahuenga studios was already more than two hundred strong. At a quarter past the hour, a phalanx of fresh-scrubbed CBS network pages began to herd the curious crowd through the sturdy metal doors that provided direct access from a quiet Hollywood side street called Lillian Way onto the lot's soundstage 5, where, in just under an hour, the pilot episode of a new comedy called *The Dick Van Dyke Show* was about go before the cameras for the very first time.

It would be a momentous night. And yet, there's little reason to believe that anyone in that opening-night crowd had the slightest inkling they were about to witness television history. As hard as it might be to conceive of today, few of the tourists, idle shoppers, and other curiosity-seekers who made up most of *The Dick Van Dyke Show*'s first-night audience had ever heard of the star, whose fame at that time had yet to travel much beyond the East Coast, where he'd been wowing Broadway audiences for the previous nine months as the star of *Bye Bye Birdie*. But if Dick Van Dyke seemed an obscure choice to headline a new TV series, it's a cinch that even fewer of those assembled to watch the filming of the show's pilot episode recognized the actress who would be playing Van Dyke's wife that night, a slightly nervous twenty-four-year-old starlet named Mary Tyler Moore.

Not that many of those in the house that night were overly concerned about the identity of the show's stars; a far more pressing topic of conversation in the moments before the filming began was almost certainly the inauguration of John F. Kennedy, who'd taken the oath of office as the nation's thirty-fifth president just a few hours earlier in Washington, DC. Though he'd been in office less than a day, political pundits on both coasts were already predicting that Kennedy's arrival would mark the dawn of a new era in American politics and culture. And yet, it's doubtful that even the most prescient member of the show's opening-night crowd could have predicted that *The Dick Van Dyke Show* itself would be viewed by future generations as a primary icon of its age—one of a handful of cultural artifacts that would come to define the start of the turbulent decade of the sixties.

By 6:25 P.M., the efficient CBS pages had already seated most of the crowd in a dozen or so rows of the stadium-style bleachers that lined one wall of the soundstage. A few feet in front of the stands were parked three mammoth 35mm movie cameras, a trio of wheeled behemoths that sat in drooped repose in the narrow limbo that separated the audience from the stage's main playing area. But while they might have appeared cumbersome at first glance, under the stewardship of the show's director of photography, Robert De Grasse, and his able camera coordinator, James Niver, those three cameras would soon prove quite nimble in their ability to chronicle the evening's comic action with an almost surgical precision. Beyond the cameras lay the stage itself, which was, for the time being, masked from the audience's gaze by a matched set of four long wooden flats that had been set end-to-end at the foot of the stage. This makeshift curtain, such as it was, was sufficient to provide the show's stagehands, prop assistants, makeup artists, carpenters, and gaffers with a semblance of privacy as they prepared the stage for the filming that lay ahead.

As was customary for the various live shows that were filmed on the nine soundstages at Desilu Cahuenga, *The Dick Van Dyke Show* pilot would be played on only four standing sets. In this case, those four sets included a convincing replica of a cluttered writers' office; the spacious living room of Alan Brady's penthouse apartment; a full kitchen; and a small boy's bedroom. Because the *Van Dyke Show* was at that point a pilot film for an as-yet-unscheduled series, the evening's standing sets were constructed in a temporary fashion, using lumber, set pieces, and even a few props that had been borrowed from *The Danny Thomas Show*, which was stage 5's usual tenant. At the conclusion of that evening's shoot, it had been arranged that the show's four makeshift sets would be quickly dismantled and their component pieces put into storage or recycled back to *The Danny Thomas Show*, which was scheduled to return to production on stage 5 the following Monday morning. This rigidly efficient—and highly economical—production arrangement was the brainchild of *The Danny Thomas Show*'s producer-director, Sheldon Leonard, who would serve as executive producer on *The Dick Van Dyke Show* pilot and the series it would eventually spawn.

At 6:30 P.M., eight or nine members of a small orchestral combo ambled up and took their places behind a bandstand that had been set up at the far end of the soundstage. There, under the direction of Earle Hagen, the studio's resident composer and conductor, the band struck up the first in an eclectic repertoire of dance numbers and hit-parade selections that had been specially chosen to boost the studio audience's energy level in the last few minutes before show time. Meanwhile, onstage, executive producer Sheldon Leonard—who would also direct the *Van Dyke Show* pilot—huddled for one last powwow with his camera and lighting technicians before the cameras were moved into their starting formation. Farther behind the scenes, makeup man Lee Greenway and his assistants were busy dabbing Mary Tyler Moore, Rose Marie, Morey Amsterdam, and the other members of the show's cast with one last touchup of the heavy reddish pancake makeup that was used to make the performers' skin tones appear normal under the harsh lights that were required in the days of black-and-white television broadcasts. The makeup artists paid particular attention to Dick Van Dyke, who would need a heavier-than-normal application of pancake that evening to cover a cold sore that had erupted on the star's upper lip earlier in the week—the most visible manifestation of the actor's opening-night jitters.

At a few minutes past 7:00, the band ended its final number with a stirring crescendo, and Leonard introduced the show's producer, Carl Reiner, who had volunteered to deliver a few informal opening remarks before the filming began. Reiner's entrance was greeted by a generous round of applause from the audience, many of whom recognized the popular character actor from his long stint as one of Sid Caesar's second bananas on *Your Show of Shows* and other variety shows of the 1950s. As the applause subsided, Reiner spoke to the crowd from a spot at the foot of the bleachers, a vantage point from which he would continue to regale the audience with spontaneous jokes and off-the-cuff patter throughout the evening. The ebullient producer began his remarks by identifying himself as the show's writer and creator, which, he explained, meant that he could—and should—be held fully responsible for anything that might go wrong that night. However, he cautioned, if the audience ended up having a good time, they were instructed to give due credit to his utterly resourceful director and executive producer, Sheldon Leonard, as well as the members of his gifted acting company, who were then introduced, one by one.

Richard Deacon. Larry Mathews. Mary Tyler Moore. Morey Amsterdam. Rose Marie. And, of course, Dick Van Dyke. As the players were introduced, each of them stepped out onto the stage for the briefest of curtain calls before they vanished back behind the scenes to prepare for their initial entrances. After the curtain calls, Reiner tossed a few more wisecracks to the audience as the camera operators wheeled their rigs into place for the first shot of the night. Meanwhile, behind the flimsy plywood partitions that continued to mask the stage from the audience's sightline, assistant director Jay Sandrich cued Mary Tyler Moore to take her place on the show's first set, a convincing mockup of a modern suburban kitchen, complete with a range and a Formica-covered counter. An instant later, Sandrich ducked behind the set to make sure that five-year-old Larry Mathews was standing on his own backstage mark, ready to make his entrance a few lines into the opening scene.

Back on the set, Mary Tyler Moore found herself struggling briefly to get a solid fingerhold on a slippery potato—the so-called practical prop that her character was supposed to be peeling at the top of the show. After a couple of false starts, the actress finally got her potato well in hand, and Sandrich issued a signal to director Leonard that all was well and ready to go on the stage. Suddenly, the long wooden flats at the foot of the stage were pushed aside, and the studio audience got their first glimpse of the kitchen of Rob, Laura, and Ritchie Petrie of New Rochelle, New York, where, at that precise moment, a somewhat jumpy young actress stood behind the Formica counter, waiting breathlessly for her impending moment of truth.

From behind the cameras, character-actor-turned-television-producer/director Sheldon Leonard barked out a few final commands to his crew in a booming baritone that carried easily to the last row of the bleachers, ending with the single word that would instantly transform the chaos around him into a few privileged moments of magic.

"Action!"

With that command, a sudden and startling metamorphosis took place on the stage, where the anxious young actress who'd been standing there not two minutes earlier vanished; in her place, the crowd saw only a confident suburban housewife behind the counter of a modern suburban kitchen, humming softly to herself as she deftly peeled a potato.

It was showtime.

For the next ninety minutes, Dick Van Dyke, Mary Tyler Moore, Rose Marie, Morey Amsterdam, Larry Mathews, Richard Deacon, and the rest of the cast and crew would perform their chores with effort that would be invisible to the studio audience, who were completely charmed from the show's opening moment. Still, it's unlikely anyone in the thoroughly delighted crowd was half as pleased by the evening's progress as Carl Reiner himself, who watched the show unfold from a discreet vantage point just beyond the harsh glare of the arc lamps that bore down on the stage.

To the uninitiated, Reiner's decision to remain on the sidelines throughout much of the evening might have seemed an odd choice, especially considering the character actor's well-established reputation as a scene stealer par excellence on *Your Show of Shows*. But, though he was happy to surrender the spotlight to Dick Van Dyke and the rest of his merry band of players on that night, there could be little doubt among those in the know that the triumphant evening belonged to Carl Reiner—regardless of where he happened to be standing while the cameras were rolling.

1

ONE MAN'S REALITY

"Any good show that you see on television is going to reflect one person's reality," says Carl Reiner, whose work as writer, producer, and creative conscience of *The Dick Van Dyke Show* certainly bears proof of his premise. If anything, Reiner's axiom seems like an understatement when applied to *The Dick Van Dyke Show*, a series that reflected the real-life events of its creator's life so closely that it plays like a comic chronicle of his early years in show business. But *The Dick Van Dyke Show* was hardly Carl Reiner's first attempt to refine the details of his life into comic fodder for his work; almost four years earlier the writer had published *Enter Laughing*, a short comic novel that provided an only slightly fictionalized look at his early days as an actor. Is it any wonder, then, that the events depicted in *The Dick Van Dyke Show* pick up almost precisely where the narrative thread in *Enter Laughing* leaves off?

It probably didn't hurt that the details of Reiner's childhood read like the treatment of some corny old Hollywood showbiz saga. Born on March 20, 1922, to a Bronx watchmaker named Irving Reiner and his wife Bessie, Carl Reiner was raised on the streets of New York at the very height of the Great Depression. According to a rather colorful account of those years that appeared in Reiner's late-fifties studio biography, the man who would grow up to create one of the most enduring popular entertainments of his era had almost no interest in show business as a child. In those days, according to the studio bio, Reiner dreamed only of a career in major league baseball, a fantasy that had been fueled by a few thousand games of stickball played on the streets of the Bronx. "I was what we called a 'three-sewer hitter,'" Reiner told his publicist in 1959. "I could belt that ball three sewer covers away—which is quite an accomplishment when you're playing ball on a Bronx street."[1]

It wasn't until he was sixteen, and his parents began urging him to find a trade, that Reiner first glimpsed that his horizons might be in show business. The teenager had already landed a job as an assistant machinist in a shop that repaired sewing machines for New York's then-thriving millinery trade when his older brother Charlie urged him to look into a drama course that was being sponsored by the federal Works Progress Administration program. Once enrolled, the younger Reiner found himself bitten by the theatrical bug, and it wasn't long before he abandoned his plan to enter the machinist's trade and embarked on a career in the theater.

Once he'd committed to the actor's life, Reiner trod a well-worn path to stardom that began with bit parts and summer stock. An extended apprenticeship at New York's Gilmore Theatre led to a few seasons of summer stock in Rochester, New York, where the young actor landed roles in dozens of venerable melodramas and light comedies of the era, including a lead role in a stock production of Philip Barry's *The Philadelphia Story*. Not long after that, he embarked on a ten-week tour with a traveling Shakespeare troupe, where the fledgling thespian got his first—and last—taste of the classics.

"I was never comfortable as a serious actor," Reiner recalled some years later. "I felt silly cavorting about in pink tights, masquerading as a Danish king."[2] And so, in the early 1940s, Reiner made his way to the Catskills, where he found more suitable employment as a sketch comedian at a Borscht Belt resort. "I fell right into the work," he would explain. "Although I hadn't been able to accept myself—a watchmaker's son from the Bronx—as a king of Denmark, I was perfectly at ease kidding kings and generals."[3] It was a quality that producer Max Liebman would admire when he later cast the young comic to play Sid Caesar's foil on *Your Show of Shows*. "He used to call that sort of performance 'stinky acting,'" Reiner recalled. "It's good bad acting. You make fun of the character and yourself at the same time."[4]

It was also during that eventful stint in the Catskills that Carl Reiner met the woman with whom he would share his life, a pretty young scenery painter named Estelle Lebost. The pair were brought together by the resort's set designer, who carefully took the young actor aside for a few words of sage advice shortly before the introductions were made. "He told me, 'Be nice to her,'" says Reiner. It was a request with which the actor would have little difficulty complying. "I took her to dinner. I took her dancing. I took her to the theater. I asked her to marry me."[5]

The couple were finally wed about a year later, in 1943, a few months after Reiner had been recruited for his most important engagement yet—an extended tour with Uncle Sam. Drafted into the armed services shortly after the outbreak of World War II, Reiner found himself stationed at Camp Crowder, near Joplin, Missouri, the real-life military installation that would also serve as the setting for some of Rob Petrie's more memorable exploits some twenty years later. Reiner was eventually assigned to a base in Hawaii, where he continued to hone his comic skills in a series of army revues designed to boost the sagging morale of GIs stationed in the South Pacific. It was there, Reiner would later recall, that he discovered he had an uncanny knack for comic improvisation. "I created my own theater by standing in front of a microphone in rec halls, telling stories and doing Hitler routines," Reiner would write.[6]

During World War II, Reiner did his bit to boost morale as a performer in the army's Special Services branch. *Courtesy: Carl Reiner*

"When I got out, I discovered that comedians were paid four times as much as actors and worked more often—so I gravitated toward comedy."

After the war, the actor and his bride made their way to New York City, where Reiner—at the ripe old age of twenty-three—landed the lead in the national touring company production of *Call Me Mister*, a role he would eventually assume in the Broadway production. That prestigious booking led to a steady stream of stage and TV assignments throughout the late forties, including work as a sketch comedian on an early TV variety series called *The Fifty-Fourth Street Revue*, as well as a prominent role in the Broadway musical comedy revue *Alive and Kicking*. It was in that show that Reiner first caught the eye of Max Liebman, the impresario who would revolutionalize television comedy in 1950 when he married Broadway revue and Borscht Belt musical comedy styles in a prime-time variety series called, appropriately enough, *Your Show of Shows*.

There's no question that Max Leibman's recruitment of Carl Reiner to join the cast of *Your Show of Shows* in 1950 represented a major turning point in the young actor's career. Almost immediately upon its premiere broadcast, on February 25, 1950, the innovative ninety-minute variety show became an institution on NBC, the network that aired the series live from New York each Saturday night. And though the versatile Sid Caesar and his rubber-faced costar Imogene Coca were the show's undisputed headliners, *Your Show of Shows* provided Reiner and his

Howard Morris, Sid Caesar, Imogene Coca, and Carl Reiner in *Your Show of Shows*, the groundbreaking series that would provide Reiner with comic fodder for five seasons of *Dick Van Dyke Show* storylines. *Courtesy: Carl Reiner*

fellow second banana Howard Morris ample opportunity to make significant comic contributions in a format that embraced the disparate styles of silent comedy, rollicking musical numbers, and exacting social parody with equal fervor. In fact, the show's brash, rapid-fire, musical comedy approach seemed ideally suited to the talents of Reiner, who would go on to lend Sid Caesar comic support through nine television seasons—five years of *Your Show of Shows* and four additional seasons on a pair of variety shows that came in its wake, *Sid Caesar Invites You* and *Caesar's Hour*, for which Reiner would earn two successive Emmy Awards as a supporting actor, in 1957 and 1958.*

DESPITE THE ACCLAIM Reiner received for his work as a performer on *Your Show of Shows*, it wasn't long before he began to grow impatient with his limited role as a supporting actor on the show. "Even though I acted once a week on Saturday and rehearsed all week," Reiner would later complain, "I didn't feel like an actor." [7] Finally, to break the monotony of his long rehearsals as a performer, Reiner cautiously poked his head into the show's noisy writers' room, where the roster on any given day might include Mel Brooks, Lucille Kallen, Mel Tolkin, Tony Webster, and Neil Simon and his brother Danny. Naturally, with some of the sharpest comic minds in America stuck in a single room for as many as eight or ten hours a day, things were rarely dull in the writers' office. Within a matter of weeks, Reiner himself became a fixture at the show's daily writing sessions, where his keen wit and gregarious nature soon earned him the respect of the show's writers. Before long, Carl Reiner found himself functioning as an active participant in the writing of the show—though it was clearly understood that his contributions were to be made strictly without attribution.

"I was a writer without portfolio," recalls Reiner. "I was in on all the sessions, and I contributed as a writer. But I didn't get my name in the credits, because actors didn't do that in those days. The writers were very solicitous of their credits." And with good reason, as he explains. "I didn't

* Though *Your Show of Shows* actually broadcast its final episode on June 5, 1954, Carl Reiner would rejoin Sid Caesar the following September on *Caesar's Hour*, an NBC variety series that borrowed heavily from the *Show of Shows* format, though without the support of Imogene Coca, who had by that time gone her separate way. A few months after *Caesar's Hour* completed its three-year run on May 25, 1957, Reiner would be reunited with Caesar in the cast of *Sid Caesar Invites You*, a half-hour version of the star's variety show that ran on ABC for a scant four months in early 1958.

blame them, because as actors, we got all the credit anyway. Everybody thought we made the lines up." As Reiner soon discovered, this tendency—coupled with the writers' own naturally aggressive personalities—often made for an intensely competitive environment in the writers' room. "If you got your joke in—fine," says Reiner. "But you knew somebody was always gonna try to improve it."

Reiner recalls a particularly vexing session at which one of the show's writers managed to blurt out no more than the first three words of a comic premise before his idea was seized upon by his colleagues and offered up for extended comic debate. "The guy started out saying, 'So, it's Thursday—'" recalls Reiner. But before the hapless scribe could stammer out the rest of his sentence, one of the other writers had already decided that the idea was ripe for improvement. "Somebody else said, 'Not Thursday—make it Friday! Friday's funnier.'" Of course, the kibitzing didn't stop there. "Then somebody else says, 'Why not make it a Saturday? Isn't Saturday funnier?'" And, as Reiner quickly discovered, as a lowly performer he was at a decided disadvantage in these debates. "I once suggested a fair joke, but not a great one," he recalls of one such meeting, "and Mel Tolkin said, 'What do you know, you're nothing but a friggin' actor!'"

Though his colleagues' frequent putdowns were invariably offered as good-natured jibes, Reiner couldn't help but take their barbed references to his scant writerly credentials as a challenge. And it was a challenge he was determined to meet head-on. After a time, whenever things grew heated in the writers' room, Reiner would simply slip out and retire to a vacant office down the hall—a quiet sanctuary that just happened to come equipped with an old manual typewriter. And it was there, in the relative solitude of an empty office, that the novice scribe began to practice his craft in earnest. "I'd learned to type on a teletype in the army," Reiner explains, "so I used to go to that office, just to see if I could still type. And I found out that I could."

In no time at all, Reiner had graduated from simple typing exercises to composing short humorous pieces for his own amusement. For his earliest comic exercises, Reiner would contrive the cast, characters, and setting for short comic plays that he had absolutely no intention of ever writing. "I would write a little one-page cast of characters for a play," he recalls. "That's all. Just the cast of characters—what they do, where the play is set. A lot

Carl Reiner in a publicity pose taken in the mid-1950s, when he was still best known to TV audiences as the second banana on *Your Show of Shows*. *Courtesy: Carl Reiner*

of them were satires of some play that already existed." Then, having created the characters and setting for an imaginary play of his own design, Reiner would simply move on to the next. "You knew from the description alone that you were going to see a crazy play," he explains. "That was all you needed. I thought they were hilarious. I wrote dozens of them. I think I might still have them someplace."

From those humble beginnings Reiner's literary career began to bloom. As his confidence grew, the writer soon moved from one-page play descriptions to three-page character studies. "Vignettes, really," as he would later describe them. From there, it was just a matter of time before he started composing full-blown short stories. One of the most memorable of those was "Fifteen Arthur Barringtons," a tale that concerned the anxieties of a young actor named Arthur Barrington who finds himself sitting at a casting call with fourteen other young actors of his exact age, weight, and physical type, any one of whom could just as easily be he. Through an odd chain of coincidence, that story wound up in the hands of a Simon & Schuster editor named Jack Goodman, who suggested that the fledgling writer develop the piece into a longer and more ambitious work about the struggles a young actor faces in the early years of his career.

But, according to Reiner, the editor's pep talk had not been the only factor that spurred him to develop his latent literary ambitions. Far more compelling was an epiphany that struck him in the late spring of 1957, as he watched his two kids—Robbie, who was then ten, and Annie, who was eight—frolic in the sand outside the family's Fire Island summer home.

"The kids were getting older," he explains, "and all of a sudden they were big enough to run around by themselves. So one day I said, 'Gee, I'm thirty-five years old. I'd better do something with my life.'" Though no one could have described Carl Reiner as lazy—he'd just completed three seasons in the cast of *Caesar's Hour*—he nonetheless felt trapped by an overwhelming sense of creative fatigue. It was a trap from which he could see only one means of escape. "It took five years of going to Fire Island and doing nothing but sifting sand until I finally wrote a novel."

BY THE MIDDLE of August 1957, Reiner had completed *Enter Laughing*, his fictional memoir of one David Kokolovitz, a struggling actor trying to break into show business despite his family's insistence that he continue to pursue a trade in the millinery business.* Though the book draws liberally from the writer's own early show business experiences, Reiner prefaced the work with a somewhat tongue-in-cheek disclaimer. "David Kokolovitz is a fictitious character," the author writes in the book's introduction. "I strongly believe I am not."[8]

Interestingly, Reiner originally planned *Enter Laughing* as a far more encompassing work. "I intended to record the life of a Bronx-born person like myself," the writer told a reporter in 1964,[9] "from his entry into the theater at the age of 17 to his mature years as an actor and writer and husband and father." But, Reiner notes, once he'd completed 250 typewritten pages and discovered that he'd barely covered a single year in his young protagonist's life, he "decided it was time to stop."[10] Even so, the economical writer had no intention of letting the rest of his vast backlog of personal history go to waste. And so, when he began work on a new autobiographical work the following summer, Reiner instinctively picked up his story almost exactly where he'd left off at the end of *Enter Laughing*. For the television scripts that would eventually be filmed as *The Dick Van Dyke Show*, the writer chose to draw inspiration from his more recent real-life experiences, as he'd earlier expressed it, "as an actor and writer and husband and father."[11] Naturally, for this new and more

* In 1963, *Enter Laughing* would be adapted for the Broadway stage by playwright Joseph Stein, who had contributed scripts to *Caesar's Hour*. The Broadway show, which starred Alan Arkin, would eventually inspire a 1967 film of the same title, which featured Reni Santoni in the leading role and was directed by Reiner from his own screenplay, cowritten with Stein.

The series may have borne the name of its leading man, but to those in the know, there was little doubt that Carl Reiner was *The Dick Van Dyke Show*'s real star. Pictured with the producer (seated) on the night they filmed the show's pilot are Dick Van Dyke, Mary Tyler Moore, Sheldon Leonard, Rose Marie, Morey Amsterdam, and associate producer Ronald Jacobs.

comprehensive work, Reiner would need an all-new protagonist. And so it was, in the summer of 1958, that Carl Reiner bid a fond farewell to David Kokolovitz and welcomed the arrival of the character who would serve as the writer's fictional alter ego for the next eight years.

His name was Robert Petrie.

2

SIFTING THROUGH SAND

When Sid Caesar's third variety series of the 1950s was canceled in May of 1958, Carl Reiner found himself out of work for the first time in nine years. But despite facing his first bout of unemployment since the end of World War II, Reiner seemed to be taking it well. And why wouldn't he? With his first novel due to hit the bookstores later that year, the optimistic performer figured he could always devote his energies to writing. Indeed, if nothing better came along, Reiner was fully prepared to spend his summer on Fire Island writing a follow-up novel to *Enter Laughing*. And had it not been for the timely intervention of his agent from the William Morris office, that's exactly what Reiner would have done.

But Harry Kalcheim had other ideas.

Writing books might make a wonderful summer pastime, the agent told his client, but it wouldn't put food on the table the way performing did. No, Kalcheim explained, writing books was not the answer. Instead, the agent consulted his crystal ball, and what he saw suggested only one possible direction for Reiner in 1958: they would have to find the actor a situation comedy to star in.

Reiner recognized his agent's point. "Variety shows were almost extinct," he observes, "so I knew I had to find something else." There was nothing stopping the former Broadway star from going back to the stage. In fact, it was around this time that Reiner's old friend Neil Simon offered the actor a leading role in the playwright's first Broadway play, *Come Blow Your Horn*. But despite Reiner's respect for his old *Show of Shows* crony, the actor had little interest in making a return trip to the Great White Way. "I'd been on Broadway," says Reiner, "and I didn't want to go back. Once you're in television, there's an everyday excitement to the work that's not there on Broadway, where you have to do the same thing three hundred and sixty-five days a year."

Of course, the greatest advantage to acting in a situation comedy, as Kalcheim was only too pleased to point out, was that it was a job in which a seasoned performer like Reiner could make a killing. To demonstrate, the agent had only to cite the careers of Jackie Gleason, Lucille Ball, and Danny Thomas, three situation-comedy headliners who, like Reiner, had all been established variety performers before they made the switch to situation comedy. And, as the agent explained, all of them wound up getting very rich in the process. There was certainly no reason why, at the age of thirty-six, Reiner couldn't make an equally successful transition to the half-hour form. All he

Howard Morris mugs with Carl Reiner, his fellow second banana on *Your Show of Shows*. *Courtesy: Carl Reiner*

had to do, Kalcheim suggested, was find a situation comedy that was reasonably well suited to his particular talents. "Is that all?" Reiner remarked. "Well, how hard could that be?"

The answer would become painfully obvious as soon as Reiner opened the first script in the stack of proposed situation comedies his agent sent for his approval. To the actor's dismay, what he read gave him pause. "It really wasn't very good," recalls Reiner. Nor did he find much to hold his interest in any of the subsequent half-dozen scripts that his agent had submitted. "None of them were any good," he says. "Or, if they were good, they weren't for me." Finally, just as the actor began to wonder if he'd ever find an appropriate vehicle to propel him to the next stage of his career, he found the answer in a stray comment made by his wife.

After a few days of listening to her husband's not-so-hushed complaints about the dismal quality of material he'd been reading, Estelle Reiner picked up a few of the scripts and began leafing through them herself. A few minutes later, she set them down, satisfied that her husband's appraisals had not been far off the mark. "You're right, these aren't very good," she volunteered, before adding, quite matter-of-factly, "I'll bet you could write a better script than any of those yourself."

It was intended as a casual remark, a statement so obvious that it hardly needed voicing. And yet, decades later, Reiner continued to marvel at the impact of his wife's simple observation. "My wife, in her infinite wisdom, said I could write better than that," Reiner would recall some years later. "Of course, I'd never written a sitcom. But when your wife thinks you can—you can."[1]

And so, with no greater preparation than his wife's encouragement, Reiner resolved to spend the summer of 1958 on Fire Island, where he would create his very own situation comedy. If he was the least bit daunted by the challenge, he doesn't reveal it as he recalls those heady days. "I'd written *Enter Laughing* the summer before," Reiner says, "so at least I knew I could type fairly well."

Once he'd made up his mind to write a situation comedy for himself, Reiner's first order of business was to decide what to write about. As he recalls it, his search for a comic premise didn't take the writer very far from home. "You always have to write about what you know," he observes. "So I just asked myself the question, on what piece of ground do I stand that no one else occupies?" The answer came to him one morning a few days later, as he was driving into Manhattan from his home in suburban New Rochelle.

"I can tell you exactly where I was the moment it came to me," Reiner insists. "I was on the East Side Highway, driving downtown, near Ninety-Sixth Street." Maneuvering his car through rush hour traffic, it suddenly struck him that his *own* life, with only minimal embellishment, would provide the ideal fodder for a compelling weekly comedy. It was an idea whose brilliance lay in its simplicity—what could be easier for a New York comedy writer from New Rochelle to write than a TV show about a New York comedy writer from New Rochelle? "I knew that scene," recalls Reiner. "Living in New Rochelle, coming home at seven o'clock, talking about what happened at the office. And then going back to the office the next day and talking about what happened at home. That's what I knew about, so that's what I wrote about."

Once he put his mind to it, Reiner had little trouble populating his proposed series with a colorful cast of characters drawn largely from people in his own life. The show would revolve around Robert Petrie, a TV writer who lives in New Rochelle with his wife, Laura, and their six-year-old son, Ritchie, much as Reiner had lived in that Westchester County suburb during his years as a writer and performer on *Your Show of Shows*, with his own wife and real-life son, who—like Reiner's firstborn TV creation—was also named Robert. In the original script for his proposed series, Reiner's alter ego works for a self-centered variety show star named Alan Sturdy, a character that many of the writer's friends would recognize as a comic exaggeration of Reiner's own longtime TV boss, Sid Caesar. Robert Petrie's cowriters, Buddy Sorrell and Sally Rogers, also had real-life counterparts. "Sally was a combination of Lucille Kallen and Selma Diamond," Reiner has said—referring to, respectively, the lone female staff writer on *Your Show of Shows* and Diamond, a *Caesar's Hour* writer and sometime actress who would find her greatest fame playing the flinty bailiff Selma Hacker on *Night Court* in the 1980s—"and Buddy was Mel Brooks."[2]

Although Reiner hewed close to reality in his fictionalized re-creation of the writers' room on *Your Show of Shows*, it's interesting to note that he chose to depart from the actuality of his own experience in one small, if telling, detail. While Reiner himself had been no more than an uncredited "writer without portfolio" on *Your Show of Shows*, the writer's fictionalized alter ego would suffer no such indignity. And so, from Reiner's very first sample script, Robert Petrie would enjoy the lofty status of head writer of his show's writing staff. Reiner's elevation of his fictional character's status represented an understandable bit of wish fulfillment on his part. If nothing else, Robert Petrie would never be shut out of a comic debate with the dismissive challenge, "What do you know? You're nothing but a friggin' actor!"

With his cast of characters firmly in place, Reiner sat down at his typewriter, where he encountered little difficulty filtering his own real-life experience through the comic prism of situation comedy. "I was with the family on Fire Island," Reiner remembers, "and the first script flies out of me in three or four days!" Buoyed on the wings of his agreeable muse, Reiner sat right back down and started work on a second script. After polishing that one off within a week, he set to work on a third. And then a fourth. In a remarkable burst of creative energy, Reiner didn't stop writing until he'd completed a full thirteen episodes of *Head of the Family*, as he'd decided to call his new TV series.

The idea that a relatively inexperienced writer would actually sit down and create a baker's dozen of half-hour comedy scripts in as many weeks struck the more established television writers in Reiner's circle as nothing short of astonishing. However, at the time, Reiner had scant notion of the magnitude of his achievement; in his mind, his productivity was the natural result of a disciplined work routine that varied little throughout the summer of 1958.

Each morning, the writer would rise, shower, shave, and have breakfast with his family. By nine o'clock, he'd be seated in the den of his family's beachfront house, typing. He'd begin his labors each day by simply typing the first words that popped into his head. "I'd sit down without a thought," he recalls, "and I'd write a first line. It didn't matter what the line was. Then I would build from that."

Because most of his storylines were drawn from the rich fabric of his own life, the writer reasoned that he was immune to writer's block. If his creativity ever did falter, Reiner figured he had only to glance up from his desk and look at the room around him, where there was no shortage of fresh inspiration. The writer's decidedly personal connection to his material goes a long way toward explaining some of the off-kilter premises that eventually found their way into what would become *The Dick Van Dyke Show*, including one show that Reiner insists he wrote to appease the family dog.

"One morning," he elaborates, "it's like the third or fourth show. And I had nothing." Suddenly, the writer looked up and noticed the family pet sitting in a corner of the room, staring at him. "I had a big German shepherd, Rinny, who just sat there looking at me. So I said, 'Okay, Rinny, I'll write you a show.' Then I wrote the show where Rob brings Buddy's dog home." Three years later, that very script would be filmed—with minor revisions—as *The Dick Van Dyke Show*'s seventh episode, "The Unwelcome Houseguest."

At two o'clock each afternoon, his day's work finished, Reiner would stack his fresh pages in a neat pile and quit for the day. Then he would make a dash for the beach, where he'd spend at least a few of the remaining daylight hours playing with his two kids. Considering the enormous amount of material he would create over the course of that summer on Fire Island, the writer's daily routine sounds positively relaxed. But, explains Reiner, it's surprising what a writer can accomplish in little more than a half-day at the typewriter, so long as he remains focused. "And," he adds, "I'd never been that concentrated in my life."

Carl Reiner's sudden dedication to the lonely life of the writer represented a marked departure for someone who had until then been viewed by his friends as a gregarious performer. And he admits that his transition from prime-time clown to man of letters was greeted with incredulity by acquaintances who'd known him only as a second banana on Sid Caesar's shows.

This was especially true of Reiner's friends in Fire Island's literary community, many of whom viewed the comedian's arrival into their ranks with a bemused skepticism that bordered on disbelief. Reiner recalls that at least one of his Fire Island neighbors—the noted screen and television writer Reginald Rose—took an uncommon delight in teasing the novice writer's literary intentions by trying to distract Reiner from his work at every opportunity. "Reggie Rose used to throw pebbles up at my window!" explains Reiner, who recalls that his neighbor's playful efforts to keep him from his labors were rarely successful. Whenever Reiner heard the distinctive clicking of tiny stones skipping off his window, he'd stop typing only long enough to part the curtains and wave his would-be tormentor away, at which point Rose—the eminent author of *Twelve Angry Men* and a few dozen of the most distinguished teleplays of TV's golden age—would drop his handful of rocks and walk on down the beach, grinning broadly at his mischief.

Comedy writer Frank Tarloff was another old friend of Reiner's who remembered being openly skeptical when he discovered the fledgling writer's plan to polish off a half-season's worth of TV scripts in a single summer. "I thought he was nuts!" Tarloff would later recall. "I said, 'Carl, nobody ever starts out with thirteen finished episodes! It just doesn't work that way.'"

Regardless of the doubts expressed by his more seasoned colleagues, Reiner's rationale for creating a thirteen-episode backlog for his new series was rooted in reason. "I knew I didn't want to do a show unless I could act in it," he explains. And since Reiner anticipated that his chores as the show's star would keep him busy enough in front of the cameras, he wanted to have a half-season of scripts written in advance, if only to make life easier on the show's eventual scriptwriters, who would at least have thirteen rock-solid examples of the show to serve as their guide. "I knew that if I wrote thirteen up front," says Reiner, "the writers would have a pretty good idea of how to take it from there. That was the idea."

Reiner maintained his remarkable pace throughout the summer, completing a new script, he says, "every three or four days," until, he recalls, "in six or seven weeks, I had thirteen shows all written." Finally, late in the summer of 1958, the writer bundled his scripts together and dropped the package off with his agent, Harry Kalcheim, whose task it would be to find a backer willing to turn them into a full-fledged television series.

While Reiner waited for his agent to work his magic with *Head of the Family*, he came to the sobering realization that he still had a wife, two kids, and a German shepherd to feed. And so, in September 1958, Reiner signed on as the host of *Keep Talking*, a lively game show that featured talkative celebrity panelists expounding at length on various humorous topics. Among the frequent panelists on the weekly show were Peggy Cass, Joey Bishop, Pat Carroll, and a popular New York nightclub comic and TV personality named Morey Amsterdam.

Although Reiner seemed happy with the light duties demanded of him as a game show host, he maintained few illusions about the job. "It was an easy way to make a good living," he later explained. "I wasn't really working at anything, creating anything. I just grabbed the money and ran."[3] For Reiner, *Keep Talking* represented little more than a temporary stopgap, something to tide him over while he waited for the happy day when Harry Kalcheim would call to report that the writer's ship had finally come in.

3

HEAD OF THE FAMILY

Carl Reiner's lucky day arrived sooner than he expected. In its September 20, 1958, issue, *TV Guide* carried the first public announcement of the series that would eventually evolve into *The Dick Van Dyke Show*. "Carl Reiner has written eight of the first thirteen chapters in a new series,"[1] read the short newsbrief, "tentatively titled *Head of the Family*, in which he will star. Peter Lawford put up the money for the test film, which will be shot in October in New York.'"*

Although the news blurb turned out to be somewhat optimistic in its projection that the pilot was set to roll in October—*Head of the Family* would not actually be filmed until two months later, in December 1958—

* It's worth noting that *TV Guide* describes the writer as having completed only eight scripts prior to the start of production on *Head of the Family*, while Reiner staunchly maintains that he'd finished thirteen complete scripts during his summer on Fire Island. "I know it was definitely thirteen," he insists. "That's what I had!" To add to the confusion, in the May 14, 1960, issue of *TV Guide*—which appeared a full year and a half after the magazine's initial blurb—Reiner told writer Dan Jenkins that he'd "knocked out 14 scripts" for *Head of the Family* before it ever went into production. Fourteen is also the number cited by Reiner's friend and longtime manager, George Shapiro, who also happens to be Estelle Reiner's nephew, and was thus a frequent visitor to the Reiners' Fire Island home when the scripts in question were composed. Of course, whatever the exact number of scripts—whether eight, a dozen, thirteen, or fourteen—no one disputes the essential fact that the enthusiastic writer generated far more material for his proposed TV series than was required by accepted industry practice.

the release correctly identifies film star Peter Lawford as the primary benefactor of Carl Reiner's pilot.

Peter Lawford's involvement came about after Harry Kalcheim discovered that the former matinee idol—who himself had recently signed to star in NBC's *Thin Man* series—was looking to get a toehold in the extremely lucrative production end of the business. Since Kalcheim was also aware of Lawford's strong ties to the Kennedy family—the movie star was at that time married to Patricia Kennedy, the sister of future President John F. Kennedy—the agent had good reason to believe that Lawford could, in fact, put his hands on sufficient capital to make a pilot film of Reiner's series. And so Kalcheim submitted the first of Reiner's thirteen scripts to Lawford, who liked what he saw well enough to request a meeting with the gifted actor/writer.

Reiner's first and only meeting with Peter Lawford took place one morning in early September 1958, in Lawford's suite in New York's swank Pierre Hotel. "It was the kind of meeting you have with a producer who's not going to do much except put up the money," Reiner says. "But I'll never forget it." As Reiner recalls, it was already past 11:00 A.M. when he and his agent arrived at Lawford's suite; even so, the suave actor answered the door dressed in nothing but a thick, plush bathrobe and a pair of matching velvet slippers. In his palm, Lawford cradled an oversized snifter of what Reiner describes as "one of those giant red drinks—something-and-grenadine on the rocks. At eleven in the morning!" As it turned out, the meeting didn't last long. "Lawford agreed to put up the money to do the original pilot," recalls Reiner. There was, however, one slight condition. "They said I had to send a script down to Joseph P. Kennedy in Florida!"

Although Harry Kalcheim had correctly surmised that Lawford's financial backing would come from the Kennedy family coffers, the agent never dreamed that Lawford's financial arrangement would be dependent on script approval from the Kennedy family patriarch himself. But apparently, that was the case. "Joe Kennedy had to read it," explains Reiner, "before any of his family's money went into the product." And so, a few days later, the script was dutifully submitted to Joseph P. Kennedy in Palm Beach, Florida. The elder Kennedy was apparently impressed—or so Reiner has always assumed, since he got the official go-ahead to start casting his pilot within a few days of the Florida submission.

Assembling a cast for *Head of the Family* posed little challenge for Carl Reiner, who already carried an indelible image of each of the show's characters in his head. As planned, the writer cast himself as Robert Petrie, and child actor Gary Morgan was signed to play young Ritchie. For his man-hungry woman writer, Reiner tagged future Oscar nominee Sylvia Miles, who was then best known for her work as a comic sketch performer on *The Steve Allen Show*. The part of comedy writer Buddy Sorrell—described in Reiner's original script as a twenty-three-year-old hypochondriac—went to New York comic Morty Gunty. And, with the addition of Milt Kamen—a character actor who had worked with Reiner on *Sid Caesar Invites You*—in the role of the Snappy Service delivery man, Reiner had every part on the show cast. Except one. He still hadn't found his Laura.

Casting the all-important role of Mrs. Petrie was proving a more difficult task than Reiner had anticipated. "I looked at about twenty girls," says Reiner, who was convinced he'd finally struck gold when he met Joanna Moore, a fetching blond who possessed the exact combination of sexiness and maternal charm that Reiner had envisioned when he wrote the part. "She was the one that I really wanted," he recalls. Unfortunately, Moore was unavailable during the time *Head of the Family* was scheduled to shoot in New York, having already committed to star in an episode of *Alfred Hitchcock Presents* that was to be filmed in California that same week.

Jenifer Lea was another actress who came close to nabbing the part of Laura Petrie—so close, in fact, that a news blurb in the November 22, 1958, issue of *TV Guide* claimed that the actress had already been signed to play the role. It was an announcement that would prove somewhat premature. When the pilot for *Head of the Family* was shot a few weeks later, the role of Laura Petrie was played by Barbara Britton,

Barbara Britton, Gary Morgan, and Carl Reiner in Reiner's 1958 *Dick Van Dyke Show* prototype, *Head of the Family*. *Courtesy: Carl Reiner*

an attractive blond actress whose previous TV credits included numerous dramatic and light comic roles on *Robert Montgomery Presents* and a number of other anthology shows of the fifties. A few years earlier, the actress had also starred as Pamela North on *Mr. and Mrs. North*, a lighthearted mystery series that had brief runs on both CBS and NBC in the early fifties.

CARL REINER'S PILOT for *Head of the Family* finally went before the cameras at New York's Gold Medal Studios a few weeks before Christmas 1958. Produced by Stuart Rosenberg and Martin Poll, the half-hour telefilm was directed by Don Weis, a veteran feature director whose credits included the Debbie Reynolds musical *I Love Melvin*, as well as the original feature film version of Max Schulman's *The Affairs of Dobie Gillis*.

Watched out of context, Reiner's original *Head of the Family* pilot film—a copy of which today holds a place of honor in the permanent collection of New York's Paley Center for Media—appears to be little more than a mildly engaging example of the kind of family-oriented situation comedy that was popular in the late fifties. As such, the show is not without its charms. However, when viewed as a dry run for the series that would be reborn as *The Dick Van Dyke Show* just over two years later, the pilot affords a fascinating glimpse of the first faltering steps of a genuine TV classic.

The show opens, as would so many episodes of *The Dick Van Dyke Show*, in the kitchen of Robert and Laura Petrie—here pronounced PEE-tree—where Laura is busy preparing a meat loaf for the family dinner. Before long, she's interrupted by Mrs. Harley, a neighbor who arrives hoping to retrieve a school bulletin that Laura's husband—big-time TV writer Robert Petrie—has promised to compose as a favor to the promoters of the local PTA bazaar. When it becomes apparent that her husband has failed to make good on his commitment, Laura stammers a halting apology, which causes her guest to turn to the door in a huff. "It'll be in the mail!" Laura calls out after her. "We'll see!" snaps the skeptical neighbor.

Returning to her domestic duties, Laura is surprised to discover that her six-year-old son, Ritchie, has sequestered himself in a kitchen cabinet. "How long are you going to stay in there?" she asks. "'Till I'm older than Roy and Freddy," he vows. Apparently, the boy is upset because his school chums have been teasing him about his dad's unorthodox occupation as a TV writer. "Why can't Daddy get a real job?" the boy demands, mortified that his father would waste his time typing all day, while all the other fathers in his neighborhood manage to find time to accompany their sons to Little League games. Laura does her best to placate the distraught lad, with little success. His frustration mounting, Ritchie is finally moved to declare, "I don't like my daddy!"

When Robert Petrie arrives home from a hard day at the office a few minutes later, he's naturally dismayed to discover that his son has suddenly turned against him. "I'm universally well liked," Robert protests. "Everybody likes me! You like me, don't you?" he inquires of Laura. "See!" he declares as she signals assent. "And you got great taste." Laura finally suggests that her husband might restore some measure of the boy's lapsed faith by taking Ritchie to the office, where the lad will at least have the opportunity to see his dad in action. Though skeptical, Robert reluctantly agrees to give Laura's plan a shot—if only to prove her wrong. "Ninety-five percent of the time you're right," he coos. "Love to lower your average just a little."

The next morning, with Ritchie in tow, Robert arrives at the Manhattan town house office where TV's *Alan Sturdy Show* is written and produced. In the moments before their arrival, we watch the show's gal writer, Sally Rogers, water her pet philodendron and exchange barbs with fellow writer Buddy Sorrell, a fastidious hypochondriac who insists on gulping five sugars in his morning coffee. "I need a lot of sugar," he whines. "I have a fluctuating metabolism and a hyperactive thyroid!" "How did you manage to get so unhealthy in twenty-three years?" Sally wonders. "I go to nightclubs" is Buddy's grumbled response.

A moment later, Robert Petrie enters and introduces Ritchie, explaining that he has brought his son to work because the boy "has no idea how his father earns a living." "And you want him to find out?" quips Sally. Not surprisingly, the child is unimpressed by his father's job. "Do you need them to help you, Daddy?" Ritchie asks, eyeing his father's two writing partners with suspicion. "Well," Petrie stammers, withering under his coworkers' steely gaze, "Yes. I need them. But," he volunteers, in a futile attempt to regain lost ground, "I'm the main one—I'm in charge. I'm like Casey Stengel!"

Ritchie is unconvinced. And the boy's flagging enthusiasm droops even lower when the Snappy Service coffee man arrives and launches into a scathing critique of the previous week's *Alan Sturdy Show*. Just when it appears that Ritchie's opinion of his father's worth could sink no further, Dad is summoned to Alan Sturdy's office. There the boy is forced to watch as his father kowtows to his boorish employer, a pitiless egomaniac who takes pleasure in browbeating his helpless head writer without mercy. After witnessing a few minutes of this demoralizing spectacle, Ritchie is reduced to tears, prompting his father to groan, "I wonder if I'm too old to start dental school?"

At breakfast the next morning, Ritchie offers a cold shoulder to his father's affections, refusing to muster even a simple good-bye kiss for the old man before the boy heads off to school. However, just as the dad begins to wonder if he'll ever regain his stature in the young boy's eyes, things take an unexpected turn. When Ritchie arrives at school, he discovers a throng of his classmates chuckling appreciatively at a clever PTA announcement that's been posted on the school bulletin board. As it happens, the announcement, which is composed in the form of a funny poem, is the handiwork of one Robert Petrie, a fact that inspires admiration among Ritchie's envious classmates. "Your father's a pretty good poem writer!" one of the kids declares, as Ritchie beams with pride.

Robert Petrie is greeted by a newly delighted son when the writer returns home that evening. Grinning like the Cheshire cat from atop the hat shelf in the family closet, the boy exclaims, "I like my daddy!" to his father's obvious pleasure. In the show's closing moments, Ritchie challenges his dad to compose a funny poem on the spot—a request with which the father cheerfully complies.

WHILE THE TRYOUT film for *Head of the Family* suffers in comparison to the fine-tooled brilliance that the same basic material would yield in its later incarnation as *The Dick Van Dyke Show*, what's surprising is just how many of the elements that would make Reiner's later show such a groundbreaker were already in place in this first, embryonic draft. Chief among those breakthroughs is the show's realistic depiction of Robert Petrie's workplace.

Reiner wasn't the first TV creator to show his leading character at work—audiences had previously seen Ralph Kramden in the Brooklyn bus depot where he labored on *The Honeymooners*; and from time to time viewers had caught glimpses of Ricky Ricardo leading the orchestra that provided *I Love Lucy*'s Cuban bandleader with the income to finance his wife's madcap schemes. But as stylized as they were, even those sketchy depictions of the modern workplace were exceptions to the norm for domestic situation comedies of the 1950s, where the breadwinner usually disappeared each morning at nine, only to return eight hours later to issue the mating cry that has become one of television's most enduring clichés: "Honey, I'm home!"

Not so on *Head of the Family*—and, of course, the later *Dick Van Dyke Show*—where you not only knew exactly how Rob Petrie earned a living, you actually watched him doing it. A stickler for realism from the very start, Carl Reiner was not about to shy away from depicting the routine details of his leading man's everyday life—indeed, in Reiner's eye, the details that most TV shows ignored provided the very fabric of his show's rich comic tapestry. By exploring the contrast of his leading man's work and home lives, Reiner was able to treat his audience to a dimension they hadn't seen before. As the writer himself would later observe, "This was the first situation comedy where, when the guy came home and said, 'Honey, I'm home,' you knew where he'd come home from."[2]

Indeed, *The Dick Van Dyke Show*'s twin emphasis on Rob's home and office settings would be one of the show's most potent legacies, providing a durable format that would inspire scores of subsequent top-drawer half-hour situation comedies, from *The Mary Tyler Moore Show* to *Frasier*, to name only two of the more outstanding examples.

Judging by the evidence on screen in *Head of the Family*, Carl Reiner's penchant for mining rich comic atmosphere from the finely observed details of ordinary life was already in full flower when he shot the historic pilot film. In one early scene, the otherwise routine staging of a husband-and-wife discussion is enlivened when Robert grabs a bunch of celery and begins stripping the stalks in the kitchen sink. It's a small detail—and yet, Robert Petrie's unbidden effort to pitch in and help out with the domestic chores provides a fascinating subtext to the marital conversation, even as it serves to ground the scene in a specific and believable reality.

One area where Reiner's pilot differs from the later *Dick Van Dyke Show* is in the technique used to film it. While *The Dick Van Dyke Show* was filmed in front of a live audience, using the so-called three-camera method first popularized by *I Love Lucy* in the early fifties, *Head of the Family* was shot "one-camera," with a single camera recording the action in separate scenes filmed piecemeal over the course of a few days, much as a feature film is made.* Unlike the stagebound three-camera system,

* Although *Head of the Family* was filmed without a studio audience in attendance, the laughter heard on the show's soundtrack was nonetheless recorded live at a special screening of the pilot that Reiner arranged for the express purpose of capturing an authentic response for the show's laugh track.

the one-camera method was well suited for outdoor and location shooting, which made it the system of choice for the producers of the more naturalistic-looking domestic comedies of the era, like *Father Knows Best* and *Leave it to Beaver*. It was a consideration that was not lost on Reiner, who freely admits his debt to both of those popular family comedies.

"I was influenced by the flavor of *Father Knows Best*," explains Reiner, "and by the fact that I could comfortably watch it." But, notes Reiner, the show that provided the greatest influence on the series that would come to be known as *The Dick Van Dyke Show* may well have been *Leave It to Beaver*, the classic late-fifties comedy that depicted small-town life through the eyes of eight-year-old Theodore "Beaver" Cleaver and his teenage brother Wally. That series, which debuted on CBS in October 1957, was the brainchild of Joe Connelly and Bob Mosher, two unsung masters of the situation-comedy form who, like Reiner, mined their greatest comic moments from simple observations of the world around them. "I remember laughing," says Reiner, recalling an exemplary *Leave It to Beaver* moment, "when two kids were arguing and one of them said, 'Aw, your sister drinks gutter water!' I said, 'That's so sweet! Your sister drinks gutter water!' That show had a sweetness to it, and a reality that I liked."

WHEN HARRY KALCHEIM finally had a chance to screen the finished workprint of Reiner's pilot film in early 1959, the agent could barely contain his enthusiasm. Before the film ended, he made the optimistic declaration that he would have no trouble convincing any one of a dozen sponsors to back the pilot as a new series for the fall 1959 season.

Unfortunately, as the agent would quickly discover, none of his potential buyers shared his enthusiasm. During the first few months of the new year, Kalcheim and his colleagues in the TV department of the William Morris Agency showed Reiner's *Head of the Family* pilot to the top media buyers at some of the biggest ad agencies in New York, as well as to the high-ranking program executives at all three networks. But despite Kalcheim's efforts, *Head of the Family* earned little more than a few curious nibbles, and in the end, the show was not picked up for the 1959 fall season.

"We got very nice mentions," insists Carl Reiner, who has long maintained that the chief reason his first pilot failed was because the networks simply weren't looking to buy situation comedies in 1959, a year when

Westerns and detective shows were all the rage in prime time. "They were looking for elaborate adventure series," explains Reiner, "and horses and guns." But, while the 1959 prime-time season did feature a high percentage of horse operas and shoot-'em-up series, situation comedies had by no means become extinct. In fact, that season saw the debut of more than a half-dozen new half-hour comedies, including a pair of hardy perennials in *Dennis the Menace* and *The Many Loves of Dobie Gillis*. Although it's certainly possible, as Reiner maintains, that *Head of the Family* got lost in the shuffle of an extremely tight market, it's equally likely that Reiner's pilot film was overlooked because it simply left the sponsors, programmers, and network executives cold.

One theory that's been bandied about over the years is that advertisers and network executives of the era may have been concerned that *Head of the Family*'s leading man, as portrayed by Reiner, seemed too Jewish for mainstream tastes of the late fifties. It's an intriguing notion—but completely unfounded, according to Reiner, who dismisses any suggestion that anti-Semitism played a significant role in the demise of his first pilot. "I never had Jewish rhythms in these shows," he insists. "I mean, even in the very first pilot I did with Barbara Britton, it was a very gentile show. I would never not admit that I was a Jew—but I wasn't going to do a show about Jewishness. I knew that the country was not looking for a Jewish ethnic show. Not yet."

William Morris agent Sol Leon keenly recalled the resistance that he and his colleagues faced when they pitched Reiner's pilot to potential buyers in the winter of 1959. "I almost had it sold to CBS," noted the agent, who remembered screening the film for a high-ranking CBS program executive named Harry Ommerle. According to Leon, when the film ended, the executive scratched his ear quietly for a good thirty seconds before he finally ventured an opinion. "It's good," the network honcho volunteered. "But," he continued, searching for the right words to express his vague sense of dissatisfaction, "it's just . . . lacking something."

Of course, the executive was right. Something *was* lacking in the series then known as *Head of the Family*. But, in the early days of 1959, it would be more than a full year before someone finally identified that the element lacking in the pilot for the series that would become *The Dick Van Dyke Show* was, in fact . . . Dick Van Dyke.

4

A BASKET FULL OF SCRIPTS

By September 1959, Carl Reiner figured it was all over. Robert Petrie was dead. Gone. In less than a year, the pilot that he'd poured his entire life into was now just another unsold reel of film gathering dust on a shelf at the William Morris office. "It was inventory," recalled Sol Leon. For his part, Reiner maintains an even more jaundiced view of those dark days in the protracted gestation of what would finally become *The Dick Van Dyke Show*. "After *Head of the Family* failed to sell," sighs Reiner, "it laid foul."

Even so, Reiner wasn't about to let this setback impede the trajectory of a career that was in all other areas very much on the rise. In the wake of his pilot's failure, the writer wasted little time relocating to California, where, by the fall of 1959, he'd already secured a steady job as a staff writer and some-time performer on *The Dinah Shore Chevy Show*. In the two years that fell between *Head of the Family*'s demise and the launch of *The Dick Van Dyke Show* in 1961, the ambitious writer/performer also found time to act in three feature films—*Happy Anniversary*, *The Gazebo*, and *Gidget Goes Hawaiian*—and to write the script for a fourth, *The Thrill of It All*. During this period, Reiner also contributed sketches and specialty material for a 1960 Debbie Reynolds TV spectacular, and managed to record the first *2000 Year*

Carl Reiner with Dinah Shore on the singer's late-fifties variety hour, *The Dinah Shore Chevy Show*. *Courtesy: Carl Reiner*

Old Man comedy album with Mel Brooks. In addition to his professional obligations, in August 1960, Reiner became a father for the third time when his wife Estelle gave birth to Lucas Reiner, who would eventually grow up to follow his father and elder brother into a career as a film director.

But despite the impressive list of creative triumphs that Reiner chalked up in the months following the dispiriting failure of his first pilot, Harry Kalcheim refused to abandon hope that his client might yet be able to retool *Head of the Family* into a viable series—and, to hear Reiner tell it, the agent spent the better part of 1959 and 1960 trying to persuade his client to do just that. "Harry Kalcheim bugged me for a year," muses Reiner, who recalls that the agent practically begged him to start work on a new, revised pilot script, despite the writer's understandable reluctance to climb back on the horse that had so decisively thrown him a season earlier. "I told him, 'Screw 'em!'" says Reiner. "'That was my best shot. I'm never gonna write a better show than that. If they don't want it, that's fine. I'm happy not to do a TV show. I'll write movies.'"

Kalcheim would hear none of that. Having been with the William Morris Agency's TV department since its inception in the late forties, the agent knew as well as anyone the rewards Reiner stood to reap as the creator/writer of a successful situation comedy—profits that would dwarf anything his client might earn as a performer and writer for hire. But even after listening to his agent's most impassioned arguments, Reiner remained squarely on the fence about whether to revive his series or not. And there he may well have stayed had Kalcheim not decided to call on one of his other clients to give the writer a gentle nudge in the right direction. As fate would have it, the nudger that Kalcheim recruited for the task turned out to be Sheldon Leonard, the talented actor/writer/ producer and Hollywood legend who would soon become a crucial player in *The Dick Van Dyke Show* saga.

Born in New York City on February 22, 1907, the former Sheldon Leonard Bershad grew up on the mean streets of the East Bronx, where he came by naturally the scrappy demeanor and thick Bronx accent that would become his Hollywood trademark in the 1930s. Though the incongruously erudite performer had earned an honors degree in sociology from Syracuse University in 1929, Leonard's pugnacious profile and imposing physical stature—combined with the unforgettable lilt of his Damon Runyonesque vocal inflections—soon won the handsome character actor steady work as one of the preeminent tough guys of the Hollywood studio era. Leonard would polish the role of the smooth-talking, multisyllabic gangster to perfection in a seemingly endless succession of strong-arm parts in stage shows, radio plays, and feature films throughout the thirties, forties, and fifties, including notable appearances in *Another Thin Man*, *To Have and Have Not*, and the movie adaptation of *Guys and Dolls*, to name only a few. Although Leonard played a handful of leading roles in a few long-forgotten B-movies of the

An early publicity shot of Sheldon Leonard, the Syracuse University sociology major whose pugnacious profile and Bronx accent ensured him plenty of work as a Hollywood tough guy. *Courtesy: Sheldon Leonard*

Comedy czar Sheldon Leonard at Desilu Cahuenga, one of the most formidable comedy factories in Hollywood in the late fifties and early sixties. *Courtesy: Sheldon Leonard*

forties, the actor may be best remembered by future generations for his relatively small supporting role as Nick, the cold-hearted bartender who turns Jimmy Stewart's George Bailey and his guardian angel out in the snow in Frank Capra's 1946 film *It's a Wonderful Life.*

Although Leonard would continue to accept the occasional acting assignment until well into his retirement years, he had already begun to focus his creative energies behind the scenes by the early fifties, when he signed on as house director—and, later, producer—of the long-running *Danny Thomas Show*, one of the first situation comedies to be filmed on Hollywood's Desilu Cahuenga lot. Leonard soon proved himself as adept behind the cameras as he'd been in front of them, and in no time at all he parlayed his success on *The Danny Thomas Show* into a burgeoning career as one of the most prolific TV directors of the 1950s. In early 1960, the already successful producer/director upped the ante when he introduced a popular humorist named Andy Griffith in the role of small-town sheriff Andy Taylor on an episode of *The Danny Thomas Show*. Eight months later—using the *Danny Thomas* episode as a "backdoor pilot"—Leonard launched *The Andy Griffith Show* as a freestanding series on the CBS network's Monday-night lineup, where the show quickly established itself as one of the biggest hits of its era and, eventually, as one of the most beloved TV shows of all time. But Leonard was not about to stop there. And so, by the end of 1960, with the top-rated *Andy Griffith* and *Danny Thomas* shows as anchors, the producer—in partnership with Danny Thomas—

stood poised to expand his production base on the Desilu Cahuenga lot into one of the most formidable comedy factories in television.

Enter Carl Reiner.

"Harry Kalcheim came to me and said that Carl Reiner wanted to break into the field of situation comedy," the producer recalled. "Would you be willing to show Carl Reiner the ropes?" the agent asked. "Of course, Carl is welcome," replied the well-established producer/director, who was already familiar with Reiner's work from the actor's tenure on *Your Show of Shows*. "He is more than welcome. Send him in," Leonard told the agent. "I'll be very happy to give him free access to anything we are doing."

But before he arranged this meeting of the minds, Kalcheim insisted that Leonard take a look at Reiner's *Head of the Family* pilot—a condition to which the producer readily acceded. And so, a few days later, the veteran producer spent the better part of a lunch hour watching Reiner's all-but-forgotten pilot in a screening room on the Desilu lot. Joining him was Danny Thomas's nephew, Ronald Jacobs, who was at that time one of Leonard's most trusted assistants. According to Jacobs, Leonard's enthusiasm for the pilot was immediate and unrestrained—with but a single reservation.

"We loved the idea of the show," recalls Jacobs, who would later serve as associate producer of *The Dick Van Dyke Show*. But despite their shared enthusiasm for the film, notes Jacobs, both he and Leonard agreed that Reiner's pilot suffered from one fatal flaw: The writer had completely miscast himself in the role of Robert Petrie. "I thought the reason the pilot had failed was principally because of the casting," remembered Leonard.

In Leonard's opinion, Reiner was hardly the show's only casting miscalculation. "Barbara Britton was a very lovely lady," Leonard acknowledged. "A beautiful lady." But in his view, Britton's cover-girl looks made her appear too glamorous to be believable in a down-to-earth role like Laura Petrie. "She was too far too beautiful for the girl-next-door kind of characterization that you need in television." Leonard was also unimpressed with Morty Gunty and Sylvia Miles as Robert Petrie's coworkers. "I thought they added nothing whatever to it," he observed. "They were there. They performed a function—but they brought nothing positive to it." Even so, it was Reiner's performance in the show's central role that earned the producer's harshest criticism.

"While I was sitting there," says Carl Reiner, "Sheldon Leonard hyphenated me. I became a creator-writer-producer." Pictured, from left, are Ronald Jacobs, Sheldon Leonard, and Carl Reiner. *Courtesy: Ronald Jacobs*

"Carl brought with him the aura of sketch comedy, of which he had been born, or more or less bred," Leonard recalled. "And that sketch comedy approach didn't work for him in the situation comedy environment."

Despite his reservations about the execution of Reiner's pilot film, the producer had nothing but praise for the show's underlying source material—the thirteen scripts Reiner had labored over during his summer on Fire Island. "I thought that basketful of scripts was the best body of material it had been my good luck to find," the producer declared.[1] "I thought the quality of the writing was very good indeed—first class," he continued, "and I realized that this was a body of material that deserved a second chance."

But before Leonard could even begin to think about reviving Reiner's moribund series, he knew that he'd first have to resolve the casting of the show's leading man. In his mind, there was simply no way the show was going to fly with Reiner in the lead—and the sooner the actor understood that, the better. "The feeling was," says Jacobs, "it's a good script. Now, let's find someone who can really do it." Of course, as a performer himself, Leonard recognized that breaking this news to Reiner would require a considerable amount of delicacy. "How do you tell an actor he's just not the type to play himself?" the producer wondered.[2]

Leonard would find out a few days later, when Reiner arrived at Desilu Cahuenga for his initial meeting with him, which most likely took place sometime during the first few months of 1960. "Carl came to my office," Leonard recalled, "and we found ourselves to be compatible. He was very self-assured. And very lively." Reiner was also quite intrigued by the veteran producer's sudden interest in a pilot that he'd all but written off himself. "Carl considered the thirteen scripts that he had written at Fire Island a dead issue," Leonard insisted. "He'd done them and they hadn't paid off—too bad, and that's that." But, of course, Leonard had other ideas, and he was only too happy to share his vision for the series with the attentive writer. "I asked Carl if he would be willing to let me try it again," Leonard recalled. "If he would let me reassemble the show in a manner that I thought would work."

Reiner admits he found Leonard's offer tempting, despite his misgivings. "I told Sheldon, 'I don't want to fail twice with the same thing.'"

"You won't," Leonard shot back, "because you're not going to act in the show. You're going to produce it."

"Produce it?" Reiner responded. "But I don't know how to be a producer."

"Sure you do," insisted Leonard, who demonstrated his point by plucking a *Head of the Family* script from a stack on his desk. "Look," Leonard exclaimed, opening the script at random. "It's all right here!"

Reiner leaned forward and read the words as the producer highlighted the text with his forefinger. The veteran producer pointed to a passage in which Reiner had described the setup and execution of a sight gag in painstaking detail, including a complete inventory of all the props, costumes, and set pieces that would be required to pull it off. "Look at the way you describe every character's reaction," Leonard explained. "Everything you need on the set is accounted for. The man who wrote this script was thinking like a producer."

"Yeah," Reiner interrupted, growing more confused. "But the reason I wrote all that stuff down like that is because I knew I *wasn't* going to be the producer—and I didn't want to leave anything to chance."

"That's the point," Leonard declared. "You don't leave anything to chance. You write like a producer. And you think like a producer. Therefore," the producer concluded with a flourish that signaled the end of the debate, "I must assume that you can produce."

According to a colorful account of that fateful meeting that Reiner related to a reporter some years after the fact, Leonard's most persuasive argument in favor of the producer's life came when the former character actor launched into an informal inventory of all the lavish adjustments he'd made in his own lifestyle since he'd abandoned the actor's trade for the producer's suite a few years earlier. "He showed me the expensive shoes he was wearing," recounted Reiner, "pointed to his extensive waistline, told me of the homes he had bought, and asked me if my two Emmys were supporting me."[3] His point well made, Leonard then added, almost rhetorically, "Where are you going as an actor?"[4] It was a question that gave Reiner a moment's pause. "While I was sitting there, thinking of an answer," Reiner recalled, "Sheldon hyphenated me. I became a creator-writer-producer. "[5]

In later years, Leonard confessed that he'd been surprised at how easy it'd been to convince Reiner to bow out of the limelight on the series that was supposed to make him a star. "I never saw anybody take that kind of blow to his ego and roll with the punch so gracefully."[6]

But, according to actress Doris Singleton, Reiner didn't abandon his dream of playing Robert Petrie without regret. "He was depressed about it," recalls Singleton, whose husband, Charlie Issacs, was then Reiner's writing partner on *The Dinah Shore Chevy Show*. "He thought it would've been great to star in the series that he created." Fortunately, adds Singleton, Reiner's blue mood was extremely short lived. In later years, Reiner freely acknowledged that Leonard's suggestion that he find another actor to fill Robert Petrie's shoes may have been the best piece of advice he'd ever been given. "I'll always be grateful to Sheldon Leonard," he has said, "for telling me I was a producer, when I thought I was an actor."[7]

With Reiner now installed as the show's producer, and Leonard taking on the responsibilities of executive producer, the pair began the arduous process of transforming a failed pilot into an entirely new and viable television series. The first item on the agenda would be to come up with a fresh title for the series, since they both agreed that the name *Head of the Family* carried too much baggage from the earlier pilot. Besides, the producers reasoned, if they were going to create a brand-new show from the ground up, it was only fitting that they start out with a brand-new title. By the spring of 1960, the producers had dubbed their new series *The Full House*, the first in a long succession of titles that would be attached to Reiner's pilot before it resurfaced the following January, by then sporting the elegant moniker by which it would become known by all posterity: *The Dick Van Dyke Show*.

5

FALL GUY

One of Sheldon Leonard's earliest and most significant contributions to the evolution of *The Dick Van Dyke Show* was his decision to put the show in front of a live audience. After watching Reiner's original pilot—which had been filmed by a single camera in the sterile confines of a movie studio soundstage—Leonard was convinced that the material would be far better served by the three-camera approach, where the scenes could be played straight through on a stage, like a play, while a trio of cameras quietly captured the action as it happened. Leonard had nothing against the one-camera method; in fact, he would employ that technique quite effectively to film eight years of *The Andy Griffith Show* throughout the sixties. But for the new Reiner series, the executive producer had a hunch that the faster pace imposed by the three-camera approach would result in a livelier, more theatrical show. And, as would soon become quite obvious, Leonard's hunch was right on the money.

The challenge of reworking Reiner's thirteen Fire Island scripts to suit the very different production demands of a three-camera show fell to Reiner himself, who admits that his only preparation for the task was a single half-hour crash course in three-camera technique conducted by his executive producer. "Sheldon showed me in one sitting how to do that," Reiner recalls. "I sat with him one day and he took a couple scripts and said, 'Look. Forget this exterior. Move this scene here. Then, take

The producers briefly considered casting Johnny Carson as Rob Petrie, until Sheldon Leonard suggested Dick Van Dyke for the part.

these lines and move them to the interior.' He showed me how one-camera shows have more scenes, but they're shorter. So, for a three-camera show, I needed fewer scenes, but I had to extend each one a little further. I learned that pretty quickly. Writing a three-camera show was more like playwriting. So I had to become more of a playwright than a one-camera film writer." Reiner turned out to be a quick study—in May 1960, the writer filed an optimistic appraisal of his recent efforts in the pages of *TV Guide*. "I've reworked all the scripts to fit a new series," Reiner told reporter Dan Jenkins, "*The Full House*."[1]

On July 19, 1960, a few months after Reiner began reworking his Fire Island scripts to suit the new series, his original pilot received its first and only network broadcast. Aired with little fanfare, *Head of the Family* surfaced as an episode of *The Comedy Spot*, a CBS anthology series that served as the final dumping ground for most of the network's more ambitious unsold pilots. "They got burned off in the summertime," said William Morris agent Sol Leon, "and then they were forgotten about."

If Reiner had any misgivings about the final disposition of the pilot of his first-born series, he wasn't losing sleep over it. By the time his agents made the deal to "burn off" *Head of the Family*, Reiner had already embarked on a search to find a different actor to star in his new and improved version of the same series. Of course, before Reiner and Leonard could begin their quest for a new Robert Petrie, they first had to decide what they were looking for.

"I knew it had to be somebody who didn't seem like a performer," recalls Reiner. "Writers are—most of them—retiring characters. These guys are as funny as comedians, only they're not comedians—except maybe when you get them in a room. So we said, we need somebody like that. And then we started throwing names around."

One of the first names to surface in their early discussions was Johnny Carson, who was at that time still best known as the host of the popular daytime quiz show *Who Do You Trust?** "But," admits Reiner, "that was just a passing idea." Far more compelling was a suggestion Leonard made, seemingly out of the blue. "There's a guy in New York," the executive producer announced. "He's doing *Bye Bye Birdie* on Broadway. His name is Dick Van Dyke."

Although Dick Van Dyke was then still largely unknown outside of New York show business circles, his talent was well known by Sheldon Leonard. The producer had been a fan of the lanky comedian since the previous November, when he first spotted Dick Van Dyke in the supporting cast of *The Girls Against the Boys*, a musical revue headlined by Bert Lahr and Nancy Walker that had a short run at Broadway's Alvin Theatre in 1959. Leonard attended the revue on the advice of Harry Kalcheim, who had been singing Dick Van Dyke's praises ever since he'd caught the show earlier that same week.† As Leonard would later tell *TV Guide*, his own first exposure to Van Dyke left an equally lasting impression. "He did a bit that fractured me," Leonard recalled, "the fella who comes home loaded from a night with the boys, but every time his wife comes in snaps

---

* Ironically, Johnny Carson would make his own bid for situation-comedy stardom that same season with a pilot for an ill-fated vehicle called *Johnny Come Lately*. Unfortunately, Carson's tryout film fared no better than did Reiner's *Head of the Family*—in fact, by an odd coincidence, Carson's unsold pilot would be "burned off" on the CBS network's *New Comedy Showcase* on August 8, 1960, just three weeks after the same network gave *Head of the Family* its single airing. Stranger yet, on August 22, 1960—exactly two weeks to the day after CBS aired Carson's forlorn pilot—the network ran yet another unsold pilot, *The Trouble With Richard*, a half-hour comedy that had been designed to showcase the talents of another would-be star named Dick Van Dyke.

† Although Sheldon Leonard gives full credit to Harry Kalcheim for being the first to bring Dick Van Dyke to his attention, Van Dyke himself says he can name at least a dozen other show business acquaintances he's met over the years who've claimed the distinction of making that fateful introduction. "It tickles me to death," says the star, "how many people take credit for having been the very first to mention me to Sheldon Leonard."

to attention."[2] Before the final curtain rang down that evening, Leonard made a mental note to keep his eye out for a TV project that would suit the singular talent he'd just discovered. "Sooner or later," Leonard boasted, "I was pretty sure I'd find something for him."

Leonard later revealed that he'd initially hoped to cast Van Dyke as Danny Williams's son-in-law on *The Danny Thomas Show*, though he never acted on that impulse, fearing that Van Dyke would appear too old for the part, which eventually went to Pat Harrington. But now, with the role of comedy writer Robert Petrie, Leonard was convinced that he'd finally found a part worthy of Van Dyke's protean abilities. And just to be sure, in the late summer of 1960 Leonard made a second trip to Broadway, where Van Dyke was starring in *Bye Bye Birdie*, which had been playing to capacity crowds at the Martin Beck Theatre since April 14. After seeing Van Dyke dazzle the audience as *Birdie*'s Albert Peterson, Leonard knew he'd found his man.

"After Sheldon saw Dick in *Bye Bye Birdie*," recalls Grant Tinker, who was then a creative executive at New York's Benton and Bowles advertising agency, "he walked into my office with a huge smile on his face and said, 'I've found Rob Petrie!'" Before the day was out, Leonard called Reiner in Los Angeles and insisted that the writer hop the next plane to New York. When Reiner finally caught *Bye Bye Birdie* himself a few days later, he left the show in absolute accord with his executive producer. "I thought, 'Geez, he's perfect!'" recalls Reiner. "It was like a great marriage of actor and role that seemed completely accidental. But that was Sheldon. He was the great matchmaker."

Despite the actor's obvious fitness for the role of Rob Petrie, Reiner admits that hiring Dick Van Dyke to anchor their brand-new series was by no means a safe choice. "It wasn't a good odds bet," says Reiner. For one thing, both Leonard and Reiner knew that their proposed series would not be Van Dyke's first exposure on national television. Far from it. As Reiner recalls, "Dick had done, like, twelve pilots in a row that had failed."

Though Reiner exaggerates the number of Van Dyke's previous times at bat, it's true that the Broadway star's television career had not exactly been charmed up to that point. In fact, long before he ever met Reiner, Van Dyke had already filmed a pilot for another series that was to be called *The Dick Van Dyke Show*, although that one was a failed variety show that bore little resemblance to the star's later situation comedy. "I did a monologue and sketches and fell down a lot"[3] is how Van Dyke later described the unsold pilot for his first *Dick Van Dyke Show*, which was created and produced by Aaron Ruben, a veteran TV writer who had worked with Van Dyke on the comedy sketches in *The Girls Against the Boys*. After their variety show failed to attract a buyer, Ruben and Van Dyke teamed up for yet another pilot, *Poor Richard*, a situation comedy, "in which," Van Dyke would later recall, "I fell a lot, too."[4] The unsold pilot for *Poor Richard* was aired—under the title *The Trouble with Richard*—on August 22, 1960, ironically, just a few weeks after *Head of the Family* received its first and only network airing on CBS.*

But the star's most tantalizing early project may well have been a TV series that never even made it to the pilot stage. According to Van Dyke, a few months before Reiner signed him to play Rob Petrie, the star had been having discussions with another producer, whose name Van Dyke has long since forgotten, who approached him with a very intriguing proposal. "Someone had an idea for a series based on the Jacques Tati character, Monsieur Hulot," recalls Van Dyke, who was flattered to be compared to the popular French director and star of the landmark comedy *Mr. Hulot's Holiday*. "There would have been a lot of mime and visual humor," says Van Dyke, recalling the premise of the proposed series. "I would've played an assistant professor from a small Middle Western college who was on a sabbatical, saddling around in Europe on a Vespa motor scooter with a typewriter on the back." But, alas, as fascinating as it sounded, Van Dyke admits that the project never got past the discussion stage. "There was no script or anything. We had simply talked about it in conceptual terms."

Even after the Tati series sputtered and died, Van Dyke refused to get too upset. Over the course of a career that had been marked by more failures than successes, the performer had developed an almost limitless capacity for patience. After all, by the time he met Reiner in 1960, the fledgling star had already spent almost five years as one of television's most promising newcomers.

BORN ON DECEMBER 13, 1925, in West Plains, Missouri, Dick Van Dyke was raised in Danville, Illinois, a small Midwestern town where his father worked as a freight agent. As a boy, Van Dyke spent countless Saturday

* After their second TV pilot failed to sell, Aaron Ruben finally gave up trying to find a vehicle for Dick Van Dyke's TV debut and moved to the West Coast, where he wound up producing *The Andy Griffith Show*, which would be filmed just a few stages away from *The Dick Van Dyke Show* on the Desilu lot.

afternoons at the local movie palaces. It was there that the future comedy star developed his lasting passion for the expressive comedians of that earlier era, including Buster Keaton, Harold Lloyd, Charlie Chaplin and, especially, Stan Laurel. When Van Dyke finally began performing his own self-styled pantomimes in local Danville variety and talent shows, it was Stan Laurel who provided the star-struck Midwesterner with his greatest inspiration, not to mention his best material, most of which, Van Dyke would later confess, he lifted directly from the vast Laurel and Hardy repertoire.

With the outbreak of World War II, Van Dyke enlisted in the air force, where his inspired clowning invariably drew the loudest response from his fellow servicemen in cadet variety shows. "He had a natural stage presence," Van Dyke's old air force chum Byron Paul would later recall. "He did a little thing—a man walking a dog in a high wind. But he was not fumble-footed."[5] Paul, who would eventually become Van Dyke's manager and close friend, was so impressed by the young cadet's extraordinary performance that he predicted then and there that Dick Van Dyke would one day be among the biggest comedy stars in the business. It was a prediction that neither of them would soon forget.

But Dick Van Dyke's day in the sun was still a long way off in 1946, the year that the future star received his air force discharge papers. After the war, Van Dyke returned to Danville, where he dabbled in advertising before deciding to renew his commitment to a life in show business. For the next few years, Van Dyke toured the country as one of the Merry Mutes, a musical pantomime act that he formed with an old friend named

Phil Erickson. Although the pair achieved some minor notoriety on the nightclub circuit in the late forties, they were not above playing third-rate supper clubs and recreation halls for twenty-five dollars a night.

By 1948, times were so tough that when Van Dyke proposed to his hometown sweetheart, the former Marjorie Willett, he and his intended had to get married under the auspices of *The Bride and Groom Show*, a then-popular radio—and, later, television—show that offered to pay for a couple's wedding ceremony and honeymoon in exchange for a few minutes of on-air chatter with the nervous newlyweds after the vows. "They bought us the ring and the license," Van Dyke later recalled, "and they gave us furniture and appliances and sent us up to Mount Hood, Oregon, for a week's honeymoon. That's the only way I could afford to get married."[6]

Now a married man with children on the way—sons Christian and Barry were born in 1950 and 1951, respectively; daughter Stacy came along in 1955, and the youngest, Carrie Beth, was born in 1961—Van Dyke decided to settle down in Atlanta, Georgia, where he'd landed a job as a morning disc jockey and radio talk show host. It wasn't long before the personable star made the leap to television, and by 1953, Van Dyke was hosting his own daily kid's show on a local Atlanta station. Though the program was ostensibly aimed at the after-school set, Van Dyke's smart combination of comedy, pantomime, and clever small talk soon earned the star a sizable following among Atlanta's adult demographic group as well. He was also having the time of his life. "I had finally achieved what I figured was my ultimate success," the actor would later observe. "I had very high ratings, and that was it for me, I was going to stay there."[7]

And there he might have remained, had not fate stepped in, in the guise of an old air force buddy. Though Byron Paul had become a successful television director for CBS in New York, he'd never forgotten Van Dyke. As soon as he was in a position to do so, Paul volunteered to set his old pal up with an audition for the CBS brass in New York. It was a tempting offer, and one that Van Dyke ultimately found impossible to resist, despite his mixed feelings about making the leap to the big leagues. "Byron Paul brought me to New York in 1955," the reluctant star later recounted, "but he had to drag me up, because I figured I didn't want any of that."[8]

As it turned out, Van Dyke's initial instincts may have been on target. After a promising start—CBS signed him to a five-year contract soon after he arrived in New York—Van Dyke ended up spending the better part of television's golden age laboring in a string of thankless assignments, beginning with an ill-fated appointment to the anchor chair of the network's *Morning Show*. By 1955, CBS's troubled morning news and chat show had already resisted the best efforts of three previous anchormen, an illustrious group that included Jack Paar, John Henry Faulk, and Walter Cronkite. When Van Dyke proved similarly unable to bolster the show's ailing format, his own stock at the network plummeted precipitously. Within a year's time he'd been assigned to host *The CBS Cartoon Theatre*, where the once-promising newcomer was reduced to playing second banana to Gandy Goose, Dinky Duck, and Heckle and Jeckle. Two years later, in 1958, Van Dyke's contract with the network was dissolved by mutual consent.

The hardworking actor spent the next few years marching through a seemingly endless parade of guest appearances on shows as varied as *The Armstrong Circle Theatre* and *The Phil Silvers Show*. But despite his near-constant exposure on television throughout the late fifties, Van Dyke's career seemed hopelessly stalled in the frustrating category of minor celebrity. By 1960, after nearly fifteen years in show business, the thirty-five-year-old star was still waiting for his big break.

Ironically, when that breakthrough finally arrived, it was not in television at all, but on the Broadway stage. And, as the noted theater director and choreographer Gower Champion might have proclaimed, television's loss was Broadway's gain. For it was Champion who took a chance on the star-to-be when he cast Dick Van Dyke as the romantic lead in the musical *Bye Bye Birdie*—despite the fact that the actor confessed he didn't know the first thing about dancing. Fortunately, Van Dyke proved to be a quick study, and the day after *Bye Bye Birdie* opened, the actor who'd spent years on the brink of stardom was surprised to wake up and discover he was an overnight success.

In spite of the acclaim that greeted his Broadway debut, the practical performer never lost sight of his long-range goal: to find regular work in television. "By that time I had three kids and I was looking for steady work," he explains. "I just couldn't take a chance on hanging around the theater and hoping to get another hit. And so a series was the best answer for me."

And so it was with more than casual interest that Van Dyke agreed to meet Sheldon Leonard not long after the producer caught the actor's head-turning performance in *Bye Bye Birdie*. According to agent Sol Leon, who remembered being present at the first meeting between Van Dyke and

Leonard, the pair met for an informal chat one Friday evening, a few minutes before Van Dyke was due to report to the Martin Beck for his evening performance. "Dick met us at six o'clock," Leon recalled. "And Sheldon said, 'I've got three scripts that I would like you to read.' Then Dick said, 'I'll read them over the weekend.'" Three days later, Van Dyke was in. "I called Dick on Monday," the agent remembered, "and he said, 'I've been offered a lot of scripts. But nothing like these.'"

"Once I saw the quality of Carl's writing," the actor concurs. "Well, that just sealed it."

A deal to secure Van Dyke's services was quickly struck with Byron Paul, who was by that time acting as the actor's manager. Under the terms of his initial contract for the series, the star was to be paid a relatively modest starting salary of $1,500 per episode, with standard raises built in for subsequent years in the event the show went beyond a single season. In addition, Van Dyke would also receive an ownership stake in the proposed series, a deal point that the actor would later credit to Byron Paul's business acumen. And a savvy move it was.

In the years since *The Dick Van Dyke Show* left the air, the star's financial participation in the series has generated far greater revenues than he ever earned as a performer on the show. Van Dyke's ownership status also ensures that the actor will continue to derive income from the show's perpetually remunerative reruns, which makes him the only member of the show's original cast to so profit, the other actors having long since exhausted the skimpy residual payments that were standard in the early sixties.*

With Van Dyke now installed as an official partner and co-owner of the new series, he and the show's other owners promptly formed a legal partnership that they christened Calvada Productions, based on an acronym that incorporated the first letters in each of the primary partner's names—*CA* for Carl Reiner, *L* for Leonard, *VA* for Van Dyke, and *DA* for Sheldon Leonard's deep-pocketed business partner Danny Thomas, who would earn a substantial stake in the company by providing the operating capital to film the pilot and subsequent episodes of *The Dick Van Dyke Show*. As things turned out, it would prove to be one of the best investments Danny Thomas ever made.

---

* In the show's later years, *Dick Van Dyke Show* co-owner Danny Thomas finally did offer Mary Tyler Moore a small ownership stake in the series in lieu of a salary increase she was due in one of the show's final seasons. Though the actress may have been tempted by the—as it would turn out—generous offer, she finally chose to forgo a minority stake in the series in favor of a higher upfront salary.

6

CASTING CALLS

With Dick Van Dyke signed to play their lead, Carl Reiner and Sheldon Leonard were ready to begin the critical task of casting the show's supporting ensemble. And when it came to the business of casting, Sheldon Leonard was in his element. As executive producer of *The Andy Griffith Show*, he had already assembled one of the strongest acting companies on television. "I'd learned very quickly on the *Griffith Show* how important it was to surround your lead with a rich, amusing, supporting cast," recalled Leonard, who was anxious to apply the lessons he'd learned on that series to the task at hand.

The first role cast—after Van Dyke himself—was also the easiest. "There's only one person to play Sally Rogers," Leonard told Reiner, "and that is Rose Marie."*

The executive producer was right, of course. Not that it required any great powers of perspicacity to envision Rose Marie playing a brash,

* Interestingly, actress Sylvia Miles, who played Sally Rogers in *Head of the Family*, insists that she was offered the opportunity to reprise the role in the *Van Dyke* series, only to turn it down to pursue a thriving career on the New York stage. "William Morris wanted to sign me to a five-year deal," says Miles, "and they were very angry with me when I turned that down." While it's entirely possible that an agent at the William Morris Agency may have approached the actress, it's doubtful that anyone directly connected with *The Dick Van Dyke Show* made any serious overtures to Miles, if for no other reason than Reiner's determination to distance the new series from the earlier pilot he'd filmed in New York. "Now that we were in California," notes Reiner, "we wanted to start over again. That way, no one at the network could say, 'Oh, we saw that show,' and turn us down a second time."

funny lady who sings and tells jokes—it was a role she'd already been playing for a lifetime. Born in New York City on August 15, 1923, Rose Marie Mazetta was all of three years old when she made her professional radio debut as Baby Rose Marie, a three-foot-tall singing and dancing dynamo. Over the next decade, Baby Rose Marie would log hundreds of appearances on stage, screen, and radio, until, by the early forties, the former child star—her name now shortened to Rose Marie—had flowered into one of America's best-known radio and nightclub entertainers. The singer would continue her tireless schedule of personal appearances throughout the decade, culminating in an extended engagement in support of Phil Silvers in *Top Banana*, a popular musical revue that opened at Broadway's Winter Garden Theatre on November 1, 1951.

By the late fifties, television had discovered the versatile Rose Marie, whose range as a singer and actress made her equally at home in variety show or situation comedy settings. Before the decade ended, Rose Marie would rack up an impressive list of credits on shows as varied as *Cavalcade of Stars*, *M Squad*, *The Many Loves of Dobie Gillis*, and *Gunsmoke*. For a brief spell in 1960, the actress also had a recurring role on *My Sister Eileen*, a short-lived situation comedy that was canceled, fortuitously, just before the *Van Dyke Show* went into production in 1961. Considering the bounty of work that had already come her

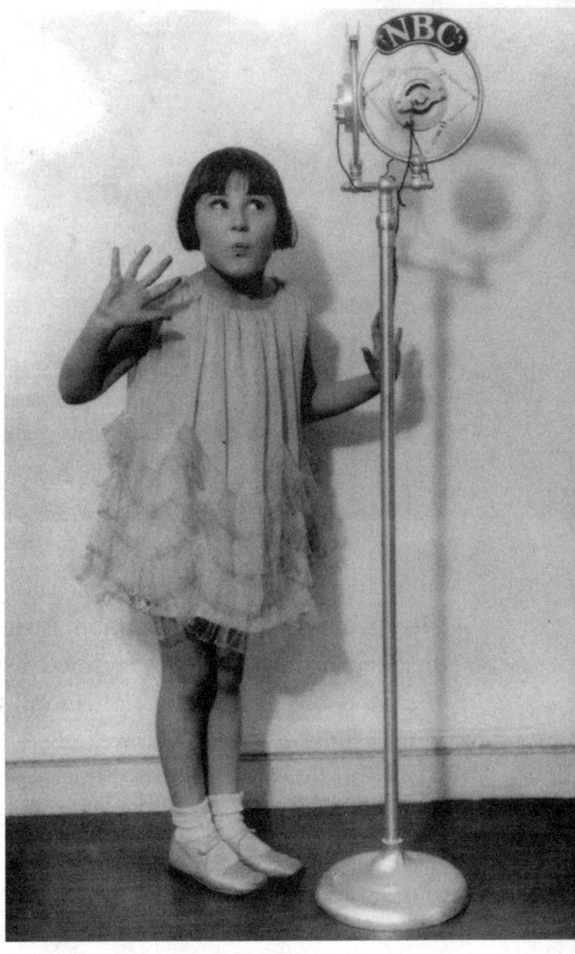

Baby Rose Marie, the singing and dancing powerhouse who would grow up to play Sally Rogers. *Courtesy: Rose Marie*

"There's only person to play Sally Rogers," Sheldon Leonard told Carl Reiner, "and that is Rose Marie."

way by the time Leonard called her in to interview for a part on his new series, it seems ironic that her first response was "Sheldon! What took you so long?"

"I'd known Sheldon Leonard for years," she explains, recalling personal and professional ties that went all the way back to radio, where Rose Marie had played Leonard's sister on *The Phil Harris Show*. In the years since, Leonard proved to be one of the entertainer's most loyal supporters. Whenever Rose Marie played a nightclub engagement in Southern California or Las Vegas, she recalls that she could count on seeing Leonard sitting ringside, often alongside Danny Thomas, another of the singer's long-standing friends. Yet for all their attention, Rose Marie found it puzzling that neither Leonard nor Thomas had ever asked her to appear on *The Danny Thomas Show*. "I used to ask Sheldon," she recalls, "'When am I gonna do a guest shot on Danny's show?'"

According to the actress, his response was always the same. "Don't worry, Rosie," he would promise. "Your time will come. Your time will come." Rose Marie had heard that refrain so often that when she finally did get a call from Leonard's casting director in the closing weeks of 1960, the actress seemed genuinely surprised. "Oh, God!" she exclaimed to Ruth Burch, Leonard's head of casting. "Does this mean I'm finally gonna be on Danny's show?"

"Oh, no, no," explained Burch. "This is for *The Dick Van Dyke Show*."

"Oh?" the actress recalls asking. "What's a Dick Van Dyke?"

No sooner had Burch answered her query than Rose Marie was out the door and on her way to the studio. "I was the second one cast on the show," she says, "after Dick." According to Reiner, it was obvious within seconds of her arrival that Rose Marie's casting interview would be little more than a formality. "As soon as I met her," he insists, "I said, 'Absolutely!'" So certain were they that they'd found their Sally Rogers, the producers never even bothered to hand the actress a copy of the script at her audition. Instead, they launched directly into a detailed description of the show's premise and her role in the series. "When they told me that I would play a television writer," recalls Rose Marie, "I said, 'Oh, my God! You're gonna let the public know that comics are not so funny on their own? That they have writers?'"

For her services, the actress was offered a generous, if not extravagant, salary of $1,000 per episode. "It was one of those things where they said, 'Well, we're paying this kind of money,'" the actress recalls. Reasoning that the figure mentioned sounded fair, the actress accepted the job on the spot. "I thought I'd made the greatest deal in the world," she remembers, "because they gave me everything I wanted. But then, as I walked down the steps, I said, 'Damn it, I should have asked for more money!'"

As her matter-of-fact interview drew to a close, Rose Marie stopped to ask her producers one additional, and, as it would turn out, significant question before she left. "Have you got anyone in mind for the third writer?" she asked.

"No," Reiner replied, "we haven't picked him yet."

"Good," she declared, "because Morey Amsterdam would be just great for this." Reiner paused to consider the suggestion as Rose Marie elaborated. "He used to be a writer for Fanny Brice and Milton Berle and Fred Allen. And he's also a comic."

The actress continued her pitch, but Reiner, who, during his tenure as host of *Keep Talking*, had already witnessed Amsterdam's comic inventiveness as a celebrity panelist, didn't need much convincing. True, at forty-eight, Amsterdam was a lot older than the character Reiner had originally envisioned as a twenty-three-year-old hypochondriac. But it didn't take the writer long to recognize the potential in recasting his third writer as a veteran comic steeped in shtick and old-school traditions. And if anyone fit that description better than Amsterdam—the self-proclaimed "Human Joke Machine"—Reiner certainly didn't know him. "Do you know where Morey is?" Reiner finally asked.

"Are you kiddin'?" Rose Marie shot back. "I'm his daughter's godmother! I've known Morey since I was eleven years old—when we did *The Al Pearce Show*—"

"Okay, Rosie," Reiner interrupted. "You win. Now, where do we find him?"

"In Yonkers," she replied. "I'll give you his number."

Reiner placed the call that same afternoon, and it was a conversation that Morey Amsterdam would never forget. "When the phone rang," the actor recalled, "I was out in the backyard, shoveling snow out of the driveway." When the comedian's wife called him in from the snow and handed him the phone, the producer got straight to the point. "Carl said, 'Morey, we're doing a show. I made a pilot on it with me playing the lead, but we're doing it again with a guy named Dick Van Dyke.' And he says, 'We want to know if you're interested. Can you get out here by day after tomorrow?' I says, 'I can leave here in fifteen minutes! I want to get out of this goddamned snow.' And that was it."

When Amsterdam arrived in Los Angeles a few days later, any reservations Reiner might've harbored evaporated in an instant. "When Morey came in," Reiner recalls, "I said, 'My God, is that right!'

"We couldn't have had a show without Morey Amsterdam," says Carl Reiner. "He literally was the Human Joke Machine." *Courtesy: Morey Amsterdam*

He epitomized every hack comedy writer in the business." In Reiner's eyes, Amsterdam *was* Buddy Sorrell—and, by all reports, the actor felt the same way. As the veteran comic was only too happy to admit, "I just played myself."

Indeed, Buddy Sorrell's biography would so closely resemble that of the actor who portrayed him that it was sometimes difficult to tell where Morey left off and Buddy began. The real-life Morey Amsterdam was born on December 14, 1908, in Chicago, but spent his formative years in San Francisco, where his father was for many years a violinist with the San Francisco Symphony. "I was raised to be a concert cellist," the comedian noted, recalling how his father would have liked nothing better than to see his son follow in his footsteps. But by his early teens, the younger Amsterdam discovered that he preferred Borscht to Bartok, and by the late 1920s, the would-be comic had abandoned the symphonic stage in favor of the noisy prosceniums of vaudeville. Perhaps as a nod to his father's wishes, the young comedian kept his cello in the act, where it would become Amsterdam's most distinctive trademark.

In the early thirties, the cello-playing comic moved his act to radio, where Amsterdam soon discovered that he had a prodigious facility for creating and cataloging jokes and one-liners, a skill that he would parlay into a substantial second income as joke doctor for some of the era's more notable stage and radio entertainers, including Will Rogers, Fanny Brice, Jimmy Durante, and Pearl Bailey, among many others. Throughout the thirties and forties, the comedian maintained a rigorous schedule of radio and personal appearances, and also found time to pen music or lyrics for a handful of popular novelty songs of the era, including the Andrews Sisters' wartime hit "Rum and Coca Cola," on which he shared credit with Paul Baron and Jeri Sullavan. With the coming of television in the late forties, Amsterdam's ability to think on his feet practically assured the versatile performer steady employment in the burgeoning medium of live TV. By 1948, he was hosting *The Morey Amsterdam Show* for CBS, an assignment that eventually led to the comic's appointment as one of the hosts of NBC's *Broadway Open House*, the pioneering 1950 late-night talk show that would serve as a prototype for the network's immensely popular *Tonight Show*. In the years between *Broadway Open House* and the start of *The Dick Van Dyke Show* a little more than a decade later, Amsterdam logged hundreds of additional appearances on a wide array of TV variety programs and celebrity panel shows, where the comedian frequently billed himself as the "Human Joke

Machine," a boastful reference to his uncanny ability to cook up a joke on any topic put to him—a talent that would, incidentally, prove a most valuable asset to *The Dick Van Dyke Show*.

"We couldn't have had a show without Morey Amsterdam," acknowledges Reiner, who happily admits that he and his writers thought nothing of plundering the comic's vast repository of jokes and one-liners whenever they got stuck. "He literally was the Human Joke Machine," says Reiner. "You'd give him a subject and he'd do five jokes on it." Adds longtime *Van Dyke Show* director John Rich, "They weren't always the best jokes. But if you weeded them out, you would get winners." And though Amsterdam would eventually provide punch lines for every character on the series, it was only natural that the comedian's vast library of punch lines proved most valuable as a source of one-liners for the character closest to him. "When the script needed a Buddy joke," Reiner recalls, "he'd give us five."

After a while, says Reiner, the actor grew so adept at supplying his own one-liners that it became a point of pride among the show's writers whenever one of them managed to think up a wisecrack that the comedian hadn't already heard. "Once in while, we'd come up with a Buddy joke for Morey," says Reiner, "and he'd be very thankful."

Carl Reiner's decision to hire the bald and bespectacled character actor Richard Deacon to round out the *Van Dyke Show*'s office ensemble was a choice as inspired as it was obvious. By the time Deacon was hired to play *The Dick Van Dyke Show*'s fastidious and high-strung Mel Cooley, the popular character actor had already burnished his reputation with dozens of similar characterizations in countless films and situation comedies of the fifties, including recurring roles on *A Date with the Angels* and *The Charlie Farrell Show*, as well as a lengthy stint as the long-suffering Fred Rutherford on *Leave It to Beaver*. In fact, it was Deacon's pitch-perfect portrayal of *Leave it to Beaver*'s easily flustered Rutherford that convinced Reiner to bring the actor in for the part of Mel Cooley in the first place. "He just looked so right," says Reiner. "He was angry and fussy. Just wonderful for that part."

Like most of the characters who would come to populate the *Van Dyke Show*, the *Alan Brady Show*'s much-put-upon producer had a real-life precedent—or, in his case, a pair of them. "Mel was based on a couple of producers we had on the *Show of Shows*," remembers Reiner. "They were good guys—nice, family guys. But they were also the kind of guys who took shit from everybody, because they were always the ones bringing us bad news. And since you couldn't go up to the vice president of NBC and yell at him, you'd yell at these guys." Naturally, Reiner recalls, it wasn't long before this constant barrage of verbal abuse began to take its toll. "One of the guys used to chew pencils," remarks Reiner, "right down to the lead. And then he'd swallow it! He always looked like he had licorice on his mouth."

Fortunately for Deacon, his character was spared that particular indignity—though Reiner may have saddled his fictional producer with an even greater cross to bear when he made Mel Cooley the star's brother-in-law. "I just invented that," says Reiner, acknowledging the fertile range of joke opportunities that Alan Brady's nepotism opened up for the show's writers. "It just made it more fun."

Of course, Mel Cooley's most striking feature could be found at the very top of his head—a hairless expanse that inspired the relentless stream of barbs that would come to define the producer's tempestuous relationship with his chief nemesis, comedy writer Buddy Sorrell. According to Amsterdam, Buddy's habit of zinging Mel with bald jokes at every opportunity was not an element in Reiner's original conception of the show, but sprang from a few on-set quips that the real-life actors exchanged during early rehearsals.

"I was always kidding Richard Deacon about his bald head," recalled Amsterdam. "One day we're kidding around, and Deac said something innocuous. And I said, 'Deac, that makes no sense at all. Sometimes I think your hair didn't fall out—it fell in and clouded your brain.' It broke up everybody on the set, and Carl came running out and said, 'Let's keep that in.' And that was the start of that relationship between me and Mel."

And, just so the Buddy-versus-Mel debates wouldn't seem too one-sided, the show's producers occasionally allowed Mel the opportunity for a comeback, the most famous of which was inaugurated in the show's third episode, "Jealousy!" Legend has it that during rehearsals for that episode, Reiner and director John Rich were searching for a suitable riposte to Buddy's latest broadside. Finally, at his wit's end, Reiner turned to Deacon and asked the actor how he would react to a tormentor like Buddy Sorrell in real life. Without a pause, Deacon uttered, "Yeecchh!" And without further discussion, the actor's monosyllabic response was duly incorporated into the script of that and many subsequent episodes.

If Deacon shared certain characteristics with his on-screen alter ego, Mel Cooley's humorlessness was certainly not one of them. "Richard Deacon was the funniest human being on the face of the earth," recalled the show's film editor, Bud Molin, who offered as evidence the surreal spectacle of the rotund actor performing an impromptu striptease for the cast and crew—an event that Molin swears actually transpired at one of the show's Christmas parties. "All of a sudden Deacon decides he's gonna do a striptease," recounted Molin. "And so he got up and started to strip—to music—for twenty minutes! He never stopped working, but at the end of that twenty minutes, all he'd taken off were his cuff links. That was it! He was just a funny, funny guy."

Another significant difference between the actor and his character on the show is that, unlike Mel Cooley, the real-life Richard Deacon was universally loved by everyone on the set. "He was a joy to have around," says Reiner, who remained on friendly terms with Deacon until the character actor's death in 1984. "Morey and Rosie loved Deacon," notes Reiner. "Everybody did. He was a dear man."

Having assembled a first-rate ensemble of character actors to populate Rob Petrie's office family, the show's producers moved on to the more exacting task of casting Rob Petrie's other clan: his wife, Laura, and their son, Ritchie. As the show's casting director, Ruth Burch, recalled, the task of finding an actor to play the Petries' six-year-old son was accomplished with a minimum of fuss. "We had interviews of children that were five and six years old," she explained. Based on those introductory interviews, Reiner quickly narrowed the field down to four or five final contenders, each of whom was asked to demonstrate his acting skill by performing one of the most rudimentary exercises of all. “Carl asked me to pretend like I was sick,” recalls Larry Mathews, who would win the role. “I was supposed to be ill in the pilot, so he wanted to make sure I could do that well.”

According to Burch, Mathews had the part sewn up after that single audition. “They just zeroed in on him,” she recalled. “He was a cute little guy. Not at all as supercilious as kids are nowadays.” As far as Reiner was concerned, Mathews's utter lack of precocity put him at a distinct advantage in the running for the role. As Amsterdam recalled, “Carl said, ‘I want a kid who hasn't done anything and who hasn't been in anything.’” In other words, what Reiner wanted was a real, live all-American boy. And, as the producer was delighted to discover, in Larry Mathews, he had found just that.

Born Larry Mazzeo, on August 15, 1955, in Burbank, California, Larry Mathews had never acted professionally before he auditioned for *The Dick Van Dyke Show* in early January 1961. A tow-headed five-year-old from the San Fernando Valley, Mathews had taken his first acting lesson only a few months earlier, when his parents, on a whim, enrolled him in a children's drama workshop. There, the outgoing five-year-old attracted the attention of a children's talent agent, who offered to recommend the young actor to Reiner, who was then looking for a real kid to join the cast of his new series. Within a few days of his audition for the show, the producer signed young Larry Mazzeo—who had by then adopted Larry Mathews as his stage name—to play Rob and Laura's son, Ritchie.

By the second week of January 1961, Reiner had cast all the principal roles on *The Dick Van Dyke Show*—save one. But with rehearsals for the show's pilot episode

scheduled to start in less than a week, the producer was growing understandably nervous that he still hadn't found an actress to play Laura Petrie, though it wasn't for lack of trying.

"I must have looked at every young actress in town," he sighs. "I saw about sixty girls for Laura. Literally—sixty!" And, as if the novice producer didn't have enough worries, he knew that he would have to solve this problem without the assistance of his mentor, Sheldon Leonard. By that point in the show's casting process, Leonard had been forced to turn his attentions to the three or four other shows he was producing on the lot, leaving Reiner to sort though the seemingly endless parade of potential Laura Petries on his own. "He left me sitting alone in a room," explains Reiner, "reading sixty actresses!"

And there Reiner would stay, for days on end, meeting, reading, and ultimately rejecting scores of hopeful ingenues who, for one reason or another, failed to live up to his exacting image of Robert Petrie's wife. "I just couldn't find the right type," he explains. After he'd interviewed at least three-dozen actresses, Reiner finally turned to Leonard for support. "Gee," he confessed to his mentor, "I don't know what I'm looking for!" But Leonard, who'd been in Reiner's spot himself on more than one occasion, knew there was little he could do to alleviate his younger partner's frustration. "You'll know what you're looking for," Leonard counseled, "when you find it."

7

THE GIRL WITH THREE NAMES

The first bright moment in Carl Reiner's marathon search to find the perfect Laura Petrie arrived when he heard about a young actress named Eileen Brennan. In early 1961, the future Oscar nominee was attracting attention in New York theatrical circles for her work as the title character in *Little Mary Sunshine*, an off-Broadway musical spoof that had been running for more than a year. "Somebody said, 'You really ought to fly her out here. She's sensational!'" recalls Reiner. But despite her glowing notices, the producer was hesitant to fly Brennan across the country to audition for him, mainly because he wasn't sure he could justify the expense of the airfare to Danny Thomas, who had by that time agreed to foot the expenses for *The Dick Van Dyke Show*'s pilot film.

"We never flew anybody out in those days," says Reiner. Even so, the producer decided that, with his shooting date less than two weeks off, and no Laura Petire in sight, he didn't have much choice. And so, inching out on what he worried was a precarious financial limb, Reiner authorized the purchase of a round-trip airline ticket to fly the young actress to Los Angeles for an interview. "I still remember the amount," he recalls. "It was five hundred dollars."

"She was a brilliant actress," Reiner recalls thinking when Brennan finally read for the part of Laura Petrie in his California office, "but it just wasn't working." To her credit, the producer notes, Brennan's interpretation of Laura Petrie was remarkably assured. But, ironically, the actress's vigorous reading of the role may have actually worked against her. As the producer would later assess it, "We knew she would be too strong for Dick."[1] And so Reiner sent the talented young actress back to New York empty-handed.

The decision left the producer feeling worse than ever. Not only had he rejected the most promising actress he'd yet seen for the role of Laura Petrie, but he'd spent five hundred dollars of his backer's money to do it! Feeling overwhelmed, Reiner finally decided to pay a call on Danny Thomas himself, if only to apprise his benefactor of his progress, or lack of it, in casting that last elusive role. "I figured Danny had a right to know how we were spending his money," adds Reiner. So, with their pilot's start date now only a few days away, Reiner and Leonard resolved to break the news to Thomas that they still hadn't found their leading lady.

When the pair finally caught up with him, they found Thomas reclining in a barber's chair in his dressing room, reading a script as the studio's barber applied a quick touch-up to the star's prematurely graying hair. "They were coloring in the part," remembers Reiner, who recalls being surprised to observe that Thomas's hair was actually quite white where the makeup man had yet to apply his brush. After a few moments of small talk, Reiner summoned the courage to broach the subject that had brought him there. "Danny," he confessed, "we just spent five hundred dollars of your money to fly Eileen Brennan out here from New York, and it didn't work out. And now we still haven't found a girl to play the wife on the show."

"Oh," the star replied, unfazed. As the makeup man continued his diligent labors, Thomas fell silent for a few very agonizing seconds, lost in thought. Finally, just as Leonard and Reiner were about to turn for the door, Thomas sat up with a start. "You know," he announced, "there was a girl who auditioned for me a couple months ago—she read for the daughter on my show. I didn't use her, and I don't remember her name. But, boy, did she read terrific!"

His curiosity piqued, Reiner listened with interest as Leonard joined Thomas in trying to remember the name of the mystery actress who had just become a front-runner in the Laura Petrie sweepstakes.

"I just remembered something else," declared Thomas. "The girl we're looking for had three names!"

"Wait a minute," said Leonard, suddenly recalling a clue of his own. "Wasn't she the one with the legs?"

"Yes!" exclaimed Thomas, "that was her!" And then, noticing the slightly confused look on Reiner's face, Thomas quickly explained this latest clue in their little mystery. A few months before she came in to read for them, Thomas recalled, the girl they were now seeking had created quite a stir in the role of Sam, the curvaceous receptionist whose legs were the most outstanding feature of the *Richard Diamond, Private Detective* show. "So now we knew that she had great legs," says Reiner. "And three names. But that was all we had to go by."

Apparently, it was enough. With the help of casting maven Ruth Burch, it didn't take the eager producers long to track down the elusive actress with the three names and great legs. Within a few hours, Reiner had arranged to meet Mary Tyler Moore in his office the very next day.

"MARY WAS PRACTICALLY out of the business when we brought her into the show," Sheldon Leonard insisted, intoning one of the more durable *Dick Van Dyke Show* legends. "She had given up on the idea of a career in acting. She was that disheartened about her career." It's a colorful story, and one that's been repeated often over the years. But despite the irresistible irony implicit in Leonard's depiction of the young

Carl Reiner interviewed more than sixty actresses for the role of Laura Petrie before he finally struck gold with Mary Tyler Moore.

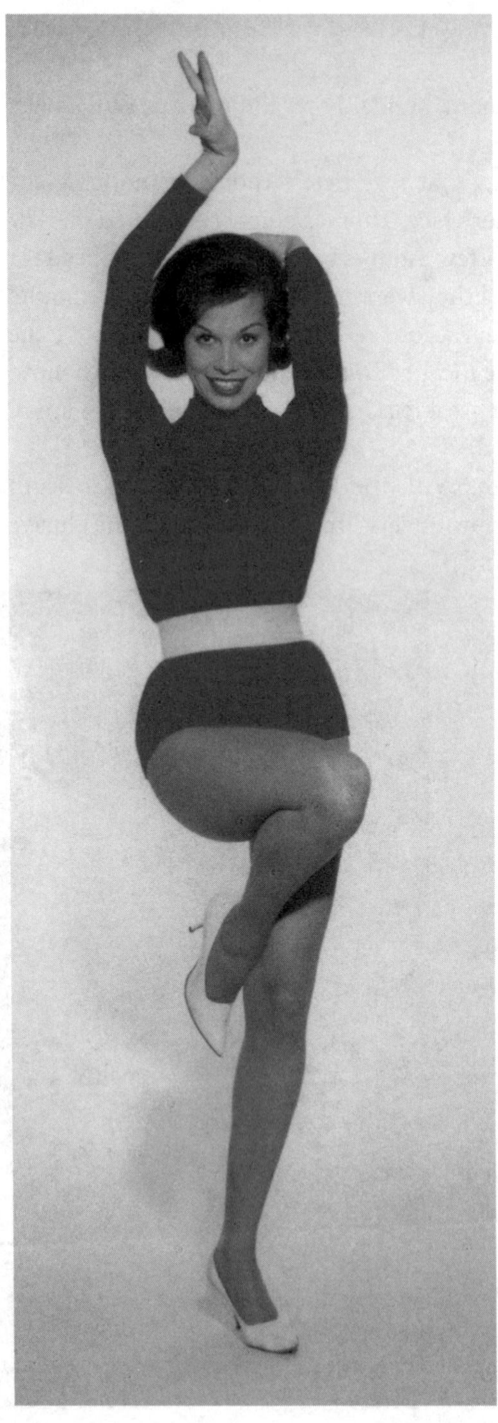

Mary Tyler Moore as a struggling outsider in the days before she was hired in the role that would make her a household name, that interpretation doesn't do justice to the tenacious young actress who arrived at Reiner's office for her eleventh-hour audition in January 1961. The fact is, Moore came to that reading armed with an impressive array of TV credits and an almost intimidating desire to succeed in her chosen field. While it's undeniable that her work on *The Dick Van Dyke Show* secured Moore's place in show business history, it's no less significant that the young actress had been determined to see her name in lights long before she ever met Sheldon Leonard, Carl Reiner, or Dick Van Dyke.

"I gave up college to learn to become a star," Mary Tyler Moore explained to a reporter early in her career. "I don't just hope for it. I work for it. I expect it."[2] In fact, Mary Tyler Moore's preparation for stardom began years before she chose to forego college to pursue her dream. Born in Brooklyn, New York, on December 29, 1936, Moore enrolled in her first ballet class while still in grammar school. When her family moved to Los Angeles in the late forties, the would-be performer studied both dance and drama throughout her elementary and high school years. The young performer's dedication paid off within days of her high school graduation, when Moore landed her first professional engagement as a TV mascot for the Hotpoint appliance company at the ripe old age of eighteen. Clad in pointy ears and a form-fitting leotard, the young dancer/actress portrayed Happy Hotpoint, an elfin sprite who danced her way through a series of commercials for Hotpoint appliances that aired on *The Adventures of Ozzie and Harriet* throughout 1955.

By the end of that year, the actress—by then wed to her first husband, Richard Meeker, a salesman seven years her senior—was forced to trade Happy Hotpoint's ears and leotard for a maternity wardrobe when she learned she was pregnant with Richard Jr., who was born in July 1956. The actress devoted the next two years to motherhood, but by 1958 she was back on television, paying her dues as a dancer in the chorus lines of a half-dozen variety shows of the era. In early 1959, Moore landed her first significant television role as Sam, the secretary on David Janssen's private-eye series, *Richard Diamond, Private Detective*. Unfortunately, the exposure Moore received on the *Richard Diamond* series was not exactly what the ambitious young performer had in mind. For it was one of the show's playful conceits that viewers never actually saw Sam—only her legs were ever shown on camera. And though Moore's shapely gams drew considerable attention to the series, the actress herself derived little personal glory from the uncredited role. To make matters worse, she wasn't even well paid for her efforts. "I was getting scale," the actress would later explain. "Eighty dollars a week."[3]

Finding the role unrewarding on every level, Moore walked away from the series at the end of her thirteen-week contract, though not before she went public with her true identity—a canny move calculated to milk as much publicity as possible from the otherwise thankless assignment. It was a brilliant ploy. Newspaper and magazine editors loved having a face to go with the most famous legs on television, and they happily obliged the actress with a gusher of favorable press coverage, including a particularly eye-catching photo layout in the pages of *TV Guide*. In the wake of this publicity blitz, the young model suddenly had casting directors clamoring for her services. "Other shows seemed to want to use the girl who played Sam,"[4] the actress

Before she became Laura Petrie, young Mary Tyler Moore extended her acting range—and paid the bills—by posing as a wide array of exotic beauties on late-fifties record album jackets.

observed. In the two years between her departure from *Richard Diamond* in 1959 and the start of rehearsals for the *Van Dyke Show* pilot in early 1961, Moore logged a string of guest roles on a variety of weekly TV shows, including *The Millionaire*, *Bourbon Street Beat*, *Surfside 6*, *The Deputy*, *77 Sunset Strip*, *Bachelor Father*, *Thriller*, and *Hawaiian Eye*, to name just a few.

But, as it turned out, Moore's most significant engagement in the months before she was signed to the cast of *The Dick Van Dyke Show* may well have been her audition for *The Danny Thomas Show* in the summer of 1959. She'd been called in to read for the part of Danny's daughter, Terry, a role originally played by Sherry Jackson, who had left the series a few months earlier. Although Moore would eventually lose the part to Penney Parker, Thomas was so impressed by the actress's audition that he finally called her back three times before he told her that she'd lost the part—quite literally—by a nose. "She had the wrong nose," as the star would later explain it to Reiner. "She had a cute little turned-up nose."[5] As much as he admired her talent, Thomas was convinced that Moore's button nose was enough to disqualify her from playing his daughter, given the size of his own prominent snoot. "Honey," Thomas reportedly told her, "people just won't be able to believe you could belong to me."[6]

According to an account of that fateful audition that appeared in the pages of *TV Guide*, when she was informed of Thomas's decision, Moore offered, only half-jokingly, to have her nose surgically altered to match the star's own. "I'll have it fixed," she supposedly volunteered, "to put a bump in it."[7] Although Thomas wisely decided not to take her up on the offer, he would not soon forget meeting the spirited actress. Nor would Reiner, who finally met with Moore himself—at Thomas's suggestion—during the second week of January 1961.

According to another of the show's oft-told legends, on the day of her audition for *The Dick Van Dyke Show*, Moore very nearly decided to stay home. "She'd already been on three or four auditions that week, and they hadn't gone well," remembers Reiner. "And we call, and she's decided not to go on another one. 'That's it!' she says. 'I'm outta this. I quit. I'm never going on another audition!' But then, at the last minute, she decided to go."

"I was so nervous when I went in to read for him," remembers Moore, recalling that fateful meeting. According to the actress, she wasn't even aware that she would be reading for Reiner himself until she arrived at the audition. "I almost blew it," she says, "because of my awe of him as a performer.

He was my hero—not only as a writer, but as a performer on *Your Show of Shows*." But if Moore was the least bit overwrought during her audition, Reiner insists that it didn't come through in her reading, which he recalls as one of the most natural he'd ever witnessed.

"I remember it as if it were yesterday," says Reiner. "She walked into the office, and she sat down. She read three lines. And they were a simple three lines—the first three lines of the opening of the pilot, 'The Sick Boy and the Sitter.'* That's all it took—three lines. And I heard the sound. And I thought, Oh, Jesus! She said hello like a real person!"

As Reiner recalls it, the minute he heard the actress read, he was on his feet, so delighted he could barely contain himself. "I started walking toward her," he remembers. "And there was only the two of us in the room—so she got scared for a moment. Then I grabbed the top of her head, and I never let go." Speechless, the startled actress rose to her feet as Reiner led her to the door. "'Come with me!' I told her. 'Just come with me.'"

Then, still grasping the frightened actress by the crown of her head, the ecstatic producer led her right out of his office, past a secretary, and across the narrow balcony that connected his office with Sheldon Leonard's private suite next door. And the giddy producer didn't stop walking until he and his slightly confused charge were standing directly in front of the executive producer's massive wooden desk. "I meant to let go, but I couldn't take my hand off the top of her head," confesses Reiner. "And when I got Mary to Sheldon's office I said, 'This is the girl, Sheldon. This is her! She said *hello* just like a real person.'"

The imperturbable executive producer glanced up from his paperwork, took a quick look at the dumbstruck actress, and shrugged his shoulders in assent. "That's fine," he muttered before turning back to his work.

"She was just right for what we wanted at the time," explained Leonard, who insists that neither he nor Reiner had any qualms about hiring the largely unknown actress on little more than their gut instinct. "She looked like a nice, attractive Westchester housewife with good legs," Leonard observed. "And she had good timing." It was only later, Leonard allowed, that he and his partner came to recognize that their latest hire was also an accomplished dancer, a gifted singer, and a trained actress of unerring

* For the record, Laura's first three lines in the filmed pilot, spoken over the phone to her neighbor, Dotty, are: "Hello," "Why are you sending him home?" and "Does Ellen have a temperature?"

comic instinct. "We discovered all that bit by bit," recalled Leonard. "But when you find it, you exploit it."

Exploit it they did. Within days of her initial audition, Leonard and Reiner had signed the young actress to a five-year contract. And, according to Leonard, owing largely to her relative obscurity, he was able to secure Moore's services at bargain basement rates. "Mary," the executive producer would later boast, "was signed up for nickels and dimes!"

Not that anyone heard any complaint from the actress. Even today, Moore recalls the joy she felt at the prospect of working with Reiner on a weekly basis. "For me," the actress explains, "Carl was every man in a young girl's life. He was my mentor, my father confessor, my teacher. I just loved that man. And still do." It didn't take long for the actress to inspire an equally passionate devotion in her mentor. "If I were a dirty old man," Reiner would later gush, "Mary Tyler Moore would be my girlfriend. But I'm not, so she's sort of my daughter. I'm just crazy about that girl."[8]

8

NERVOUS WRECKS

"The total cost of *The Dick Van Dyke Show* pilot was forty thousand dollars from start to finish," Sheldon Leonard once bragged, with justifiable pride. And though Carl Reiner remembers a slightly higher figure—in his recollection, the total was closer to $47,000—at either amount the figure seems quite modest by today's standards, when that kind of cash barely covers a week's pretzels and petty cash on the average Hollywood set.

Most of the credit for the *Van Dyke Show*'s cost efficiency goes to executive producer Leonard, whose genius for maximizing *The Dick Van Dyke Show*'s relatively limited resources began with the show's very first episode. "By that time I had already learned the technique of making cheap pilots," recalled Leonard, who had caused industry observers to sit up and take notice the year before, when he managed to sell *The Andy Griffith Show* to CBS without making a pilot film at all. Instead, the canny producer had contrived to introduce Andy Griffith's Sheriff Andy Taylor character—along with some of Mayberry's other notable citizens—on an episode of *The Danny Thomas Show*. Then, using that episode of the *Thomas Show* as a working sample of his proposed new series, the producer was able to convince CBS and General Foods to add *The Andy Griffith Show* to the

Carl Reiner and Sheldon Leonard flank Danny Thomas, the deep-pocketed star who agreed to foot the bill for *The Dick Van Dyke Show* pilot in exchange for a hefty ownership stake in the series. *Courtesy: Ronald Jacobs*

network's fall 1960 schedule—all without having invested a cent to make an actual pilot for the series. By creating this "backdoor pilot" for *The Andy Griffith Show*, Leonard executed one of the earliest and most successful examples of the television spin-off, a cheap and effective means of generating new prime-time programming that is still employed, for better or worse, by budget-conscious TV producers to this day.

Despite his successful sale of the *Griffith Show* without a pilot in 1960, Leonard knew that he would have to develop a different strategy when it came time to pitch the *Van Dyke Show* to potential networks and sponsors a season later. Owing to complex legal and creative restrictions, Leonard ruled out the possibility of simply introducing the *Van Dyke Show*'s cast and characters on an episode of *The Danny Thomas Show*. Instead, he did the next best thing when he arranged to shoot his *Van Dyke* pilot on *The Danny Thomas Show*'s stage during a temporary layoff in that show's weekly production schedule—an ingenious scheme that allowed the thrifty producer access to Thomas's fully staffed and well-equipped studio, without having to spend a dime on the overhead charges and costly start-up expenses that are usually incurred when shooting a pilot. And because his above-the-line talent expenses on *The Dick Van Dyke Show* were relatively modest, Leonard

PRODUCTION SCHEDULE FOR WEEK OF JAN. 16 Thru JAN. 21, 1961 PAGE 2

NO.	SHOW	NO. & TITLE	UNIT PROD.MGR. &	ASST.DIR.	LOCATION
DESILU CAHUENGA					
6203	ANDY GRIFFITH SHOW	#23 ANDY & OPIE HOUSEKEEPERS #24 THE NEW DOCTOR	MYERS-	BILSON	STAGE 1-2 1/16,17,18 STAGE 1-2 Reh. 1/19,20
6230	DANNY THOMAS SHOW	LAYOFF (1/16 thru 1/20/61)	MYERS-	SANDRICH	LAYOFF
6230	CARL REINER SHOW	#800 ALL IN A DAYS WORK-Pilot	MYERS-	SANDRICH	STAGE 5 Prepare 1/16 STAGE 5 Reh. 1/17,18 (AUD.PREV.) Bl. 1/19 Sh. 1/20
6275	ANGEL	#26 FRENCH LESSON #27 PHONE FUN		ALDWORTH	STAGE 4 Reh. 1/16 Bl. 1/17, Sh. 1/18 STAGE 4 Prep. 1/19 STAGE 4 Reh. 1/20
6269	ONE HAPPY FAMILY	#8 CHARLIE, EXECUTIVE AT LARGE #9 RAINY AFTERNOON		J.McEVEETY	STAGE 3 Bl. 1/16, Sh. 1/17 STAGE 3 Prep. 1/18 STAGE 3 Reh. 1/19,20
DESILU CULVER					
6118	THE UNTOUCHABLES	#49 THE LILY DALLAS STORY	STUART-	PETSCHNIKOFF	STAGE 4,2,3 1/16 STAGE 2,3(PROCESS)&40A 1/17 STAGE 3,4 1/16
		#47 THE NICK MOSES STORY (Pickup on #47)			STAGE 3 (6118-49) & CULVER LOT (6118-47) 1/19
		#50 MAN UNDER GLASS	STUART-	V.McEVEETY	STAGE 3,4,RAMP ? 1/20
6130	GUESTWARD HO	#21 BILL, THE CANDIDATE		SCHILZ	40A COMPOUND, GUEST. RANCH & STAGE 11 1/16 STAGE 11 1/17
		#23 HAWKEYE, THE MOTHER (Read & Reh. only) 1/18 #22 BABS, THE GUEST (Reh. 1/17,20)			STAGE 11 Read & Reh. 1/18 STAGE 11 Reh. 1/19 STAGE 11,40A GUEST. RANCH Reh. 1/20
6233	THE REAL MC COYS	#129 THE HORSE EXPERT	DONAHOE-	EVANS	40A McCOY FARM 1/16 40A W.ST.BARN 1/17 STAGE 14 1/18
		#130 (TO BE DETERMINED)			STAGE 14 Reh. 1/19 40A MC COY FARM 1/20
6267	MIAMI UNDERCOVER	#400 AUTO MOTIVE ROOM 9	POWER-	WHELAN	CULVER CITY HIGHWAY & STS.1/19 (SEE GOWER SCHEDULE)

JIM PAISLEY

The pilot for the show that would soon be rechristened *The Dick Van Dyke Show* was still identified only as "Carl Reiner Show: *All in a Day's Work*" on the original Desilu Studios production roster for the week ending January 21, 1961. *Courtesy: Bart Andrews*

was able to bring in the tryout episode for less money than he spent to shoot an average episode of *The Danny Thomas Show*. All of which must have come as good news to Thomas himself, whose financial commitment to *The Dick Van Dyke Show* would extend well beyond the show's pilot episode.

Under the terms of the financial arrangement he'd worked out with Leonard, Thomas agreed to pick up the show's per-episode production tab even after the *Van Dyke Show* went to series, which was no small proposition. With estimated expenses of around $40,000 per episode, the investment required to capitalize the show's first season alone was projected to fall somewhere between 1.25 and 1.5 million dollars.*

* Of course, that 1.5-million-dollar figure looks downright paltry when viewed from the perspective of the modern TV marketplace, where the cost to film a single episode of a filmed situation comedy can easily approach or exceed that amount. For example, by the early 2000s, the cost to produce a high-end sitcom like *Frasier* exceeded $3 million per episode, an amount approximately equivalent to what it cost Danny Thomas, in 1961 dollars, to finance the first *two seasons* of *The Dick Van Dyke Show*!

Although future star Dick Van Dyke seems to exude self-confidence in this publicity still taken shortly after his arrival in California in 1961, he later confessed that he'd been a nervous wreck the week he filmed his show's pilot episode.

Naturally, that kind of support didn't come cheap. As Leonard observed, "You have to give up something for that kind of financing." In the case of *The Dick Van Dyke Show*, what the executive producer gave up was a substantial ownership stake in the series. In exchange for fronting the show's initial start-up budget and production costs, it was agreed that Danny Thomas would be entitled to a sizable share of any profits the show might eventually earn in syndicated rerun sales, which could be substantial. For Thomas, the arrangement turned out to be a good investment. More than a half-century later, *The Dick Van Dyke Show* still generates substantial revenues for the late star's heirs, even as it continues to enrich the bank accounts of the surviving members of the show's original partnership to this day.

THE DICK VAN DYKE SHOW pilot finally went into production on stage 5 of the Desilu Cahuenga Studios the week of January 16–20, 1961, during a relative lull in activity on the normally bustling lot. With *The Danny Thomas Show* on hiatus, only four shows—including the *Van Dyke Show* pilot—were in production on the facility's nine soundstages that week. On stages 1 and 2, Andy Griffith and his cast were hard at work on the twenty-third episode of *The Andy Griffith Show*, an episode titled

"Andy and Opie, Housekeepers." According to the studio's official production roster for that week, the other two shows in production on the lot were a pair of now long-forgotten situation comedies: *One Happy Family*, a domestic comedy that starred Dick Sargent and Jody Warner as newlyweds, and *Angel*, another domestic situation comedy, this one starring

Though Dick Van Dyke and Mary Tyler Moore shared a chemistry unmatched in television, the actor was initially skittish. "She was still in her early twenties, and I was thirty-five," he says, "I just thought, 'God Almighty, this is never going to work!'"

Marshall Thompson and Annie Farge. Curiously, that same Desilu Studio production manifest lists *The Dick Van Dyke Show* pilot, somewhat cryptically, as "Carl Reiner Show: #800, All in a Day's Work—Pilot."

According to Dick Van Dyke, the week he shot the show's pilot happened to fall at the very height of the Broadway theater season, a fact not lost on the producers of *Bye Bye Birdie*, who were naturally reluctant to allow their leading man to leave the play for a week during one of their busiest months. Under the circumstances, Van Dyke was released from his *Birdie* contract with the strict proviso that he take off *one* week and *one* week only: the star was to be back on stage at the Martin Beck for the following Tuesday night's performance. While he was gone, understudy Charles Nelson Reilly filled in for the star, allowing Van Dyke to fly three thousand miles to experience what he would one day describe as the five scariest days of his career.

"I was a nervous wreck," insists Van Dyke, recalling his general state of mind during rehearsals for the *Van Dyke Show* pilot. "I think I lost five pounds that week." According to Reiner, Van Dyke's weight loss wasn't the only malady to plague the actor during that fretful week. "He developed a cold sore," recalls Reiner. "If you look at the pilot, you can see that Dick's got a cold sore on his lip." It's a memory that still makes the star wince. "I remember that they had to use a lot of makeup on me," says Van Dyke, "because I had about four fever blisters that had popped up just from pure nerves."

As Dick Van Dyke recalls it, he had a big shock waiting for him when he finally laid eyes on the youthful actress who had been hired to play his wife. "She was still in her early twenties, and I was thirty-five!" explains the actor, who remembers leaving the show's first rehearsal convinced that his producer had made a terrible casting blunder. In Van Dyke's opinion, there was simply no way audiences were going to accept a mere sprig of a girl like Mary Tyler Moore as the wife of a man who was—in reality—eleven years her senior. "I just thought, 'God Almighty, this is never going to work!'" says Van Dyke. And at the first opportunity, the star took his producer aside and told him so.

"Dick kept saying, 'Mary's too young for me!'" recalls Reiner, who insisted that the show's audience would hardly notice the disparity in their ages. After all, as Reiner explained to his leading man, "No one ever says Cary Grant is too old for his costars."

"Yeah," came Van Dyke's retort, "but *I'm* not Cary Grant!"

Though Dick Van Dyke was hardly a household name when the actor won the part of Rob Petrie, the show's producers were so determined to make him a star that they named their show after him anyway.

Despite his leading man's initial—and, as it would happen, short-lived—skepticism, Reiner was convinced he'd made the right choice in casting Mary Tyler Moore as soon as he saw the sparks she and Dick Van Dyke generated on stage. It was a rare example of perfect chemistry between two actors, and it was a quality that the producer encouraged at every opportunity. "Carl told us, 'I want you both to go away and spend the weekend together,'" recalls Van Dyke, who hastens to add, "Which we didn't! But he was making a point—that if you don't really like each other, no amount of good acting or writing is gonna make people believe you do."

Ironically, even as Reiner and his actors worked to foster Rob and Laura's onstage rapport, the seeds of another offstage romance were planted when Sheldon Leonard introduced Moore to a handsome young advertising executive named Grant Tinker after one of the show's first run-throughs. Although Tinker insists he didn't ask Moore out on a date until after the actress separated from her first husband a few months later, at least one eyewitness to the couple's protracted courtship suggests that the pair's romantic paths were on a collision course well before they ever started going out.

According to an anecdote that *Van Dyke Show* associate producer Ronald Jacobs delights in retelling, he got his first hint that Moore and her future husband were fated to come together one evening early in the show's run, after Tinker joined the cast for an informal post-show dinner at a small restaurant near the studio. As the evening's festivities drew to a close, recalls the former associate producer, the party moved out to the sidewalk in front of the restaurant, where most of the cast milled about while they waited for the parking attendants to retrieve their cars. Finally, the valet drove up in Moore's vehicle. "Mary said good-bye and jumped in her car," recounts Jacobs. Then Tinker's car arrived, and he waved and drove off in the same direction the actress had driven a few seconds earlier. That was just before they heard the crash.

Jacobs and the rest of the company were still standing at the curb when they heard the thud of metal hitting metal, a sound that seemed to emanate from down the street. "We all laughed," notes Jacobs, "and said, 'Ha! Grant must've run into Mary!'" Jacobs insists that he was only joking at the time, which is why he was so surprised when he finally poked his head out into traffic and saw that his jest had not been far from the mark. "Mary had stopped suddenly," says Jacobs, "and Grant plowed right into the back of her car!"

Fender benders notwithstanding, Tinker maintains that he and his wife-to-be didn't finally get together until much later that year, after the actress traveled to New York on a promotional tour for the show—which would have put the date somewhere in the early part of October 1961. The morning after the couple's first date, the New York columnists dutifully reported that the pair had taken in the Broadway show *Mary, Mary* before they wound up the evening dancing at New York's then-trendy Peppermint Lounge. It was only the couple's first date, but it would certainly not be their last. As Moore would later confess in the pages of *TV Guide*, "I woke up the next morning and knew I was in love."[1]

As a creative executive at an ad agency with strong ties to Leonard, Tinker was a frequent visitor to the *Van Dyke* set even before his friendship with the show's female star began to blossom in the latter part of the show's premiere season. Even so, as more than one observer would note, the frequency of the ad man's visits increased significantly in the months that followed Moore's trip to New York in the autumn of that year.

"Grant would come and pick Mary up after rehearsals during the day," noted *Van Dyke Show* costumer Harald Johnson, who insisted that despite such occasional clues, the couple maintained a low profile throughout the early days of their courtship. In fact, so discreet were Tinker and Moore that when the pair finally wed on June 1, 1962, more than a few of her coworkers expressed surprise on hearing that the couple had paired up in the first place. Even so, the union was greeted by near unanimous enthusiasm by their friends on the set, most of whom agreed that the two were an ideal match.

"Everyone liked Grant when they met him," remembered Johnson. "He had a lot of class and a sophisticated look about him." According to actor Bill Idelson, who played Herman Glimscher on the show, "Grant was like the perfect goy—a white-bread goy from beginning to end, and perfect for Mary Tyler Moore. The ultimate shiksa and the ultimate goy. They made a perfect pair."

BY THE MIDDLE of January 1961, with their cast poised to begin rehearsals for the pilot episode of their brand-new series, Leonard and Reiner decided that the time had come to settle on a permanent title for the show. The producers had discarded the show's first working title, *The Full House*, almost as soon as they'd come up with it the previous spring. In the intervening months they'd tried at least a half-dozen different monikers on for size, though none of them seemed to last more than a few days, or, in some cases, hours. *Double Trouble*, a title that was intended to reflect the show's twin-arena setting, was an early favorite, though it would finally be rejected as too obscure; *All in a Day's Work* was also popular, until the producers decided that it was too prosaic a title for a situation comedy. But finally, with the pilot's start date looming and the show still without a name, Reiner and his creative partners had to admit they were stymied. "We just couldn't come up with a name," recalls Van Dyke.

It was Reiner who finally broke the deadlock by suggesting that the new series be called *The Dick Van Dyke Show*, following the pattern already established by the *Andy Griffith* and *Danny Thomas* shows, both of which had been self-titled to capitalize on the name value of their respective stars. Of course, the only problem with titling their new series to capitalize on Dick Van Dyke's star power was that he didn't really have any. As Van Dyke himself was gracious enough to insist as soon as he heard the newly proposed title, his was not exactly a household name in the homes of America in 1961. "At that time," Van Dyke admits, "nobody knew who I was!"

No matter—as far as Reiner was concerned, his leading man's obscurity was about to become a thing of the past. "In my mind, Dick Van Dyke was a star," recalls the producer. "And I said, 'If the rest of the world doesn't know it yet, let's tell them.'"

"Dick was a relative unknown at the time," Leonard would concede, although he, too, viewed Van Dyke's relative anonymity as a transitory proposition. "I thought that part of our job," he would later observe, "to make the show popular, was to make Dick popular." And so, in a bit of circular logic that speaks to the underlying optimism of its two producers, the show was named after its star, at least partially in an effort to make him famous enough to have a situation comedy named after him.

ALTHOUGH *THE DICK VAN DYKE SHOW* was not officially christened until late in its gestation, the series had already found its indelible signature in the snappy theme song that had been composed for the show by Earle Hagen, the resident musical genius on the Desilu Cahuenga lot. As Sheldon Leonard's house composer, the former big band trombonist had long been responsible for scoring, orchestrating, and often conducting most of the incidental music that found its way into the shows in the producer's ever-expanding stable. But Hagen's most lasting claim to fame would be the distinguished catalog of TV themes he created for some of the most enduring shows of his era, including the melodies that kicked off each episode of *The Andy Griffith Show*, *That Girl*, *I Spy*, *The Danny Thomas Show*, and *Gomer Pyle, USMC*, to name just a few of the prolific composer's better-known works.

In Reiner's opinion, Hagen's masterpiece was the unforgettable theme song the composer crafted for *The Dick Van Dyke Show*. "That was a wonderful theme he wrote for our show," acknowledges Reiner, who still recalls the thrill he felt when Hagen arrived at his office with a demo tape of the freshly composed tune. "He played it," recalls Reiner, "and as soon as I heard, 'Tah-dah da-da-da-dada-da,' I said, 'That's it! That's Dick!' It sounded like him!"

Today, after being heard in countless repetitions on *Dick Van Dyke Show* reruns that continue to play throughout the world, the show's theme is one of the most instantly identifiable melodies in Western culture. But according to its composer, the durable theme song was hardly composed with posterity in mind. In fact, the composer insisted, he wrote the *Dick Van Dyke Show* theme quickly—after only a cursory reading of Reiner's pilot script—and then arranged and recorded the song a few days later in a single take. "You hear the orchestra in your head," the composer explained, struggling to define a creative act that he perceives as purely instinctual. "And then you put it down on paper. For the *Van Dyke* song I was just trying to find something in that particular show that was contemporaneous for the time."

Hagen finally recorded the song one afternoon, on a whim, he recalled, when he realized he had a little time left on an orchestral session that he'd called to record incidental music for a *Danny Thomas Show* episode. With the musicians already in place, the composer decided he might as well use the remaining time productively, and so, a few minutes later, the composer produced and distributed copies of his latest composition to the waiting band members. "I had already made the arrangement of the *Dick Van Dyke* theme," recalled Hagen, "so when that session was over, I just ran it down and recorded it."

As die-hard fans of the series are almost certainly aware, a variant arrangement of Hagen's well-known *Dick Van Dyke* theme song was played under the opening credits of the show's first fourteen episodes. This alternate version of the show's theme—which is easily distinguished by its brassier fanfare arrangement and a prominent conga line backbeat—would be retired in the middle of the show's first year, a casualty of the midyear facelift that accompanied the show's midseason move to Wednesday nights. It was only then that the more familiar version of the show's theme—which until that time had been used only as the show's closing theme, appearing exclusively under the end credits on the show's first fourteen installments—was moved to the top of the show, where it would remain for each of the show's remaining 144 episodes.

Curiously, despite its prominent placement at the start of the show's first fourteen episodes, the song's composer would later claim no memory of having written, recorded, or conducted this variant arrangement of the show's signature tune. In fact, when Hagen heard this alternate version of the *Van Dyke Show* theme song some years later, he expressed his disdain for the arrangement in no uncertain terms. "I must've made it," he allowed, "but I'll be damned if I remember doing it. And, as a matter of fact, it shocks me to hear bongos on there, because I hate them!"

9

CASTING OFF PEARLS

At a few minutes past 10:00 A.M. on the morning of January 16, 1961, Carl Reiner and Sheldon Leonard assembled their newly hired acting company around a pair of folding tables on an otherwise vacant stage on the Desilu Cahuenga lot and called to order the first official rehearsal for the pilot episode of *The Dick Van Dyke Show*. Because the studio's carpentry crew was still hard at work constructing the show's standing sets on the lot's soundstage 5, where the pilot would be filmed, the company would spend their first day of rehearsal a few doors away on this adjoining stage. Of course, where they met for their initial rehearsal was of little consequence, since they would remain seated for most of that first day, which was to be devoted to a painstaking read-through of the script that had been chosen as the series' maiden effort, "The Sick Boy and the Sitter."

Once his cast was seated, Reiner picked up his copy of the script and, clearly savoring the moment, announced, "Page one!" Then, inaugurating a ritual that would be repeated at the first reading of each of the following 157 episodes, the company opened their scripts to the first page and began reading aloud. Over the next two or three hours, the actors and their producers scrutinized every line in the script, laughing out loud at the jokes

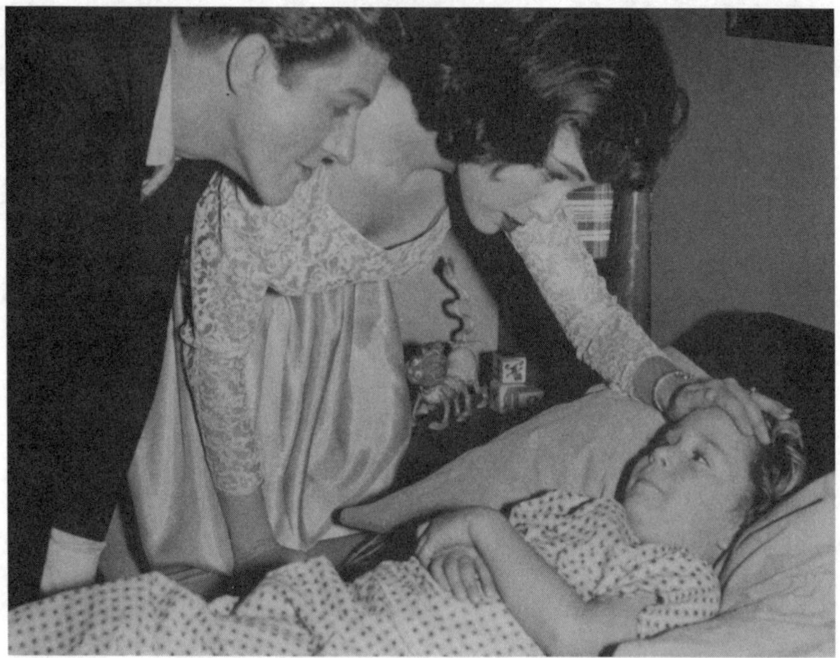

Dick Van Dyke and Mary Tyler Moore comfort Larry Mathews in "The Sick Boy and the Sitter," a script that Carl Reiner chose to film as his show's pilot episode because it was the one that best explained the characters.

that worked, and tossing out the ones that didn't. Whenever they ran into a stumbling block, they would halt their reading until the problem was fixed. Once they'd stopped, it was understood that the floor was open to anyone at the table who wanted to kibitz, complain, or simply offer helpful suggestions on how the show might be made better.

From the start, no one in the *Van Dyke Show* company was ever shy about tendering a suggestion that might improve their show. One idea adopted without debate at that first reading was Van Dyke's proposal that they alter the pronunciation of his character's name, which Reiner had pronounced PEE-tree when he played the role in the *Head of the Family* pilot. "Dick asked if it wouldn't be PEH-tree," says Reiner. "And I said, 'Sure!'"

Coincidentally, the name of Rob Petrie's employer would also be changed after it, too, came under scrutiny during that initial script reading. In Reiner's *Head of the Family* pilot, Rob's boss was named Alan Sturdy—an appellation that the writer hastened to revise after Morey Amsterdam identified a peculiar tendency in the pronunciation of the name as written. "I told

Carl that if you said 'Alan Sturdy' fast," explained Amsterdam, "it sounded like you were saying 'Alan's dirty!'" The producer conceded the point and promptly rechristened the character Alan Brady—a name that Amsterdam insisted was borrowed from a delivery boy who happened to pass through the rehearsal hall in the midst of the debate. "We were trying to come up with a name when this guy walks in delivering coffee," Amsterdam recalled. "Carl says to him, 'Excuse me, what's your last name?' The guy says, 'Brady.' And Carl says, 'That's perfect. We'll call our guy Alan Brady.'"

The script that Reiner and Leonard picked to launch their new series, "The Sick Boy and the Sitter," was not an arbitrary choice, but was carefully selected from among the thirteen that Reiner had written more than two years earlier during his summer on Fire Island. Nor was it chosen because it was the best script of the bunch. Far from it. In the episode's storyline, Rob convinces Laura to attend a dinner party at Alan Brady's penthouse, despite the fact that her maternal instincts seem to be telling her to stay home and tend to their ailing six-year-old son, who has come down with a slight fever. It was not a terribly compelling premise, as Reiner himself is the first to concede. "It wasn't our strongest one," he admits.

While the episode might've lacked the comic bite that would invigorate many of the writer's later efforts, Reiner insists that his script for "The Sick Boy and the Sitter" possessed a quality that was vital for the inaugural episode of a brand-new series: it had heart. In his opinion, the domestic conflict of a husband who's torn between twin loyalties to his boss and his six-year-old son offered a more compelling introduction to the show and its characters than the slapstick situations that propelled many of his more comical efforts. "We picked that show," notes Reiner, "because it was the one that best explained the characters."

Leonard was equally keen to inaugurate the series with "The Sick Boy and the Sitter," though for different reasons. While Leonard undoubtedly appreciated the gentle domestic interplay that Reiner felt did so much to define the show's characters and setting, the executive producer was even more excited by the potential inherent in the party sequence that dominates the episode's second act, where Buddy, Sally, and Rob find themselves drafted into performing an impromptu variety show for the guests at Alan Brady's penthouse. In Leonard's view, the sequence provided a perfect showcase for the talented trio of Amsterdam, Van Dyke, and Rose Marie, each of whom could be counted on to shine in the self-contained musical

Dick Van Dyke's amazing physical capabilities were a source of constant amazement on the set. As one crew member described it, "He was like a human waterfall."

variety block that the producer felt certain would anchor the pilot with a ten-minute sequence of sure-fire entertainment.

"I thought it was brilliant that they came up with that party scene," says Van Dyke, who was only too happy to borrow from his own repertoire of specialty material to ensure the success of the sequence. In this case, Van Dyke's contribution was a short pantomime in which he plays a drunk husband trying to sneak into the house after a bender. It was very similar to a piece the star had performed to great acclaim in *The Girls Against the Boys*, the 1958 revue that brought him to Leonard's attention in the first place. Not surprisingly, Van Dyke's cheerful plundering of his own comic backlog was an act of creative larceny undertaken with Leonard's unquestioned endorsement. "Dick's personal repertoire of bits and shtick were an asset," as the executive producer saw it, "and we simply exploited them until we'd used them up."

Once his cast concluded their first table reading, Reiner grabbed his notes and beat a retreat to his office on the second floor of the studio's Building A, where the writer labored well into the night to remove all the bugs that had suddenly become evident during the script's first read-through.

The next morning, after the carpenters had finished their labors on stage 5, director Leonard and the cast moved down to the set, where they would spend most of their second rehearsal day putting Reiner's newly revised script on its feet. By the end of day three, Leonard and the cast had finished working out the show's preliminary camera blocking, and the company was ready to face their earliest moment of truth: the first-ever run-through of the entire show, from start to finish.

Although this initial run-through was supposed to be a primarily technical exercise—a dry run performed mainly for the benefit of the show's sound, camera, and lighting crews—associate producer Ronald Jacobs recalls that the cast, who could hardly be expected to rein themselves in, would invariably play the first run-though with all the stops out. "They were trying to test the material out," explains Jacobs.

Still, trying to get a rise out of a crew of distracted stagehands, dolly grips, and other jaded Hollywood professionals could be a daunting prospect. "They were a tough crowd," acknowledges Jacobs. "These guys had seen it all." And yet, in one of their earliest professional triumphs, by the end of that initial run-through, Van Dyke and his fellow players managed to make a fan of every focus puller, key grip, and gaffer in the studio that day. "The crew was supposed to be watching it very technically," notes Jacobs, "but they ended up laughing. A lot. They really enjoyed themselves."

"I never will forget watching Dick Van Dyke," concurs camera coordinator James Niver, who was present at that first *Van Dyke Show* run-through. "I remember the bit where Dick flows down off that chair," he recalls, referring to the moment in the comedian's tour de force drunk act where his inebriated character seems to slide off his chair into oblivion. "I'd never seen anyone do anything like that," adds Niver. "He was like a human waterfall." But of all those on the set that day, no one was more impressed by the star's pantomimic artistry than Reiner himself. "Dick's ability to move amazed me," notes the producer. "He could do things that nobody in the world could've done like him. He had the kind of body that would not quit."

ON THE EVENING of Thursday, January 19, 1961—a scant twenty-four hours before *The Dick Van Dyke Show* pilot was scheduled to go before the cameras—the company presented a final onstage dress rehearsal for an invited audience of friends, family, and other assorted well-wishers who'd wandered over from other stages on the lot. Also in the crowd that night was a small clutch of agents from the William Morris office, who had arrived to check the status of a show whose progress many of them had already been following for more than two years. If the show's cast and producers had been gratified by the response they'd earned at the Wednesday-afternoon run-through, they were positively flabbergasted by the uproarious laughter and applause that greeted their first run-through before a live studio audience, most of whom seemed genuinely taken with the evening's performance.

Most. Though not all.

According to Sheldon Leonard, one particular attendee at the *Van Dyke Show*'s final dress rehearsal held an opinion of the show that was at odds with the majority of the crowd—and he wasted little time before sharing his viewpoint with the executive producer. "Some people from the William Morris Agency came to see the final dress rehearsal," Leonard explained. "And one of the men from the agency—who will be nameless, but who considered himself the guardian of my career—was greatly disturbed."

"That was fun," the agent told Leonard a few minutes after the actors had taken their final bows. "And it's a very nice show. But—" At that point, Leonard recalled, the agent lowered his voice to a whisper before continuing in a conspiratorial tone. "You've got to back out of this," he insisted. "I cannot allow you to do this show."

"What?" Leonard responded.

"It's a loser," the agent explained. "A sure loser."

According to Leonard, the agent then proceeded to identify what he imagined to be the show's most insurmountable stumbling blocks. "You've got material that's already failed once," the agent elaborated. "A star who's made a number of pilots before—none of which have sold. And," the agent concluded, "you've got Morey Amsterdam and Rose Marie—two stars from *radio*! This show cannot make it. And I cannot let you do it."

In Leonard's recollection, his conviction was hardly shaken by the agent's well-meaning advice. "I told him to sit down and take a Valium," Leonard recalled. "He was only trying to protect my career. But I rejected his excellent advice nonetheless. You gotta respect your own opinion."

THE PILOT EPISODE of *The Dick Van Dyke Show* that was filmed the following evening, on Friday, January 20, 1961, was a triumph by any measure. Under the careful supervision of producers Leonard and Reiner, the show's writing, direction, and production values were conspicuously assured. But an equally noteworthy factor in the pilot's success—and, significantly, the key element that had been missing from Reiner's first pass at the material in *Head of the Family*—was the tangible sense of ensemble that the producers had somehow managed to instill in their diverse company of players after a scant five days of rehearsal. In Van Dyke's view, the company's ineffable chemistry was the result of chance—pure and simple. "It was just luck in casting that it worked that well," observes the star. "It was pure serendipity. From the very beginning, the chemistry between us all was so good. Everyone in that cast had the right rhythm and the right character from the very first day."

Nowhere was the show's fabled chemistry in greater evidence than in Van Dyke and Moore's depiction of Rob and Laura Petrie, who emerge as a convincing married couple from their first moments on-screen. The extended sequence where Rob bargains to convince Laura to attend a dinner party that she'd just as soon skip offers a prime example of the acting team's camaraderie at work. Where a typical situation comedy might show us a bickering couple locked in pitched battle over a forgotten anniversary or a burnt pot roast, Reiner and his actors offer a knowing depiction of real-life marital compromise that is instantly familiar—and thus terribly funny—to anyone who has ever conducted petty negotiations with a loved one of his or her own. "I'll tell you what I'll do for you if you come with me," Rob barters. "I'll go to two decorator shows and three PTA meetings."

"Five PTA meetings," Laura counters.

"You'll go?" asks Rob, his mood brightened by the apparent ease of his unexpected victory.

"Well, all right," Laura replies. "But," she adds, raising the stakes with a final emotional gambit, "I refuse to enjoy myself!"

It's a funny exchange—and a remarkably assured piece of comic writing. In this deceptively simple patch of dialogue, the writer succeeds in moving his storyline forward, even as he offers a knowing glimpse into the subtle emotional stakes at play in any modern marriage. If nothing else, Reiner's perceptive snapshot of an everyday marital debate served as the perfect antidote to the slapstick hijinks that had come to define married life on prime time until that point in time. And that was no accident. Reiner has long maintained that he created Rob and Laura Petrie at least partially in response to the retrograde domestic reality he'd observed on *I Love Lucy* and at least a dozen other situation comedies from the era that preceded his show. "The battle of the sexes was the big plot device," he explains. "It's the easiest one to write—you scream at me, I'll scream at you. And a lot of people identified with that. More people lived like that than lived like Rob and Laura."

As for the immensely popular *I Love Lucy*, Reiner confesses that the brand of marital politics routinely practiced by Lucy and Ricky Ricardo left him cold. "I didn't like their premise," the writer says. "They were hilarious—no doubt about it—but it was always Lucy fooling Ricky. Lucy and Desi made you wonder why they stayed together. You'd say, 'How could they love each other? He never caters to her, he always calls her a dope!'" When it came time to create his own series, Reiner was determined to shoot for a different sort of truth: a verisimilitude rooted in a reality that he knew.

"My show was based on a mutually respecting husband and wife," says Reiner. "It was two against the world. And even when it was one-against-one, it was the kind of one-against-one you have in a family that loves each other." As the writer admits, he discovered the perfect model for Rob and Laura's emotional truth in his own durable marriage. "I was trying to pattern it off a life that I knew."

It's also noteworthy, in light of Rob and Laura's obvious affection for each other, that Reiner rarely had his onscreen couple utter the words "I love you"—mostly because he viewed such overt displays of emotion as too easy. "I always objected to that kind of schmaltziness," asserts Reiner, who saw little point in telegraphing his leading couple's devotion through words when there were so many more interesting ways to communicate their attraction to one another.

And, as anyone who's watched more than a few episodes of *The Dick Van Dyke Show* will confirm, it was always quite clear that Rob and Laura's feelings for each other were never strictly spiritual. That there was a strong physical aspect to the couple's relationship is a fact that Sheldon Leonard readily acknowledged. "This was the first show to star an attractive young couple," he explained. "And a certain element of romance was inherent in these two attractive young people." Although it was rarely addressed directly in the show's scripts, the series owed much of its appeal to that fact. "With Van Dyke and Mary," Leonard observed, "it was implicit that those characters had a certain degree of a sex life, which was a novelty. So

"It was implicit that those characters had a certain degree of a sex life," says Sheldon Leonard, recalling one of the more fortuitous by-products of Dick Van Dyke and Mary Tyler Moore's chemistry.

the show was very popular—very popular—with young people."

Viewers requiring further proof that Rob and Laura's union included a physical component need look no further than the show's pilot episode, which concludes with a sequence that leaves little doubt. In the playfully suggestive scene that takes place in the couple's kitchen late at night, Laura attempts to explain the source of her uncanny intuition to her starry-eyed husband. "Darling," she purrs, pausing just long enough to tease him with the barest hint of a kiss, "I'm a woman!" And then, in a single seductively fluid motion, she reaches back and unhooks the clasp on her string of pearls, which begin to slip from her neck, stone by stone, as she slinks off in the direction of their bedroom.

"Yeah!" replies Rob. And the lascivious glint in his eyes as he follows Laura offstage leaves little question about what's really going on.

Interestingly, the multitextured sequence works on another level as well. In casting off the ubiquitous string of pearls that had symbolically condemned so many earlier prime-time wives to a life of sexless domesticity, Laura Petrie and her creators offer a long overdue farewell to the era of June Cleaver and her perfectly matched jewelry, tasteful coiffures, and sensible pastel dresses. Whether or not Mary Tyler Moore and her collaborators were consciously aware of the symbolic defiance of Laura Petrie's openly seductive closing gesture, there can be little doubt that the seeds of a prime-time revolution had been planted that night, and there would be no turning back.

10

SOFT SOAP

By the middle of February 1961, with a freshly developed 16mm print of *The Dick Van Dyke Show* pilot under his arm, Sheldon Leonard was ready to begin the potentially arduous process of shopping his new show's sample film to potential sponsors—a task that, even for a producer with his considerable track record, could quickly turn into a time-consuming and demoralizing process. Fortunately, in the case of *The Dick Van Dyke Show*, it was neither.

The first name on Leonard's list of potential *Van Dyke Show* suitors was Lee Rich, the senior vice president in charge of Media and Programming at New York's Benton and Bowles Agency. As Leonard was well aware, one of Benton and Bowles's prize clients happened to be the Midwestern soap company Procter & Gamble. And in the early months of 1961 the Procter & Gamble company had made it known that they were very interested in doing business with Leonard.

Actually, to refer to the Procter & Gamble Company of Cincinnati, Ohio, as a soap company is an understatement. A sprawling multinational corporation, Procter & Gamble was one of the largest manufacturers and distributors of detergents and other household products in the free world. If you lived in the United States in 1961, chances were good that somewhere in your kitchen, pantry, or bathroom you had at least one product made or marketed by Procter & Gamble, be it a carton of Blue Cheer in the laundry room, a bottle of Joy detergent in the kitchen, or a tube of Crest

Executive producer Sheldon Leonard at work in his office at Desilu Cahuenga in the early sixties.

toothpaste in the medicine cabinet. Naturally, the advertising required to support that kind of market saturation didn't come cheap, and even in those preinflationary days, Procter & Gamble's annual expenditures for television advertising alone ran into the multimillions. Of course, much of that was devoted to daytime programming, where the presence of household-products manufacturers' advertisements was so pervasive that the broadcast industry had come to think of the afternoon serials that were the detergent makers' mainstay as "soap" operas.

But by the late 1950s, having established itself as a formidable presence in daytime, Procter & Gamble was anxious to increase its nighttime visibility as well. So it was only natural that the company's aggressive efforts to gain a greater foothold in prime-time advertising would eventually lead to Leonard, who was at that time the prime mover behind a handful of the most popular half-hour comedies on television. And it probably hadn't slipped past the soap company's notice that Leonard's *Andy Griffith* and *Danny Thomas* shows were selling an awful lot of Maxwell House coffee and other products for Procter & Gamble's rivals at General Foods. Recognizing that it was already too late to buy into any of the producer's existing hits—most of which were already locked into long-term sponsorship commitments to General Foods—Procter & Gamble's executive decision makers decided that the next best thing would be to get in on the ground floor of Leonard's next series, whatever that might be.

"Procter & Gamble were prepared to finance anything I wanted to do," Leonard recalled. "*Any* subject. *Any* project. And, at the time, what I was about to come up with was *The Dick Van Dyke Show*."

Under the circumstances, the producer had little trouble convincing the soap manufacturer to snap up the sponsorship rights to *The Dick Van Dyke Show*. "They bought it right off the first look at it," noted Leonard, recalling how Procter & Gamble pledged a full year's sponsorship commitment for the series based on a single viewing of the show's pilot film.

Once they'd signed on as sponsors of the new series, Procter & Gamble offered the program to CBS, where—in light of Leonard's track record and Procter & Gamble's own well-established clout—obtaining a berth for the show on the broadcaster's upcoming fall schedule should have been a foregone conclusion. Still, Leonard allowed himself only guarded optimism. He knew that before the *Dick Van Dyke Show* could earn a slot on the network's fall schedule, it would have to pass the scrutiny of CBS President James T. Aubrey. And that, as the producer understood only too well, could be a problem.

In a line of work that's never been particularly dependent on personal congeniality, the network boss had earned a reputation for performing his executive duties with such cold-hearted dispatch that even Aubrey's colleagues routinely referred to him as the Smiling Cobra—though never, of course, to his face. As someone who'd locked horns with the formidable executive on more than one occasion, Leonard was already familiar with Aubrey's steely demeanor. "I had a very hard relationship with Aubrey," Leonard remembered. "I didn't dislike him—but we didn't think the same way."

As the producer recalled, one of the principal areas where he and the executive failed to see eye to eye was in the field of situation comedy. "I had a chip on my shoulder about him because he had expressed his dislike for *The Danny Thomas Show* in too many places," admitted Leonard. And, as the producer would discover shortly after the network president finally got a chance to screen the *Van Dyke Show* pilot, Aubrey was not exactly enamored of the producer's latest effort, either. "It was his opinion that a series with a show business background would have no popular appeal," Leonard explained, recalling the network president's chief criticism of *The Dick Van Dyke Show*.

According to Leonard, Aubrey was not pleased that Reiner had chosen to create a leading character who was a TV writer, an occupation that was, in the network executive's opinion, far too exotic for the average television viewer. "He told us to make him something that people can identify with," recalled Leonard, "like a real estate agent or an automobile salesman. But I wouldn't do that." As Leonard expected, his antipathy to the network chief's creative suggestions for *The Dick Van Dyke Show* wound up costing him—and the series—no small amount of goodwill from the network. "Aubrey said, in effect, 'If you won't cooperate with me, I won't cooperate with you. The hell with you.'"

Despite almost certain odds that he'd incur the executive's wrath by doing so, Leonard stood his ground—though it must be conceded that, in this particular skirmish, Leonard held the upper hand. "If I needed support," explained Leonard, "I could always go to Procter & Gamble and say, 'Look, the network is giving me trouble.' And Procter & Gamble would rear up over Jim Aubrey's head and say, 'What in the hell are you trying to do to my show?'"

Naturally loath to risk alienating one of his network's most powerful advertisers, Aubrey set aside his own personal and creative reservations about the *Van Dyke Show* and gave his programming chiefs the nod to slate the series into the CBS network's fall lineup, where it premiered in the Tuesday 8:00 P.M. time slot on October 3, 1961.

Reiner still remembers the exact moment he discovered that *The Dick Van Dyke Show* had finally been given the green light. A few days before CBS issued their formal announcement, Reiner was back in New York, where he happened to run into a high-ranking executive from Procter & Gamble's ad agency on a Manhattan-bound commuter train. "He sat across the aisle from me, and didn't say a word," as Reiner would later recall. "But then I noticed that he made a little 'okay' sign with his hand. That was when I knew we were going to be okay."[1]

Once the series was officially announced on the network's fall schedule, William Morris agent Sol Leon made sure he was the first to call Dick Van Dyke with the news. "I told Dick, 'You're on the air!' And he couldn't believe it," the agent later recalled. "He moved out to California in—like—thirty seconds. He couldn't get out here fast enough."

WITH HIS SERIES scheduled to go into production in June 1961, Dick Van Dyke dutifully notified the producers of *Bye Bye Birdie* that he would be leaving the show for good once his contract to star in the musical expired in mid-April 1961. Although *Birdie*'s producers had little choice but to accept the star's resignation, they didn't hesitate to let the actor know what they thought of his decision. "They said I was crazy to do television," notes Van Dyke, who acknowledges that his Broadway producers weren't the only ones to take a dim view of his choice to abandon the Great White Way. "Everybody," says Van Dyke, "tried to talk me into staying in New York."

According to Van Dyke, the person most opposed to the actor's pursuit of television stardom was Gower Champion, the Broadway legend who had directed the star's breakout performance in *Bye Bye Birdie*. Says Van Dyke, "He told me, 'This is where you belong! You're born to do theater!'" In the end, not even Gower Champion could sway the determined actor. "I wasn't listening to any of them," he says, "because I knew you just couldn't work steadily in theater."

Dick Van Dyke finally left *Bye Bye Birdie* on April 15, 1961, exactly a year and a day after he'd opened the show. In his wake, the role of Albert Peterson was assumed by Gene Rayburn, a light-comic actor who would eventually achieve a degree of celebrity as the host of TV's long-running *Match Game*. According to writer Norm Liebmann, who later became a contributor to the *Van Dyke Show*—and who was then writing scripts for *Flair*, a daily syndicated radio series that Van Dyke hosted during his final days in New York—the star-to-be was so anxious to begin shooting his situation comedy that he was literally counting the days that remained before his eventual departure for the West Coast. "Dick was anxious to be done with *Bye Bye Birdie*," recalled Liebmann, who remembers watching with amusement as the star gleefully ticked off each of the remaining performances in his *Birdie* contract. "Every time I'd see him," observed Liebmann, "he'd go, 'Only nine—or eight or seven—more to go!'"

It wasn't that Van Dyke had anything against starring in *Bye Bye Birdie*. On the contrary, the performer has always spoken of the show as a turning point in his career. But, after a year of six-day weeks, the actor had simply begun to grow weary of the drudgery of performing the same show every night. "After six or eight months," the star would later observe, "a Broadway show gets to be a grind. You've tried everything you can think of in the first half-year, then you run out of fresh approach ideas."[2] Fortunately, that was a dilemma Van Dyke would not face in his chosen medium. "With

TV," he explained, "there's a new script each week, a new challenge, something fresh to concentrate on."[3]

But if it was a fresh challenge Dick Van Dyke sought as he and his family prepared for their cross-country trek from New York's Great White Way to Hollywood's Cahuenga Boulevard, he would not be disappointed. Though the road maps pegged the distance between the two points at a shade less than three thousand miles, the actor would soon discover they were worlds apart.

"They said I was crazy to do television," recalls Dick Van Dyke, who had personal reasons for walking away from a potentially lucrative career on the Broadway stage. "By that time I had three kids," he explains, "and I was looking for steady work."

11

THE BEST OF TIMES

The lot that was once familiarly known as the Desilu Cahuenga studio is still in business at 846 Cahuenga Boulevard in Hollywood, although it has operated under a variety of different names over the years, including the decidedly less resonant moniker of Ren-Mar Studios. But in most other ways, the modest seven-acre facility has remained surprisingly unchanged since its heyday as Hollywood's sitcom mecca in the late fifties and early sixties. The lot's stages have been engaged in the manufacture of dreams since the silent-movie era; and yet, like most factories, it isn't much to look at from the outside. From the street, the place appears to be little more than an unassuming string of industrial edifices, fronted by a nondescript entrance gate. Gleaming Hollywood tour buses streak past this treeless stretch of Cahuenga Boulevard every single day—but rarely do the coaches pause to allow their cargoes of curiosity seekers to stop and take a peek inside those walls, despite the fact that some of our culture's most cherished collective memories were born there.

It was there, on the lot's soundstage 9, that Lucy's Little Ricky grew up before our eyes. Desilu Cahuenga also provided the setting for the fictional hamlet of Mayberry, North Carolina, during the eight seasons that *The*

"It was the best of times," says writer Sam Denoff, recalling the extraordinary working conditions that prevailed on the *Van Dyke* set, "but the worst of times just were not there."

Andy Griffith Show was in residence on the studio's stages 1 and 2. And, of course, from 1961 through 1966, the lot also served as the home base for five seasons of *The Dick Van Dyke Show*.

There were others, as well. Hundreds of them, from *Our Miss Brooks* and *I Married Joan* in the fifties, through *That Girl*, *The Mothers-in-Law* and *Gomer Pyle, USMC*, in the sixties, *Soap* in the seventies, and—in more recent years—*Ally McBeal* and *Lizzie McGuire*. In fact, the former Desilu Cahuenga studio has played host to so many countless hours of television comedy since the 1950s that it's difficult to comprehend the magnitude of laughter generated by comic material originally filmed on the lot's nine soundstages. Still, it's a safe bet that no other parcel of real estate on Earth can lay claim to inspiring as much human mirth as the seven square acres that lie beyond the gates at 846 Cahuenga Boulevard.

The rich history of Hollywood's liveliest little studio dates to 1915, when it was founded as a back lot by Metro Pictures. The studio underwent major construction after the Second World War, when it was rechristened

Motion Picture Center Studios, a B-movie lot that did a brisk business providing rental stages for the producers of the low-budget features and quota quickies that Hollywood churned out during the postwar years of the late forties. With the arrival of television, the owners of the Motion Picture Center Studios, quick to react to changing times, had little trouble adapting their facility to suit the needs of TV's earliest producers—a transition made somewhat easier by the fact that many of those early TV pioneers were former B-movie moguls who were only too happy to continue cranking out their formula Westerns, detective melodramas, and domestic comedies for the hungry new medium.

It wouldn't be until 1953 that an enterprising television producer arrived on the lot with a revolutionary approach to the production of filmed television entertainment that was geared to the exacting demands of the bold new medium. That producer's name was Desi Arnaz, and the technique that he brought to the Motion Picture Center Studios was the three-camera system. A groundbreaking method for filming half-hour comedies, the three-camera system had been perfected during the early years of *I Love Lucy*, the immensely popular comedy that starred Arnaz and his real-life wife, Lucille Ball.

By 1953, after completing two phenomenally successful seasons of *Lucy*, the Arnazes were looking for a permanent home base for their ever-expanding Desilu empire, which had already generated a pair of *I Love Lucy* clones, *Our Miss Brooks* and *I Married Joan*, both of which debuted in 1952. It was Desi's dream to transform an entire studio into a state-of-the-art television factory dedicated to the assembly-line production of half-hour comedies forged in the Desilu style. And to his mind, the modest facility at 846 Cahuenga seemed ideal.

By the summer of 1953, Lucy and Desi Arnaz had negotiated a long-term lease with the owners of the Motion Picture Center Studios, which would eventually come to be known as the Desilu Cahuenga studios. No sooner was the lease signed than the Arnazes initiated a multimillion-dollar facelift of the sleepy production facility.

Employing all the technical advances that he'd pioneered with *I Love Lucy* staffers Al Simon, Karl Freund, and Jess Oppenheimer, Arnaz retrofitted the lot's largest soundstages into so-called Desilu Playhouses: highly efficient, audience-friendly stages that would come equipped with stadium-style bleachers, as well as special, acoustically sealed doorways that would provide the lot's audiences direct access from street to studio, the better to accommodate the teeming crowds that were such a vital element in the three-camera Desilu process. At the same time, Arnaz also constructed plenty of new offices to house the influx of writers, producers, designers, and directors that he envisioned working side by side on the soon-to-be-thriving lot. As a final touch, Arnaz installed a suite of offices and dressing rooms adjacent to the studio's soundstage 9, where he and his wife would film more than 125 episodes of *I Love Lucy*, including the thirteen infrequently screened hour-long installments that would complete the show's run in the late fifties.

With *I Love Lucy* as an anchor, the newly refurbished studio quickly attracted the attention of TV producers all over town. In no time at all, the tiny lot was bursting with activity, hosting production of scores of situation comedies and dramas, including *December Bride*, *The Ray Bolger Show*, *Love and Marriage*, *Desilu Playhouse*, and *Whirlybirds*, to name just a few. But with the notable exception of Lucille Ball herself, the lot's most conspicuous tenant throughout the fifties was a song-and-dance man of Lebanese extraction named Danny Thomas, who would begin filming his own long-running series, *Make Room for Daddy*—later retitled *The Danny Thomas Show*—on the lot in 1953.

Like Lucy and Desi before him, Thomas did quite well in weekly television. By the end of the decade, Thomas and producing partner Sheldon Leonard were able to parlay the success of *The Danny Thomas Show* into a thriving production dynasty that would eventually rival even Desilu's own interests on the lot. In fact, when the Arnazes finally departed the facility in 1960, Thomas and Leonard were poised to fill many of the studio's newly vacant soundstages with products from their own rapidly expanding production slate—a bountiful roster of programs that would eventually grow to include *The Danny Thomas Show*; *The Andy Griffith Show*; *The Bill Dana Show*; *The Joey Bishop Show*; *Gomer Pyle, USMC*; *Mayberry RFD*; and, of course, the series that Danny Thomas would refer to as the Cadillac of his entire empire, *The Dick Van Dyke Show*.

BY THE TIME the *Van Dyke Show* arrived on the lot, the Desilu Cahuenga studio's golden age was already in full flower. According to the firsthand recollections of many of those who worked on the lot during that halcyon era in the early-to-mid-sixties, they were heady days indeed. "It was the best of times," insists Sam Denoff, who started out as a lowly freelancer on the lot before he finally worked his way up to producer of *The Dick Van Dyke Show*. "But," he adds, "to paraphrase Dickens, the worst of times just were not there"—a circumstance Denoff attributes to the enlightened management policies practiced by Thomas and Leonard. "The working conditions on that little lot were extraordinary. Sheldon and Danny set up a work ethic that was so positive and rewarding that no one ever felt afraid to say exactly what was on their mind—or to fight for it. Which is probably why most of those shows were so good."

"It was a wonderful, open atmosphere," agrees director Jay Sandrich, who recalls that the constant flurry of activity on the bustling lot promoted a healthy cross-pollination of creative ideas among the writers, directors, and actors who worked on the various shows in production. "Everybody would wander in and watch everybody's show and make suggestions. There was no jealousy."

"It wasn't cutthroat at all," observed Harvey Bullock, who cowrote *The Dick Van Dyke Show*'s thirty-third episode, "Bank Book 6565696," and would also contribute many classic scripts to *The Andy Griffith Show*. "The writers all knew each other, so there was no bloodletting. If one guy got a job producing a show, he'd be sure and use all the other guys. There was a lot of communal thinking then. And a lot of good, good feelings."

"It was a very collegial atmosphere," adds Sandrich, who retains particularly fond memories of the studio's campus-style cafeteria, a lively little lunchroom that also served double duty as the hub of social activity on the lot each weekday afternoon. "It was like high school," recalled Bullock. "You'd plop down at a table and you'd see all the people you knew. Danny Thomas would come by and we'd kid him. And then he'd kid us. It was very egalitarian."

Director Al Rafkin was another Desilu regular who nurtured warm memories of the studio commissary's convivial atmosphere, if not the food. "It was the worst cafeteria in the world!" he recalled. Even more questionable than the food was the commissary management's peculiar tradition of naming menu items after whoever happened to be a reigning celebrity on the lot at that time. "They would name sandwiches after the guys on the shows," said Rafkin, who noted that the honor was flattering, so long as a celebrity's star remained on the rise. But, for someone whose celebrity status happened to be on the wane, that same studio menu board could quickly change into an equally adroit indicator of his rapidly withering stature. "Bill Dana had a sandwich named after him," remarked Rafkin, "until his show got canceled." When that happened, the director recalled, the commissary management's response was both swift and sure. "They ripped his name right off the board!" Before the day was out, the director insisted, the Bill Dana sandwich had been permanently retired. "It went right back to being just plain bacon, lettuce, and tomato."

According to Jay Sandrich, the Desilu commissary's management initiated an even stranger practice when the lot's eatery became the only private studio cafeteria in the history of Hollywood to encourage the general public to eat within its walls—a disastrous and short-lived open-door policy, says Sandrich, that the commissary actively promoted by installing a public entrance that opened directly onto the sidewalk on Cahuenga Boulevard! "It was called Hal's Eat with the Stars," says Sandrich, "and people could wander right in off the street to eat there." Despite the fact that the gimmick somehow earned the endorsement of studio honcho Danny Thomas, Sandrich recalls that few others on the lot were as enthusiastic about the prospect of sharing their lunch hour with a roomful of camera-toting tourists. "It was terrible," remembers Sandrich. "You're sitting there having lunch with Danny or somebody, and people would wander right in off the street and ask for autographs!"

IN THE WEEKS before the *Van Dyke Show* company was due to arrive for their first regularly scheduled rehearsal on June 14, 1961, art director Kenneth Reid was already hard at work designing and supervising construction of the four standing sets that were to be erected more or less permanently on the lot's stage 8, the studio that would serve as the show's home base for the next five years. For the show's pilot, Reid had already built prototype versions of *The Alan Brady Show* writers' room and the Petries' kitchen. For the show's second episode, "The Meershatz Pipe," the art director would introduce an early version of Rob and Laura's bedroom, which would end up as the setting for much of the show's domestic interplay through episode 4, "Sally and the Lab Technician," when Reid would unveil his proudest achievement—the Petries' sprawling, split-level living

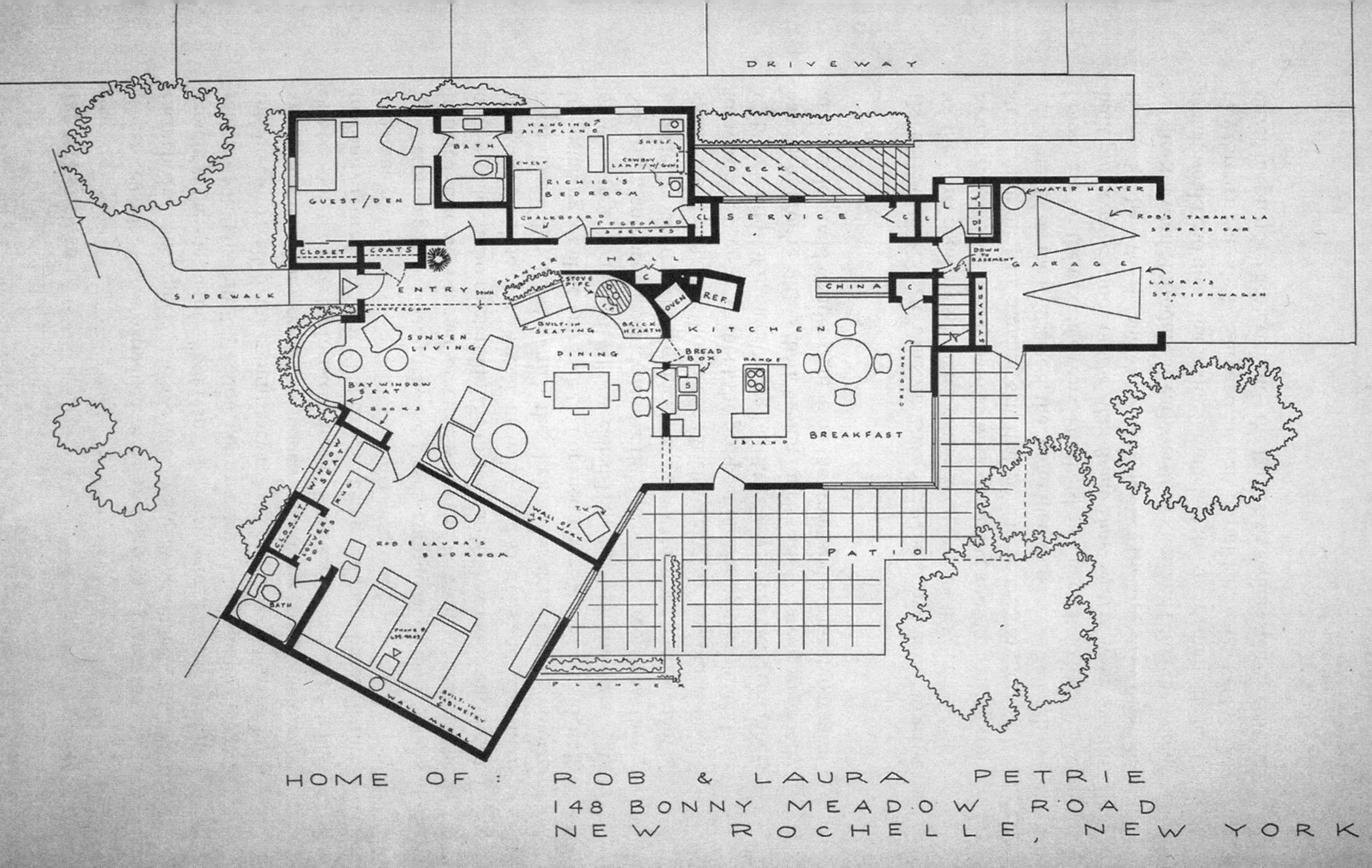
DRIVEWAY
GUEST/DEN
BATH
HANGING AIRPLANE
SHELF
COWBOY LAMP w/ GUNS
CHEST
RICHIE'S BEDROOM
CHALKBOARD
PEGBOARD
SHELVES
DECK
CL
SERVICE
C
L
WATER HEATER
ROB'S TARANTULA SPORTS CAR
CLOSET
COATS
HALL
SIDEWALK
ENTRY
DOWN
PLANTER
STOVE PIPE
OVEN
REF.
CHINA
DOWN TO BASEMENT
GARAGE
LAURA'S STATIONWAGON
INTERCOM
SUNKEN LIVING
BUILT-IN SEATING
BRICK HEARTH
KITCHEN
STORAGE
DINING
BREAD BOX
RANGE
CREDENZA
BAY WINDOW SEAT
BOOKS
S
ISLAND
BREAKFAST
WINDOW SEAT
RUG
T.V.
WALL OF ART WORK
CLOSET
LOUVER DOORS
ROB & LAURA'S BEDROOM
PATIO
BATH
BUILT-IN CABINETRY
WALL MURAL
PLANTER
HOME OF: ROB & LAURA PETRIE
148 BONNY MEADOW ROAD
NEW ROCHELLE, NEW YORK

room/dining room, a spacious and attractive setting that would serve as the show's center stage for the next five years.

Reid would have good reason to be proud of his design for the Petrie living room, whose chief virtue—beside its remarkable versatility—was its verisimilitude. Here was a soundstage on which it was possible to imagine that people might actually live—which is not surprising, since Reid insisted that the entire house be carefully appointed with the specific details of Rob Petrie's lifestyle in mind, right down to the amount of money the character was likely to spend furnishing it. "I wanted to be sure that Van Dyke's character could afford anything I designed," the art director observed, "so I asked Sheldon and Carl what kind of money a guy like that would make. They gave me an estimate of thirty thousand dollars a year or something like that. So I knew I couldn't get ridiculous."

In a fascinating sidelight of *Van Dyke Show* lore, Reid would one day reveal that his efforts to instill a convincing lived-in look in the Petrie home may finally have been more successful than he had dreamed. Or so the art director would discover a few years later, when he got a phone call from an enterprising real estate developer who actually hoped to incorporate the floor plan for Rob and Laura's fictional TV house into his designs for a real-life housing development that he was building on the East Coast. "He asked me to send him the plans for the *Dick Van Dyke* house," said Reid, who was so flattered by the request that he forwarded the blueprints without a second thought. Although he never heard from the builder again, the art director had no reason to believe that his blueprints weren't finally incorporated into the contractor's plans. "Somewhere out there," the designer insisted, "there's a whole bunch of *Dick Van Dyke* houses around."

Ken Reid created a floor plan for the Petries' house so appealing that a home builder once asked the art director to borrow the plans. In more recent years, the Petrie home inspired fine artist Mark Bennett to create this rendering of New Rochelle's most famous fictional house. *Credit: © Mark Bennett, Courtesy Mark Moore Gallery*

12

MOVING THE FURNITURE

On June 20, 1961, the *Van Dyke Show* company kicked off their first regular production season with the filming of episode 2, "The Meershatz Pipe." Despite its prime position in the production order, the episode itself was no groundbreaker—a fact not lost on the show's producers, who would bury it as their tenth episode when they finally got around to arranging the shows for broadcast. Based on the evidence on screen, it's not hard to see why.

In the episode's lackluster storyline, Rob becomes consumed by jealousy after he discovers that Alan Brady has rewarded Buddy Sorrell with a rare Meershatz pipe from his own private collection, a conspicuous display of approbation that leaves head writer Rob feeling more than a little slighted. Rob's insecurities are aggravated a few days later when flu forces him to remain bedridden while his able colleagues polish off a perfectly brilliant script without his help. It's only after Alan Brady publicly acknowledges the vacuum created by the head writer's absence that Rob realizes his fears were without merit—a conclusion driven home a few days later when Buddy finally confesses that he fabricated the story about the Meershatz pipe, which turns out to be a worthless trinket the writer picked up at the corner drugstore.

Based on a staple premise of late-fifties situation comedy—that of the insecure husband/wife/coworker who finally comes to discover how truly indispensable he or she really is—it's safe to say that "The Meershatz Pipe" was not one of Carl Reiner's most inventive scripts for *The Dick Van Dyke Show*. But if the premise for the show's second installment seems a tad on the shopworn side, it should be borne in mind that—like most of the show's earliest efforts—"The Meershatz Pipe" had begun life as one of the thirteen scripts that Carl Reiner composed on Fire Island during the summer of 1958. Which meant that by the time it was finally shot in June 1961, the script for "The Meershatz Pipe" was already practically three years old.

The episode that followed offered little improvement. Episode 3, "Jealousy!"—in which Laura goes a little crazy after she discovers that Rob will be working overtime with a gorgeous movie starlet—offers slight variation on the time-tested motif of the jealous sitcom wife. But while the episode's script might not have added any particular luster to the nascent *Dick Van Dyke Show*'s reputation, the third show would nonetheless bear the distinction of introducing a pair of notable additions to the series' teeming cast of characters—Jerry and Millie Helper.

"Jerry and Millie were friends of ours," explains Reiner, who recalls that he based his characterization of Rob and Laura's next-door neighbors on Jerry and Millie Schoenbaum, a real-life couple who'd been Carl and Estelle Reiner's best friends and neighbors during the years they lived in New Rochelle. In fact, notes Reiner, he and his wife first befriended the Schoenbaums in the early fifties, long before they moved to New Rochelle, when both couples still lived in the Bronx. So close were the couples that when the Reiners finally decided to pull up stakes and leave the old neighborhood for the tree-lined security of New Rochelle, the Schoenbaums weren't far behind. "We moved up to New Rochelle, and then they moved up to New Rochelle," says Reiner, describing a scenario that would serve as the springboard for the *Van Dyke Show*'s fourth season episode "Your Home Sweet Home Is My Home Sweet Home," in which the Helpers and Petries go househunting together and wind up in New Rochelle. "They were funny people," says Reiner, recalling his longtime friends. "We laughed with them for a lot of years."

Despite the obvious parallels between Reiner's fictional next-door neighbors and their off-screen counterparts, the writer hastens to add that he employed a healthy dollop of dramatic license in his televisual

Ann Guilbert and Jerry Paris made their first appearance as Millie and Jerry Helper in the show's third episode.

rendering of his real-life best friends. Although Reiner depicts the show's Jerry as a boisterous dentist with a weakness for practical jokes and a penchant for lodging his foot squarely between his molars, the writer insists that those traits bore little resemblance to the character's real-life namesake. In fact, confesses Reiner, Jerry Helper bore a far greater resemblance to the actor who would play him for five years: Jerry Paris, a man who was—by most accounts—every bit as outspoken and high-spirited as his on-screen alter ego.

"Jerry Paris was a wild man," recalled Bill Idelson, who'd been a close friend of the performer for many years before Paris's passing in 1986, "he took lithium to keep himself on an even keel." But the actor's most distinctive personality quirk, Idelson insisted, was an almost total inability to hold his tongue. "Jerry would just say whatever was on his mind."

"He had absolutely no editor in his brain," concurs Dick Van Dyke, who also counted himself among Paris's closest friends. "Whatever Jerry thought or felt fell right out of his mouth. He was that spontaneous. And very often he'd say something that was inappropriate and make people mad." And yet, notes Van Dyke, even though the actor's unchecked outbursts left some people ill at ease, Paris's indefatigable exuberance was a quality that few could resist. "He just ate up life in great big bites," reminisces Van Dyke. "I tell you, I loved him dearly. He was a unique human being."

As a character actor of vast and varied experience, he was also an ideal choice for this key supporting role on *The Dick Van Dyke Show*. Born in

San Francisco on July 25, 1925, Jerry Paris got his start as a bit player on the Broadway stage in the late forties. Like so many other stage-trained actors of his generation, Paris made an easy transition to the live television environment of the early fifties, where his list of credits would include dramatic roles on many of the era's top anthology shows, including *Playhouse 90*, *Studio One*, and *The Kraft Television Theater*. Paris's feature film roles include appearances in *The Wild One* and *The Naked and the Dead*, as well as notable bits in the big-screen adaptations of *Marty* and *The Caine Mutiny*, among others.

According to Ann Guilbert, who'd been friends with Jerry Paris for years before she signed on to play his wife on *The Dick Van Dyke Show*, the show's producers began scouting for actors to play the Petries' next-door neighbors shortly after the pilot was shot the previous January. "They had another couple in the pilot," Guilbert explains, referring to Michael Keith and Barbara Eiler, the actors whose appearance as neighbors Sam and Dotty in "The Sick Boy and the Sitter" consisted of little more than a walk-on. "But they weren't comedians. And Carl wanted comedians." By Guilbert's account, Jerry Paris had been Sheldon Leonard's first and only choice to play dentist Jerry Helper. "Jerry was a friend of Sheldon's," recalls Guilbert, "and they were at the track, and Sheldon said, 'Why don't you come and do the neighbor on this show?'"

The actor promptly took the producer up on his offer, says Guilbert, who insists that it was Paris who finally recommended her for a role on the show—after a little judicious prodding from Guilbert's then-husband, TV producer George Eckstein. "Jerry kept saying, 'Oh, Annie, they need a funny person. You should be doing my wife!" recalls Guilbert. "Finally my ex-husband said, 'Why don't you quit *saying* it and just get her an interview?' So Jerry took me down, and I auditioned for Carl."

While Paris may well have been responsible for bringing Guilbert to his producer's attention, Reiner recalls that the actress was no stranger to him when she walked in to audition for the show in the early summer of 1961. The producer first spied the comic actress two years earlier, when she was in the cast of *The Billy Barnes Revue*, a musical-comedy romp that played repeat engagements in different versions on Broadway and in Hollywood throughout the late fifties and early sixties. A big fan of the revue in all of its incarnations, Reiner was especially fond of Guilbert's contributions. "She was a sketch performer," notes Reiner. "And funny!

Really funny. She had a way about her, a sound in her voice that made me laugh."*

Like most of the auditions for *The Dick Van Dyke Show*, Guilbert's reading for the part of Millie Helper was a simple affair, straightforward and mercifully short. "Carl had me read a scene from an upcoming show," the actress recalls. "I read it with Jerry. And that was it." The producer hired the actress on the spot—a decision he would have little reason to regret. "Annie," he observes, "turned into a great actress."

IN HIS PATERNAL zeal to give *The Dick Van Dyke Show* its strongest possible send-off, Leonard had insisted on directing the show's pilot and first two episodes himself. It was not until the show's fourth episode went into production during the last days of June 1961 that the executive producer felt confident enough in the show's progress to surrender the directorial reins to John Rich, a consummate craftsman whose arrival would mark a significant addition to the show's crack creative staff.

But then, it hardly took a producer of Sheldon Leonard's keen instincts to recognize that Rich was ideally suited to direct *The Dick Van Dyke Show*. Born in Rockaway Beach, New York, on July 6, 1925, John Rich came to the *Van Dyke Show* with a weighty resume that dated all the way back to 1952, the year Rich got his start in TV as a director of live variety shows for singers Dennis Day and Ezio Pinza. By the mid-fifties, Rich had moved into the three-camera arena, where he served as a house director at Desilu, eventually helming multiple episodes of *Our Miss Brooks* and *I Married Joan*. By the end of the decade, the versatile Rich had mastered the art of directing one-camera drama and adventure series as well—a skill he would demonstrate throughout the late fifties and early sixties as director of dozens of episodes of *Gunsmoke*, *Twilight Zone*, *Bonanza*, *Bat Masterson*, and *General Electric Theater*, among many others. "Getting John Rich was one of those lucky things," observes Reiner. "He was a highly intelligent man. And he was a good, solid director."

Far more important than Rich's impressive credits—at least as far as the fledgling company of players awaiting his direction on *The Dick Van Dyke*

---

* Nor would Ann Guilbert be the only member of the *Billy Barnes* troupe to strike Reiner's fancy. Over the years, the *Van Dyke Show*'s guest cast would be studded with names drawn from *The Billy Barnes Revue*'s illustrious alumni list, including Ken Berry, Jackie Joseph, Patty Regan, Joyce Jamison, and Len Weinrib.

Show was concerned—was his rock-solid reputation as an actor's director. Unlike many, if not most, TV directors of the era, Rich had cultivated an unusual degree of respect for actors, and he prided himself on his ability to communicate with performers in a language they understood. "John was the best comedy director in the world," says Rose Marie, who maintains that Rich's keen directorial instincts were in evidence from his very first week on the set. "He would always tell me, 'I gotta find the relationship between you and Dick. And Dick and Mary. And Dick and Buddy. I gotta find out what the relationships are, so I can tell the audience.' So John spent the first couple shows telling everybody in the cast who we were and what our relationships were with one and other. And it was brilliant."

If Rich favored the kid-glove approach with his actors during those early rehearsals, the show's cast and crew would quickly discover their new director could also be an extremely demanding perfectionist come shooting night. As Bud Molin, the show's film editor, recalled, "He would shoot all night—the same thing forty times, until he got it the way he wanted it. John was a 'let's do it again' type—and he sometimes kept the actors there to the point of people getting very uptight about it." As Reiner would soon come to appreciate, Rich's penchant for perfectionism was by no means limited to the areas of staging and direction. "I would write a scene," recalls Reiner, "and John would say, 'This could be better.' But he never told you how! So I used to go back and rewrite. And rewrite. He'd force you to write more and better. Sometimes better . . . sometimes just more. He would carpet everything." But if Rich occasionally got carried away with his critiques, Reiner concedes that the director's criticisms were invariably intended to improve the show. "I think he was just insecure that the show should be the best it could be," recalls the producer. "But everybody had great faith in him."

"John Rich was the kind of guy you always got an answer out of," says James Niver, who served as the director's camera coordinator on the show. "Other people might say, 'It doesn't matter.' But with John you always got, 'You're right!' Or, 'No, it works much better this way.'" And if Rich earned the respect of his crew, he was practically revered by the individuals in his acting company. "Johnny Rich was brilliant," declared Morey Amsterdam some three decades after the show's debut. "I learned so much from that guy."

"Everyone looked up to John," states Rose Marie, "because he knew. He just knew." And, adds the actress, the director took particular pleasure in sharing that knowledge. "He used to explain everything to me. John would say, 'I'm using a 70mm lens here, because this will cut you at this angle. Then I'm gonna cut to Dick with this.' He even let me go into the editing room, where he'd ask me, 'Where would you cut this scene? What camera would you cut to?' I'd say, 'The party scene's over—I think we should cut to the master shot.' And he'd say, 'You're right.' And he'd cut it that way. He taught me so much."

Despite the accolades he would eventually earn as director of *The Dick Van Dyke Show*—including the 1963 Emmy for Outstanding Directorial Achievement in Comedy—Rich insists that his first week on the job very nearly turned out to be his last. The problem, as Rich relays in an anecdote that seems to grow more colorful with each retelling, was that, after three

Dick Van Dyke and Mary Tyler Moore huddle with director John Rich, the man Rose Marie has called "the best comedy director in the world." *Courtesy: John Rich*

years in the fast-paced world of one-camera TV, he'd all but forgotten how to direct a live three-camera situation comedy by the time he arrived on the *Van Dyke* set. "In a single-camera show like *Gunsmoke*," he explains, "you're always in a hurry. You rehearse a sequence—sometimes maybe as long as two or three pages—and then you commit it instantly to film." Which, the director emphasizes, is a far cry from the relatively relaxed pace of a three-camera situation comedy, where the director often has as many as five days to rehearse with his actors before a single frame of film is shot. It's an important distinction, says Rich, and one that had, unfortunately, temporarily eluded him by the time he started work on *The Dick Van Dyke Show* in the summer of 1961.

"On my first day," recalls the director, "I put everyone on their feet and said, 'Let's start to work.'" And work they did! Moving along at the same breakneck pace that the director had grown accustomed to on one-camera shows like *Gunsmoke* and *Bonanza*, the director practically flew through every scene in the show. "They're very quick actors," he says, "and we got a momentum going that was terrific." By the end of that first frenetic day, the cast had completely rehearsed Reiner's entire forty-five-page script. "The show was ready," insists the director. "It was up. It was terrific!"

Indeed, it was nothing short of a miracle. In a single day's rehearsal, the director had whipped the entire show into shape, and it was now ready to roll. The only problem was, the shooting date was still four working days away—which left the overzealous director and his hard-working cast with absolutely nothing to do on the four days of rehearsal remaining. Driving home from the studio that night, Rich could smell disaster. "I was like the coach of a football team who's got his players all ready to go a full week before the big game! I thought, 'What am I gonna do now?'" Finally, the director decided, there was only one solution.

He had to move the furniture.

It was a brilliant, if risky, idea. The next morning, Rich would arrive at work early. Then, before any of the cast members arrived, he would simply rearrange every stick of furniture on the set. He would put sofas where there weren't sofas before. He'd drop end tables in where the sofas were. And then, once he'd rendered the set so confusing that it was practically impossible to navigate without a compass, he would invite the actors to resume their rehearsals, feigning innocence all the while. If everything went according to plan, the actors would be so disoriented by the reconfigured set that they would spend the better part of the next day stumbling around as they tried to reblock their original stage movements from scratch. Then, having successfully burned off a full day of slack time in the week's rehearsal schedule, the director would simply move all the furniture back to into the original positions, leaving the actors just enough time to re-rehearse the show before the Tuesday-night filming. It was a desperate ploy, and the director knew it. But, at that point, Rich just didn't see any other way out of the corner into which he'd so neatly painted himself.

When the actors arrived at the studio the next morning, they were puzzled to find their director seated in the middle of the set, where he'd already moved every piece of furniture on the stage to a different spot than it had been the day before. "I've had a few second thoughts on the set," the director announced to his by-now-dumbstruck actors. "Indulge me."

"I turned the entire room around," admits Rich, who promptly resumed rehearsal on the haphazard new floor plan. And, just as he'd hoped, the actors did their best to recapture the magic of the first day's rehearsal—to no avail. With unfamiliar furniture blocking their every move, the actors did little more than bump into each other for most of the afternoon. By the end of the day, the show was in a complete shambles—just as Rich had planned. "I just wouldn't let them rehearse effectively," recalls Rich.

The next morning, after wasting an entire day of rehearsal, Rich ordered his stage crew to move every piece of furniture back into its original position on the set. And, just as he'd hoped, the company spent the rest of the week retracing their footing, until finally, by the time the show went before the cameras the following Tuesday evening, they were secure enough to film the episode without a hitch. Of course, it was only after the shooting was finished that Rich let the company in on his little secret. "After the show," says Rich, "I finally took them aside and told them what I'd done."

Curiously, as much as Rich delights in recounting the story, Reiner insists that he didn't hear the director's harrowing account of his first week on the *Van Dyke Show* until many years after the fact—which may have been just as well. "When I heard that story," says Reiner, "I told John, 'If I'd known you did that, I woulda killed you!'"

13

COURTSHIP

The show's sixth episode, "Oh How We Met the Night That We Danced," filmed on July 18, 1961, was a milestone in the annals of *The Dick Van Dyke Show*. The first episode to feature an extended flashback to the stormy early days of Rob and Laura's courtship, "Oh How We Met the Night That We Danced" also gave us our first peek at Rob Petrie's days at Camp Crowder, Missouri, where he'd been stationed in the army's special services unit. The lighthearted episode details Rob's frustrated attempts to date a striking young USO showgirl named Laura Meeker, who—as his pal Sol Pomeroy is only too eager to warn him—has a reputation around the base as "a real cold potato." As Sergeant Petrie discovers when the dancer rebuffs his every advance, her reputation is well earned. Undaunted, Rob conspires to join the young dancer on stage during her act, where the enterprising serviceman vows to tender a marriage proposal during an impromptu soft-shoe. But even this romantic gesture ends in disaster when the over-eager staff sergeant accidentally steps on his reluctant partner's toe—and ends up sending her to the infirmary with a broken foot! Of course, as the flashback ends, Laura reveals that she eventually did revise her opinion of her clumsy suitor, to his obvious, and everlasting, delight.

Inspired by the success of "Oh How We Met the Night That We Danced," Reiner would return frequently to the continuing saga of Rob and Laura's courtship and early married life. In later years, Reiner would rank the *Van*

Rob stutters a halting proposal in "The Attempted Marriage," one of the show's most memorable flashback episodes.

Dyke Show's army episodes among his favorite shows. It's not hard to see why. Taken as a group, this remarkable subset of *Van Dyke Show* flashback episodes would trace the fitful progress of Rob and Laura's romance in an unfolding saga rich in comic detail and poignant romantic observation. And, as should surprise no one familiar with Reiner's self-reflexive style, most of those observations were inspired, with only minor embellishment, by the writer's own experiences. "Those army shows were all based on real things," acknowledges Reiner. "I just invented the details."*

* One significant detail in this episode that was not made up was Laura Petrie's maiden name. Early in the teleplay, Mary Tyler Moore's character is introduced as Laura Meeker—an in-joke of sorts, since Meeker was the surname of Moore's first husband, to whom the actress was still married when this episode was shot. After Moore and Richard Meeker divorced a few months later, Laura's family name in future scripts would be changed—without explanation—from Meeker to Meehan.

As a quick glimpse at Reiner's personal dossier reveals, the *Van Dyke Show*'s army flashback episodes were indeed rife with autobiographical echoes of Reiner's own life and career. Like Rob Petrie, the writer/producer had also been stationed at Camp Crowder, Missouri—though Reiner's hitch began a bit earlier than Rob's, in 1943, not long after the real-life writer met his own wife, the former Estelle Lebost. "She wasn't in the USO," says Reiner. "But she did used to visit me at Camp Crowder."

Reiner would continue to explore the axiom that truth can be stranger—and often funnier—than fiction when he returned to the army setting for the show's second-season classic, "The Attempted Marriage." The highlight of that episode was the unforgettable sequence where Rob stutters his faltering marriage proposal to Laura in an open-air jeep—a scene, says Reiner, that was a thinly veiled takeoff on his own quaking proposal to Estelle. "I proposed to my wife at home," says Reiner, who recalls that, like Rob, he was fighting off flu at the time. "I was shivering, just like he was. I was twenty-one years old, and I was so scared! And I remembered that emotion when I wrote the scene. So that's why I had Rob say, 'Do y-y-you want to get m-m-married?' It was all felt."

Reiner's next army script, episode 47, "Will You Two Be My Wife?"—in which Sergeant Petrie bids farewell to the girl he left behind—was largely a fiction, though Reiner would be back on the autobiographical track by the show's eighty-fifth episode, "Honeymoons Are for the Lucky." That episode described how Rob and Laura's honeymoon was nearly ruined by army regulations and the postwar housing crunch—another plot torn directly from the Reiners' own wedding album. "I wouldn't give those shows to anybody to write," insists Reiner, "because even though they were invented, the feelings had to be right."

Ironically, the one scene in "Oh How We Met the Night That We Danced" that Reiner admits he fabricated from whole cloth was the climactic soft-shoe number—where Rob attempts to tender his flippant marriage proposal to Laura in between verses of "You, Wonderful You"—which may well be the best sequence in the episode. As Reiner observes, "That was pure Dick and Mary."

"I invented that because I wanted to see Dick and Mary dance together," says the writer, who admits he'd been pleasantly surprised to discover a few weeks into rehearsals that his two leading players shared an uncanny knack for song and dance. "Mary and Dick were incredible," notes Reiner, "the way they did those complicated dance numbers." It was a feat that was all the more impressive in light of the show's tight rehearsal schedule. "They'd have three, maybe four days to learn the number, do it, and shoot it."*

Although Van Dyke and Moore pull off their soft-shoe number with fluid grace, Reiner insists that the effortless quality of the performance was hard earned. "They came to me," says Reiner, "and said, 'We can't do this! It's just too hard!'" Fortunately, the producer refused to heed their protests. "We had choreographers," says Reiner, "and they pushed them. No one made it easy for Dick and Mary, because we knew they were both so good." And, he notes, the results of that extra effort are still paying dividends all these years later. "I saw that number, 'You, Wonderful You,' on TV the other day. And—gee!—they were both right on the button."

DICK VAN DYKE'S musical comedy skills came as little surprise to Reiner, who was well aware that the actor had dazzled Broadway audiences for more than a year in *Bye Bye Birdie*. But, he confesses, his discovery that Mary Tyler Moore was similarly gifted came as a pleasant revelation. "I already had Dick Van Dyke when I found out Mary could sing and dance," Reiner remembers. "And that was serendipity, because we didn't know that when we hired her." But if the producer was pleased to witness Moore's emergence as a musical-comedy star in the show's sixth episode, he was still completely unprepared for the eye-opening performance she would turn in three weeks later, when the talented young performer finally came into her own as a comic actress in the show's ninth episode, "My Blonde-Haired Brunette."

The episode that would provide Moore's breakthrough opens in the Petrie bedroom, where Rob has rebuffed Laura's good-natured attempt to rouse him from sleep with a good-morning kiss. In the face of her husband's startling romantic apathy, Laura comes to the conclusion that the spark has finally drifted out of their marriage. Her fears appear to be confirmed a few moments later, when Rob arrives at their breakfast table clad in a shabby

---

* It probably came as some small consolation to the busy performers that they wouldn't actually have to worry about singing their various musical numbers live at the show's Tuesday-night filming, since it was a common practice on *The Dick Van Dyke Show*—as it was on almost every other audience show of that era—to have the actors lip-sync to their own prerecorded vocals during the live performance.

"I had no experience in comedy," admits Mary Tyler Moore, whose comedic skills were nonetheless in full display by the show's ninth episode, "My Blonde-Haired Brunette."

sweater and jeans, which Laura interprets as further evidence of his growing marital disinterest.

Faced with such incontrovertible evidence of decline in her marriage, Laura works herself into a serious funk. It's in this vulnerable state that she allows Millie to talk her into bleaching her hair blonde in a last-ditch effort to recapture her husband's waning attentions. Naturally, Millie's harebrained scheme goes awry, and Laura ends up with a hideous two-tone dye job that leaves half of her hair blonde and the other half brunette. And that's how she appears when she finally comes face-to-face with her thoroughly confused husband. When Rob makes the mistake of asking for an explanation, Laura barrages her hapless husband with a tearful monologue that is a masterpiece of confused, if heartfelt, emotional logic.

"Why?" Laura finally sobs, struggling to find words that might sum up the depth of her self-inflicted malaise. "Well . . ." she sniffs, "yesterday morning . . . ." And then, before she can even stammer out the rest of the sentence, she has shifted gears completely. "And I *kissed* you, and you said 'Don't *do* that!' And you came down to breakfast in your *yecchy* shirt!" On and on she goes, sobbing in utter exasperation all the while, until her monologue has finally dissolved into a long string of barely comprehensible—though heartwrenchingly funny—non sequiturs. Finally, at her wit's end, Laura sobs, "and . . . the . . . general *yuck-i-ness* . . . ." Then, with no better way to communicate her desperate need for comfort, she collapses into Rob's waiting arms. "I understand, honey," he coos soothingly. "I understand." And, through some inspired combination of acting, writing, and direction—so do we.

It's a remarkably written scene—unsettling, poignant, and wildly funny, all at the same time. Moore's reading of the monologue is nothing short of a revelation—a performance of such unerring emotional truth that we find ourselves chuckling reluctantly at the sweet despair of the insecure young wife's folly.

The monologue is also notable in that it marks the inaugural appearance of what would come to be one of *The Dick Van Dyke Show*'s most durable comic staples: Laura Petrie's extended comical crying jags. In fact, boasts Reiner, it was under his personal tutelage during rehearsals for this episode that Moore actually perfected her trademark technique of sobbing her way through entire paragraphs of comical exposition. As Reiner recounts it, "Mary always said I taught her how to cry and make it funny."

"Mary always had a question of being real or being funny," explains the producer, who recalls that the actress had experimented with a number of more down-to-earth readings of the episode's hilarious closing monologue before he finally stepped in to correct her. "If you cry for real," he cautioned the actress, "it's not going to be funny." As Reiner observes, "There's a way to do a scene like that where you make people feel sorry for you—but you still get your laugh. And it's one of the things I can do." Which is essentially what Reiner told Moore at that early rehearsal for "My Blonde-Haired Brunette." Naturally, as soon as the actress heard Reiner's boast that he'd mastered the art of stage crying, she demanded a demonstration. "When I told her that was something I could do," recalls Reiner, "she said, 'Do it!' So I did it."

Without further prompting, Reiner proceeded to act out the entire monologue—tears, hysterics, and all—to Moore's obvious delight. Once the actress recovered from the extended bout of giggles that Reiner's rendition inspired, she reworked the piece until it was unmistakably her own. "That was a tour de force for Mary," says Dick Van Dyke, recalling the actress's showstopping performance in "My Blonde-Haired Brunette." "She was brilliant."

Van Dyke wasn't the only one to notice the attention that Moore had begun to attract by the show's ninth episode. Director John Rich suggests that Moore's breakout performance in "My Blonde-Haired Brunette" was so outstanding that it forced the show's producers to rethink their conception of her character, which the director maintains had up until that time been far more limited. "When Mary came to the show," Rich elaborates, "she was supposed to be what we call an 'ear' for Dick Van Dyke—an ear being somebody to whom you turn at night and say, 'This is what happened at the office today, and this is what my problem is.'" But, notes the director, that limited approach to the character became outmoded the instant Moore stepped into the role. "It soon became apparent," says Rich, "that Mary was a whole lot more than just an ear."

Just as the show's producers would come to recognize that they got more than they bargained for when they signed Moore, so, too, would the actress come to appreciate the exceptional opportunity the show afforded her. "Producers all over town had let me wear the same bangs and the same pants on their shows that I wear on this one, but nothing great ever happened," the actress later explained. "I think Laura came off because of a combination—what rubbed off on me before I came to the show, and the effect Carl and his cast had on it."[1] As the actress would acknowledge, she was not about to take this opportunity lightly. "With Dick and Rose Marie and Morey Amsterdam to play to, I think I also felt I'd better make something out of Laura, or *The Dick Van Dyke Show* would be the last of Mary Tyler Moore."[2]

Although Mary Tyler Moore thrived in the creative atmosphere fostered by Carl Reiner and her fellow players, the actress could not fail to notice the pressures that came with being the junior member of such a highly experienced ensemble. Decades later, the actress still recalled the insecurity that dogged her in those early days. "I had no experience in comedy," she admits. "I was a dramatic actress. I started out as a dancer and went from that straight into working as an actress on a lot of episodic dramatic shows." Moore admits that with her slim comic resume, stepping into a company of established pros—some of whom had roots dating all the way back to vaudeville—was not easy. "It was very intimidating, because they all had this comedy knowledge and background." And yet, to hear Van Dyke tell it, his costar took to situation comedy like she'd been born to the calling. "She was a serious actress when she came on the show," the star observes, "but she kind of picked up the rhythms from everybody else. And then, before you knew it, she could hold her own with no trouble at all. That's just how bright she was."

Ironically, Moore's lack of comedic training might actually have been an asset. Without a polished comedienne's bag of tricks to fall back on, she was forced to build a character based entirely on her own instincts—which, as it turned out, wasn't such a bad idea. "I was a housewife and mother myself," she acknowledges. "So I thought, 'Well, I can bring to this something from my own background—and that's honesty.'" She certainly got no argument from Reiner, who encouraged his cast to draw on the raw material of their own lives at every opportunity.

"I think Carl would back me up when I say that I kept him honest," volunteers Moore, who admits that she rarely hesitated to venture an opinion whenever she felt her character's integrity might be at stake. "I would go to Carl and say, 'We can't do this joke, because last week we said thus and such about Laura, and this would be contradictory.'" Although Reiner didn't accept all of her suggestions, the actress recalls that both he and Sheldon Leonard always found time to hear her out. "I generally made a pain in the ass of myself," she confesses, "but they took it with fond, fond acceptance."

If only to shed light on a fascinating corner of the colorful history of *The Dick Van Dyke Show*, it's worth noting that the actress did lock horns with her executive producer over at least one suggestion that she offered in the show's first year. As difficult as it may be to believe today, one of the show's earliest tempests stemmed from Moore's seemingly innocuous request that she be allowed to wear capri pants on the show. However innocent, that simple request set off a chain of events that would have a lasting impact not only on *The Dick Van Dyke Show*, but on every domestic situation comedy to follow in its wake.

14

CAPRI PANTS

It may not seem a particularly radical choice today, but Mary Tyler Moore's insistence on wearing her own form-fitting slacks on television was little short of revolutionary in 1961. In the days before *The Dick Van Dyke Show* rewrote the prime-time dress code, the costume of choice for women in situation comedies was still a freshly pressed full-skirted dress worn with a single, tasteful string of pearls. "Little frocks," as Moore describes them, "that were sweet and cute but didn't bear any resemblance to reality." And, as costumer Harald Johnson remembered it, Mary Tyler Moore was not about to let Laura Petrie be straitjacketed into a sweet little frock for five years.

"Mary liked to wear tight-fitting slacks," said Johnson, who would be responsible for dressing the cast of the *Van Dyke Show* throughout the life of the series. "And a lot of Mary's own personality was in the character that she played, so those capri pants were one of the things she pushed for." According to Johnson, it was a decision he supported wholeheartedly. "We wanted a more natural look, and we knew that ladies didn't sit around at home wearing pearls."

But neither did they lounge around the rec room wearing the extremely tight-fitting wool jersey slacks that the actress favored. Or so went the argument of Sheldon Leonard, who wondered if the dancer's form-fitting slacks might be a tad too revealing for a character on a family show—especially when that character was as naturally curvaceous as Mary Tyler Moore.

Mary Tyler Moore models her trademark capri pants—a wardrobe preference that would spark one of the show's most protracted behind-the-scenes controversies.

Nonsense, responded the actress, who argued that the capri pants Laura wore on-screen were the same slacks she herself wore to shop and run errands every day of her life—and she'd yet to hear anyone in the supermarket line accuse her of undermining their moral fiber.

Despite his reservations about Moore's choice of wardrobe, Leonard stopped short of actually forbidding his leading lady from wearing slacks on the air. But the capri pants controversy continued to rage throughout rehearsals for the show's early episodes, when it would invariably resurface as a hot topic whenever the actress showed up on the set clad in slacks. "We'd have three-way conversations about it," recalled Johnson, "right on the set, in front of everybody. Sheldon's argument was that the sponsors wouldn't like it—that they had certain ideas about what was protocol for shows of this type. There was a type of unwritten censorship in those days—and he wanted her to wear dresses."

"It wasn't Sheldon so much who was nervous," explains director John Rich, who holds the opinion that Leonard's stand on the capri pants controversy had nothing whatsoever to do with the executive producer's personal feelings, but was motivated almost entirely by a sense of responsibility to the show's sponsors. "Sheldon was just transmitting a feeling that had been expressed to him by Procter & Gamble. They were afraid that the housewives around America would get nervous because Mary was wearing pants."

"The sponsors were upset," concurs Moore, "because they started getting letters from housewives—probably older housewives—who were a little upset at the *clingy* aspects of those capri pants." According to Harald Johnson, the sponsors continued to apply pressure—via the show's executive producer—until late in the first season, when Moore and Leonard reached a truce. "They finally compromised and let her wear the pants every now and then," recalled Johnson, "just so long as they seemed natural for the scene." But, in Moore's recollection, she was held to a far more exacting quota. "They restricted me to wearing them in only one scene per show," she recalls.

Whatever the precise terms of Moore's capri pants embargo, any restrictions that might have been placed on the actress were quickly forgotten once the show landed in the top twenty a year or so later. In the meantime, suggests Rich, Moore's tenacity may have had a more far-reaching impact than anyone on the *Van Dyke* set imagined. "What she did," postulates the director, "was set a style trend. Partially as a result of Mary, women started to wear pants." And, as Rich is quick to point out, the fabric of our society hardly suffered as a result. "It didn't destroy the American family."

HARALD JOHNSON'S ROLE as Mary Tyler Moore's chief advocate in the capri pants debate was hardly the costumer's greatest concern in the show's earliest days. A far more urgent quandary—for him, anyway—was the question of how he was supposed to clothe an entire company of actors on a wardrobe budget that he would later describe as paltry beyond belief. "Sheldon was a wonderful producer," the costumer acknowledged, "but he didn't loosen his purse strings in my department. And because we were on a low budget, I was always encouraged to save." One of the costumer's most effective cost-cutting measures was simply to require many of the show's performers to appear on the air in their own clothing. "Most of the men who appeared as guests on the show would be encouraged to wear their own clothes," noted Johnson. "And Morey always brought in his own stuff. So did Richard Deacon."

Ann Guilbert was another *Van Dyke* regular who was obliged to wear her own clothes on the air. "If I needed something very special for a show," she observes, "like an evening dress, they would get it for me. But they didn't have a big clothes budget, so I almost always used my own clothing." Even Moore was encouraged to do her bit to help the show's wardrobe austerity program after her capri slacks fell under the scrutiny of the show's budget-conscious wardrobe director. "Those pants were very expensive," noted Johnson. "So Mary would wear her own slacks on the show all the time."

Dressing Dick Van Dyke presented its own unique set of challenges for the busy costume supervisor. For one thing, the star required an above-average supply of clean shirts on shooting day, or so reported *TV Guide* in a 1962 profile that described the star as a "highly strung worrier" who "still perspires through six shirts on the day of the performance."[1] And then there was the problem of the star's physique, which was so slender that Johnson found it almost impossible to find an off-the-rack suit that would fit Van Dyke's six-foot-one, 147-pound frame. As a result, almost everything the lanky star wore on the show had to be custom tailored. "Dick was very, very particular about his clothes," said Johnson. "He never wore off-the-rack suits. The only things he ever wore that were not custom made were sportswear items. I might buy him sweaters or sports shirts. But even his casual slacks were usually custom made."

Naturally, all that custom tailoring cost money. But, owing to an ingenious promotional arrangement that Sheldon Leonard worked out with the Botany 500 line of men's wear, Van Dyke's wardrobe ended up not costing the show's producers a single penny. Under Leonard's deal, Botany 500 agreed to supply the star's wardrobe free of charge, in exchange for a promotional acknowledgment in the show's closing credits that stated, "Mr. Van Dyke's wardrobe furnished by Botany 500."

It was an ironic credit, and more than a little misleading, considering that a clotheshorse like Van Dyke would not have been caught dead in department store ready-to-wear. In fact, according to Johnson, Botany 500 didn't actually manufacture any of the suits that the star wore on camera, which were all custom tailored by a prominent Beverly Hills tailor—at Botany 500's expense. "They were all custom made, and very expensive," said Harald Johnson.

If the arrangement with Botany 500 saved the show's producers a bundle on wardrobe costs, it was also a boon for Van Dyke, who was allowed to take his custom-fitted suits home after he'd worn them on the air. And, recalls Johnson, Van Dyke wasn't the only one to reap benefits from this particular perquisite of the Botany 500 setup. "Part of the deal," he revealed, "was that Sheldon Leonard and Carl Reiner also received suits made by the same tailor."

Once Johnson got Van Dyke's wardrobe problems squared away courtesy of Botany 500, the costumer set to work organizing a similar scheme to obtain the steady parade of smart dresses and sporty outfits that would be required to keep Rose Marie and Mary Tyler Moore poised on the cutting edge of early-sixties fashion. Using the Botany 500 plan as a guide, the costumer negotiated deals with a variety of California-based women's clothing designers, most of whom were only too happy to loan samples of their latest fashion lines to the show's female stars in exchange for the exposure and, of course, a prominent plug in the show's closing credits.

As Johnson remembered it, the only real drawback he encountered in borrowing clothes for the show's two female stars was that it occasionally engendered rivalry between them. "There was always jealousy about who got the better things to wear," he recalled. According to the costumer, that competition didn't always end in the dressing room.

"They never were close friends," said Johnson, who insisted that he detected the first signs of jealousy between the show's female stars shortly after the producers began to feature Moore more prominently in the series. "In the beginning," explained Johnson, "Rose thought that she would be the female star of the show. Then Mary actually became the female star, because the public just took to her. And Rose Marie fell into second place."

If a rivalry existed between the show's leading ladies, Rose Marie insists that she was never aware of it. "There was never any problem or anything," says the actress, who nonetheless acknowledges that she and her costar did keep their friendship at arm's length. "We were pleasant enough," she says. "We always got along—but very, very sparingly, so to speak. I don't know why. We just never hit it off."

Reiner dismisses out of hand the notion that jealousy ever played a significant role in the social dynamic of *The Dick Van Dyke Show*, onstage or off. The closest thing to competition that Reiner ever observed on the *Van Dyke* set came early in the show's run, when Rose Marie and Morey Amsterdam would occasionally lobby for more scenes set in *The Alan*

Brady Show's writers' room, where they had most of their lines. "It's funny," says Reiner, "in their heads, it was a show about a comedy writer. But I never thought it was a show about writers. In my head, it was a show about a husband and father who happened to be a comedy writer. And I had to explain that to them over and over again. They never felt their part was big enough in the first year—but it was just like in any show, everybody wants a bigger part." But if Rose Marie and Amsterdam openly acknowledged their hunger for increased stage time during the show's early days, the producer insists they never got their feathers in a ruffle over it. "They finally fell into the fact that the show was what it was," says Reiner, "and then they were both very happy."

Ruffled feathers of any sort were an extremely rare sight on the set of *The Dick Van Dyke Show*. "We never had an argument," observed *Van Dyke Show* director Al Rafkin. "It was always settled with a laugh, with a smile.

Morey Amsterdam and Rose Marie frequently lobbied Carl Reiner to include more scenes set in the writers' room, despite his insistence that the show wasn't really about writers at all. "In my head," says Reiner, "it was a show about a husband and father who happened to be a comedy writer."

Because that was Dick's temperament, and so it became the temperament of the show." Reiner agrees it was rare that anyone heard the sound of raised voices at a *Van Dyke* rehearsal—unless they happened to drop by on one of those mornings when he and his executive producer failed to see eye to eye.

"Sheldon and I had a lot of fights," says Reiner. According to the producer, the vast majority of their battles were staged at the show's Wednesday-morning script readings, where Reiner recalls that he and his "worthy adversary" would frequently lock horns over the finer points of comic theory. "They used to have some wonderful arguments," recollects Van Dyke. "Sheldon had a background in three-camera, and when it came to story—he was a strict constructionist. But Carl came in with some different ideas about comedy. So they were at odds a lot." And yet, even in combat, Van Dyke insists, his producers were never less than entertaining. "We'd all just sit and listen to them," recalls the actor.

Writer Sam Denoff—who with his partner Bill Persky would eventually write many of the show's finest third-, fourth-, and fifth-season episodes—recalls that he used to watch with nervous fascination whenever his producers engaged in heated debate. "They would have these tremendous fights," recalls Denoff. "And Billy and I would sit there in terror. Sheldon would say, 'No, Carl. Don't you see? Goddammit, don't you see?' And Carl would say, 'No, Sheldon, you're wrong, for chrissake!' Then Sheldon would say, 'Well, Carl—you're crazy! I don't think it'll work.' And he'd walk out."

Reiner hastens to add that Leonard's frequent abrupt departures from the *Van Dyke Show* set were never the result of pique, but merely the most visible manifestation of his overwhelming workload. "Sheldon always disappeared after the readings," says Reiner. "When you've got five shows on the air, you can't pay attention to the minutiae on every one of them." Naturally, Leonard's habit of making sudden exits was not lost on the *Van Dyke Show*'s observant cast, who came to view their executive producer's disappearing acts as the stuff of legend. "We used to call him the Shadow," says Moore, recalling the Lamont Cranston character from the classic radio show. Adds Rose Marie, "We even had a welcome mat made up for Sheldon with the name 'Lamont Cranston' printed on it."

If the *Van Dyke Show*'s producers occasionally engaged in spirited verbal sparring during the weekly script meetings, most observers agree that these blustery debates—which were, after all, invariably waged on the show's behalf—posed little threat to the show's otherwise unflappable creative harmony. In fact, it's one of the minor miracles of *The Dick Van Dyke Show*'s production history that the set remained practically free of strife throughout five full seasons of production—a remarkable record, especially considering the extremely diverse and highly opinionated group of talents that assembled there each week.

"Morale was very important on that set," explained Leonard, who insisted that he and Reiner worked hard to foster an atmosphere of creative harmony on the *Van Dyke Show*, if only because they knew that a buoyant mood made for a better show. "If you weren't happy when you came in," noted Leonard, "something would be missing. And it would show up on the screen."

To many observers, the infectious spirits that prevailed on the set could be traced directly to the show's producer, whose own indefatigable personality was legendary even then. "Carl was ebullient," recalled writer Harvey Bullock. "He was open—always jumping around. You could tell he was in love with being there." Camera coordinator James Niver seconds that sentiment, adding, "With Carl, it was always like he'd just been let out of a cage. There was always excitement. 'Here!' he'd say, 'here's a new thing! A new idea!' Great enthusiasm—that's Carl."

Reiner was also, according to Niver, a tireless booster of new talent.

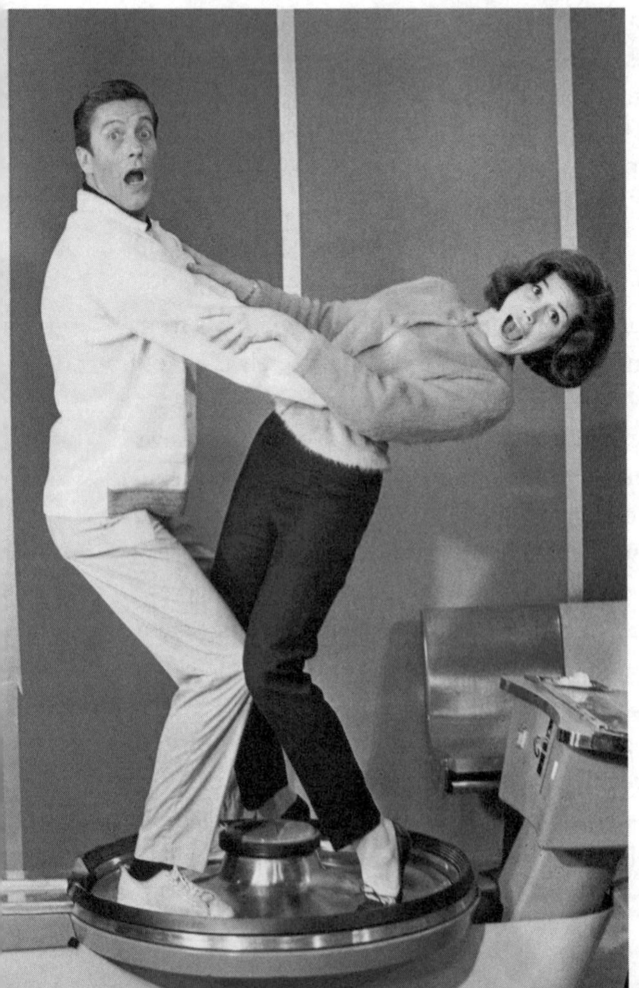

"There was always a little bit of pandemonium on the set," observes Dick Van Dyke. "Sheldon Leonard used to say we looked like otters playing in a pond."

The producer was never so happy, notes Niver, as when he brought some awestruck young comic or singer he'd just discovered to the *Van Dyke* set, where the flabbergasted newcomer would invariably be introduced to the show's entire cast and crew, usually with great fanfare. "Carl was always bringing somebody in," says Niver. "He would walk in like he'd just found a new toy that we all had to stop and listen to. He'd stop rehearsal and we'd all say, 'Oh, what now?' Then he'd say, 'Oh, you gotta hear this person!' Then somebody'd start telling stories."

One of the show's more notable visitors was a talented young comedian named Bill Cosby, who'd been invited by Reiner to drop by the set of *The Dick Van Dyke Show* one afternoon in the show's fourth year. Though Cosby was still far from a household name at the time, Reiner denies that he played more than a passing role in the discovery of the soon-to-be superstar. As it happens, the producer recalls, his then-teenaged son, Rob, was the first Reiner to recognize the comedian's substantial gifts.

"When [Rob] was about sixteen," Carl Reiner recalled in 1985,[2] "I came home from the *Van Dyke Show* one night about one in the morning. Rob was awake. I said, 'What are you doing awake? You have school tomorrow.' And he said, 'I just saw the greatest comedian on *The Tonight Show*, a guy named Bill Cosby.' And he proceeded to get out of his bed and do Cosby's whole routine for me, the voices, everything. I just got hysterical." So impressed was the elder Reiner by his teenaged son's facsimile of the comic's act that he finally invited Cosby himself to the *Van Dyke Show* stage, where the comedian was only too happy to provide a sample of the genuine article for the show's cast and crew. "I invited Cosby to visit us on the set," recalls Reiner. "He was there for the whole Wednesday reading, and we didn't get a bit of work done that day, we were laughing so hard. He did all of his act, and he was hilarious."

"He was just a young guy," remembers Van Dyke, who harbors similarly fond memories of Cosby's unscheduled visit to a *Van Dyke Show* rehearsal, "but he came in and did this piece about Noah and the Ark—and he absolutely threw us all on the floor." Perhaps no one was more taken with Cosby's electrifying performance than Sheldon Leonard, who declared to all within earshot that they hadn't seen the last of Bill Cosby. Sure enough, within the year, Leonard himself would play an instrumental role in Cosby's transformation from comedian to prime-time commodity when he cast the rising comic opposite Robert Culp in

I Spy, an innovative adventure series that Leonard executive produced for NBC beginning in 1965.*

"THERE WAS ALWAYS a little bit of pandemonium on the set," observes Van Dyke, recalling the giddy spirits that occasionally overcame the cast during rehearsals for the show. "Sheldon Leonard used to come down to the set and say we looked like otters playing in a pond." And, it must be admitted, the cast's irrepressible esprit de corps did have its mischievous side as well. Van Dyke himself confesses that he wasn't above enlivening a dull rehearsal with a good practical joke if the opportunity presented itself.

One of Van Dyke's favorite rehearsal pranks was the vanishing cast trick, a bit of organized whimsy that began with the star leading the entire cast off the set just split seconds before one of the show's hapless guest stars was scheduled to make his or her entrance. "We'd vacate the studio," explains Van Dyke. Then, hidden at a safe distance, the star and his coconspirators would watch their victim squirm as he or she waited in vain for someone onstage to cue his or her entrance. "We'd leave them standing out there, all alone on an empty soundstage," recalls Van Dyke, "until they finally decided to open the door and find out what the hell was going on."

Ann Guilbert recalls that, despite the good-natured hazing that awaited the show's more tolerant guest stars, *The Dick Van Dyke Show* stage was still one of the most popular destinations in Hollywood for character actors. "Every actor in town wanted to work our show, because it was so damn much fun," the actress recalls. "They were all such funny people that working there was just a ball." However, Van Dyke insists that despite the conviviality the show engendered, his company's freewheeling approach was not for everyone. "Sometimes we'd have a guest star who

* By coincidence, Reiner recalls that he was also responsible—in a roundabout way—for Robert Culp's casting in that same series. According to Reiner, Culp was already an established leading man when he approached the producer for advice on breaking into the writing end of the business. "Culp loved the *Van Dyke Show*," explains Reiner, "so he asked me to comment on some writing he'd done." No sooner had Reiner begun to read the actor's writing sample than he realized that Culp had written a sample script for an hour-long adventure series—a genre for which Reiner professed little expertise. Rather than try to critique it himself, Reiner passed the script along to his partner Leonard, who at that precise moment happened to be casting his own hour-long adventure series, *I Spy*. As fate would have it, Leonard was more impressed by Culp's acting skills than his potential as a writer. And so, although he took a pass on the actor's sample script, Leonard wound up signing Culp to a long-term contract to star in *I Spy*, making him the second actor—along with his costar, Bill Cosby—to land a role on the series courtesy of Carl Reiner.

just didn't know what the hell to make of us," confesses the star, who cites Robert Vaughn—the actor who played Laura's old flame on episode 59, "It's a Shame She Married Me"—as one of the few *Van Dyke Show* guest stars to cast a scornful eye on the cast's hijinks. "I think our silliness kind of got on his nerves a little bit," says Van Dyke, who recalls that the visiting actor spent most of his week on the set eyeing the cast with a mixture of curiosity and disdain. "He just kind of sat and studied us," says Van Dyke. "Like an anthropologist."

Actor Ross Elliott had no such qualms about the highly charged creative atmosphere he observed on the *Van Dyke* set. "Rehearsals on that show were a kind of free-for-all," remembered the actor, who appeared as a psychiatrist in episode 82, "The Brave and the Backache," and reprised the role two years later in episode 129, "Uhny Uftz." "If anyone had an idea for a line, you threw it in and they'd use it."

"Everybody had input," agrees Ann Guilbert. "Carl was really great about that. Anybody could think up a gag or change their line. Sometimes the new lines were funny, sometimes they weren't. But you always felt as though you were contributing."

Naturally, rehearsals for *The Dick Van Dyke Show* were not all fun and games. As on any TV or movie set, there were the unavoidable hours of waiting for lights to be adjusted, cameras to be blocked, or any one of the ten thousand other details that go into filming a weekly TV series. But, notes actor Frank Adamo, even during these inevitable lulls, the cast had little trouble coming up with diversions to keep themselves occupied. "There was no sitting around," says Adamo. "If we found ourselves just sitting there, we'd be filling our mouths with cookies. You know, noshing and giggling and scratching." According to Rose Marie, there was rarely a shortage of edibles on the *Dick Van Dyke* set. "We could've had a party anytime we wanted it," says the actress, who remembers that the show's prop man, Glenn Ross, always kept his office refrigerator well stocked with goodies. "If you wanted a sandwich, you'd say, 'Glenn, I'm hungry. I can't wait for lunch.' He'd say, 'What do you want? Ham and cheese?' He'd have soda and snacks around all the time."

"They had anything you can imagine," recalled Morey Amsterdam. "Sandwiches of all kinds, and coffee and cake and fruit, and everything else." Ironically, in spite of the show's well-stocked cupboard, the actor insisted that he actually lost weight over the course of his years on the show—no thanks to Carl Reiner. "Carl was a food tout!" the actor exclaimed. "He was always saying, 'Taste this! Taste that!' If I'd let myself go, I'd've gained four hundred pounds!"

Of course, snacking was by no means the only distraction available to actors on the *Van Dyke* set. Mary Tyler Moore and Ann Guilbert, both fans of a then-popular word game called Perquackey, would frequently organize on-set Perquacky tournaments to keep the cast and crew entertained during breaks in the show's rehearsals. Conspicuously absent from the wordplay would be Van Dyke, who preferred to while away his downtime in pursuit of more contemplative activities, such as sketching or playing the piano. "When we used to rehearse," notes Rose Marie, "Dick would sit in a corner and doodle."

An accomplished amateur cartoonist, Van Dyke delighted in skewering his fellow players with exaggerated caricatures, many of which eventually found their way on-camera. The Petrie family portrait that's sketched on the bottom of a turtle shell in episode 73, "Turtles, Ties, and Toreadors" is an original Van Dyke, as is the scathing depiction of Mel Cooley that graces Buddy's dartboard in show 79, "The Lady and the Tiger and the Lawyer." And the hilarious big-mouthed caricature of Laura in episode 132, "Draw Me a Pear," offers another prime example of the show's resident cartoonist at work.

According to Morey Amsterdam, Van Dyke's passion for cartooning was matched only by the star's devotion to classical music. "He was a very good piano player," noted Amsterdam,

Dick Van Dyke's lighthearted caricatures frequently popped up on the show, including this sketch of Richard Deacon from "When a Bowling Pin Talks, Listen."

who recalls that when Van Dyke wasn't rehearsing or off in a corner sketching, he could usually be found noodling away at the keyboard of the studio's practice piano, where the star's tastes ran heavily toward the baroque. "He was a real nut for Bach," observed Amsterdam, himself a classically trained cellist. According to the comic, Van Dyke was surprisingly reverent in his playing—at least until he came to the end of a piece. Then, the comedian recalled, the star would often pop up from the piano bench and throw himself to the floor, where he would launch into a vigorous calisthenics routine. "He was a tremendous athlete," said Amsterdam. "I've seen Dick do a hundred pushups and get right back on stage and do a scene."

As in any workplace, at the end of the day the show's hardworking actors would bid each other adieu before heading their separate ways. For despite the affection they shared on the set each day, the men and women who created *The Dick Van Dyke Show* rarely saw each other outside of the studio. "We never socialized too much or anything like that," recalls Ann Guilbert. And though associate producer Ronald Jacobs insists that the show's actors and producers frequently dined together after the show's Tuesday-night filmings—at Martoni's on Cahuenga, Friscatti's on Sunset, or any one of a half-dozen other local eateries—most observers agree that even these celebratory functions grew increasingly rare after the first few weeks of the show's initial season. "We had a lot of fun on the set," says Ann Guilbert, "and then we'd all get in our cars and go home to our families."

15

WEDNESDAY NIGHTS

"The higher the quality of a show," Sheldon Leonard was fond of saying, "the longer it will take to catch on with the general public." Unfortunately, by the middle of its first season, *The Dick Van Dyke Show* was well on its way to proving him right. In its first year on the air, the show averaged a pitiful Nielsen rating of 16.1, which means that the series was, on average, tuned in by only 16.1 percent of America's television households over the course of the season. By contrast, the year's top-rated series, *Wagon Train*, commanded a whopping year-end average rating of 32.1. By the end of the season, *The Dick Van Dyke Show* was firmly docked in eightieth place, near the very bottom of the A. C. Nielsen Company's year-end ratings chart. Applying the logic of Leonard's axiom, *The Dick Van Dyke Show* must have been of extremely high quality indeed.

When word of the *Van Dyke Show*'s dismal ratings first reached Leonard, he remained remarkably unfazed. Despite the show's low numbers, the executive producer knew there was nothing wrong with *The Dick Van Dyke Show*—or at least nothing he and his producer couldn't fix with a little judicious tinkering. The problem, in his view, was their time slot—it was killing them.

When *The Dick Van Dyke Show* premiered on October 3, 1961, it was broadcast on Tuesday nights at 8:00 P.M.—a time slot that Leonard insisted was too early in the evening for a program with such obvious appeal to grown-up sensibilities. Moreover, the executive producer was convinced his show would never find its target audience of sophisticated adult viewers as long as it remained in so early a time slot.

Confident that his logic was unassailable, Leonard presented his argument to a team of CBS program executives a few weeks into the show's run. Remarkably, they agreed. Or they were at least impressed enough by his reasoning to order a midseason time change for the series. Effective January 3, 1962, *The Dick Van Dyke Show* would move from Tuesday nights at 8:00 EST to Wednesday nights at 9:30 EST.

When Leonard heard about the move, his sense of relief was tempered by apprehension. On the one hand, he was delighted that the show might finally have a chance to attract the older, more sophisticated audience that had so far eluded them. On the other hand, he was equally aware that the time change raised the stakes. If the series didn't start reeling in better numbers, and fast, the network's midseason reprieve could very quickly turn into the show's last gasp.

As it turned out, the time change would do little to boost the show's anemic ratings. But, still blissfully unaware of their fate, the show's producers were determined to inaugurate their new time slot with a bang, and so, as their first Wednesday-night entry, Leonard and Reiner scheduled a show they both agreed was one of the funniest episodes they'd ever made.

"Where Did I Come From?" which debuted on January 3, 1962, as the first

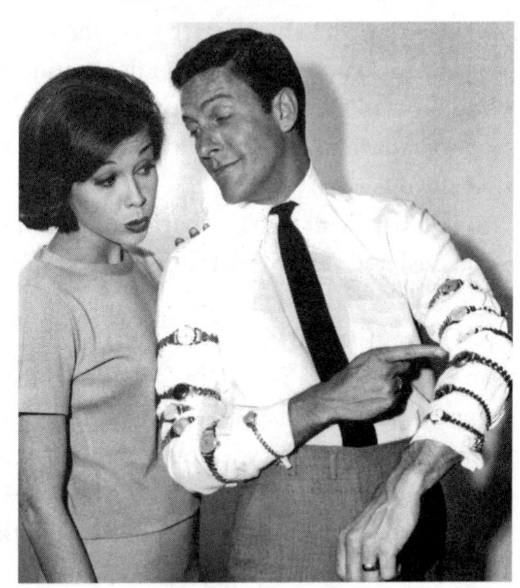

Dick Van Dyke and Mary Tyler Moore alert viewers to the first year's midseason time change.

entry in the show's new Wednesday-night time slot, is still considered a high-water mark by many fans of the series. A charming flashback story that's enlivened by some of the show's most outrageous slapstick, the episode reveals the comedic chaos that gripped the Petrie household in the days leading up to Ritchie's birth. The flashback opens in the Petries' bedroom, where Rob is driving his wife to distraction with his overanxious behavior during the final days of her pregnancy. The overzealous husband climbs into bed wearing jacket and pants, on the off chance he might have to pop up for a middle-of-the-night run to the maternity ward. When Rob finally does drift off to sleep, his dialing finger remains poised over the telephone on his chest—just in case.

Of course, when the stork does come calling, Rob is caught completely unaware. When Laura calls him at work to announce that the big moment has arrived, her husband is standing over a tray of prune Danish, clad only in a rumpled shirt and boxer shorts, having dispatched his wrinkled pants and suit to the local dry cleaner for a quick pressing. In a panic, Rob demands that Mel Cooley surrender his trousers—a suggestion that is quickly rebuffed. "I really need my pants today," Mel explains. "I'm having lunch with the sponsor."

Rob finally arrives home—wearing Buddy's pants hiked high above his ankles—only to lock bumpers with the taxicab that's been waiting to whisk Laura off to the hospital. Fortunately, Charlie the laundry man saves the day when he offers to ferry the soon-to-be mom to the maternity ward in his truck. "Honey, you don't mind going in a laundry truck, do you?" Rob asks his long-suffering wife. "No," she replies, "as long as you're with me, darling." Turning to the laundry man, she adds, "This is very nice of you!"

"Oh, that's all right," Charlie quips as he escorts Laura and her nervous husband out to his waiting truck. "You know our motto, 'We pick up and deliver.'"

One of the show's undisputed classics, "Where Did I Come From?" also ranks high on Dick Van Dyke's own list of all-time favorites. "There was an awful lot of slapstick in that one," the star reminisces. "But I had an absolute ball. They let me do everything I wanted to." Director John Rich also counts the episode among his favorites, citing Van Dyke's standout performance as reason enough to treasure the hilarious half hour. As the director observes, "Dick was just superb."

When CBS asked Dick Van Dyke to host its broadcast of *The Wizard of Oz* in 1961, the star brought his family along for the ride. Pictured with Dad are Barry and Stacy, with the star's eldest son, Chris, on the right.

The actor cheerfully admits that playing the part of a nervous poppa wasn't exactly a stretch for the real-life father of four. In fact, Van Dyke had just returned from his own most recent trip to the maternity ward—where his daughter Carrie Beth was born on October 18, 1961—less than a month before this episode was filmed. Naturally, Reiner had no qualms about incorporating the actor's comical perspectives on his own blessed event into the week's script. "Everybody brought up all the crazy things that happened when their kids were born," says Van Dyke, "and we put 'em all in one show."* As it happened, Dick Van Dyke wasn't the only cast member to come to the show with brand-new expectant-parent material—on the night "Where Did I Come From?" was filmed, Ann Guilbert was herself seven months pregnant.

Ironically, when Ann Guilbert had first become aware of her pregnancy the previous summer, she'd been reluctant to let Reiner in on her secret—with good reason. Since the show had been in production only a few weeks at that time, Guilbert was understandably concerned that Reiner might decide to replace her with an actress who was not so likely to grow visibly pregnant within the year. When the actress finally did summon the

---

* Dick Van Dyke would further embellish his paternal credibility a few weeks later when he hosted that year's annual CBS telecast of *The Wizard of Oz* on December 10, 1961, joined for the broadcast by his three eldest kids, Barry, who was then ten; Chris, then eleven; and Van Dyke's six-year-old daughter, Stacy. According to a report that appeared under Cecil Smith's byline in the *Los Angeles Times* on the day of the broadcast, CBS had wanted to include Van Dyke's newborn in the telecast as well, as they informed the star on the day Carrie Beth was born. "How d'ya like that?" Van Dyke reportedly quipped, "Carrie was only born three hours ago, and already they want to book her for *The Wizard of Oz*!"[1]

courage to break the news to her producer, she was pleased to discover that Reiner had no intention of replacing one of his key supporting players over a little thing like pregnancy. "He apparently didn't mind having a big, fat neighbor," the actress later joked.[2]

Since it wasn't practical to integrate the actress's real-life pregnancy into the show's continuity at that late date, Reiner chose instead to mask Ann Guilbert's increasingly visible condition in oversized blouses and loose-fitting dresses for the remainder of her appearances that first year—with the notable exception of "Where Did I Come From?" in which Guilbert's real-life pregnancy merged perfectly into the story's flashback segment. After the episode was filmed, Guilbert left the series for a temporary, and well-earned, maternity leave. Guilbert's daughter, Hallie Eckstein—who would eventually launch her own acting career under the stage name Hallie Todd—was born two months later, in January 1962.

IF CARL REINER had been able to predict what he was getting himself into when he agreed to serve as producer of *The Dick Van Dyke Show*, he might have thought twice about taking the job in the first place. But it was only after the series was well into its first season of production that the hapless writer got a sense of the enormity of the task.

In addition to his responsibilities as the show's story editor, Reiner was also responsible for supervising the casting, staging, scoring, and editing of as many as thirty-two entirely new half-hour episodes of the *Van Dyke Show* each season—most of which he also wrote. As incredible as it seems, of the sixty-three scripts filmed in the first two years of *The Dick Van Dyke Show*, Reiner would receive a solo writing credit on forty of them—or just slightly less than two-thirds of the entire output of the show's first two seasons. And that's not counting the editing, polishing, and uncredited rewrites that he performed on the remaining twenty-three episodes filmed in the show's first two seasons—a prodigious feat by any measure.* As Reiner's friend and longtime manager George Shapiro observes, "To do what he did! Carl's like Lou Gehrig. An iron man!"

* Incredibly, Reiner also found time to moonlight as an actor in four films during his years as producer of *The Dick Van Dyke Show*, logging cameos in *The Thrill of It All* and *The Art of Love*—both of which he also wrote—as well as more substantial parts in *It's a Mad, Mad, Mad, Mad World* and *The Russians Are Coming, the Russians Are Coming*.

"For two solid years, I wrote all day—every day, " says Reiner, describing his working method during the show's early days, a routine so relentless that it allowed no time off, not even on weekends. "On Saturday and Sunday I'd work on rewrites to get the show in shape for Monday's rehearsal." No sooner would the writer polish off one script than he'd have to start to work on the next week's show. Perhaps the only thing more remarkable than the dedication Reiner displayed during the show's first few years was the remarkable patience that his family extended to their absentee husband and father. But, as Reiner would later explain to a reporter, he made certain that he had his wife's unstinting support well before the show ever hit the air. "Before I started it, " said Reiner, "my wife and I agreed I'd have to devote my entire time to it if it was to be the best possible show."[3]

Given Reiner's daunting workload, he remained on constant lookout for freelance scriptwriters to augment his own efforts. "People would submit scripts to me," says Reiner. "And Sheldon was terrific at finding writers, because he knew a lot of them from his other shows. So he'd bring in people that he knew." Of course, since the vast majority of these outside writers lacked Reiner's insights into the *Van Dyke Show*'s unique character and rhythms, most of the scripts he received required extensive reworking before they met his exacting standards for the series. Still, the producer was so delighted to get any help at all that he didn't mind the extra work the freelance submissions created—at least not at first. "If they could just give me pages to work on, I would be so happy." But, before long, Reiner discovered that rewriting an outsider's script often took longer than it did to compose one of his own from scratch. "It took me four to five days to write a script," says Reiner. "But I found myself taking eight days to rewrite someone else's show!"

The worst scripts were those that arrived, as Reiner describes it, "with the bones buried in the wrong place." And, he observes, the task of retooling a structurally unsound script could be a vexing process. "Those were the ones that drove me nuts! I'd have to take *this* out, and when you take *this* out, *that* falls out. I finally decided it's easier to write a show myself. So that's why I wrote forty of the first sixty, because I could work faster that way."

Of course, it would be some consolation to Reiner that, by writing the lion's share of the show's first two seasons himself, he was ensuring that his unique autobiographical vision would remain woven deep in the

Laura ponders opening a package in "The Curious Thing About Women."

show's DNA. "The show was *my* reality," Reiner explains unapologetically. "That didn't mean you got a better reality in my scripts than somebody else might've written. Or that I wrote better than anybody else. But my reality was my reality."

One early episode that Reiner thinks may have fallen beyond those boundaries was "The Curious Thing About Women," an episode that many fans regard as a highlight of the show's first season. Written by Frank Tarloff—under the pen name David Adler—the episode revolves around a domestic squabble that erupts after Rob exploits Laura's habit of opening his mail as fodder for a comedy sketch. What's really got Laura steamed is Rob's depiction of her as an incurable snoop, which she insists is an unwarranted accusation. But Laura's resolve is tested a few days later when a mysterious package arrives at the Petrie house addressed to her husband. Not surprisingly, Laura proves unable to restrain herself, and in less than sixty seconds the curious homemaker has unleashed the parcel's volatile cargo: a giant, inflatable life raft, which naturally swells to its full ten-foot length in the middle of the Petries' living room floor just as Rob walks in the door!

The gargantuan life raft—and Mary Tyler Moore's priceless reaction as she tries to physically restrain it—provides the episode with one of *The Dick Van Dyke Show*'s more spectacular comic set pieces, a superb example of slapstick mayhem that calls to mind the physical comedy that Lucille Ball perfected a decade earlier on *I Love Lucy*. Which might explain Reiner's lukewarm reaction to the episode, whose comic premise may have hewed a bit too close to traditional sitcom conventions for his sensibilities. "I didn't love the fact that we made Mary so silly that she had to open the package," says Reiner, who confesses that his biggest problem with Tarloff's script was that he simply couldn't imagine his own wife—or anyone else's, for that matter—behaving as Laura Petrie does in the episode. "I made Laura a little sillier than my wife," explains Reiner, "but I was still basing things on Estelle. And I never liked that show particularly, because that wasn't my wife."

The fact that "The Curious Thing About Women" calls to mind the basic mechanics of an *I Love Lucy* episode was no coincidence. As it happens, Tarloff's script was actually based on a similar plotline that the writer first composed for the Joan Davis sitcom *I Married Joan*, which itself was little more than an *I Love Lucy* knock-off from the Desilu assembly line of the early fifties. "Curiosity"—which was the title of the script that Tarloff penned for the Davis show—was first telecast on December 3, 1952. The *TV Guide* synopsis for the Davis episode—which was coauthored by Tarloff, Arthur Stander, and Phil Sharp—reveals a striking similarity to Tarloff's later *Van Dyke Show* script. "Joan's husband forbids her to open his mail," reads the blurb. "She follows his order until the next day, when a large parcel arrives."[4]

Tarloff's mild act of self-plagarism was hardly uncommon in an era when situation-comedy writers routinely dusted off scripts from as far back as radio in their search for fresh springboards. Ironically, in later years, Tarloff would retain little memory of writing either version of his durable storyline. Speaking of "The Curious Thing About Women" some years later, Tarloff confessed, "I saw it about six months ago, and I didn't even remember that I'd written it until I saw my name on it at the end."

Despite his reservations about the episode's lack of fidelity to his reality, Reiner was not about to take a pass on a script with such obvious comic potential. "I mean, I couldn't say no to it," he acknowledges, "because I needed a show to do." Long after the dust has settled, the producer admits that he has no regrets. "It was a very successful show," admits Reiner. "And very funny. But it always bothered me that I would never have come up with that premise. That show was written by another person—it was somebody else's reality. And I didn't like that."

Eagle-eyed *Van Dyke Show* fans will no doubt recognize the delivery boy who drops off Laura's mystery parcel in this episode as Frank Adamo, a gangly character actor who would prove to be a durable addition to the show's unofficial stock company—a select group that also included Ross Elliott, Jamie Farr, Herbie Faye, Jerry Hausner, Allan Melvin, Isabel

Randolph, Johnny Silver, Doris Singleton, and Amzie Strickland. Unlike the other members of the *Van Dyke Show*'s loose-knit repertory company, Adamo also enjoyed the rare status of regular employment on the series. In addition to the dozens of bit parts and uncredited walk-ons that Adamo contributed during his five seasons on the show, the skinny bit player also served as Dick Van Dyke's full-time rehearsal stand-in—a job that came about as the result of Adamo's long-standing friendship with the star, which predated *The Dick Van Dyke Show*.

Adamo was a struggling junior advertising executive when he met Van Dyke during the star's lean years in New York in the late 1950s. "I was working for J. Walter Thompson at the time," recalls Adamo. "And Dick used to come up to J. Walter to rehearse and do Rinso commercials, or some damn thing like that. So we got to be friendly up there." As fate would have it, Adamo found himself out of work a few months later—just as Van Dyke's fortunes were about to take a turn for the better. "I had left J. Walter Thompson," Adamo says, "and I read in the trades that Dick was going to be doing *Bye Bye Birdie*." Figuring he had nothing to lose by asking his old friend for a job, Adamo gathered the courage to pay an unannounced call on the fast-rising star. "I knew he was in rehearsal at the Phyllis Anderson Theatre down on Second Avenue," recalls Adamo, "so I went and stood by the stage door. It was a very snowy, cold day. And when Dick came out, I told him very frankly that I needed work." To Adamo's surprise, Van Dyke offered him a job on the spot.

For the next year, the former ad man enjoyed steady employment as Van Dyke's backstage assistant on *Bye Bye Birdie*. "During that year we became very close," recalls Adamo. "Like family. I met Dick's wife, Marge, his grandparents, and his whole tribe of kids. And we all got along like peas in a pod." When Van Dyke finally left *Bye Bye Birdie* for his weekly television show, he invited his capable assistant to join him. "Dick said to me," remembers Adamo, "very casually, 'Would you like to go to California? I don't know what we can pay.' I said, 'Don't worry about it. I'll just go along on good faith.'" Once Adamo got to California, his faith was rewarded when Leonard—struck by the rail-thin personal assistant's striking physical resemblance to the show's star—immediately put Adamo to work as Van Dyke's rehearsal stand-in.

Of course, the stand-in work—which basically required Adamo to do little more than stand under the set's hot lights in Van Dyke's stead

Dick Van Dyke poses with his rehearsal stand-in, stock player Frank Adamo, who enjoyed the distinction of logging more appearances on the series than anyone outside of the show's central cast.

during the show's arduous technical rehearsals—was not the most glamorous job on the show. To break the monotony, Adamo would often sit in on the show's table readings, where he would sometimes be asked to read one of the small parts that hadn't yet been cast. When the time finally came to hire an actor for one of these minuscule parts, the producers would frequently just hand the role to the stand-in. "Sheldon would say, 'Frank's already doing the part, let's just give it to him,'" recalls Adamo. "That's how I ended up doing all the little parts on the show."

While it's true that most of Adamo's on-camera work on the show flashed across the screen in the blink of an eye, the bit player did manage to take center stage on at least a few occasions. Adamo's personal favorite of all his *Van Dyke Show* parts was H. Fieldstone Thorley, the pretentious poet who does his bit to bruise Rob's ego in episode 55, "I'm No Henry Walden!" Equally memorable was Adamo's turn in episode 101, "Romance, Roses, and Rye Bread," where he played an actor who brazens his way through a dismal production of an off-Broadway travesty called *Waiting for an Armadillo*.

But Adamo's finest moment—or at least the one that drew the biggest laughs—came in the show's eighteenth episode, "Punch Thy Neighbor," where he played a singing telegram man hired by a peeved Jerry Helper to deliver a scathing assessment of Rob Petrie's writing talent to the unamused writer. "Look how far this man has gotten," Adamo's telegram man sings in a grating monotone, "Writing shows that are really rotten."

16

BAD OLD DAYS

By the first week of 1962, the cast and crew of *The Dick Van Dyke Show* had returned from a well-earned two-week holiday hiatus to begin work on the show's twenty-fourth episode, "The Twizzle," a show that has the distinction of being one of Carl Reiner's least favorite episodes of the series. "There're about eight shows where one or two or three members of the cast were not happy with it," he confesses. "And 'The Twizzle' was one of them."

Little wonder, since Reiner's offbeat script—which depicts Sally Rogers's improbable discovery of a new singing sensation in a Connecticut bowling alley—reads more like an extended sketch from *Your Show of Shows* than a fully realized *Van Dyke Show* plotline. According to Reiner, the episode was designed to be a starring vehicle for a virtually unknown singer named Jerry Lanning, whose main claim to fame was that he happened to be the son of the now all-but-forgotten fifties pop singer Roberta Sherwood.* "That was one of those things where somebody came to me and said, 'Can you do a show for Roberta Sherwood's son?'" explains Reiner. "It was written for him." Despite the writer's valiant push, Jerry Lanning proved to be no Ricky Nelson, and "The Twizzle" remains a rare example of that scarcest commodity, a *Dick Van Dyke Show* misfire.

---

* In addition to the small measure of immortality he earned by appearing in this episode of *The Dick Van Dyke Show*, Jerry Lanning would resurface in the late 1970s in regular roles on the daytime dramas *Search for Tomorrow*, *The Guiding Light*, and *Texas*.

Carl Reiner gives coexecutive producer Danny Thomas a VIP tour of the bowling alley set of "The Twizzle," while their wives sit nearby. Pictured, center, is Rose Marie Thomas; to her left is Estelle Reiner, Carl Reiner's real-life Laura.

Dick Van Dyke's own candidate for the show's all-time stiff is episode 27, "The Bad Old Days," which was filmed on January 30, 1962, just three weeks after "The Twizzle." "That was the worst one we ever did!" declares Van Dyke, recalling the episode's well-worn plotline, in which Buddy attempts to convince Rob that the modern American male is being systematically emasculated by tyrannical wives. Gullible husband Rob nearly falls for Buddy's line, until he imagines—via an elaborate dream sequence—just how lousy things really must have been in "The Bad Old Days."

The idea that a young husband's masculinity would be threatened by his wife's domestic tyranny was already a wheezing premise in 1962—a fact that did not pass Van Dyke's notice. But what really gave the actor heartburn was the episode's dream sequence, a creaky turn-of-the-century costume piece in which the star was forced to don Gay Nineties garb and sport an oversized handlebar mustache to no apparent comedic purpose.

Mary Tyler Moore in "The Bad Old Days," the episode that earns Dick Van Dyke's vote for worst *Van Dyke* show ever.

"It was just awful," sighs the star, "just incredible!" The show's only saving grace, says Van Dyke, is that production requirements for the dream sequence dictated that it be shot separately from the rest of the episode, thus sparing him and Moore the indignity of having to perform the travesty in front of a live audience. "We shot it during the day," Van Dyke recalls, still cringing at the memory. "I don't know what the hell we thought we were doing," he says. "It didn't work, and we all knew it. But by that time we were too far into it to stop!"

In defense of the show's hard-working cast and crew, it's probably only fair to point out that by the time they began rehearsals for the pair of ill-conceived episodes cited above, the show had already been in active production for well over six months—an exhausting stretch during which the actors had enjoyed only minimal time off, and writer/producer Reiner none at all. In fact, by the end of January 1962, Carl Reiner had already been producing, writing—and rewriting—one new half-hour *Dick Van Dyke Show* teleplay every week for the previous eight months. Considering the enormity of the producer's workload, what's surprising is that the show's quality remained so high that the occasional less-than-perfect entry like "Bad Old Days" remained an anomaly. As the show's third-season story editor Bill Persky would observe, "Our worst shows were better than most people's best."

Besides, as longtime *Van Dyke Show* writer Sam Denoff contends, with a production schedule that demanded at least thirty new shows every year, no one expected the series to score an out-of-the-park home run with each episode. "Out of twenty-six or thirty shows a year," says Denoff, "you know you're gonna have six that are fantastic, twelve that are pretty good, and three or four clunkers that—for one reason or another—don't work."

If the *Van Dyke* company had to contend with one or two "clunkers" as their first year rolled to an end, it was hardly cause for alarm. Far more damaging to the cast's usually buoyant morale was the very real threat that, despite all their hard work and struggle, *The Dick Van Dyke Show* might not be returning for a second season. By the beginning of 1962, rumors of the show's demise—spurred on by the series' disappointing Nielsen standings—had been circulating for months. As costumer Harald Johnson recalled, "We were sort of, like, walking on grapes the whole first year."

According to *Van Dyke* stock player Doris Singleton, who logged her first appearance on the series in episode 22, "The Talented Neighborhood," cancellation jitters were already in the air when that episode was filmed during the first week of December 1961. "Everyone was very worried," recalls the actress, "because the show was in trouble at that time." In the eyes of many of those on the *Van Dyke Show* set that week, Singleton was something of an authority on the subject of premature cancellation, having recently survived the abrupt termination of *Angel*, a sitcom on which she'd enjoyed steady employment until it had been axed after a single season on CBS. Singleton recalls that her show's then-recent cancellation was a topic of especially keen interest to Mary Tyler Moore, who was concerned that her own show might be facing a similarly ignominious end. "Mary asked me, 'When did you know that you were going off the air?'" says Singleton. It certainly didn't lift the young actress's spirits when Singleton informed her that, in her case, the end came swiftly and without warning. "Mary was very depressed," recalls Singleton, "because it didn't look like the *Van Dyke Show* was going to be renewed."

As the youngest and least established member of the *Van Dyke Show* company, Moore had good reason to be nervous, if only because she had the most to lose. But if the show's demise would have dealt a blow to her burgeoning career, Moore had equally compelling personal reasons to pray for *The Dick Van Dyke Show*'s continued success. In late 1961, the actress and her first husband filed for divorce, and the dissolution was finalized in February 1962. So, by the time the show's debut season rolled to an end that same month, the newly single twenty-five-year-old mother had come to depend on the familial surroundings of the *Van Dyke Show* set for emotional, as well as professional, support. "They *were* my family," she acknowledges. "They were my first experience with a feeling of family outside of my own blood relations."

IN SPITE OF the doubts that hovered over the *Van Dyke* soundstage during the final weeks of the show's first season, the cast managed to rally their energies for the outstanding two-part saga that would comprise their penultimate effort for the year: "I Am My Brother's Keeper" and "The Sleeping Brother." The twin episodes would be fondly remembered as the segments that introduced the final branch of the show's family tree, Rob's brother Stacey Petrie, who was played by the star's real-life sibling, Jerry Van Dyke.

According to Reiner, that inspired bit of stunt casting was not the result of any grand design but was merely "one of those happy accidents." As Reiner tells the story, he didn't even know his star had a younger sibling until Van Dyke happened to mention in passing one day that his brother was opening a nightclub act at Chicago's Playboy Club. "Your brother's a comic?" Reiner asked, already weighing the possibilities. "Is he funny?"

"Oh, sure. He's very funny," Van Dyke replied. That was all Reiner needed to hear.

"Are you sure your brother can act?" Carl Reiner asked Dick Van Dyke before the writer scripted the show's first two-parter as a showcase for Jerry Van Dyke.

"Well, then," the producer proposed, "I'll write a show for your brother. And then I'll fly him out here to star in it!"

Reiner went right to work. "Tell me a little about your brother," he asked, fishing for any clues that might lead to a suitable storyline. Van Dyke proceeded to rattle off a thumbnail profile of his younger brother, ending with a little tidbit that his producer found irresistible. "Dick said, 'Oh, yeah, as a kid he was a bit of a somnambulist,'" Reiner recalls. "And I said, 'That's it!' I knew I could make something out of a brother who walks in his sleep!"

Inspired by the high-concept springboard he'd been handed, Reiner had little trouble shaping his storyline. In the first half of what would become the show's first two-parter, Rob's ebullient brother Stacey pays an unexpected call on the Petrie home and announces he'll be staying for a few days. Although Laura and Ritchie are quickly won over by Stacey's clever jokes and confident patter, Rob appears less impressed by his brother's irrepressible vitality—a fact that does not go unnoticed by Laura. Once Stacey is safely sequestered in the family's guest room, Laura holds Rob to account for his diffidence to their guest. "My brother Stacey has a problem," Rob explains. "He's a somnambulist."

And not just any garden-variety sleepwalker, Rob elaborates, but a world-class schizophrenic sleepwalker with two entirely independent personalities. "When he's awake he's very shy," says Rob. "But when he's asleep, he's very friendly and outgoing." Suddenly, as if to demonstrate the curious extremes of his malady, Stacey walks into the room, now wide awake and shy as a dormouse. It's in this sorry state that Rob's bashful brother confesses the secret ambition that brought him to New York in the first place. "I've been thinking," he stammers, "well, that maybe I'd like to be a . . . a comedian!"

Rob has his doubts, of course. But he sets them aside and agrees to introduce his brother to Mel Cooley and the rest of his friends at a party a few nights later. Rob's worst fears come to pass when his brother shows up at the party in a state of sleep-induced euphoria—and proceeds to dazzle the assembled guests with the high-octane charm of his comedy act. When Mel offers the young comic an audition for *The Alan Brady Show*, it puts Rob in a tight spot, since he knows that his brother will never be able to make it through the audition—unless he happens to be asleep. And it's on that cliffhanger that the episode's first installment comes to an end.

Reiner didn't set out to write a two-part tale. But once he sat down at the typewriter, he says, the story seemed to take on a life of its own. "I had all this fun stuff," he says, "and I'm not gonna throw it out! So I knew I had to do a second part."

It was only after he'd polished off the second installment of his ambitious two-parter that it finally dawned on Reiner that he was about to commit two half hours of network prime time to spotlight the singing, acting, and comedic talents of an actor he still hadn't even met! It would be one thing to work the star's brother into a single episode—but now, with two full shows suddenly resting on Jerry Van Dyke's untested shoulders, Reiner realized that the stakes had just gotten a lot higher. If the star's younger sibling didn't turn out to be everything that Dick Van Dyke had promised, the producer would now have not *one* but *two* very dull episodes of *The Dick Van Dyke Show* on his hands. It was in this state of low-level panic that Reiner placed an eleventh-hour call to his star player. "Dick," Reiner asked, "are you sure your brother can act?"

"Yeah," Van Dyke responded. "Why?"

"Because the show's hysterical," Reiner replied. "Only it's gonna be a two-parter. So your brother's gotta be a good actor. You're sure he can act?"

"Oh, absolutely! " Van Dyke answered.

"Great," Reiner answered with audible relief. Then, after a short pause, the producer sought further confirmation, "How can you be so sure?"

"Because," Van Dyke replied, oozing conviction, "if he can't—I'll have to kill him."

Jerry Van Dyke finally did prove worthy of his brother's confidence. But not before he put John Rich through what the director describes as one of the most trying weeks of his career. As Rich relates the story, his troubles began at the table reading for "The Sleeping Brother," where he got his first inkling that their guest star may have been in over his head.

"I can tell this story because Jerry and I are very good friends," says Rich. "He was scared stiff!" That much was clear, says the director, from the younger Van Dyke's line readings, which were bland and colorless throughout the early rehearsals. "He read his lines without anything on them," recalls Rich. "Uncurved. Flat."

Reiner also noticed the actor's stiffness at that initial rehearsal, but remained confident that with Rich's reputation as an actor's director, he would be able to bring the star's brother around. For his part, the director wasn't so sure, but he decided to reserve judgment. "You listen to the first reading," says Rich, "and you say, 'This'll get better.'"

But to his mounting dismay, it didn't. By the time Rich began blocking scenes on stage the next day, he'd noticed little improvement in the neophyte actor's shaky confidence level. "We started to put the thing on its feet," says Rich, "and Jerry was really a stumbler." By the third day of rehearsal, the director recalls, he sensed panic setting in among the other actors.

"Taking nothing away from Jerry," says Rose Marie, recalling those early rehearsals for the show's twenty-eighth episode, "he was bad." According to Rich, the veteran actress wasn't the only one to hold that opinion. In fact, notes the director, the only member of the cast who didn't seem concerned about Jerry Van Dyke's flailing performance was his brother, who invariably ended each morning's rehearsal by giving his younger sibling a hearty clap on the back as they walked off together to the studio commissary. "Dick looked very cool," acknowledges Rich, while he, on the other hand, was growing more frantic with each passing hour.

The turning point finally came after the show's Friday-night run-through, an affair so lackluster that it caused Rich to embark on a course of action he'd been hoping to avoid all week. With only two rehearsal days left before the Tuesday-night filming, the director decided the time had come to pull Dick Van Dyke aside for a short offstage consultation. "I think Jerry might need a little help," the director suggested to his star. Then, having made his point, he decided the most prudent course of action would be to leave the matter in Dick Van Dyke's hands. "That's all I said," states Rich.

It was enough. "When Jerry came in on Monday, he was a heckuva lot better," recalls the director, who was overjoyed to observe a vast improvement in his guest star's performance. "Suddenly he got it just right," says Rich, "that shy, self-deprecating, lovely quality that was the character." And, notes Rich, the younger Van Dyke's performance continued to grow right up till showtime. "By Tuesday night, he was a smash. It was extraordinary. A triumph!"

"I never did ask what happened," says Rich, who admits he still has no idea what Dick Van Dyke might've said or done to inspire his brother after his slow start. In the opinion of at least one observer, the younger Van Dyke may have initially kept his performance under wraps in deference to his older brother. "It wasn't Jerry's show," explains Dick Van Dyke's stand-in, Frank Adamo, who was also on the set that week, "and he knew that. So I think Dick finally had to tell him, 'Look Jerry, just go out there and do what you do best. Don't worry about me.'"

With characteristic modesty, Dick Van Dyke dismisses speculation that he played any role in his younger brother's triumphant debut on the show. "He was very nervous," acknowledges the elder Van Dyke. "But his comedy instincts were good, particularly when he had an audience to work with. And by the time we hit the audience, he was doing great."

Dick Van Dyke was by no means alone in his glowing assessment of his younger brother's telegenic promise. "He came in, and he was delightful," recalls Reiner, who was so impressed with the younger Van Dyke's talents that he would eventually try—without success—to develop a separate TV vehicle for Jerry Van Dyke. "We tried to do a pilot with him two years later that didn't work."

No matter. In the wake of his debut on *The Dick Van Dyke Show*, Jerry Van Dyke found no shortage of job offers. In 1963, he signed on as Judy Garland's second banana for the early episodes of the excitable diva's now-legendary CBS variety series. In the years since, the popular character actor has logged an untold number of appearances on television variety shows and situation comedies, including featured roles on *My Mother the Car*, *Accidental Family*, and a long run as assistant coach Luther Van Dam on the ABC situation comedy *Coach* from 1989 to 1997.

ON FEBRUARY 14, 1962, the cast gathered to begin rehearsals for the final show of their first season, "The Return of Happy Spangler." But there would be little happiness on the show's normally sunny set that Valentine's Day. A few days earlier, the cast got wind of scuttlebutt that CBS had already decided not to renew the series for a second season. Although unconfirmed, the rumor was enough to send company morale plummeting to an all-time low.

Although he said nothing to his cast and crew, Sheldon Leonard had already run the rumor by a friend of his at the network, who'd unfortunately confirmed the worst. CBS President James Aubrey had met with his top programming brass a few days earlier to hammer out a first draft of the network's fall schedule, the insider reported, and *The Dick Van Dyke Show* was nowhere to be found. The show's much-ballyhooed move to Wednesday nights had failed to improve the program's low ratings, and that, apparently, was that. The executive producer thanked his spy for the intelligence, hung up the phone, and began planning his next move.

17

ON THE BANKS OF THE OHIO

As unsettling as the news of his network's defection had been, Sheldon Leonard refused to accept that *The Dick Van Dyke Show* was dead, even if it did appear to be on life support. CBS had not officially announced the show's cancellation, and until they did, he reasoned, he still had time to change their minds. Failing that, he could always count on his friends at Procter & Gamble to back him up.

In an era when big advertisers like Procter & Gamble still held sway over the television networks, Leonard was confident that his strong ties to the Cincinnati soapmaker would give him the upper hand in any negotiations with CBS. "With the support of powerful sponsors like Procter & Gamble," the producer explained, "it was possible to bully and manipulate the networks." Now, if Procter & Gamble suddenly lost faith in the show—that would be different. That would be nothing short of calamitous.

The producer would discover just how calamitous when he received an urgent call a few hours later from Lee Rich, the Benton and Bowles executive who oversaw Procter & Gamble's television advertising. The ad man told Leonard he wanted to talk about Procter & Gamble's advertising plans for the coming season—and he warned him the news wasn't good. After a thorough review of *The Dick Van Dyke Show*'s first-year ratings, explained Rich, Procter & Gamble had developed serious doubts about the show's continued viability as an effective advertising vehicle for the company's household products lines.

"And?" Leonard asked, anxious to cut to the chase.

And, the ad man continued, as a result, Procter & Gamble had decided to end their sponsorship commitment to *The Dick Van Dyke Show* effective with the show's final first-season broadcast.

Leonard paused for a moment to absorb this latest setback. The news was clearly disastrous. But what made his sponsor's decision especially alarming was the timing—coming, as it did, just as the producer was preparing to go toe to toe with CBS over the network's impending cancellation order. Clearly, if *The Dick Van Dyke Show* ever needed the support of its sponsor, it was now. Without it, the show didn't have a prayer.

"There must be something we can do," Leonard declared, "something we can say to Procter & Gamble to make them change their minds."

"Probably not," came the weary reply from Rich, who suggested that the time to act had passed. The final decision would be made in a matter of hours, he explained, at a high-level meeting of the company's product managers that he was, in fact, planning to attend the very next day at the company's Cincinnati headquarters.

"In that case," Leonard announced decisively, "save me a seat on the plane. Because I'm going to Cincinnati with you."

It was an outrageous suggestion, as Rich was quick to inform him.

"I realize," the producer admitted, "that what I'm proposing is unorthodox."

No, protested the advertising executive, it was worse than unorthodox. The idea that a television producer would consider crashing a high-level

To save his beloved *Dick Van Dyke Show* from extinction, Sheldon Leonard drew on charm he'd polished over three decades of playing touts, con artists, and strong-arm men in Hollywood.

powwow at his sponsor's corporate headquarters to deliver a personal plea for one of his own shows was—well, it was nothing short of preposterous.

And yet . . .

After a moment's consideration, Rich had to admit that—as outlandish as it sounded—the producer's scheme was not without a certain roguish charm. Then, too, there was always the chance it might actually work. It was just possible that the Procter & Gamble executives would be so flattered by the unexpected arrival of a bona fide Hollywood celebrity on their corporate doorstep that they would grant their glamorous visitor a sympathetic audience. If nothing else, the ad man reasoned, Leonard would provide the staid Midwestern executives with a show that none of them would soon forget.

And so it was decided. Rich would go along with Leonard's scheme. An extra seat was booked on the overnight flight from Los Angeles to Cincinnati, where Rich had arranged for Leonard to meet with the soap company's top executives the very next day.

Early the following morning, the pair arrived at Procter & Gamble's corporate headquarters, where—still bleary-eyed from the all-night flight—the ad man and the TV producer were ushered into the company's wood-paneled executive boardroom. There, standing before a select audience of Procter & Gamble's top marketing executives, Leonard reached into his actor's bag of tricks and launched into one of the most effective performances of his career. "I went back East," as he would later describe it, "got down on one knee, and sang 'Mammy.'"[1]

"Sheldon made a big, long, impassioned speech," recalls Rich, "a typical Sheldon Leonard speech." In Leonard's recollection of the meeting, he began his pitch with a confession. "I told them that I knew the show had been a little rusty in its first year," he recalled, "that it had not yet hit its stride—that it was not the show we knew it could be." After disarming the executives with this opening gambit, the producer quickly segued into a candid appraisal of *The Dick Van Dyke Show*, with an emphasis on the series' future potential, which the producer insisted had barely been tapped. "I loved the show," he would later elaborate, "and I loved the material. And I simply explained to them my deep gut feeling that, if given a chance for people to gain some familiarity with the characters, the show would catch on."

By this point in his spiel, the wily showman knew he had earned their rapt attention, even though he was just warming up. Drawing on persuasive skills that had been sharpened by thirty years of playing con artists, touts, and strong-arm men, Leonard charmed, wheedled, and cajoled the roomful of hard-nosed executives until, finally, he had every last one of them nibbling from his hand.

Or almost every one.

Unfortunately, there was a lone holdout. And, as fate would have it, he would prove to be the most troubling exception of all. For of all the executives in the Procter & Gamble boardroom that morning, only Lee Rich himself remained visibly unmoved as Leonard wrapped up his pitch. The ad man's studied neutrality was particularly unnerving to the producer, who knew that without Rich's okay, he was sunk, since Procter & Gamble would be unlikely to approve a major sponsorship commitment without the consent of their Madison Avenue media guru.

Fortunately, the suspense would be short lived. It was no more than a few seconds before one of Procter & Gamble's management team turned and put the question to Rich directly. "Well, Lee," the executive queried. "What do *you* think? What does Benton and Bowles think we should do?"

Rich paused only an instant before he finally ventured his opinion, a split second that nonetheless seemed an eternity to the anxious executive producer. "The Benton and Bowles Agency," Lee Rich announced, "recommends that you renew *The Dick Van Dyke Show*." Though the words had been long in coming, the ad man's declaration sounded like poetry to Leonard. And, just as the producer predicted, Rich's vote of confidence was all that was needed to usher the Procter & Gamble executives into his camp.

"Procter & Gamble agreed to pick up the show for another year," recalled Leonard, who flew back to Los Angeles that same afternoon. But no sooner had his plane touched down in California than Leonard discovered that his travels were not over yet. Back on the ground, the producer was handed an urgent message from Lee Rich, who had stayed behind in Cincinnati to iron out the remaining wrinkles in the Procter & Gamble sponsorship deal. Judging from the grave tone of his dispatch, it was apparent that the ad man had run into some pretty big wrinkles. "I came back to Hollywood very happy," the producer recalled, "only to learn that Procter & Gamble had had second thoughts. Suddenly they were only willing to sponsor half the program!"

The news came as a devastating blow to Leonard, since it meant that, after all his efforts of the past twenty-four hours, he was suddenly back at square one. "I now had to go back out and find another sponsor to pick up the other half of the show," he recalled. Worse yet, he had to find a second backer quickly, before word of his primary sponsor's defection leaked to the executives at CBS, who would surely view this latest turn of events as all the justification they needed to proceed with the show's cancellation, which—through some miracle—was still not official. And so, with the clock ticking, Leonard turned around and boarded another jet—this one bound for New York City.

By the time the producer landed at New York's Idlewild Airport early the next morning, Sol Leon of the William Morris office had already arranged the first appointment in what promised to be a busy day of meetings. The producer's first pitch had been scheduled at the headquarters of the P. Lorillard Tobacco Company, the makers of Kent cigarettes. "They interrupted a board meeting to bring me in there," remembered Leonard, who returned the courtesy by opening his presentation with a gesture of deference calculated to earn him the instant respect of the busy executives.

"Sheldon took off his gold watch," recalls Grant Tinker, who attended the meeting as Lorillard's ad agency representative, "and he put it on the desk. And he said to them, 'How much time do I have?' They said, 'Twelve minutes.' And he said, 'Well, gentlemen, here's what I want to tell you.'"

With that, recalls Tinker, the producer began pitching his wares in his own inimitable fashion. "He's one of the most articulate guys in the world," says Tinker, who testifies to the peculiar effectiveness of Leonard's trademark Damon Runyon–inflected speech patterns in a straight business setting. "He just said what he had to say so well that it was like music."

True to his word, Leonard wrapped his presentation exactly twelve minutes later, at which point the producer retrieved his watch from the table and hurried on to his next appointment. "We left Lorillard," recalled Leon, "and the executives went back into session by themselves." Meanwhile, Leonard and his agent moved on to the offices of the Compton Advertising Agency, where the producer wasted little time launching into his now well-rehearsed presentation for an executive of the Alberto-Culver Company.

As fate would have it, the producer's pitch to the hair-products company executive promised to be the easiest presentation of all. "I find out that his children are already familiar with the show," the producer recalled, "and he's already strongly biased in favor of it. You know, I've already got him lined up. He's gonna be a cinch." But, in an ironic twist, the Alberto-Culver executive never even got to hear the end of his visitor's spirited pitch.

About a minute and a half after he'd started talking, Leonard noticed that Sol Leon had been called to the phone for what was obviously an urgent message. Ignoring his agent's momentary defection, the producer continued his spiel. A minute or so later, Leon walked back into the conference room and, smiling broadly, called the meeting to an abrupt end.

"Sol Leon gives me this signal for 'Cut!'" recalled Leonard. "So the only thing I can figure is that it is no longer necessary for me to continue pitching the show, because obviously the phone call had said that Lorillard was gonna buy it. Which is what had happened."

"In the intervening twenty minutes after we left the Lorillard boardroom," Leon confirmed, "they had enthusiastically decided to buy the other available half of the show. So that was it."

WITH LORILLARD TOBACCO and Procter & Gamble now signed to share the advertising tab for *The Dick Van Dyke Show*'s second season, Leonard assumed that persuading CBS to drop their saber-rattling stance and restore the series to a prominent spot on their fall schedule would be a simple matter. Unfortunately, such was not the case.

Despite the pair of lucrative sponsorship commitments that he'd sewn up for the show's second season, the producer was surprised to discover that the programmers at CBS continued to profess little interest in renewing their option for a second year of *The Dick Van Dyke Show*, sponsored or not. According to Leonard, the network's official excuse was that there were simply no open slots left on their fall schedule. While the producer had been shuttling back and forth across the country, the programmers explained, they'd promised the *Van Dyke Show*'s time slot to another series, and the network's fall lineup was now booked to capacity.

Pictured at the first-season wrap party are, from left, Richard Deacon, costume assistant Marge Makau, Larry Mathews, script supervisor Marge Mullen, associate producer Ron Jacobs, Morey Amsterdam, Mary Tyler Moore, Dick Van Dyke, film editor Bud Molin, Rose Marie, prop man Glenn Ross, Carl Reiner, director John Rich, assistant director John C. Chulay, composer Earle Hagen, an unidentified visitor, and Sheldon Leonard.

Or so they said—but Leonard didn't buy it for a second. In his opinion, the network's resistance to renewing the *Van Dyke Show* was residual fallout of the petty antipathy to the show that network president James Aubrey had expressed from the very start. But petty or not, for a few days in the late winter of 1962, that antipathy threatened to play the deciding role in the fate of *The Dick Van Dyke Show*.

That it didn't was largely due to the timely intervention of Leonard's friends from Procter & Gamble, who made short work of the stalemate when they finally added their booming voice to the debate. "The argument from Procter & Gamble to Aubrey was, 'Do you want to keep our daytime business?'" explained Leonard, who noted that Procter & Gamble was one of the primary sponsors of the network's lucrative daytime lineup. "'Well, if you like our daytime business—the soap operas that are the backbone of your daytime operation—then you'd better find a time spot for *Dick Van Dyke*!'"

It was a persuasive argument. A few days later, under the headline, "Van Dyke Show Renewed," the industry trade paper *Daily Variety* carried news of the show's renewal on the front page of its March 21, 1962, issue. "One of the few freshman shows to be renewed for next season," wrote *Variety*, "is the Dick Van Dyke half-hour comedy."[2] The blurb went on to explain that the show would be returning to its old Wednesday-night time slot, and concluded with a brief mention of the show's new sponsorship arrangement. "Procter & Gamble," noted the trade paper, "will have Lorillard sharing the tab."[3] And so it was official: *The Dick Van Dyke Show* was back in business.

18

NEVER NAME A DUCK

Like most of those on *The Dick Van Dyke Show*'s first-year payroll, the show's star player had written off any chance of the series returning after they filmed the first season's final episode in late February 1962. "I think most of us just assumed that that was it," he says. "We had pretty much given up hope that there was any recourse." Which is why the actor was so surprised when Carl Reiner called a few weeks later to inform him that he would indeed have a show to come home to the following season. "I didn't even know that Sheldon had gone to Cincinnati," confesses Van Dyke. "I didn't know that he'd saved our necks until it was over. I had gone into a movie over at Columbia, and I figured that my career was gonna have to go somewhere else."

As it happens, the actor would've had little reason to worry about his professional prospects even if his show hadn't been renewed. If *The Dick Van Dyke Show*'s first season had done nothing else, it established its namesake as a star of the first magnitude: a singing, dancing dynamo whose services were already in demand before he wrapped his TV show's freshman year. In February 1962, Van Dyke had been summoned by Walt Disney, who was anxious to cast the rising star in one of his pet projects:

a musical comedy film that was to be adapted from a series of children's books about a spellbinding English nanny named Mary Poppins. Intrigued, Van Dyke gave Disney an immediate thumbs-up on his involvement, though he hastened to explain that he wouldn't be able to start work on the movie for at least a year, since his feature film calendar for 1962 was already booked solid.

On May 1, Van Dyke reported to Columbia Pictures, where he was set to reprise his stage role in the studio's big-screen adaptation of *Bye Bye Birdie*, which would be the first film in the actor's nonexclusive five-year, seven-picture contract with the studio. *Birdie*'s three-month shooting schedule would keep Van Dyke hopping through the end of July, leaving him just enough time to shave and shower before he returned to Desilu Cahuenga to start rehearsals for the second year of his own series on August 1.

In spite of the scheduling complications that inevitably ensued, Van Dyke would find time to complete five feature film assignments during the four summer breaks in the *Van Dyke Show*'s five-year production schedule.

No sooner did he wrap the show's first season than Dick Van Dyke reported to Columbia Pictures to costar with Janet Leigh in the big-screen adaptation of his Broadway smash, *Bye Bye Birdie*.

In addition to *Birdie* and *Mary Poppins*, the star would also appear in *What a Way to Go!*, *The Art of Love*, and *Lt. Robinson Crusoe, USN*.

Even more intriguing than the star's actual early-sixties filmography is the fascinating list of projects that he considered but, for one reason or another, never made. High on this roster of films that never were is *Zoomar*, a comedy that was to have been based on a novel by the late Ernie Kovacs. Also discussed during Van Dyke's tenure as star of *The Dick Van Dyke Show* was a big-screen biography of Laurel and Hardy, in which Van Dyke would have portrayed his boyhood idol Stan Laurel. The star also briefly entertained the notion of playing the blacklisted talk-show host John Henry Faulk in a film biography based on Faulk's memoir, *Fear on Trial*, a project that would eventually surface a decade later as a TV movie starring William Devane.

Despite the number of big-screen roles that Van Dyke added to his resume during that busy period, the star made no secret of the fact that he was happiest on the set of his own series. "I've found movies the hardest and dullest work," the actor confessed a few weeks after he began work on *Bye Bye Birdie*.[1] After viewing the rushes of his first scenes from *Bye Bye Birdie*, the actor came to the conclusion that—in his opinion, anyway—his talents were better served on his own small-screen series. "I seemed so stiff to myself," the star would later confess, "and only about sixty percent as effective as I feel I am on my TV show, where I'm relaxed and at home."[2]

A FEW DAYS after Carl Reiner wrapped the first season of *The Dick Van Dyke Show*, the busy writer checked into an office on the Universal-International lot, where he'd been contracted to write *The Art of Love*, which would be filmed—with Dick Van Dyke in a leading role—in 1964. After the nonstop rigors of writing, producing, and story editing the *Van Dyke Show*, writing a single sceenplay seemed like a vacation to Reiner. If so, his respite would be short lived. In May 1962, with the first production date of the *Van Dyke Show*'s second season looming, the writer began splitting his workday between his office at Universal and his writer's cubicle on the Desilu Cahuenga lot, where he would arrive each afternoon at three to start work on one of the twenty-two original *Van Dyke Show* scripts that he would write during the show's second year.

As busy as he was, there was one Hollywood springtime ritual that the writer wasn't about to miss. And so, on May 22, 1962, Carl Reiner took a break from his labors to attend the fouteenth annual Emmy Awards ceremony, where he and director John Rich had each been nominated for one of the coveted statuettes. As it happens, Rich lost the award for Outstanding Directorial Achievement in Comedy to Nat Hiken, the director of *Car 54, Where Are You?* However, Reiner was genuinely stunned to hear his name announced as the recipient of that year's Emmy award for Outstanding Writing Achievement in Comedy. The startled writer didn't attempt to disguise his shock as he stumbled to the dais to deliver a brief acceptance speech that many saw as the high point of the evening's festivities. "I wish somebody would have told me," Reiner quipped from the podium, his bald pate gleaming under the bright stage lights. "I'd have worn my hair!"

WELL BEFORE THE show made its second-season debut on September 26, Sheldon Leonard had been predicting that *The Dick Van Dyke Show* was on the verge of a spectacular comeback. But it's unlikely that even the show's optimistic executive producer was prepared for the overwhelming response that would greet the show in the first weeks of its sophomore season. The program's second-year premiere garnered the series' highest rating to that time—and that was just the beginning. By the fourth week of the season, the show cracked the Nielsen top ten for the very first time, when the October 17 broadcast squeaked into ninth place with an average audience rating of 24.8, the first crest in a ratings tide that would continue to rise right through the end of the 1962–1963 season, when *The Dick Van Dyke Show* would finish the year as the ninth-highest-rated show in prime time, racking up an impressive average audience rating of 27.1 for the season. Not a bad comeback for a series that finished its freshman year in eightieth place.

According to Dick Van Dyke, the show's astonishing second-year turnaround was attributable to the legion of new viewers who had discovered the series over the summer, when—at the urging of Carl Reiner—CBS had agreed to rebroadcast many of the show's first-season episodes. "We did rather well during the summer," explains the star. "They put us into reruns, when we didn't have such stiff competition. And so we hit the air the next fall with a little bit of an audience, which we hadn't had at all in the first year."

However effective the show's summer rerun campaign might have been in attracting new viewers to the show, longtime *Van Dyke Show* observer Jay Sandrich suggests a simpler explanation for the show's sudden surge in popularity. "In the *Van Dyke Show*'s second year," says Sandrich, "CBS put a new show called *The Beverly Hillbillies* on in front of it. It was an immediate smash and went straight into the top five. The *Van Dyke Show* followed it—and so it too became an immediate hit."

It may seem hard to fathom that *The Dick Van Dyke Show*—the smartest, most sophisticated half-hour comedy of its age—could have broken into the top ten on the coattails of *The Beverly Hillbillies*, a series that many prime-time pundits rank as one of the least sophisticated shows in history. But a cursory glance at the Nielsen charts of the era bears that scenario out.

The Beverly Hillbillies wasn't merely a hit—it was a phenomenon. In the weeks following the backwoods comedy's debut in the time slot right before *The Dick Van Dyke Show* on CBS's Wednesday-night lineup, *The Beverly Hillbillies* blazed up the Nielsen ratings charts. By the close of the Nielsen weekly ratings period ending October 21, 1962, *The Beverly Hillbillies* had grabbed the number-one spot, making it the first series ever to top the ratings chart within five weeks of its premiere. Because viewers in the pre–remote-controlled early sixties were notoriously reluctant to get out of their chair to change the channel after their favorite program ended, *The Beverly Hillbillies*' ratings bonanza came as a godsend to the producers of *The Dick Van Dyke Show*, who stood to inherit a spillover audience of millions from their popular rural lead-in. It's a testament to the *Van Dyke Show*'s own staying power that the series soon established a dedicated audience whose loyalty would ensure the series a regular berth in Nielsen's top twenty for the remainder of its run.

If *The Dick Van Dyke Show*'s producers hoped to attract a broader audience at the outset of their second year, they made a smart choice in scheduling "Never Name a Duck" as the inaugural episode of their sophomore season. A funny and tender entry in the long-running saga of the Petrie family, the bittersweet comedy gets under way when Rob arrives home with a pair of cute baby ducklings that he presents to Ritchie—over Laura's pointed objections. "Those cute little balls of fur," she warns, "are going to grow into big, fat, noisy, dirty, dumb ducks!" Sharing none of his mother's concerns, Ritchie promptly christens his new pets Stanley and

Oliver, at which point Laura is forced to relent, acknowledging the unwritten rule that a pet, once named, cannot be turned away.

Laura's worst fears come to pass a few weeks later when Oliver dies, leaving Stanley—now fully grown—alone and looking a bit peaked himself. Fearing that the grief of losing a second pet might be too much for Ritchie to bear, Rob takes the surviving duck to the local veterinarian's office, where he hopes to discover a cure for the ailing bird.

At the vet's office, Rob is surprised to find the waiting room teeming with eccentric pet devotees of every variety. On one side sits a talkative poodle fancier; on the other, a cat owner who seems more down to earth—until she looks Rob in the eye and assures him that "a duck is a duck, a dog is a dog, and a cat is *a person*!" Rob's visit veers further into the realm of the surreal when another patron in the doctor's office turns out to be the doting owner of a full-grown kangaroo.

In the show's penultimate scene, Rob returns home without the duck and then tries to explain to Ritchie why he set their pet loose in a local pond. "It's very selfish of us to make Stanley stay in that kitchen sink when he'd much rather be in the park with his friends," Rob explains, struggling for the words to convey a set of very grown-up concepts to a distraught seven-year-old. Rob finally wins the boy over with a bit of anecdotal evidence that suggests the bird might do okay after all. As soon as he put Stanley in the water, Rob explains, their former pet spied a beautiful white female duck and promptly took off after her, "like a jet speedboat." Satisfied that nature has taken the proper course, Ritchie resolves to visit the pond with a pair of wedding presents for the feathered couple: a box of oatmeal cookies and a jar of his father's favorite caviar!

"The actual story was absolutely true," insists Carl Reiner, who cites the episode as yet another *Van Dyke Show* script inspired by a page in the Reiner family scrapbook—although in this case, the writer admits, he had to employ more than a little poetic license in the retelling. For one thing, the real-life writer had already moved from New Rochelle to Beverly Hills by the time he brought home a pair of cute baby ducklings and presented them to his son, Lucas, who was then a toddler.

"We put them in the sink," says Reiner, "and they ate Rice Krispies." Like Rob and Laura, Carl and Estelle Reiner soon discovered that even the most adorable baby ducks don't stay cute forever. "They'd go swimming in the pool," Reiner recalls. "And I said, 'Look at that, how pretty! They're

Dick Van Dyke and his feathered costar from "Never Name a Duck."

swimming in the pool!' Then we looked in the pool, and the bottom of it was covered with shit! Those two ducks shat more than our German shepherd. So we knew we had to get rid of them."

The writer finally decided to set his ducks loose in the waters of Los Angeles's MacArthur Park lagoon, just as he would later have the fictional Rob Petrie set his pet free in a local pond. But, in stark contrast to the waterside pastoral that Rob Petrie describes to his seven-year-old son on the show, Reiner and his own young son found their encounter with nature a far more harrowing experience. "The other ducks didn't want ours in the pack!" recalls Reiner, who was shocked to observe a display of fierce territorial behavior among the park waterfowl. "One duck came out of the pack—he was almost flying, with his legs hitting the water. He came over and he grabbed one of our ducks by the neck and shook him like he was gonna knock his head off!"

By then in tears, young Lucas Reiner was nearly beside himself after witnessing the cruel pageant of nature being enacted before his eyes. Fortunately, the elder Reiner saved the day by tossing a handful of breadcrumbs onto the water, creating a diversion sufficient to give his ducklings time to blend into the flock unmolested. "Luckily," notes Reiner, "I brought a lot of bread with me."

CARL REINER WOULD not be the only *Van Dyke Show* company member to come away from the making of "Never Name a Duck" with a renewed respect for the unpredictability of the animal kingdom. *Van Dyke Show* stock player Jerry Hausner would not soon forget his own run-in with Duke, the headstrong kangaroo who turned what was supposed to be a simple sight gag into a lively on-set improvisation that pitted actor against animal in a hilarious onstage tug-of-war. But while Hausner acknowledged that the unscripted tussle earned big laughs on the night of the performance, things didn't look nearly so comical from his vantage point on the set. "I was scared to death," recalled the diminutive character actor. "That animal was mean!"

Oddly enough, the actor acknowledged with a chuckle, everything had gone perfectly well at dress rehearsal. As written, Hausner was simply supposed to grab the kangaroo's leash and lead the animal quickly out of the veterinarian's office. At least that's how the scene played at the afternoon rehearsal, when the kangaroo appeared calm and well behaved. Unfortunately, by the time they let Duke out of his cage for the evening show, the marsupial star was in a fighting mood.

"He was angry about something," said Hausner, who noticed the alarming shift in his costar's disposition only after he was on stage with the animal. "Suddenly, he was obstreperous," recalled Hausner. "He didn't want to do anything that I wanted him to do." But with the cameras rolling—and the audience howling—the actor had little choice but to play out the impromptu tug-of-war, even if his 185-pound costar did seem to be getting the better of him. "We got big laughs," Hausner remembered. "But all I could think of is how they train kangaroos to box in the circus. And how they usually win."

19

STUMBLING

When The Dick Van Dyke Show returned to the air on September 26, 1962, fans of the series were no doubt surprised to discover that the show sported an entirely new opening-title sequence. Gone was the primitive still-photo montage that had appeared under the opening titles of the show's first thirty episodes; in its place was a whimsical introductory sequence that would, with slight variation, open each of the show's remaining 127 episodes. In the now-classic opening that debuted that night, Rob Petrie breezes jauntily into his living room, only to take an unplanned nosedive over an ill-placed ottoman that sits squarely in his path.

According to the show's director, John Rich, no one who was involved in the creation of the iconic sequence—which was filmed, almost on a whim, at the end of a full day's shooting—had any idea it would become one of television's most indelible visual signatures. Ironically, Carl Reiner didn't even think the show needed new opening titles until one of the program's sponsors suggested the idea to him a few weeks before the series returned to the air for its second season.

"The sponsors," explains Reiner, "were always saying, 'We've got to catch them at the beginning. We've got to make sure they stay with you.'" In the eyes of the skittish advertisers, the show's original opening titles were not compelling enough to keep the fickle viewing public glued to their seats through the all-important first commercial.

Dick Van Dyke and Mary Tyler Moore join producer Carl Reiner in welcoming their studio audience back for a second season.

While Reiner sympathized with his sponsor's desire to rope viewers into the show as early as possible, the producer didn't see how he could hope to hold a viewer's interest week after week with something as inherently predictable as the opening titles of a TV show. "I said, 'People are never going to stay with you for the main titles,'" recalls the producer. "'They're the same every week!'"

But, the producer wondered, what if the opening titles *weren't* the same every week? What if the show had two opening credit sequences? In the first version, Reiner would show his star taking a pratfall over a living room ottoman. Then, just to keep the audience guessing, he would film a second, nearly identical take, in which the actor *doesn't* stumble. The two versions would be attached to the episodes in random order, so the audience would never be sure, week to week, whether Van Dyke was going to take a fall or not. "One week he trips," explains Reiner. "And one week he doesn't. Then the people at home were supposed to say, 'I wonder if he trips this week?' It was silly. I don't think it ever worked. But that was the idea."*

Both variations of the *Van Dyke Show*'s celebrated opening sequence were filmed on the evening of August 14, 1962, just a few minutes after the cast finished shooting their thirty-second episode, "The Two Faces of Rob." The two versions of the soon-to-be immortal sequence were filmed in record time, says director John Rich, if only because, after a full day's work, none of the show's cast and crew were anxious to hang around the set any longer than they had to. And no one was more eager to wrap the evening's shoot than the director himself, who had already arranged a dinner date for later that night. "I had someone waiting for me in the Pacific Palisades or something," recalls Rich, "and I was irritated, frankly, about having to shoot this thing on a night I didn't want to."

But with the second-season premiere less than six weeks off, the show's producers were anxious to get the new title sequence in the can. So, after discussing the game plan with Reiner, Rich went right to work. "Okay, let's go," barked the director, rallying his cast and crew to the stage in his best no-nonsense voice. "Can we do this *now?*"

The actors obediently took their places on the set, where—still clad in the outfits they'd worn in the final scenes of the episode they'd just shot—the cast filmed the entire sequence in little more time than it would take to watch the twenty-second clip when it debuted on the air a few weeks later. "I set up a camera very quickly," says Rich, explaining his strategy for the shot. "All I wanted was something where Dick had enough room to come in and trip, and everybody else would have room to cluster around him, so that it made a comfortable shot. And it was set up about as fast as I just said it."

* To confuse matters even more, eagle-eyed viewers will note that a third variant of the show's familiar opening title sequence pops up in season three. In this variation—which is easily distinguished from the first two because the cast is wearing dressier evening wear in this third version—Van Dyke successfully negotiates the troublesome ottoman, only to get tripped up a few steps later when he stumbles, and almost falls, a second time. Shortly after this third variant was filmed, Reiner finally decided that the game of musical chairs he'd been playing with the show's titles was having no impact whatsoever on the show's viewership, and he curtailed the practice in the show's final years. During the fifth season, the take where the star sidesteps the ottoman was used almost exclusively under the show's opening titles.

Not surprisingly, the director made sure that he got everything he needed in the first take. "Dick came in, fell over the thing, and we shot it. And I said, 'That's fine, let's go home.'" According to Rich, it was while standing there on the set that Reiner actually came up with the inspiration to film a second, alternate version of the sequence. "Carl said, 'Hey, wait a minute! Let's do a variation, so that some nights Dick doesn't trip.' I said, 'Oh, good idea.'"*

At the director's signal, the actors dutifully repeated the sequence, with Dick Van Dyke substituting a deft sidestep around the ottoman in place of his earlier pratfall. "We shot it," says Rich, "and I went off on my date. The whole thing took about three minutes. I don't think we gave it any more thought than that. I just set the camera and said, 'Let's go.' Sometimes it works better that way."

Despite the extemporaneous circumstances of its shooting—or, perhaps, as Rich indicates, because of them—the show's classic opening title sequence achieves a casual spontaneity entirely appropriate to the material. Much of the credit for the sequence's visual elegance—indeed, for that of the entire series—must go to the show's director of photography, Robert De Grasse, a veteran cinematographer who'd been capturing rich and varied visual textures on film for more than three decades by the time he signed on to shoot *The Dick Van Dyke Show* in 1961.

"Robert De Grasse was wonderful," gushes Reiner, who considered himself fortunate to have at his disposal the services of a master lensman who, as a cinematographer at RKO Pictures during the thirties and forties, had distinguished himself as director of photography on many of the studio's most prestigious pictures, including *Stage Door*, *Alice Adams*, and *Carefree*. But despite his gilded resume, De Grasse had little trouble adjusting to the arena of three-camera television, where—as Reiner observes—the medium's inherent technical, budgetary, and time restrictions posed a very different set of challenges than those found on a feature film set.

"A three-camera set could look very flat," explains the producer. "You didn't have a lot of depth to the set. And here you had three cameras working, so you had to light all three angles at once." None of these potentially

* According to camera coordinator James Niver, the final decision of choosing which variation would appear on a given episode was left entirely to film editor Bud Molin. "None of us ever knew whether Dick was going to trip over the ottoman or not until we finally saw it on television," recalls Niver, "same as everyone else."

Under the watchful eye of veteran director of photography Robert De Grasse, even the most mundane scenes were imbued with a rich visual elegance. Says Carl Reiner, "He was the best guy for making a three-camera show look good with shadows and light."

daunting technical limitations seemed to deter the show's talented director of photography, who skillfully employed lighting to manipulate the show's black, white, and gray palette to achieve a surprisingly rich texture with the illusion of three-dimensional depth. "He was," says Reiner, "the best guy for making a three-camera show look good with shadows and light."

Like most of those who worked behind the scenes on any of executive producer Sheldon Leonard's cost-efficient situation comedy sets, De Grasse actually split his workweek between two shows. Under an ingenious system that the thrifty executive producer had devised to maximize his studio labor force, De Grasse would work as director of photography on the *Van Dyke Show* for the first two days of the week only; then, the morning after that show's Tuesday-night filming, the cinematographer would shuttle next door to Desilu's stage 9, where he would spend the remainder of his workweek performing similar duties on *The Danny Thomas Show*. All of which kept the sexagenarian cinematographer hopping throughout the three years that both shows were in production on adjoining Desilu soundstages. "We used to walk back and forth between the shows," recalls James Niver, who—like De Grasse and many other members of the *Van Dyke Show*'s behind-the-scenes crew—also split his own time between the two series. "The minute there was a layoff on one show, I'd usually go right over and watch the other show in rehearsal. It was a busy time. But it all worked, quietly and efficiently."

Indeed it did. By the middle of *The Dick Van Dyke Show*'s second season, the show's production machine fairly hummed along, fueled by the dedicated efforts of a crackerjack team of skilled troubleshooters that included associate producer Ronald Jacobs, production manager Frank Myers, and assistant director John C. Chulay. Another unsung hero on the show's production side was its tireless script supervisor, Marge Mullen, who managed script continuity on all but two of its 158 episodes.

AS *THE DICK VAN DYKE SHOW* moved into its second full season of production, it had become clear to Carl Reiner that at least one member of his creative team—director John Rich—might not be long for the series. By the end of his first year as house director of the *Van Dyke Show*, Rich had already begun to attract the attention of some of the biggest producers in Hollywood's feature-film community, most notably Paramount's Hal B. Wallis, who was anxious to sign the director to make movies for him at that studio. Although Rich would not officially leave the series until a few weeks into the show's third season, Reiner was already aware that he wasn't going to be able to keep his ambitious young director pinned down to the rigors of a weekly series forever. "We knew John was gonna have to take a rest sometime," says Reiner, "so we started to develop other directors."

Most of the responsibility for recruiting and training new directors for the *Van Dyke Show* fell to executive producer Sheldon Leonard, who accomplished the task—in typically paternal fashion—by establishing an informal apprenticeship program designed to attract talented newcomers. "If Sheldon Leonard saw somebody he thought had good timing," notes associate producer Ronald Jacobs, "he'd let them come in and observe us." At the end of a reasonable apprenticeship, during which the novice would watch Rich or one of the lot's other experienced directors at work, the newcomer would be given a shot at directing an episode or two on his own. "John Rich trained five of us who were essentially out to get his job," observed director Al Rafkin, an early graduate of Leonard's unofficial apprentice program. "There was me," Rafkin recalled, "Lee Philips, Hal Cooper, Jerry Paris, and maybe a couple others."

Ironically, one name conspicuously absent from Leonard's list of potential *Van Dyke Show* directors was his top assistant director and right-hand man, Jay Sandrich. Although Sandrich would eventually carve out a distinguished career as house director of *He & She*, *The Mary Tyler Moore Show*, *The Cosby Show*, and *Soap*, among others, he never did get a shot at directing *The Dick Van Dyke Show*—though he insists it wasn't for lack of

Carl Reiner (top, center) in a crew photo taken during the show's second season. Pictured in the row below Reiner are, from left, stand-in Frank Adamo, director Jerry Paris, assistant director John C. Chulay, CBS publicist Bruce Pennington, and second assistant director Bud Messinger; in the middle row stand makeup artist Tom Tuttle, music editor Donn Cambern, camera coordinator James Niver, director of photography Robert De Grasse, Dick Van Dyke, and Morey Amsterdam; and, finally, kneeling in the foreground are camera operator Harry Webb and costume supervisor Harald Johnson.

trying. "I begged Sheldon to let me direct a couple," he recalls. "I loved the *Van Dyke Show*. Still do. That was always, to me, a really wonderfully written, very sophisticated show. And that was the show I wanted to direct. But for whatever reason, Sheldon just never felt that I was ready or capable."

Although Sandrich has long since forgiven his mentor for what must, in retrospect, be viewed as one of Leonard's few questionable judgment calls, the former assistant director of the *Dick Van Dyke* and *Danny Thomas* shows still remembers how frustrating it was to watch less experienced hands get their shot at directing the *Van Dyke Show* while he was forced to look on from the sidelines. "That was a hard thing," says Sandrich. "A lot of directors were coming in who didn't understand how to do cameras, or they didn't understand the show, or whatever."

Fortunately, director-trainee Al Rafkin wasn't one of them. A former stand-up comic, Rafkin had played second banana to Van Dyke on an ill-fated variety show pilot that the star shot in the late fifties—an experience that gave the director a head start when he was assigned to direct the show's thirty-seventh episode, "My Husband Is Not a Drunk."

The centerpiece of this well-loved episode is Van Dyke's hilarious reprise of the inebriated-husband character that he played to such riotous effect early in his career. The episode's clever storyline describes the complications that ensue when Rob falls prey to a posthypnotic suggestion that he become a falling-down drunk every time he hears a bell ring. "It was just a magnificent piece of material," said Rafkin, who recalled that Van Dyke kept him in stitches all week long. "Every time that bell went off and Dick would get drunk again, I'd get hysterical," Rafkin confessed. "I mean, it just made me laugh every time. And it never stopped making me laugh. He could do it for me tonight—in my living room—and I would still laugh."

Reiner was an equally enthusiastic fan of Van Dyke's drunk-husband character, the trademark comic premise that the star introduced in *The Girls Against the Boys* on Broadway in 1959 and later revived for a short comic interlude in the *Van Dyke Show* pilot. In fact, it was after seeing his star perform the character in the show's pilot that Reiner became determined to revive the hilarious characterization at the earliest opportunity. The question then became how to depict Rob Petrie in a state of public drunkenness without betraying the integrity of the character, who was, of course, firmly established as an upstanding husband, father, and all-around pillar of the community. In

A posthypnotic suggestion provided a socially acceptable excuse for straitlaced Rob Petrie to appear in a state of comic inebriation in "My Husband Is Not a Drunk."

other words, not the sort of guy who would spend the better part of an episode in a drunken state, no matter how comical. Unless . . .

Unless Rob only *thought* he was drunk, but was in fact under the influence of hypnosis. It was the perfect solution. By letting Rob slip into a posthypnotic trance at the top of the show, the writer created a plausible rationale for putting his straitlaced star into a drunken stupor without having him touch so much as a drop of booze. "That's how we got away with me playing a drunk," observes Dick Van Dyke.

Like most of the directors who got their start behind the camera on *The Dick Van Dyke Show*, Al Rafkin would parlay his early experience on the show into a long and profitable career as a prolific director of half-hour comedies. In addition to directing three additional *Van Dyke Show* episodes and numerous installments of *The Andy Griffith Show*, Rafkin would eventually serve as house director on a number of highly regarded series over the course of a long and distinguished career, including *The Bob Newhart Show*, *One Day at a Time*, and *Coach*.

Despite the success of star pupils like Rafkin, it should be noted that not every recruit to Leonard's directorial apprenticeship program experienced so smooth a transition from novice to full-fledged director. "It's always difficult for a new director to come in and direct a show that's already established," observes Ronald Jacobs, who served as *The Dick Van Dyke Show*'s associate producer for all five seasons. One problem that frequently presented itself to anxious young directors assigned to the *Van Dyke Show* was how to deal with a cast that was so comfortable in their roles that they could essentially direct themselves. "You didn't have to tell that cast what to do," says Jacobs. "Rosie would already know if she had to get up and go to the desk on this line, or that she had to stand up on that line." The real secret to directing the *Van Dyke Show*, notes Jacobs, was simply knowing when to get out of the way and let the performers soar.

One freshman director who learned that lesson the hard way was Coby Ruskin, a Sheldon Leonard protege who came on board to direct the show's fortieth episode, "The Secret Life of Buddy and Sally." Though Ruskin would go on to a respectable career as a director of *The Andy Griffith Show* and *Gomer Pyle, USMC*, the novice director's first week on the *Van Dyke Show* would amount to a trial by fire.

As Morey Amsterdam told it, the new director's troubles began at his very first rehearsal, when Ruskin, anxious to flex his directorial muscles, rather courageously dared to second-guess one of Amsterdam's line readings. The line in question came early in the episode, during a short exchange where Buddy is supposed to be protesting the idea of having to work late at the office. After watching a preliminary run-through of the sequence, Ruskin decided that the scene could use a little more pizzazz. "He stopped me," recalled Amsterdam, "and he said, 'You're not aggravated enough. Jump up and down! You're furious this happened! You're a disgruntled citizen!'"

As soon as he heard that direction, the actor know he had a problem. Like all of the show's regular players, Amsterdam had come to view himself as the gatekeeper of his character's reality. And, as the actor politely informed the director, the overblown reaction that Ruskin asked for simply didn't fit the actor's conception of Buddy's reality. "I can't do that," replied Amsterdam. "I wouldn't know how. I've never been a disgruntled citizen in my life."

But Ruskin was insistent. Finally, the actor reluctantly agreed to give the suggestion a try—with one caveat. "I'll do it your way," Amsterdam volunteered. "But," he warned, "when Carl and Sheldon come down to watch the run-through, I don't know what they're gonna think."

They would both find out soon enough. The cast staged their first run-through for the show's producers not long after, and when Amsterdam got to the scene that had earlier caused so much controversy, he played it with wild-eyed abandon—just as he'd been directed. And, just as he'd anticipated, Leonard took one look at the scene and stopped the rehearsal cold.

"Morey!" the executive producer exclaimed. "What are you doing?" As Amsterdam recalled it, he quickly assumed his straightest poker face and explained that he was simply playing the scene as if he were a disgruntled citizen. "That's ridiculous!" came Leonard's retort. "You've never been a disgruntled citizen in your life!" Needless to say, the apprentice director restaged the scene that same afternoon, this time taking full advantage of his actor's instinctive reactions.

WHEN ANN GUILBERT left *The Dick Van Dyke Show* for an extended pregnancy leave midway through the show's first season, the actress was not sure there would be a job waiting for her when she was ready to return to work a few months later. "When I left, I didn't even know if the show was going to get picked up for another year," she says. "And when it did, I didn't know if they were going to use me again." But according to Carl Reiner, there was never any doubt that he would find room for Guilbert, whose place in the show's ensemble was, in his mind, unassailable. As proof, the producer offered to sign her to a long-term employment contract within a few days of her return to the show in October 1962. It was an attractive offer: in exchange for her commitment to continue with the series through the end of its run, she would be guaranteed a specified number of weeks of work each season. Which was a considerable improvement over the status Guilbert had labored under during the show's first year, when she had been called in to work on a show-by-show, as-needed basis. But despite the proposed contract's obvious advantages, Guilbert left her producer astonished when she informed him that she actually preferred working without a contract.

"With two youngsters at home, I didn't want to work all the time," she explains. "I was happy doing about as much as I did. I thought, if I'm under contract, I'll just have to come in and sit around to do two or three lines. And for a three-camera show, you've got to come in and work for four or five days, even if it's just a little bitty scene." On the other hand, the actress reasoned, if she continued to book her appearances on the series on a show-by-show basis, her producers would almost certainly make better use of her time. "If they have to hire me as a guest star every time they use me," she surmised, "they'll only call me in when they really want to use me."

Looking back, Guilbert is convinced she made the right decision. "It worked out fine for me—I don't think the pay scale was that different whether you were a continuing character or a recurring character, like I was."* As far as the actress could tell, her freelance status had little impact on the frequency of her appearances on the series. "They used me a lot," she says, "because my character figured in the house scenes. Dick had Morey and Rosie to talk to in the office scenes, but Mary needed someone to talk to—and that's why Millie was always there."

If, as Guilbert suggests, Millie Helper's status as Laura Petrie's best friend and chief sounding board guaranteed the actress playing her a constant visibility, she was aware that the role of next-door neighbor

* Like most of the actors on the show, Guilbert was paid modestly. In her recollection, her shooting fee at the series' start in 1961 was a mere five hundred dollars per episode, though she recalls that her weekly rate had risen to about double that amount by the time the *Van Dyke Show* left the air in 1966.

imposed its own set of limitations as well. "I was the door opener and door closer," she observes with bemused detachment. "I'd stick my head in, and they'd say, 'Go home, Millie!' or something like that. It was always in and out—in and out." Equally frustrating for the actress were those scenes where her character functioned as a device to keep the show's plot purring along. "I hated the part where I had to sit around the living room and say, 'And then what happened, Rob?'"

But, if the character of Millie Helper was occasionally deployed more sparingly than Guilbert might've wished, the actress would have little to complain about in the show's forty-first installment, in which Millie takes center stage as the lone witness to an aerial attack by a giant woodpecker!

The decidedly nondisgruntled Morey Amsterdam and some of the cast strike an irreverent pose.

20

SNEEZING FUNNY

The series of giant woodpecker attacks that propel the plot of episode 41, "A Bird in the Head Hurts," must surely rank as one of the show's more outlandish comic premises. And yet, implausible as it sounds, Carl Reiner insists the episode's absurd storyline was drawn almost verbatim from a true-life tale described to him by Millie Helper's real-life counterpart, Millie Schoenbaum of New Rochelle, New York.

"Nobody's gonna believe it!" Reiner told his former New Rochelle neighbor when she called him in Beverly Hills to share the harrowing tale of how an oversized woodpecker had taken to attacking her son. "The kid wouldn't go to school, because every day a bird pecked his head!" swears Reiner. "When she told me that story, I said, 'Write it up, Millie.' I'll use that one on the show."

The script that Reiner finally drafted from his old friend's notes turned out to be one of the writer's best, a bizarre foray into suburban surrealism rendered all the more fantastic because it was based on the truth. In the episode's opening scenes, Rob and Laura scoff at Ritchie's hysterical claim that he's been singled out as an object of attack by a giant woodpecker. The skeptical parents are fully prepared to dismiss the boy's outrageous tale as the fanciful product of an overstimulated imagination, until Millie arrives

The show's thrty-sixth episode explores the origin of Ritchie's one-of-a-kind middle name in another flashback to the early days of the Petries' marriage.

to report that she witnessed one of the attacks with her very own eyes. That's when the Petries decide it's time to call in an expert.

Unfortunately, the concerned parents derive little satisfaction from the Westchester County game warden who arrives only to inform them that the county's animal protection laws are skewed overwhelmingly in the bird's favor. Eschewing the animal specialist's suggestion that they send the boy to school in pith helmet and sunglasses, Rob eventually deduces that it might not be Ritchie that the woodpecker is after but the boy's hair, which—as Rob cleverly surmises—the bird has somehow identified as an ideal nesting material. Finally, using a few hairs from his son's comb as bait, the resourceful father successfully lures the bird into captivity. By episode's end, the once-troublesome predator has found a new and safer home in the aviary of the Bronx Zoo.

"All of that really happened," says Reiner, who was surprised at how little embellishment was required to recast his neighbor's anecdotal account as a comic teleplay. In fact, the writer insists that at least one scene in his script was transcribed almost verbatim from the actual event. "Those were the game warden's actual lines," says Reiner, noting the similarities between the Schoenbaums' real encounter with their local game warden and the show's fictional re-creation of the same event. "He told them, 'There are no woodpeckers in New Rochelle.' Then, when they saw the bird, he said, 'You're not allowed to shoot it.'" Finally, adds Reiner, when the distraught Schoenbaums inquired what they might do to protect their child, the real-life game warden answered exactly as the writer would later portray it in his script. "He told them, 'Have your kid wear a pith helmet!'"

Of course, it wasn't every week that one of Reiner's friends was kind enough to phone up with as rich a story premise as the one that inspired "A Bird in the Head Hurts." Most weeks the producer was forced to look elsewhere for comic stimulation. According to Reiner, one of his most fertile sources of inspiration was Dick Van Dyke himself, whose inventive improvisations provided comic fodder for more than one classic *Van Dyke Show* episode. One of the more memorable examples is "Gesundheit, Darling," the episode where Rob develops an apparent allergic reaction to his wife and child—a storyline that Reiner insists was inspired by little more than his star's ability to sneeze funny.

"I loved the way he sneezed!" exclaims Reiner, who recalls that he first became aware of Van Dyke's theretofore unknown sternutationary skills when he noticed the star regaling the crew with an impromptu demonstration of a dozen or more comical sneezes during a lull in rehearsal one afternoon. Within a week's time, Reiner had written "Gesundheit, Darling," a half-hour script designed to capitalize on what must surely qualify as Dick Van Dyke's most unusual ability.

But Van Dyke's uncanny facility for sneezing funny would not be the only previously unheralded talent to emerge from the star's frequent on-set

The in-laws squabble their way through "What's in a Middle Name?" Pictured with Mary Tyler Moore and Dick Van Dyke are Cyril Delevanti (seated), Geraldine Wall, J. Pat O'Malley, Isabel Randolph, and Carl Benton Reid.

improvisations. "Dick could do pantomimic things that nobody else in the world could have done," says Reiner, who delighted in testing the limits of his star's capabilities every chance he had. "Just to see if he could do it," says Reiner, "I once challenged Dick to sneeze, cough, belch, fart, and hiccup—to do everything that the human body could possibly do—all within one second! And he did it! All at once. 'Ugh-da-cough-wheez-hick-ah-bloo!'"

"They were always coming up with stupid physical ideas," recalls Van Dyke, who insists that Reiner wasn't the only member of the show's writing staff to derive pleasure from this form of benign torture. "One time," recalls Van Dyke, "Sam Denoff said, 'You're a tap dancer, but you've got a broken leg and you've got to do a number. Let me see you do that!'" "And then," adds Bill Persky, who swears he was present at the rehearsal where Van Dyke attempted to conquer that particular challenge, "Dick did a guy tap dancing with a broken leg on a shot of novocaine! I mean, you would just throw this stuff at him, and he would then do it. You'd give Dick a challenge like that, and he just couldn't resist."

"It was just fun," allows the star. "That's the whole idea. I think that's why the show worked so well, because—on top of the good writing and everything else—we had such a good time."

In a town where the frequency and volume of a star's on-set temper tantrums are often viewed as a barometer of his or her celebrity standing, Van Dyke's unfailing congeniality on the set of his own series was viewed with awe by many Hollywood observers. "Dick was a doll," observed character actor Jerry Hausner, a regular member of the show's unofficial stock company.

"He never seemed to worry about anything," echoes director John Rich, who claims he never heard a single harsh word emanate from the star's lips in all their years together. According to Rose Marie, "Dick just sort of relaxed and did what he wanted to do." "He never got angry," concurred writer Bill Idelson. "Dick just sort of floated above it all."

By the star's own recollection, that's not exactly true. As Dick Van Dyke confesses, his legendary patience *was* tried to the breaking point on at least one occasion. As the actor recalls it, this rare display of pique occurred early in the show's second year, shortly after he made the ill-considered decision to appear, in character as Rob Petrie, in a series of in-house commercials that touted the virtues of Kent cigarettes, whose maker sponsored the show. According to Van Dyke, he agreed to appear in the advertising spots only reluctantly, after Leonard requested he participate as a favor for

Rob suspects he may be allergic to Laura when he can't seem to stop sneezing in the second-season episode "Gesundheit, Darling."

their sponsor. The actor recalls that he would come to regret that decision almost immediately.

Despite Van Dyke's misgivings about appearing in the half-dozen or so Kent cigarette pitches that he and the other cast members filmed during the show's second season, the brief, self-contained advertisements present a fascinating snapshot of the show's cast members at work in a dreamily odd context. One of the more memorable spots features Rob and Laura lounging around their familiar living room as they extol the virtues of Kent cigarettes in a conversation so stilted that no one was likely to mistake it for dialogue written by Reiner.*

"I have the two things that would make any man happy," boasts Rob in the almost surreal exchange that opens the spot. "A gorgeous wife, and I'm smoking a Kent!" When Laura inquires which of the two he prefers more—her or the cigarette, Rob's answer comes without a moment's hesitation. "Let me see . . ." he says, "For cooking and for dancing and kissing—you satisfy best. But, for filter and taste, Kent satisfies best!" "I'll accept that," Laura replies—somewhat improbably—before she, too, relaxes into a

* Indeed, executive producer Sheldon Leonard took full credit for the content, script, and direction of the Kent spots, which—like similar integrated commercials he prepared for General Foods on his *Andy Griffith* and *Danny Thomas* shows—were produced as a gesture of goodwill to the show's sponsors, who paid little or no additional cost for the custom-made endorsements. "I did integrated commercials free," Leonard boasted. "I made them up, wrote the commercial, used my cast of characters and crew. I gave the sponsor a complete one-minute commercial—and it never cost them a dime."

chair to enjoy the soothing taste of her own freshly lit cigarette. And, on that oddly disconcerting image, the commercial fades out.

Never comfortable in the role of cigarette pitchman, Van Dyke recalls that he grew so livid once he finally saw one of the Kent spots on the air that he was moved to put his foot down for the first and only time during the show's five-year run. "I told Sheldon, 'This is a family show. Kids are watching, and I just cannot be telling kids to smoke cigarettes.'" According to the actor, the executive producer offered no argument, and the cast's in-house Kent endorsements were eventually phased out. "And," assures Van Dyke, "we never did another one."

The star's principled reaction to his on-air endorsement of their sponsor's tobacco product was ironic in light of the fact that both he and Mary Tyler Moore were heavy smokers throughout the years *The Dick Van Dyke Show* was in production—though, it must be admitted, neither of them favored their sponsor's brand. "Mary smoked Pall Malls," recalled costumer Harald Johnson. "I know, because she was always bumming cigarettes from me, and I smoked Pall Malls."

While Kent may not have been the preferred brand of either of the show's stars, Johnson insisted that that didn't stop them—or any of the other smokers on the show's staff, himself included—from accepting the free cartons of Kents that the sponsor willingly supplied to the show's cast and crew. That Kent was not the brand of choice for most of them made little difference, according to Johnson, who recalled that he and his backstage coconspirators devised an effective way around that obstacle. "I'd take my carton of Kents down to the local market and exchange them for Pall Malls," confessed the costumer, who insisted that he wasn't the only one to perpetrate this scam at his sponsor's expense. "Mary did the same thing," said Johnson, "and so did Dick."

Sure enough, many years after the fact, Mary Tyler Moore—by then a confirmed nonsmoker—cheerfully confirmed her participation in the petty larceny Johnson described. "Oh, exactly!" she confessed, "I used to take mine to my local market and just automatically trade 'em in."

AFTER MORE THAN a decade of toiling in the vineyards of episodic television, John Rich finally got his shot at the majors in the closing weeks of 1962, when Hal B. Wallis closed a deal to secure the director's services for a five-picture contract to direct movies for his unit at Paramount Pictures. But though Wallis's offer looked like a once-in-a-lifetime opportunity to the ambitious director, Rich was also aware that accepting the movie deal would mean leaving *The Dick Van Dyke Show*. And that, he insists, was not an easy decision to make. "I was very happy there," says the director, recalling his days on the *Van Dyke Show*. "But the fact is, I had a chance to do films."

The director's first film for Paramount would be the Van Johnson–Janet Leigh comedy *Wives and Lovers*, which was set to go before the cameras in the early months of 1963. In all, Rich would direct four additional features over the next four years—*The New Interns*; *Boeing, Boeing*; and the Elvis Presley vehicles *Roustabout* and *Easy Come, Easy Go*; but ironically, after spending a few years in the supposedly greener pastures of feature film-making, the veteran TV director admits he couldn't wait to get back to the bustling world of weekly television. "Films bored me," says Rich, who found the tedium of feature-film production especially frustrating after the break-neck pace he'd maintained as director of *The Dick Van Dyke Show*. "I was used to going so fast with them—it was all snap-snap-snap! In five days, you knew what you had. On a film, you'd work for a year—and by the time you were done, whatever was funny initially would quickly grow stale."

Although Reiner and Leonard had no interest in standing in their director's way, they were understandably concerned that Rich's sudden departure might have a deleterious effect on company morale. "John was like the father figure on the set," observes Reiner. "When he left, everybody was afraid we couldn't do it without him."

But Rich harbored no such fears for the show's future, as he explains in his own fabled account of how he came to appoint actor Jerry Paris to be his successor. "Carl and Sheldon were worried about what would happen to the show," he explains. "But it was already firmly on the tracks. The cast and the writing were so solid, I told them, that anyone could direct the show—I turned around, and Jerry happened to be standing there—even *him*." In Rich's recollection of the events that followed, he summoned the slightly startled actor over and tendered a job offer on the spot. "I said, 'Jerry, you want to be a director?' And Jerry says, 'Yeah, I guess so, why?' So I turned to Carl and said, 'How about if Jerry watches me very carefully as a director for the next six weeks?' Carl said, 'If you think he can do it.' And, of course, he turned out great. So Jerry became a director because I needed an out to do a film."

Though no one denies Rich's ability to spin an entertaining tale, Reiner takes exception to a few of the particulars in the director's account of how Jerry Paris came to discover his calling as director of *The Dick Van Dyke Show*. Despite Rich's assertion that serendipity played a primary role in the future director's big break, Reiner insists that the decision to move Paris behind the cameras in the *Van Dyke Show*'s second season was hardly random. In fact, notes Reiner, Paris had been lobbying for the chance to direct *The Dick Van Dyke Show* almost from the day he arrived. "Jerry Paris bothered me to become a director for two years," says Reiner. According to Paris's friend Ann Guilbert, the actor's ambition to direct had been so strong that he even attempted to make it a condition of his employment to work as an actor on the show. Before Paris agreed to play Jerry the dentist, insists Guilbert, "he told Sheldon Leonard, I'll do the part, but only if you'll let me direct later."

Despite the actor's determination to move behind the scenes, Reiner was not entirely convinced that directing a weekly TV series was the best job for a man of Paris's wide-ranging temperament. "Jerry was so flaky," the producer admits with a laugh. "No one thought he'd be very good as a director. We said, 'Oh my God, they're not gonna listen to you!'"

Though Reiner insists that he also took the actor's considerable strengths into account—"He was hilarious," acknowledges Reiner, "and very bright"—in the end, it was the actor's unwavering confidence in his own abilities that would sway the producer most decisively. "Anybody who wants to direct that badly," says Reiner, "you know he's going to be able to direct. So I said, 'We'll give him a shot.'"

Of course, even after Reiner set his own misgivings aside, Paris still had to prove himself on the set, where the former actor's credibility remained a topic of concern among his fellow company members well into his first few days on the job. "Nobody came up to my office and said, 'Hey, what are you doing?'" recalls Reiner. "But there was talk. 'Hey,' they'd whisper, as they took you aside. 'Is this gonna work?' And I'd say, I dunno, let's take a chance. We'll see.'"

To those who knew Jerry Paris well, there was never any doubt that the actor had found his true calling. "Jerry loved directing," observed actor Bill Idelson, who'd known Paris since the late forties, when the pair attended acting classes together in New York. "Jerry loved being in control of people," Idelson added. "He would take over. He told you what to do, he told you what to wear. You went to a party, he directed the party. If you had him at your wedding, he would direct your wedding. He would direct anything. He was a natural born director."

Paris's natural affinity for the job soon became apparent to the show's cast, who would eventually develop a fierce loyalty to their new coach. "Jerry loved actors," said Idelson, "and actors always felt comfortable with him, because they knew he loved them. He was with you every second. He got very involved—he was *in* your body. He could tell you to jump through a wall and you'd try it, because you knew that it might be funny." "Jerry was our greatest audience," concurs Van Dyke, who credits the director with inspiring him to new heights of slapstick invention on more than one occasion. "He invented a lot of good moments on the show."

As Reiner observes, Paris wasn't shy about taking credit for those comic moments that bore his signature. "When we'd watch the rehearsals," recalls Reiner, "Jerry would say, 'Did you see that? I put that joke in.'" Finally, after a few week's exposure to Paris's relentless self-promotion, the producer felt obliged to bring his overeager director into check. "I finally said, 'Jerry, don't say, "I put that in." Because if you say, "I put that in," that's *all* I'll think you put in! If you don't tell me every time you put something in, I will give you credit not only for that, but for everything that happened on the stage that Dick put in, or that Mary put in!' And he said, 'Yeah, you're right! You're absolutely right.'"

Despite his overbearing personality, the cast and crew took note of the way Paris invariably approached his work with intelligence and an infectious enthusiasm, and it wasn't long before the director had earned the respect of the show's entire staff, including many of his former detractors. "Jerry did better than anyone dreamed," acknowledges Reiner. "He finally surprised us all." As proof of their confidence, the show's producers would assign the journeyman director to helm no fewer than ten second-year episodes, including such standout entries as "Ray Murdock's X-Ray," "I Was a Teenage Head Writer," "Give Me Your Walls!," "I'm No Henry Walden!," "When a Bowling Pin Talks, Listen," and a curious little science-fiction parody that bore the unlikely title "It May Look Like a Walnut!"

21

NUTS

In the years before his death in 1986, Jerry Paris usually cited "It May Look Like a Walnut!" as the debut episode of his tenure as director of *The Dick Van Dyke Show*. But while that's not strictly true—Paris received credit as director of "Ray Murdock's X-Ray" and "I Was a Teenage Head Writer," two episodes that were filmed weeks before "It May Look Like a Walnut!" went before the cameras on January 15, 1963—it's not hard to see how the walnut show might have eclipsed its predecessors in the director's recollection. With its half-dozen interweaving plotlines, a handful of the show's most elaborate sight gags, and a cameo appearance by Danny Thomas himself, "It May Look Like a Walnut!" easily ranks as one of the show's most fondly remembered episodes.

"I was searching for things to do to stay current," explains Carl Reiner,

"I was doing my version of *The Twilight Zone*," says Carl Reiner, recalling the show's unforgettable fifty-first episode, "with seventeen hundred walnuts."

recalling the genesis of his script for the walnut show, "and I loved *The Twilight Zone*." So, for the *Van Dyke Show*'s fifty-first episode, the writer concocted a surrealistic takeoff that drew liberally from Rod Serling's classic science-fiction TV anthology series as well as a number of other sources, most notably Don Siegel's classic 1956 sci-fi shocker *Invasion of the Body Snatchers*, which was scripted by Daniel Mainwaring from a novel by Jack Finney.

In Reiner's spoof, Rob Petrie wakes up one morning to find himself surrounded by extraterrestrials from the planet Twilo, who, in their nefarious quest for world domination, have somehow taken on the physical forms of his best friends. Stranger yet, the invasion is led by a general who just happens to bear an uncanny resemblance to *The Dick Van Dyke Show*'s own coexecutive producer, Danny Thomas. "I was doing my version of *The Twilight Zone*," insists Reiner, "with seventeen-hundred walnuts."

Those walnuts would play a key role in the episode's brazenly silly plotline, which opens in the Petrie bedroom, where Rob is gradually reducing Laura to a nervous wreck with his scene-by-scene reenactment of the creaky plotline of a late-show thriller in which aliens plot to take over the world by tampering with the earth's walnut supply. Rob's chilling blow-by-blow sends Laura to bed scared out of her wits, but in the end it's he who has the nightmare—or so it would appear when Rob awakes the next morning to find his house strewn with walnuts. At first, the hapless husband assumes that his wife is simply playing a joke on him, but he's forced to think twice when he arrives at work and Buddy offers him a snack from a sack of . . . walnuts!

Things go from weird to worse for the beleaguered comedy writer when his coworkers and Mel Cooley begin to pace around the office like a trio of mindless zombies. When they're joined by a Danny Thomas lookalike who is introduced as Kolac, the evil emissary from the planet Twilo, Rob becomes convinced he's having a bad dream. Hoping to jostle himself awake, he rushes home—only to confront the most bizarre sight of all. No sooner does he go to hang up his coat than his wife comes sliding in headfirst from the hallway closet, grinning malevolently from atop a mountain of thousands and thousands of walnuts! Suddenly, from out of nowhere, Buddy, Sally, and Mel appear, flanked by the alien Danny Thomas—forming a tableau so fearsome that it forces the drowsing writer from his slumbers once and for all. Now awake, Rob barely has time to regain his composure before he makes the startling discovery that Laura has had the same dream!

Rob induces nightmares in the setup to the second-year classic "It May Look Like a Walnut!"

Reiner's script for "It May Look Like a Walnut!" was, of course, an exercise in whimsy from start to finish. Even so, the show's cast was savvy enough to appreciate the comic potential in the writer's broad parody from their very first reading of the script. Which was more than could be said for executive producer Sheldon Leonard, who didn't share the cast's enthusiasm for Reiner's tongue-in-cheek spoof. "Sheldon didn't like that one," recalls Dick Van Dyke. "He thought it was a little too bizarre, and he didn't think it would be funny."

"Sheldon and I had a big argument about that show being no good," concurs Reiner, who recalls that his executive producer pronounced the script unsalvageable after a single table reading. "It was," notes Reiner, "the only time we had one of those arguments." But Reiner held firm, and finally—after the requisite amount of around-the-table haggling—the executive producer gracefully bowed to his producer's instincts. And when Leonard finally saw how well the episode played before the audience at the show's Tuesday-night filming, he was the first to admit he'd misjudged the effort.

"I was 100 percent wrong," the executive producer would later observe, "and Carl was 100 percent right on that one."[1] "Sheldon was terrific," recalls Reiner, "a mensch. He just said, 'You were absolutely right!'"

According to *Van Dyke Show* writer Sam Denoff, Leonard's handling of the debate that surrounded the walnut show provides a revealing glimpse of the executive producer's evenhanded managerial style in action. "Sheldon was really the boss," says Denoff. "But he never, ever said, 'You do it my way.' All of his producers would fight with him, and he'd always say, 'Okay, if that's the way you wanna do it. But I'm telling you it's gonna stink.' And when it didn't stink, he'd admit it didn't stink. He was that kind of gracious man."

From their first day of rehearsal, cast members knew they would have a ball putting the walnut show on its feet. And by all accounts, they did—despite the somewhat complicated technical setup required to facilitate Laura's dramatic third-act entrance from atop the monstrous pile of walnuts that pours forth unexpectedly from the Petries' front-hall closet. According to Michael Ross—the son of *Van Dyke Show* prop man Glenn Ross—that memorable sight gag was accomplished using real walnuts. Sacks and sacks and sacks of them, in fact, which were poured into the closet a few hours before showtime through a chute that had been specially rigged above the set. "We packed the closet with walnuts before the show," explains Ross, who was still a teenager when he arrived on the set to help his father assemble the mechanics of this sight gag in 1963.

On the night of the filming, Mary Tyler Moore sat perched on a backstage ladder, from which she was to leap onto the waterfall of walnuts at the precise split second that Van Dyke unleashed them onto the stage. On another ladder stood an additional pair of stagehands, whose job it would be to drop a few hundred additional walnuts into the mix, for good measure, once the closet door was opened. It was a complicated setup but—to everyone's amazement—when the moment of truth arrived, the sight gag went off without a hitch. As soon as Van Dyke opened the closet door, the walnuts came tumbling out on cue, and Moore slid onto the stage from atop an enormous pile of hard-shelled walnuts to make one of the grandest comic entrances in television history.

In case you've ever wondered whatever became of all those walnuts after the episode was filmed, according to one firsthand observer, the ones that didn't crack went right back to the store! Or so claimed film editor Bud Molin, who insisted that after the episode was shot, the show's penny-wise producers had arranged to return any undamaged walnuts to the nut wholesaler from whom they were purchased in the first place. "The deal was," explained Molin, "they could return the ones that weren't broken and get their money back." By Molin's reckoning, the unbroken walnuts eventually found their way back to the shelves of local supermarkets and, it can be assumed, were finally purchased and consumed by Southern California nut aficionados—few of whom, presumably, had the slightest notion of their snack's distinguished pedigree.

According to Van Dyke, more than a few of these tasty morsels were also consumed by the show's hungry cast and crew, many of whom continued snacking freely on the walnuts all week—until it finally dawned on someone that a surfeit of walnuts might have an adverse effect on one's digestive tract. But, says Van Dyke, by then it was too late. "We all got really bound up," the star confesses. "The entire cast and crew were constipated—we were in bad shape for days."

When the words "It May Look Like a Walnut!" appeared on television screens during the opening credits sequence of *The Dick Van Dyke Show*'s February 6, 1963, broadcast, it marked the first time the title of an episode of the series actually appeared on the air. According to Reiner, he would have begun the practice of running on-screen titles earlier if the idea had only occurred to him. "The titles were always on the scripts," he explains. But it was not until the cast was reading "It May Look Like a Walnut!" around the rehearsal table, maintains Reiner, that "some smart person said, 'This is a funny title. Why not put it on the air?'" The producer instantly agreed, and it was decreed that, effective immediately, the titles for that and all subsequent episodes of *The Dick Van Dyke Show* would be offered up for public consumption. "And we did it till the end," says Reiner. "It was like an extra bit of entertainment."

FOR *THE DICK VAN DYKE SHOW*'S fifty-fourth episode, "The Sam Pomerantz Scandals," Reiner returned to that most durable *Van Dyke Show* format, the comedy-variety episode. "Those musical shows were always easier on my heart," explains Reiner, who had discovered early on that it took considerably less time to craft a script in which Rob, Laura, Buddy, and Sally spend the better part of the episode singing, dancing, and telling old jokes—whether at a party, a neighborhood variety show, or an old friend's Borscht Belt nightclub—than it did to write an entirely new plot-driven episode from scratch. "It was a pleasure when we did those shows, because I didn't have to write a forty-page show," observes Reiner. "I could write a twenty-two-page show, since I knew there were gonna be three musical numbers."

As effective as the show's musical-variety format could be in helping the writer meet his annual script quota in the show's first two or three seasons, Reiner also recognized that it was a device best used sparingly. "You couldn't do 'em too often, or it would turn into a musical show," says Reiner. "But I knew that once every thirteen weeks or so I could do a musical show." And so it was that Reiner dropped Rob, Laura, Buddy, and Sally into the Borscht Belt for the show's fifty-fourth episode, which is set in a Catskills resort managed by Rob's old army buddy Sam Pomerantz.

"The Sam Pomerantz Scandals" opens as Rob, Laura, and the rest of the gang arrive for what they expect to be a leisurely vacation in the mountains. But all thoughts of a relaxing weekend are dashed after Rob accidentally incapacitates the club's headliner in a tennis match, and he, Laura, Buddy, Sally, and Mel are drafted into service as the featured entertainment in the club's main room. Sally rises to the challenge with a rousing rendition of Johnny Mercer's "I Wanna Be Around." Next, Buddy provides a few minutes of comic relief before he introduces Rob and Laura, who wow the audience with an impromptu soft-shoe to the tune of "Carolina in the Morning." For their big finale, the cast regroups on stage to perform "The Musicians," the classic bandleader number that would be reprised memorably a few months later on the *Van Dyke Show*'s Christmas episode.

But as far as Van Dyke was concerned, the real highlight of the episode was the show's Laurel and Hardy sketch, an extended pantomime in which the star got to play Stan Laurel to costar Henry Calvin's Oliver Hardy—a piece that was quite clearly intended as a tribute to one of Van Dyke's most esteemed boyhood idols. "Stan Laurel was my hero," says Van Dyke, who counts among his most cherished memories the afternoon he finally got a chance to meet the former silent-film star at Laurel's home in Santa Monica, an event that took place not long after Van Dyke first moved to California.

"When I started the series," Van Dyke reminisces, "I asked a lot of people whatever became of Stan. But nobody was sure where he was." Then, one day, he recalls, as he was looking up a phone number in the Santa Monica city directory, he happened across a listing for a Stan Laurel. Van Dyke nervously dialed the number and was thrilled when the voice at the other end turned out to be Stan Laurel himself.

As Van Dyke began to stammer out a halting introduction, he was relieved to discover the screen star already knew who he was. "He was familiar with the show," says Van Dyke, "and he said he liked my work."

Before Dick Van Dyke dared impersonate Stan Laurel on the show's fifty-fourth episode, "The Sam Pomerantz Scandals," the star called his boyhood idol for pointers. Pictured with Van Dyke is Henry Calvin.

Before the call ended, Stan Laurel had invited his enthusiastic fan to drop by for a visit the following Sunday afternoon. "He lived in an apartment on Ocean Avenue in Santa Monica," remembers Van Dyke. "I just went over there, knocked on the door, and couldn't believe I was in his presence." The two comic actors exchanged small talk for no more than a few minutes before the conversation finally—and inevitably—turned to the business of comedy. "Of course, all I did was pump him with questions," confesses Van Dyke. "We talked about physical comedy a lot."

When Van Dyke rose to leave at the end of the afternoon, the aging comedian extended his hand in friendship and offered a compliment that the younger comic would not soon forget. "He said," recalls Van Dyke, "'If anybody ever decides to do a film on my life, I would like you to play me.' It was the greatest compliment I'd ever had in my life. That made my day."

Van Dyke would finally have the chance to fulfill his idol's wish when he and Henry Calvin performed their homage to Laurel and Hardy on the *Van Dyke Show*'s fifty-fourth episode. Surprisingly, Van Dyke insists that until the night he filmed "The Sam Pomerantz Scandals" he'd never performed his impression of Stan Laurel in public—which only made the actor all the more anxious to hear the great man's response to his tribute, which arrived a few minutes after "The Sam Pomerantz Scandals" received its first network broadcast on March 6, 1963.*

* Though it's unlikely Stan Laurel ever saw it, Dick Van Dyke did log at least one earlier public appearance in the guise of his comedy idol when he performed a remarkably similar Laurel and Hardy sketch—with Chuck McCann in the Hardy role—on the July 24, 1958, broadcast of *The Chevy Showroom Starring Andy Williams.*

"I called him as soon as the show went off the air," Van Dyke would later recall.[2] As the star relayed the conversation to Bob Thomas of the Associated Press, Laurel had been extremely complimentary, offering the younger comedian, in Van Dyke's words, "25 minutes of notes and criticisms."[3] The only element of Van Dyke's act that the screen legend found amiss was the actor's choice of hat, which, in Laurel's opinion, curled a little too sharply at the brim for authenticity's sake. "I did everything I could to get a flat brim like Stan's," Van Dyke observed at the time, "even had the brim pressed out. But it still didn't look right, and Stan said so. 'I would have loaned you mine,' he said. That just killed me."[4]

Van Dyke would stay in contact with his idol until Laurel's death in February 1965, at which time Van Dyke was asked to prepare a eulogy for the legendary screen star—a task that he undertook with an understandable mixture of sadness and pride. Later that same year, Van Dyke was again called upon to pay tribute to Stan Laurel when he hosted a CBS television special honoring Laurel and Hardy—to benefit the Motion Picture Relief Fund—that aired on November 23, 1965.

AFTER AN EIGHT-MONTH stretch that would see the creation of thirty-three entirely new episodes of *The Dick Van Dyke Show*, the show's cast and crew finally wrapped their second production season on April 9, 1963, with the filming of the show's sixty-third episode, "All About Eavesdropping."* But though the *Van Dyke Show*'s cameras had shut down for the season, there would be little rest for the show's star player. A few days later, Dick Van Dyke reported to the Walt Disney studios in Burbank, where the actor would spend the better part of the late spring and summer filming his scenes as Bert the chimney sweep in Disney's musical fantasy *Mary Poppins*, which costarred Julie Andrews.

While many of the show's hardworking cast and crew viewed the show's springtime hiatus as a well-deserved rest from the relentless

---

* Although it was filmed as the last episode of the show's second season, "All About Eavesdropping" would be held over for broadcast until the following year, an efficiency measure designed to give the busy company a one-episode head start when they reported back to begin work on their next season's shows a few months later. This scheduling sleight of hand would be repeated to similar effect at the end of the program's third and fourth seasons as well, when the show's ninety-fifth episode, "My Two Show-Offs and Me" and episode 127, "A Farewell to Writing," would each be filmed at the end of their respective production years and broadcast in the subsequent season.

Despite the tutoring he received on the set, child actor Larry Mathews returned to public school at the end of each production season.

pressures of putting on a weekly television series, for young Larry Mathews the show's final day of shooting marked the start of a routine he found far more stressful than acting: public school. For a youngster who enjoyed the luxury of his own on-set tutor for eight months out of each year, the thought of being thrust back into the world of hallway passes, absence notes, and regimented recess for the final six weeks of each school year was nothing short of demoralizing.

"You go back into school," says Mathews, "and all of a sudden there's a teacher hassling you. When you have a private tutor, one on one, it's real easy to learn, and you can learn quickly. It's much easier than being in a classroom of forty or fifty kids." The fact that Mathews had skipped a grade didn't make the child actor's annual readjustment to public school any easier. "I went from first to third grade," recalls Mathews, "so I was always coming back to children that were older than me in age. And yet, I felt like I was older than them." As Mathews observes, the most difficult challenge of returning to school may have been relearning how to talk to kids his own age. "Every so often I would not be able to relate to the kids in my class, simply because I spent most of my year around adults. And when I would get back in a school situation, it was like regressing."

BY THE TIME the membership of the Academy of Television Arts and Sciences gathered to pass out their annual Emmy Awards on May 26, 1963, they'd already bolstered the spirits of the *Van Dyke Show*'s cast and crew with award nominations in almost every major category for which the show was eligible. Before the awards night was over, Carl Reiner would accept two statuettes, including the Emmy for Outstanding Program Achievement in the Field of Humor, as well as his own second consecutive Emmy for Outstanding Writing Achievement in Comedy. After being left standing at the altar the previous year—when he'd been nominated, but did not win, in the director's category—John Rich was especially gratified to accept the evening's Emmy for Outstanding Directorial Achievement in Comedy.

In the acting categories, Dick Van Dyke was nominated for, but did not receive, the award for Outstanding Continued Performance by an Actor in a Series, which went to E. G. Marshall for his work on *The Defenders*. Mary Tyler Moore also nabbed a nomination for the top acting trophy for an actress, though the Emmy for Outstanding Performance by an Actress in a Series would be won by *Hazel*'s Shirley Booth. Also nominated for an acting trophy that evening was Rose Marie, who faced especially stiff competition in the supporting actress category, where the comedic performer was at a distinct disadvantage in a field dominated by actresses in traditionally showy dramatic roles. Although Rose Marie could take pride in the fact that she'd been the only comedy player to earn a nomination in the extremely competitive supporting actress category, the award for Outstanding Performance in a Supporting Role by an Actress would go to Glenda Farrell, who was recognized for her dramatic turn as a guest star on an episode of *Ben Casey*.

22

UNLIKELY SAVIORS

By the start of the show's third year, there could be little doubt that Carl Reiner's efforts as the head writer, producer, story editor, and resident genius behind *The Dick Van Dyke Show* had paid off in handsome dividends. The series had achieved success beyond anything its creator ever dreamed when he sat down to pound out the first draft of his *Head of the Family* pilot script on Fire Island five summers before.

After spending its first season as a dark horse in the weekly Nielsen sweepstakes, *The Dick Van Dyke Show* had bounded into the top twenty near the start of its second year, where it would remain throughout the rest of its five-year run. Even more impressive was the fact that, after two years on the air, *The Dick Van Dyke Show* had earned the near-unanimous endorsement of television critics across the land, many of whom took pleasure in citing the show as the leading exemplar of that rarest of prime-time programming forms: a situation comedy for grown-ups. Equally heartening to the show's creator/producer was the unstinting support he'd received from his peers within the industry, who had thus far honored his show with four Emmy Awards—with many more to come.

Bill Persky and Sam Denoff, the writers Carl Reiner credits with saving his life, are seated on either side of the show's associate producer Ronald Jacobs and fellow Desilu Cahuenga writer Jack Elinson, who's holding the script in this snapshot. *Courtesy: Ronald Jacobs*

Although Reiner's ceaseless devotion to *The Dick Van Dyke Show* during its first two seasons had yielded a show of exceeding vibrancy, the effect of those labors on his personal well-being wasn't nearly so salutary. In fact, the producer would later insist, it practically killed him. "If I hadn't found someone to help me in that third year," he would one day observe, "I wouldn't be here. I would've had a heart attack."

Which may explain why Reiner ascribes such importance to the addition of a pair of writers named Bill Persky and Sam Denoff to his staff at the start of the show's third season—an arrival that the producer insists came not a moment too soon. "Bill Persky and Sam Denoff," asserts Reiner, "saved my life." Even so, he acknowledges, the young writers hardly appeared to be knights in shining armor the day they arrived on his doorstep, with a sample script in hand, in 1962. In fact, when the pair approached the producer with their earliest *Van Dyke Show* tryout script late in the show's second season, they had never written a situation comedy before—or much of anything else, for that matter.

Persky and Denoff became a comedy-writing team in the late fifties, after meeting at New York's WNEW radio, where they'd worked together in the programming department. Like many comedy writers of the late fifties, the pair got their start as joke writers, contributing material and routines to Don Rickles and other nightclub comics of the era. Lured to California by the promise of writing jobs on Steve Allen's short-lived 1961 variety show, the pair would spend the next two years drifting through a wide array of short-term assignments, including a one-season stint as sketch writers on NBC's *Andy Williams Show*. "We had some odd jobs," says Denoff, recalling their early years in Los Angeles, "and stood in a lot of unemployment lines."

Considering their skimpy professional resumes, it's a wonder Persky and Denoff managed to get in to see Reiner at all. But then, it probably didn't hurt that the team's agent at the William Morris office was Reiner's close friend, adviser, and nephew by marriage, George Shapiro, an aggressive booster of talent who was not above using his privileged position to land his young clients a meeting with the busy producer. "You're gonna love these guys," Shapiro promised Reiner as he handed him the sample *Van Dyke Show* script that the team had prepared. "They've written a funny, funny script."

"All right," sighed Reiner, who decided to reserve judgment until he'd read the script himself. Not that he had any reason to doubt Shapiro—but, after two years of combing through freelance *Van Dyke Show* submissions, experience had taught the producer not to expect much. And, alas, Persky and Denoff's initial effort hardly gave Reiner cause to revise those expectations.

"They wrote a show that was so wrong," observes Reiner, recalling Persky and Denoff's writing sample. "It was a battle of the sexes kind of thing," he elaborates, "and it wasn't funny—at least not my kind of funny. And, if it wasn't my kind of funny, I didn't care how funny it might be to someone else—it wasn't right for the show." But despite his harsh judgment of their work, as a favor to Shapiro, Reiner agreed to meet Persky and Denoff for what turned out to be a very short conference. In the producer's recollection, his first meeting with the pair consisted of little more than a couple of handshakes and a few polite words of rejection. "I just said, 'No, it's not right for us,'" says Reiner.

As Denoff recalls it, Reiner's summary dismissal of their earliest attempt at writing a situation comedy came as a painful blow, especially since—after nearly two years of irregular employment as variety show writers—the team had been anxious to make the leap to the more respectable arena of situation comedy. "We wanted to be more like real writers," remembers Denoff, "rather than sketch guys."

Determined to learn from their mistakes, the writers sat down and analyzed their rejected *Van Dyke Show* script line by line, joke by joke—and quickly came to the sobering conclusion that Reiner's assessment of their work had not been far off the mark. "Basically," admits Denoff, "it was a stupid script." Their biggest error, he recalls, was writing a sample script that failed to capture the show's specific comic rhythms and tone. "That's what happens with a lot of writers. They look at something on television and they say, 'Oh, this is what it is!' But they miss the point." Which is exactly the trap that Denoff and his partner fell into when they set out to write their initial *Van Dyke Show* sample. "We didn't understand what they were going for on that show."

Resolving not to make that error a second time, the pair began studying *The Dick Van Dyke Show*'s weekly broadcasts with an almost scientific concentration. Sitting in front of their television sets each Wednesday night, they examined the show's storylines, dissected the jokes, and analyzed the dialogue until they were as familiar with the program's characters as anyone this side of Carl Reiner himself.

In addition to their self-taught Wednesday-night seminars, Persky and Denoff continued to hone their situation-comedy writing skills by contributing freelance scripts to other sitcoms of the era, including *McHale's Navy* and *The Joey Bishop Show*, among others. Although happy for the work, the writers couldn't fail to notice that none of the other sitcoms they wrote for demanded a fraction of the wit, intelligence, and craft on display in any given episode of *The Dick Van Dyke Show*. Finally, their frustration mounting, the writers felt they could defer their dream no longer. "We decided," says Denoff, "why write for these other kinds of shows? We wanted to write for *Dick Van Dyke*. So we decided that we would try and go back to Carl again."

They called George Shapiro, who called Carl Reiner.

"George came to me," recalls Reiner. "And he said, 'They watch the show, they know what your sensibility is now. They know who your people are. And they got a great idea for a show. Promise me you'll go talk to them.'"

"So we got a meeting with Carl," Denoff continues. "And we went in with a shopping list of ideas." But, as it turned out, Reiner was hooked on their very first pitch. "We want to do a flashback episode," Persky proposed, before launching into a detailed outline of a story that takes place in the days immediately following Ritchie's birth, a comedy of errors in which Rob becomes convinced that he and Laura have been given the wrong baby. "I don't remember where the mixed-up babies idea came from," recalls Denoff. "But Carl liked the idea."

"They came in with the baby show," concurs the producer, "and I said, 'Oh boy! This is heaven!'"

A few days after Reiner gave the story his go-ahead, Persky and Denoff reconvened in the producer's office for their first full-fledged story conference with Reiner and Sheldon Leonard, which is where, the writers recall, their real education began. "Bill and I started pitching how we would do the story," recalls Denoff, "and then Carl and Sheldon broke the story down, scene by scene by scene by scene. We weren't talking dialogue—unless, once in while, a joke or an idea would come up, and then we'd write it down." But, as Reiner reminded them more than once that afternoon, the purpose of that initial session was simply to hammer out a road map for the writers to follow once they went off to start writing the script on their own. "And," says Denoff, "we didn't leave the office until Carl and Sheldon were satisfied that we had that structure."

With their story outline in hand, Persky and Denoff went right to work, driving directly from the Desilu Cahuenga lot to their office, which in those days was a tiny cubicle that the pair rented in a rundown West Hollywood office building at 8228 Sunset Boulevard. "Neither of us could ever write at home," explains Denoff, who still chuckles at the thought of their first abysmal office, a windowless room whose most arresting feature was a wall-sized mural of Japan's Mount Fuji mounted behind a set of venetian blinds, presumably to give the impression that the volcano was just outside the nonexistent window. Although the room was barely wide enough to contain their single desk and chair, the young writers took solace in the fact that their office was one of the few in the building to

Executive producer Sheldon Leonard menaced his cast, in character, when he played Big Max Calvada in an early Persky and Denoff script.

have its own private bathroom—which Persky and Denoff soon came to view as an extension of their hopelessly inadequate workspace. "One of us literally had to sit in the bathroom while the other one sat at the desk typing," recalls Denoff.

"Sam sat at the typewriter," reminisces Persky, picking up his partner's description of their early work routine. "And we'd talk through the script. We'd play all the parts—just talking it out, back and forth, like a conversation. We'd type stuff, and then we'd go back and fix it." "And," adds Denoff, "after we wrote it, we rewrote it. And rewrote it. With all the great pain that you go through when you're trying to get something right that you want to be right. We just stayed in that room and wrote the script—with one guy sitting at the chair and the other guy in the bathroom."

After three or four weeks of these painstaking labors, Persky and Denoff finally had a script that they felt was good enough to show Reiner. The only problem was that their script ran about ten pages longer than the standard half-hour teleplay. "We knew it was too long," notes Denoff, "but we didn't know what to cut. We wanted to leave in all this wonderful stuff that we wrote." After making one more futile attempt to edit the script, they finally decided to turn it in as it was and let their producer decide what to delete. And so, on May 22, 1963, Persky and Denoff delivered a slightly long draft of their first script for *The Dick Van Dyke Show*, "That's My Boy??"

Then came the hard part.

"We sat in our office and waited," recalls Denoff. "And we waited. And waited. We were going crazy, just waiting to find out whether Carl liked it." Finally, says Denoff, after two or three days that seemed positively endless, the phone rang.

Rob and Laura leave the hospital with their new baby—or is it?—in "That's My Boy??"

"I remember it like it was yesterday," says Persky, recalling that life-changing phone call. "Sam sat at the little typewriter table, and I was sitting in the hall." A few seconds after Denoff picked up the receiver, he shot a glance at his partner. "It's Carl!" he whispered. "And he's read the script!"

"We both held our breath," continues Persky. "And then Sam started to smile, and he said, 'Oh my God! That's great!'" Denoff still remembers Reiner's exact words. "Carl said, 'Fellas, it swings! It's terrific!'" Moments later, the jubilant Denoff hung up the phone and leapt to his feet to embrace his partner in a celebratory hug. "We laughed," says Denoff, "and then we did whatever dance we could do in that limited space."

CARL REINER WOULD hardly be alone in his admiration for "That's My Boy??," one of those *Dick Van Dyke Show* episodes that seems to have found its way onto the ten-best lists of almost everyone involved with the series. A no-less-discerning critic than John Rich—who had returned to direct this and the following three episodes as his valedictory run on the show—lists "That's My Boy??" among the top two or three *Dick Van Dyke Show* episodes of all time. And it's not hard to see why.

An unofficial sequel to the saga of Ritchie's birth outlined in the show's nineteenth episode, "Where Did I Come From?," "That's My Boy??" traces Rob and Laura's adjustment to parenthood in the days that follow Laura's arrival home from the maternity ward.

The comic complications set in almost immediately, as Rob gets it into his head that, owing to a clerical mix-up at the hospital, he and Laura have somehow arrived home with someone else's baby. Try as she might, Laura is unable to dissuade her husband from his preposterous assumption. "Do you know that one out of every fifty million women has the wrong baby?" Rob asks his skeptical wife. "That's a cute trick," she answers, unfazed. "How does she manage it?"

Rob finally gets his comeuppance later that evening, when he comes face to face with Mr. and Mrs. Peters, the couple whose child he's sure that the hospital has switched with their own. But it's only after the other parents arrive at his doorstep that Rob recognizes the magnitude of his error. For, as becomes obvious the minute the visiting couple walks into his living room, there's simply no way the hospital could've confused their baby with Rob and Laura's—because Mr. and Mrs. Peters are black!

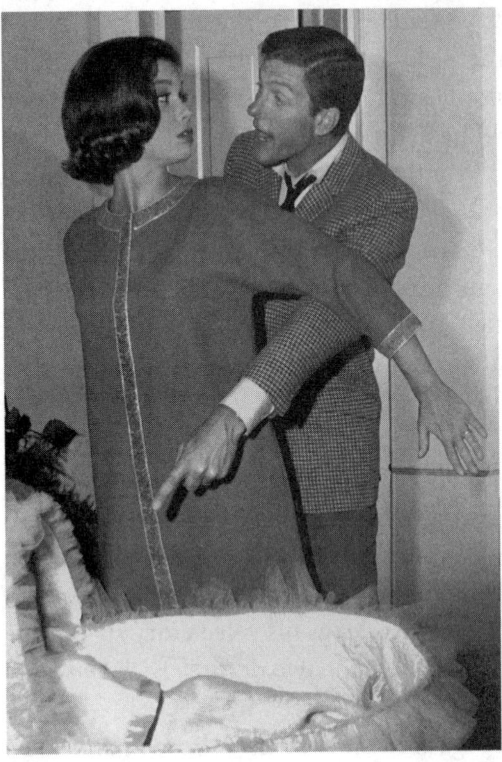

Rob insists that he and Laura took home the wrong baby in "That's My Boy??," the inaugural *Dick Van Dyke Show* script by Bill Persky and Sam Denoff.

"Why didn't you tell me on the phone?" Rob stammers to his guest, who's clearly enjoying the spectacle of Rob's embarrassment. "And miss the expression on your face?" replies Peters, savoring the moment to the last.

Rob's stunned reaction to his guests' arrival was indeed a sight to be savored. The flabbergasted take that Van Dyke summoned for the black couple's climactic entrance would stand as one of the actor's crowning achievements—a brilliantly modulated take in which his character's protean foolishness is revealed in the actor's deft combination of shock, relief, and, finally, bewildered embarrassment. Judged purely by the length of the riotous ovation that greeted the entrance of actors Greg Morris and Mimi Dillard on the night the show was filmed, many *Van Dyke Show* staffers identify that scene as the funniest single moment of the entire series. "That," maintains Van Dyke, "to my recollection, is by far the longest laugh we ever got."

Yet, according to Sheldon Leonard, until just a few hours before showtime, it looked doubtful that the scene would make it before the cameras at all. In one of the strangest behind-the-scenes ironies of the entire series, the sight gag that would provide *The Dick Van Dyke Show* with its longest single laugh was filmed under protest from the show's sponsor and the CBS network itself.

"Procter & Gamble had been very frightened about that episode," observed Leonard, who recalled that he got his first whiff of an impending storm at the show's Friday-night run-through, which was, as always, attended by representatives of the show's sponsors. As Leonard remembered the events of that evening, his actors had barely left the stage before an emissary from Procter & Gamble approached him to voice his reservations about what he'd just seen. According to Leonard, the sponsor's worries were well intentioned, if completely misguided.

After watching the show's climactic twist, the sponsor was convinced that viewers would misinterpret the producer's intentions and assume that the black couple was the butt of a joke. "It's gonna look like we're making fun of the black man," the sponsor complained. To which the executive producer quickly replied, "No, it's not! It's gonna look like we're making fun of Van Dyke, because he's an idiot! The black man is smarter, more self-contained. And he has more dignity."

Leonard's reasoned argument seemed to placate the sponsor for the time being, and it was finally decided that Procter & Gamble would defer to the producer's judgment. Thinking the issue settled, Leonard went on to other matters. But as the executive producer might have guessed, the controversy surrounding the episode was not about to go away. That much became clear the following Tuesday afternoon, when—with only hours to go before the show was to be filmed—Leonard heard from an anxious CBS executive who'd developed a bad case of cold feet. "Won't people think we're ridiculing the black couple?" the well-meaning network executive queried.

With time running short, Leonard decided not to argue the point, but instead offered a compromise. Why not, he proposed, let the audience judge? The executive producer suggested they simply allow the cast to perform the show as written when the audience arrived that evening. If at that time, even *one* member of the crowd failed to embrace the show's closing gag—if anyone in the stands let out so much as a single groan when Greg Morris and Mimi Dillard made their entrance—the executive producer promised to reshoot the entire ending, at his own expense, in any fashion the network dictated.

With showtime looming ever closer, the network agreed to Leonard's compromise, and the climax of "That's My Boy??" was filmed, exactly as written. And, just as Leonard predicted, no one in the gallery groaned, moaned, or otherwise complained. But they did laugh. And laugh. And laugh, until, finally, the audience registered what many feel was the longest laugh in the show's history. And no one from the network ever mentioned Leonard's offer to reshoot the ending.*

Director Rich insists he never had a moment's doubt that the sight gag that ends "That's My Boy??" would deliver a whopping response—and his sense of confidence was apparent in the last-minute instructions he offered to Greg Morris and Mimi Dillard just before the episode went in front of the cameras. "I told Greg and Mimi to wait for the laugh," recalls the director. "I said, 'Just walk in, let Dick do the take, and then stand there.' And I told Greg Morris, 'The only mistake you can make is to speak too soon after Dick's initial reaction.'"

It was good advice. According to Rich, the prolonged ovation that followed the entrance of the black actors was like nothing he'd ever heard. "First there was a gasp," he recalls. "Then there was a laugh. And then protracted applause. And that applause was the most gratifying sound I'd ever heard in my life. It was just wonderful. It was quite a piece of vindication."

In Van Dyke's recollection, the laughter went on so long that he began to feel the queer sensation, in his own words, of "being suspended in time." "They would not stop laughing," he recalls. "We stood there forever." The audience's thunderous ovation was so extensive, in fact, that film editor Bud Molin had to cut it down for the finished episode. The response, the editor recalled, was so protracted that it threw the show's timing off, with the result that he was forced to lop a few precious seconds of laughter from the finished show in order to squeeze the scene into the allotted running time. And so, ironically, when viewers at home finally got a chance to see the episode on the air, they were treated to *The Dick Van Dyke Show*'s longest laugh ever . . . give or take a few seconds.

---

* Ironically, though the network acquiesced to the executive producer's wishes on the racial gag, director John Rich remembers another punch line—equally innocuous by today's standards—that failed to make it past the show's various censors in 1963. The joke in question originally occurred during the exchange where Rob is chiding Laura for trying to do too much as they're preparing to leave the hospital. "Honey, you shouldn't exert yourself," he cautions, reaching for the babe in arms. "You'd better not carry the baby." In the version that was shot, Laura dutifully hands the infant over. But, in the episode's original script, Laura's response to her husband's solicitousness is far more pointed—and much funnier. "I carried him for nine months," Laura answers. "I think I can carry him out of the building." Although the line got a resounding laugh at every one of the show's early run-throughs, it was finally deemed unacceptably suggestive by the CBS Standards and Practices Department, which insisted that the line be dropped entirely before the episode was filmed—a demand to which Reiner and his writers reluctantly complied.

23

CHANGING OF THE GUARD

Carl Reiner knew the minute he read Persky and Denoff's first draft of "That's My Boy??" that the writers had crafted a first-rate script. The plotting was good, the jokes were clever, and the script's style and pacing were right on the money. But what had impressed the producer more than anything else was how closely Persky and Denoff's script resembled one of his own. And for the overworked story editor, producer, and chief scriptwriter of *The Dick Van Dyke Show*, that was cause for celebration.

Indeed, it was a dream come true. After two years of trolling through freelance story submissions to dredge up raw material for the show; after the countless story conferences that had been required to structure and polish that material; and after the dozens of last-minute rewrite sessions that were necessary to get those scripts into shape—the weary producer's prayers had been answered. Here, at last, was a pair of writers who could craft a workable *Dick Van Dyke Show* script from the ground up! Even more significantly, in Bill Persky and Sam Denoff, Reiner recognized a pair of young, hardworking writers who could—with a little faith, patience, and guidance—be trained to serve as the show's full-time story editors. Which is exactly what he had in mind.

As Persky remembers it, the producer left little doubt that he had big plans for his young proteges. "Carl told us our first script was great," recalls Persky. "And then he asked us to write as many shows for him as we could handle. And that's when everything changed for us."

The initial terms of Persky and Denoff's employment on the series were quite modest. As the producer explained to them, his budgetary restrictions were such that he couldn't afford to pay the writers a salary beyond the script fees they would earn for every episode they actually wrote.* Even so, the producer promised, if the writers were willing to hang around the studio and listen and learn as much as they could about the show and the way it was put together, he would guarantee them a rent-free office on the lot, and as many script assignments as they could handle.

Were they interested?

It took the writers all of two hours to move their typewriter over from the cubicle they rented on Sunset Boulevard to their brand-new office on the ground floor of the Desilu Cahuenga studio's Building A. Ironically, it was only after they'd taken up residence on the lot that it dawned on the writers that their new space wasn't much of an improvement over their former digs. "The office they gave us was from, like, 1920," recalls Denoff. "It was painted a dingy green," he continues. "And everything stunk. It smelled like some silent movie star had died in there."

But as the writers cheerfully acknowledged, whatever their new office may have lacked in amenities was more than made up for by its proximity to Reiner, whose office was not far from theirs. According to the producer, that was no accident. "I put them next door to me," says Reiner, "so I would be able to walk in the room every day and stop them if they started going in the wrong direction." And, as Persky observes, he and his partner had no qualms about working under the watchful eye of so attentive a mentor. "It was a wonderful education," says Persky, who looks back on his years as a writer and story editor for *The Dick Van Dyke Show* as the most reward-

---

* Incredible as it seems—considering the amount of material that Persky and Denoff would generate during the show's final three seasons—the writers would not actually be under contract to the show until well into the series' fifth year, when they were engaged to fill in as producers during a brief leave of absence by Reiner. Prior to then, the team was paid strictly on a per-script basis, at prevailing fees that hovered in the neighborhood of $3,000 for a finished first-draft script, with an additional $1,500 for a second-draft rewrite or final polish of their own or another writer's script. Of course, like any other *Van Dyke Show* writers—including Reiner—Persky and Denoff would also collect nominal residual payments for the initial rerun cycles of the episodes that carried their names as primary writers.

Director John Rich walks into a surprise party after his final night on the show. *Courtesy: John Rich*

ing period of his career. It's a sentiment that's echoed by his former writing partner. "It was utopia," observes Denoff. "A situation comedy writer's utopia."

IN ONE OF those ironies that are common in the mercurial world of television, Bill Persky and Sam Denoff began their association with *The Dick Van Dyke Show* in August 1963, the same month that John Rich would end his own long and fruitful tenure as the show's director. Rich, who had left the series some months earlier to pursue opportunities in the feature-film arena, had taken advantage of a four-week gap in his movie directing activities to shoot his last four episodes of the show at the start of season three.

By odd coincidence, the director would film his final *Van Dyke Show* episode, "Very Old Shoes, Very Old Rice," on August 27, 1963, the night before his first feature film, Paramount's *Wives and Lovers*, had its world premiere in New York City. "That last episode was particularly emotional," says Rich, "I knew that I had done very nice work with a very extraordinary group of people. And now I was leaving them."

The cast, who shared Rich's melancholy on the eve of his departure, decided to commemorate the occasion by throwing a surprise party for their departing general at the end of his final night of service. According to Rich's account of that memorable evening, he didn't know what a surprise was until he'd been surprised by that gang. As the evening's filming drew to a close, the director—still without a clue to the revelries that his cast was planning for him later that night—became concerned at his company's apparent lack of sentiment on what was, for him, a very difficult night. "I said, 'Cut! That's a wrap,'" recalls Rich, "and then everybody just kind of drifted away. There were a lot of quick, 'G'bye, g'bye's,' and then suddenly, I was all alone on the stage."

By then thoroughly confused by his cast's uncharacteristic diffidence, the director resigned himself to a bittersweet exit and started gathering his personal belongings from the now deserted soundstage. "I thought, 'Gee, everyone's gone home, and we never got a chance to mark the occasion,'" the director recalls. "It was sad. But that's show business." Then, just as the director's melancholia threatened to get the better of him, Van Dyke stepped out from the shadows of the darkened studio—right on cue.

"Dick came out of his dressing room," Rich continues, "and he said, 'Hey, John, you still here?' I said, 'Yeah, yeah. I'm feeling a little nostalgic.' He said, 'Yeah, me too. You want to go across the street and have a beer?' Naturally, I jumped at the chance."

A few minutes later, recalls the director, the pair arrived at a neighborhood watering hole not far from the studio. "When I came through that door with Dick," exclaims Rich, "my mouth dropped open four feet." For there, jammed elbow to elbow into every available corner of the tiny neighborhood tavern stood the entire cast and crew of *The Dick Van Dyke Show*—along with a few dozen other well-wishers—all standing with their mugs raised high in cheerful salute to their beloved director. "It was

The cast cuts the cake at John Rich's farewell party, which was convened on August 27, 1963, immediately following the filming of the director's valedictory episode, "Very Old Shoes, Very Old Rice."

a remarkable send-off party," Rich observes, and a perfect capper to two of the director's most rewarding years in television. "Those were really among my happiest days," notes Rich, "I must say, in the theater."

With Rich's departure now official, Leonard and Reiner began to give serious thought to choosing his permanent replacement. With ten first-rate episodes already under his belt by the start of the show's third year, Jerry Paris seemed the obvious choice to inherit the mantle from Rich. Or so thought the show's cast, who made no secret of their preference for Paris when the time came to pick Rich's successor. "They used to complain whenever we brought anyone else in to direct," recalls Reiner, who was finally only too happy to accede to his acting company's demands. And so, a few weeks into the show's third season, Paris finally landed his sought-after appointment as the second—and, as it would turn out, final—house director of *The Dick Van Dyke Show.*

No one was more pleased to see Paris finally achieve his due than his longtime friend and Pacific Palisades neighbor Ann Guilbert, who recalls that the only downside to Paris's promotion was that it cost her a car-pooling partner. "When we were both just acting, we'd be in the same scenes," recalls the actress, "so I would usually drive down with Jerry." But once Paris took on the more labor-intensive duties of director, the actress found herself making the thirteen-mile trek from the Palisades into Hollywood on her own. "Sometimes Jerry would have to stay late," says Guilbert. "And I just didn't feel like hanging out."

In the second week of November 1963, the cast of the *Van Dyke Show* put a fresh spin on the series' variety-show format when they filmed their first—and only—holiday episode, "The Alan Brady Show Presents." In the clever show-within-a-show premise that writers Persky and Denoff concocted for the episode, Alan Brady decides to turn the asylum over to the inmates when he invites Rob and his staff—aided and abetted by Laura, Mel, and Ritchie—to create and stage the holiday edition of *The Alan Brady Show* on their own, a paper-thin premise that nonetheless provided the framework for one of the series' most satisfying variety-show episodes.

Drawing on skills they'd honed during their stint as writers for musical star Andy Williams, Persky and Denoff crafted a half-hour of specialty material for the show's versatile cast—including a handful of songs composed especially for this episode. "It was a welcome change from the ordinary half-hour show," says Denoff.

Although the writers were accorded a rare on-screen credit as composers of the show's entire program of songs, Persky and Denoff admit they had nothing to do with the composition of the episode's rousing finale, "The Musicians." The delightful musical number—in which each of the cast members, in turn, takes on the persona of a marching band instrument—made its *Van Dyke Show* debut some nine months earlier, when it was a high point of the show's fifty-fourth episode, "The Sam Pomerantz Scandals." But, according to Van Dyke, the origin of the song goes back even further than that.

"I suggested that song," says Van Dyke, who recalls that he first heard the catchy little ditty on a novelty record that he found when he was scouting material for a kids' TV show he hosted in Atlanta in 1953.* "I did little mimes and sketches on the show," the star explains. "And I had a little band, and we used to do that song." A decade later, when the performer was looking for musical selections to fill out the show's fifty-fourth episode, he suddenly remembered the bouncy little tune, which turned out to be such an ideal fit for the show's cast that they revived it again for this holiday special. The original record's composition was credited to songwriters Tom Glazer and Charles Randolph Grean, who were no doubt thrilled to see their novelty song achieve instant immortality by its inclusion in not *one* but *two* episodes of *The Dick Van Dyke Show*. "It's funny how long that little song has lasted," observes Van Dyke, "*everybody* knows that song."

Another fascinating sidelight to the filming of the *Van Dyke Show*'s Christmas installment is that—despite the camera crew's diligent efforts to re-create the live ambience of a TV variety spectacular—"The Alan Brady Show Presents" was, ironically enough, one of the few episodes of the series to be filmed without a live audience in attendance. With six full-costume musical numbers and a flashback scene set in the writers' office, the *Van Dyke Show* producers recognized that it would be impractical to film the technically demanding episode straight through for a live audience. And so

---

* Although "The Musicians" made its first appearance in the United States on a 1949 collection of folk songs released on the Young People's Records label—where it was identified as a folk song of German origin with English lyrics by Raymond Abrashkin—the version that inspired Dick Van Dyke was almost certainly a 1951 RCA Victor recording of the song by Dinah Shore, Betty Hutton, Tony Martin, and Phil Harris, who sing an arrangement almost identical to the one that later appeared on *The Dick Van Dyke Show*. Although that 1951 recording was credited to songwriters Tom Glazer and Charles Grean, the song's roots as a European folk tune suggest that "The Musicians" may well have been around, in one form or another, for hundreds of years before Van Dyke finally stumbled upon it in 1953.

Before it became a *Van Dyke Show* standard, "The Musicians" was an early-fifties novelty record that Dick Van Dyke found when he was hosting a kids' TV show in Atlanta. *Courtesy: David Bonner*

the decision was made to shoot the episode scene-by-scene, with no audience present. "That one was shot piecemeal on a different stage," recalls Larry Mathews, "because of the way we had to edit the show together."

Although the cast didn't know it when this episode was filmed, "The Alan Brady Show Presents" would not be the last *Van Dyke Show* of that season to be filmed without a studio audience. In fact, just two weeks later, the company would choose to perform another episode to an empty house, though in that case the decision to do so was made under more sobering circumstances. Three days into rehearsals for the episode titled "Happy Birthday and Too Many More," the world was shocked by the news that the thirty-fifth president of the United States had been shot in a Dallas motorcade. By the time the company regrouped to film the episode four days later, they were hardly surprised to discover that nobody was in much of a mood for laughing—onstage or off.

24

PLAYING TO AN EMPTY HOUSE

When news of the Kennedy assassination reached the cast of *The Dick Van Dyke Show* on the morning of November 22, 1963, they were already on stage rehearsing the opening scenes of "Happy Birthday and Too Many More," an elaborately silly exercise that revolved around Rob and Laura's efforts to keep sixty-three unruly kids entertained at Ritchie's birthday party. As Carl Reiner remembers it, the cast had just started to walk through a scene when Glenn Ross, the show's prop man, emerged from his backstage office, ashen-faced and sweating.

"He's been shot . . ." Ross announced in slow, even tones addressed to no one in particular.

"What?" asked Reiner, looking up from his script. "*Who?* Who's been shot?"

"The president . . ." came the prop man's response. "Kennedy."

Audible gasps swept through the studio, as the cast instinctively moved to the closest radio, which was just offstage, in the prop man's tiny office. There, crowded shoulder to shoulder amidst the incongruous collection of party hats and tin horns that the prop man had gathered for the upcoming episode, the cast of *The Dick Van Dyke Show* stood in horrified silence as the announcer intoned the devastating details of the tragedy in Dallas. "The guy on the radio said the president had died at one o'clock," recalls Rose Marie. "And then we all just looked at one another."

After a very long pause, Reiner broke the stony silence when he dropped his script on the prop man's cluttered desk and turned to leave. "Well, that's it for today," he announced. "Ain't no one gonna get any more work done. Let's go home."

"I called my husband," says Rose Marie, remembering the sense of desolation that gripped the entire company that morning. "I told him, 'I'm coming home.' And then everybody drove home crying."

In one of the day's stranger ironies, director Jerry Paris had already planned to take the afternoon off. Earlier that week, Paris had cast his seven-year-old son, Tony, in a bit part as one of the guests at the party in that week's episode—and the director had already set the remainder of that Friday afternoon aside to register Tony with the Social Security office in preparation for his first day of work that Monday. "It was the first job I'd ever had," recalls Tony Paris, who confesses that he was too young to grasp the significance of the day's events at the time.

"My dad was obviously shaken when he picked me up at school," recalls the younger Paris. "And the next thing I knew, we were driving around Hollywood, getting all this business stuff taken care of with Social Security, and joining the Screen Actors Guild and all that. I just remember my dad taking me down to this office where you had to sign all these papers. And all I knew was that something really horrible had happened that day."

Dick Van Dyke and Mary Tyler Moore in "Happy Birthday and Too Many More," one of a handful of shows filmed without a studio audience.

In the wake of the tragedy, the *Van Dyke Show*'s producers were understandably concerned that the events in Dallas might have a less-than-positive effect on their audience's morale at the filming that was scheduled to take place the following Tuesday night. Over the weekend, Reiner and executive producer Sheldon Leonard considered canceling the week's episode altogether. But finally, invoking the oldest show business maxim of all, Reiner and his producing partner agreed that the show would go on—though, under the circumstances, it was decided that it would go on without the benefit of a live studio audience. As much as he bristled at the thought, Reiner reluctantly agreed to use canned laughter on the episode's soundtrack, the assumption being that even prerecorded laughs would be preferable to the shell-shocked response they were likely to elicit from any live audience they would get that week.

On the Monday following the Kennedy assassination, the cast and crew regrouped to resume rehearsals for "Happy Birthday and Too Many More." And, as anyone who was there will attest, the show's final two days of rehearsal were certainly no party. "We just sat around all week in a stupor," recalls Van Dyke. "There *was* a pretty somber mood on the set," concurs Tony Paris. But even discounting the cast's emotional state, Paris insists that "Happy Birthday and Too Many More" would have been a difficult shoot even under the best of circumstances.

"There were forty kids on the set that day," explains Paris, referring to the large number of child extras who'd been brought in for the episode's birthday party scene. "And almost all of them were really high strung."

Given the high level of hyperactivity shared by the cast of underaged extras, Tony Paris recalls that his father didn't have to push them very hard to incite the state of pandemonium required for the sequence where the kids run rampant through the Petrie house. In fact, according to Paris, at least one of the show's high-spirited extras seemed to spend the better part of his two days on the set in preparation for that sequence. "There was this one kid who just kept running around the set screaming," says Paris. "Literally screaming! I really grew to hate that kid."

"The show didn't turn out that badly on the air," maintains Van Dyke, offering an even-handed assessment of "Happy Birthday and Too Many More" that would be shared by few others among the show's cast and crew, most of whom were only too eager to put their ill-fated seventy-eighth episode behind them. "That was a pretty bad episode," acknowledges Tony Paris. “But even if Kennedy hadn’t been killed,” he adds, “it probably still would have been a pretty bad show.”

AFTER THE LOGISTICAL trials of the Christmas episode and the tumultuous complications that attended the filming of the birthday party show a few weeks later, the company was greatly relieved to discover that their very next episode would be a mercifully straightforward comedy of domestic manners titled “The Lady and the Tiger and the Lawyer.” The episode’s brisk storyline pits Rob against Laura in an ill-fated competition to find a suitable mate for the seemingly perfect bachelor who just moved in down the street. Laura sides with her maiden cousin, Donna, while Rob submits Sally Rogers as the natural matrimonial choice. An awkward romantic triangle results when the bachelor appears to be equally smitten with both of them—an intriguing dilemma that is resolved rather abruptly when the bachelor confesses that he won’t be calling either woman again, on doctor’s orders. “I have this bad, bad temper,” he confesses. “I’m prone to hit people that I love.” Until he gets his problem under control, he explains, his therapist has suggested he never date any woman more than once.

The episode’s bizarre resolution aside, what makes “The Lady and the Tiger and the Lawyer” a noteworthy entry in the annals of *The Dick Van Dyke Show* is that it was the first episode written for the series by Garry Marshall and Jerry Belson, two writers whose work would make a substantial impression on the show. Like so many of the outstanding comedy writing talents of their era, Belson and Marshall honed their craft writing sitcoms on the Desilu Cahuenga lot in the early 1960s. Garry Marshall

Mary Tyler Moore confers with associate producer Ronald Jacobs during a lull, while director Jerry Paris looks on from the couch. *Courtesy: Ronald Jacobs*

hailed from New York, where he'd earned a respectable living as a joke writer for Jack Paar and some of the era's more popular nightclub comics, including Joey Bishop. In 1962, Bishop lured Marshall to the West Coast with a job offer to write for *The Joey Bishop Show*, a Sheldon Leonard sitcom filmed on the Desilu Cahuenga lot. It was there that Marshall met Jerry Belson, a would-be comedy writer in his early twenties who'd earned his entree to the lot on the strength of a sample script he'd tossed over Leonard's transom in early 1962. According to legend, it was Leonard's inspiration to pair Belson and Marshall as a team. But in later years, Belson admitted that that's not exactly how it happened.

"Garry and I already knew each other," the writer confessed. In fact, Belson acknowledged that he and Marshall had already decided to form a writing partnership when the producers of *The Dick Van Dyke Show* brought the pair together for what Leonard and Reiner thought was the future writing team's first meeting—an illusion that the young writers did little to dispel. "Sheldon and Carl wanted it to seem like they put us together," Belson explained, "so we pretended like we'd never met."

Whatever its origin, the team of Belson and Marshall would prove to be a most fortuitous pairing. Over the course of the *Van Dyke Show*'s final three seasons, Garry Marshall and Jerry Belson would contribute eighteen scripts to the show, including the texts for such classic episodes as "Talk to the Snail," "Odd But True," "No Rice at My Wedding," "Baby Fat," and at least a half-dozen other shows that are among the series' smartest half hours. "They were really funny, brilliant guys," observes Reiner, who admits that Belson and Marshall's only real shortcoming as writers was that they shared a common weakness for one-liners.

"They loved jokes," remarks Reiner, who was never quite sure if the team's dazzling facility for the comic one-two punch was an asset or a liability on his character-driven series. "You had to watch them," says Reiner, "because they could slip in a joke that would destroy your character in a minute. And we had to be very careful of that."

When Reiner ran across a joke that he didn't approve of, observed Belson, he could be ruthlessly direct in communicating his displeasure. "When Carl didn't like something in your script, he'd write 'RR' next to the joke." As Belson discovered shortly after he got one of his own early scripts back from the producer and noticed the curious annotation scrawled liberally throughout the margins, the dreaded initials were Carl Reiner's shorthand for "rotten 'riting." "It meant you'd written a bad joke," said Belson, who would cringe whenever the mark appeared on one of his and Marshall's submissions. "Carl was such a nice guy, he'd never tell you that you stunk. That's why we always hated to see that little 'RR' in the margin when we got our scripts back from Carl."

Belson recalled that another one of the producer's favorite self-coined literary appellations was "the realie," a term that, as defined by Reiner, referred to any one of the countless moments of carefully observed reality that the producer insisted his writers include in their scripts for the show. "He was always saying, 'We need more realies! Give me more realies!'" Belson recalled. "Carl would ask us, 'How do you use that rubber thing on the end of a toothbrush? Well, put that in the show!'"

As the writer soon discovered, his producer's thirst for such privileged moments of reality was all but unquenchable. "Carl didn't care about funny," Belson insisted, "he wanted realies. If you sat down with Carl, instead of saying, 'What's funny?' he would sit you down and say, 'Okay, what happened to you this week? What'd you fight with your wife about?' And those things that happened to you were the realies that Carl wanted. And so we were always searching for more realies."

"Carl encouraged us to take incidents from our personal lives and turn them into scripts," Garry Marshall would write in his autobiography.[1] "We would relate the most horrifying and embarrassing moments from our childhood and adult lives and then try to weave them back into a plot for the show."[2] *Dick Van Dyke Show* story meetings could get so confessional, the writer would observe, that they sometimes felt like group therapy. "Our pitching sessions on the show didn't involve a group of guys swapping snappy one-liners, but a roomful of men with sad faces."[3]

Even after the addition of Marshall and Belson to Carl Reiner's short list of favored freelancers, the producer's own script tally decreased only slightly in the show's third year, when his byline would still appear on close to a quarter of the season's total production output. Still, the producer viewed having to script only a fourth of the year's *Van Dyke Show* episodes as a picnic compared to the Herculean schedule he'd maintained during the show's first two seasons.

By the middle of the show's third year—as Persky and Denoff began to assume a greater role in the show's scripting and story-editing chores—the producer suddenly found himself with extra time to devote to his own contributions to the series. Reiner obviously put his added writing time to good use, crafting episodes that display a richness of style, content, and subtext that would greatly enrich the series as it moved into its middle years.

One noteworthy example is a third-season show that bears the ungainly title "Who and Where Was Antonio Stradivarius?" In Reiner's script for this classic episode, he employs a time-tested amnesia plotline to surprising effect, when we discover what happens to a staid suburban husband when his bearings are unmoored by an unexpected bump on the head. For Rob Petrie, anyway, what results is a hilarious "lost weekend" in which his deepest subconscious impulses are played out with a dolefully trusting blonde named Graciella in the unlikely environs of Red Hook, New Jersey.

A few episodes later, Reiner provided equal time for Mrs. Petrie in his script for the show's eightieth installment, "The Life and Love of Joe Coogan." In this wholly unpredictable scenario, Laura is compelled to examine a road not taken in her early romantic life after Rob meets a handsome stranger from her past on the golf course. In the episode's touching climax, Laura discovers that her onetime suitor has come to rededicate his life to the priesthood. In a poignant twist, she and Rob find themselves reexamining one of the cleric's old sonnets in light of their deeper understanding of his piety. Rob's tender reading of the poem sets the stage for the episode's effective—and affecting—closing moment, which offers a sweet meditation on the fleeting quality of youthful desire and the unpredictability of human yearning.

It's perhaps not surprising that in later years Reiner would cite his script for "The Life and Love of Joe Coogan" as among his favorites, expressing a particular fondness for the poem he composed to anchor the episode's deeply felt ending scene. "I don't write poetry," he explains. "But I wrote that poem. And I had to write it so it had a double meaning, since the priest was talking about God, but Laura thought he was talking about love between a man and a woman. Took a long time. I fussed with that an hour or so. And then I got it right."

Nor would Reiner be the only writer for whom this episode would strike a chord. In 2007, Pennsylvania composer Paul Salerni was so impressed by a chance viewing of the show that he decided to build an opera around it. As the composer tells the story, he was casting about for inspiration for his second short opera when he and his wife happened to

In 2010, Carl Reiner's script for "The Life and Love of Joe Coogan" inspired an opera. Pictured in the debut performance are James Bobick as Rob (seated), David Gordon as Buddy, and Cherry Duke as Sally. *Courtesy: Allen Kingsbury*

see "The Life and Love of Joe Coogan" on television one night. "As soon as it ended," he recalls, "[my wife] said, 'That's it! That's your second one-act!' And she was right."

In May 2007, the composer and his librettist, Kate Light, sought and received Reiner's blessing to adapt this episode's script into musical form. On September 25, 2010, *The Life and Love of Joe Coogan* premiered at the Zoellner Arts Center at Lehigh University in Bethlehem, Pennsylvania, distinguishing the show's eightieth installment as the first sitcom episode in history to inspire an opera.*

Reiner returned to his ongoing tale of Rob and Laura's early married life in the show's eighty-fifth episode, "Honeymoons Are for the Lucky," in which the couple finally consummate their nuptial vows—or attempt to, anyway. Like the previous chapters in Reiner's show-within-a-show, this flashback is set against the backdrop of Camp Crowder, Missouri, where Rob and Laura's honeymoon plans are severely cramped after Sergeant

---

* The cast of the world premiere performance of *The Life and Love of Joe Coogan* included James Bobick and Nancy Allen Lundy as Rob and Laura Petrie, with Branch Fields singing the role of Joe Coogan. Also appearing were Cherry Duke as Sally, Jacquelyn Familant as Millie, Jan Opalach as Mel, David Gordon as Buddy, and Sarah Caldwell Smith as a waitress.

Petrie's wedding furlough is unexpectedly canceled. Undaunted by his official orders, Rob concocts a foolproof—if foolhardy—scheme to get off the base. Under cover of darkness, Rob sets off across the drill field in a disguise that includes Laura's black chiffon dress, a pair of white sneakers, and a set of false eyelashes that the hapless soldier has unwittingly affixed to his eyelids with a permanent adhesive.

Like the earlier flashback episodes that unfold the saga of Rob and Laura's romantic life, the plot of "Honeymoons Are for the Lucky" was borrowed from the annals of the writer's own early days of marriage to the former Estelle Lebost—right down to the absurd details of Rob's AWOL scheme. "That stuff where he wears eyelashes—I didn't do that," assures Reiner, "but I did sneak out over a fence. And a guy caught me." Once apprehended, Reiner tried to talk his way out of the fix, much as his fictional alter ego would do in Reiner's retelling of the incident two decades later. "The guy didn't believe me," insists Reiner. "So I went around the drill field."

In Reiner's televisual treatment, the honeymoon couple finally ends up in a ramshackle boarding house where, as the landlady explains, the wedding suite is so-named because "it's the only room that people don't have to go through to get to their own rooms." Incredible as it seems, Reiner insists that the spartan accommodations he depicts in his script describe the cramped room where he and his wife spent their own honeymoon, right down to the sign that prohibited the couple from using a rocking chair after 8:00 P.M.! "We got a room in an apartment that had three rooms in a row," explains Reiner, recalling his own early days of marriage during a military housing crunch. "The toilet was out in the hall, so people were coming through our room all night. Actually, they were very nice. They made sure they only came through once the whole night. But we kept a screen around our bed anyway." By the end of Reiner's teleplay, the landlady has had a change of heart, and everything finally works out for newlyweds Rob and Laura, who enjoy their first night as a married couple in the seclusion of the apartment manager's private room.

Things didn't go too badly for the Petries' real life counterparts either. In the years following the honeymoon that inspired this episode, Carl Reiner and his late wife Estelle would celebrate sixty-four years of wedded bliss. It's a love story that would make a great romantic comedy—if Reiner hadn't already written it.

25

PICTURING MARY NAKED

By the end of their debut season as *The Dick Van Dyke Show*'s de facto writing staff, newcomers Bill Persky and Sam Denoff had more than fulfilled Carl Reiner's early confidence in their promise. In the show's third year alone, the team's byline would appear on a dozen scripts, including such hardy *Van Dyke Show* perennials as "Big Max Calvada," which featured Sheldon Leonard's only on-screen appearance in the series, playing—no surprise here—a gangster; "The Pen Is Mightier than the Mouth," in which Sally departs *The Alan Brady Show*'s staff for a stint as second banana on Stevie Parsons' late-night talk show; and "October Eve," an episode that Persky and Denoff rank high on their own list of personal favorites. The writing team's pride in "October Eve" is understandable—if Persky and Denoff had done nothing else to merit their mentor's faith during their first season, that script alone would have justified their fees for the year.

In the episode, Laura confronts a long-forgotten skeleton in her closet when a nude oil portrait of her unexpectedly surfaces in a prominent midtown gallery. The awkward circumstances surrounding the painting's origin are explored in a flashback to the studio of a petulant painter named Serge Carpetna—played, with appropriately hammy gusto, by

Laura is distraught when Sally discovers a revealing portrait of her hanging in a midtown gallery in "October Eve."

Reiner—where Laura has come to have her picture painted as a keepsake for Rob.* The well-dressed newlywed has a nice, representational portrait in mind, but the artist has other ideas—as Laura discovers when she gets a glimpse at the canvas and sees that the painter has rendered her sans clothing. "How dare you!" she gasps. "That's not me! That's not the way I was standing there!"

"I painted you as a goddess," Carpetna counters, "and you're acting like a peasant!" When Laura protests that she expected him to paint a conventional portrait, the artist is incensed. "For *that* kind of a picture," he shouts, "you take a camera, you go to Central Park, you get on a pony, and snap your brains out!" In a fit of pique, the artist chases the ungrateful philistine back to New Rochelle—without the painting.

Returning to the present, Carpetna, now a darling of the art world, has renamed Laura's fifty-dollar commissioned portrait "October Eve," and upped its price to $5,000. Once Laura finally confesses all to Rob, he pays a call on the artist's Greenwich Village loft and straightens everything out. After a bit of haggling, the painter agrees to sell the work to a reclusive

* "I loved that part," confesses the producer, who says that writers Persky and Denoff conceived the role with him in mind. "They said, 'You gotta play this guy!'" he remembers. "I guess they thought I was going to do it as well as anybody else." Reiner's modest appraisal aside, the show's associate producer, Ronald Jacobs, insists that the producer's decision to cast himself in the part was a sound one. "Carl's such a good comic actor, how could you not use him? He would have to be a bad producer not to hire Carl Reiner the comic actor."

South American millionaire, who will presumably display it in surroundings more discreet than a Madison Avenue gallery.

When Persky and Denoff dreamt up "October Eve," they knew they'd never be able to show Laura's revealing portrait on television. In fact, notes Dick Van Dyke, the actual painting didn't exist. "That's right," the star confirms, "there was nothing there." On the night the show was filmed, he explains, the actors played their scenes to a prop painting that was, in reality, a blank canvas.

It's a testament to the show's graceful direction—and *mis*direction—that viewers conjured a more vivid picture in their imaginations than anything the show's art department might have depicted in oil on canvas. According to Van Dyke, there are still those who refuse to believe the work was an illusion. "People *swear* they saw that painting," he observes. "There were a number of shows we did where the audience would insist they'd seen something they hadn't, and that was one of them. People think they saw the painting, but nobody ever saw it—that was just artful writing."

For their part, Persky and Denoff confess that the challenge of persuading the show's viewing audience to picture Mary Tyler Moore posed in the altogether never struck them as a daunting task. "I figured that everybody wanted to see Mary naked," says Sam Denoff, "because I certainly did."

"He would have to be a bad producer not to hire Carl Reiner the comic actor," says Ronald Jacobs, recalling Reiner's decision to cast himself as a bohemian artist in "October Eve."

The Dick Van Dyke Show wrapped its third production season with the filming of their ninety-fifth episode, "My Two Show-Offs and Me," on April 3, 1964. A few days later, Van Dyke boarded a plane for London, where he and his wife Marjorie hoped to squeeze in a three-week vacation—their first in four years—before the actor was due in Paris to start shooting *The Art of Love*, a Universal Pictures comedy written by Reiner, who also had a cameo role in the film.

Van Dyke's big-screen career would get a boost later that summer, when *Mary Poppins* opened to widespread acclaim—and strong box office—after a star-studded world premiere at Grauman's Chinese Theatre on August 27, 1964. The runaway success of the Disney film cemented Van Dyke's reputation as a bona fide movie star, and also sent his fee—reportedly $100,000 for the Disney film—soaring to a then-staggering $250,000 per picture. By comparison, the actor's *Van Dyke Show* salary at the start of the show's fourth season was a relatively paltry $5,000 a week.

Carl Reiner also stayed busy during the four-month hiatus that fell between the show's third and fourth seasons. After completing work on his script for *The Art of Love*, the hyperactive writer made a deal to write three additional comedies for Universal Pictures over a four-year period. In April, Reiner also began hosting *The Celebrity Game*, a weekly panel show that appeared on the CBS network's prime-time schedule throughout the summers of 1964 and 1965. When the *Hollywood Reporter*'s Hank Grant wondered if the producer might be spreading himself too thin, the writer/producer/actor/game-show host dismissed the columnist's concerns out of hand. "Every other Friday night I

Laura stands by her man in "Dear Mrs. Petrie, Your Husband Is in Jail," the second script from *Van Dyke Show* stalwarts Garry Marshall and Jerry Belson.

tape two shows within three hours at CBS," Reiner quipped. "This is work?"[1] As if he weren't already busy enough that summer, Reiner also found time to produce a comedy album called *The First Nine Months Are the Hardest*, which was written by Persky and Denoff. The record cast a comedic eye on the trials of pregnancy and early parenthood, an arena that had provided fertile ground for the writers when they penned "That's My Boy??" a year or so earlier.

AS IN PREVIOUS years, the cast and creative staff of *The Dick Van Dyke Show* maintained a high profile at the 1963–1964 Emmy Award ceremonies, which were held on May 25, 1964. For the second year in a row, the series dominated the nominations in the Television Academy's comedy awards categories, with a total of six. By evening's end, *Van Dyke* personnel would walk away with five of the coveted statuettes, including the series' second consecutive Emmy for Outstanding Program Achievement in the Field of Comedy. In his second nomination in the top actor's category, Dick Van Dyke picked up his first Emmy for Outstanding Continued Performance by an Actor in a Series, an honor that was echoed by a win for Mary Tyler Moore in the category of Outstanding Continued Performance by an Actress in a Series. Also honored that night were Jerry Paris, for Outstanding Directorial Achievement in Comedy, and Bill Persky and Sam Denoff, who shared an Emmy with Carl Reiner for Outstanding Writing Achievement in Comedy or Variety.

Though Rose Marie and Morey Amsterdam were each nominated for Emmys for their work on the series, neither of them ever won the award, owing largely to complicated Emmy-nomination procedures of the era that tended to favor dramatic actors in the supporting actor categories.

The evening's only disappointment came when Rose Marie, nominated for the second year in a row, was again shut out in the fiercely competitive supporting actress category. In a field once again dominated by actresses nominated for showy dramatic performances, the award for Outstanding Performance in a Supporting Role by an Actress was given to Ruth White, for her work in a *Hallmark Hall of Fame* special.

The loss of an Emmy Award seemed a matter of very small consequence to Rose Marie, who missed that year's ceremonies so she could be at the bedside of her gravely ill husband, trumpeter Bobby Guy, who had contracted a rare blood infection that would take his life a few days later. The news of his passing came as a blow to members of the *Van Dyke Show* cast, who had come to know the musician through his frequent stints in the show's onstage combo. Rose Marie was so torn by grief that she briefly considered retiring from acting. "I was devastated when he passed away," explains the actress, who had taken stock of her life in the wake of her tragedy and decided that show business was no longer important. "I can't sing anymore," she told friends at the time, "and I can't go back to work." Finally, after some painful soul-searching, she called her friend John Rich to break the news that she'd decided to leave the cast of *The Dick Van Dyke Show* before the series returned to production in late July.

Rich was floored by his friend's announcement. As the *Van Dyke Show*'s founding director, he knew as well as anyone that Rose Marie played a vital role in the show's chemistry. The director also recognized the equally vital role *The Dick Van Dyke Show* played in Rose Marie's life—even if the actress had apparently lost sight of that fact herself. "Rosie," the director beseeched her, "please don't make any final decisions until I have a chance to talk to you."

As Rose Marie tells it, the director arrived at her house that very evening, determined to persuade her to reconsider her decision. The marathon conversation that followed lasted far into the night, until Rose Marie's mother finally tiptoed in at two the next morning to bring the talk to a close. "My mother came into the living room," recalls Rose Marie, "and she said to John, 'You oughta go home now.'" At which point, says the actress, the director dutifully rose from his chair to leave. But before he got to the door, he turned to ask his old friend one final question. "He said, 'Rosie, have I convinced you to stay with the show?'" she recalls. "And I said, 'Yes.' And then John said, 'Then I've done my job.' And he left."

The Dick Van Dyke Show family as they appeared during rehearsals for episode 110, "Brother Can You Spare $2,500?" Pictured, clockwise from left, are guest stars Tiny Brauer and Jimmy Cross, director Jerry Paris, Rose Marie, Mary Tyler Moore, Dick Van Dyke, guest star Gene Baylos, story editor Sam Denoff, Carl Reiner, story editor Bill Persky, script supervisor Marge Mullen, guest star Sheila Rogers, Morey Amsterdam, second assistant director Bud Messinger, and guest star Herbie Faye.

Rose Marie returned to the *Van Dyke* set in the last week of July 1964, as the cast gathered to start rehearsals for the first show of their fourth season. According to the actress, Richard Deacon was so concerned she be spared any emotional awkwardness on her return that he took it upon himself to deliver a short pep talk to the rest of the cast a few moments before she arrived. "Whatever you do," Deacon cautioned, "don't make a big fuss when Rosie walks in. What she really wants is for everyone to treat her the same as always." Most important of all, he added, the cast was to avoid indulging in any overt displays of sentimental affection. "If everyone puts their arm around her," the actor warned, "she'll only start crying."

The cast listened politely to their colleague's well-intentioned instructions and then proceeded to disregard every one of them as soon as Rose Marie walked onto the set. When the actress suddenly found herself once again surrounded by the laughter and warmth of her beloved company, she didn't even try to stem the tears. Nor did anyone else—least of all Richard Deacon. "When I got back they were so wonderful," says Rose Marie. "They were truly, truly a family that really cared. Every one of them."

In the months to come, the actress would often be touched by her company's ongoing regard for her still-tender emotions. "They used to take things out of the scripts that they thought might upset me," she recalls. Nor did their concern end at the studio gates. As the actress later recalled, Van Dyke frequently took it upon himself to check in with her once she got home in the evening. "Sometimes when I'm home at night," the actress told a reporter in early 1965, "he'll call and say, 'What are you doing?' And I'll say, 'The dishes.' And he'll say, 'Why don't you come over and have a drink? We're just sitting around.' If you can say you love somebody without being mushy, I say we all love that man."[2]

"WE SHUT UP a lot in the beginning and just watched," says Bill Persky, recalling his and Sam Denoff's early days of apprenticeship on the staff of *The Dick Van Dyke Show*. "But," he adds, "by the end of our first season, we pretty well knew what we were doing." It was an opinion shared by Carl Reiner, who rewarded the team's diligence with a promotion in title at the start of the show's fourth season, when Persky and Denoff were appointed *The Dick Van Dyke Show*'s official story consultants, a post they would hold throughout the show's fourth and fifth seasons.

As story editors, it would be Persky and Denoff's job to generate a brand-new script every week, either by writing it themselves or by assigning a story idea to one of the show's ever-increasing stable of freelance contributors. Once a script's first draft was complete, it would be up to the story editors to hone and polish it—or, in some cases, totally rewrite it—until that early draft was as close to perfect as humanly possible. Next, they would serve it up for the scrutiny of the entire company at the show's Wednesday-morning table reading, which, in many ways, was when their real work began.

"We'd go through the whole script very slowly," explains Rose Marie, describing the ritual that would take up the better part of the show's first rehearsal session each Wednesday morning. "Word for word. And we'd make all the little changes. Morey would say, 'I can get a better joke in here, let me try something!' And we'd all have something to say."

"We'd spend the whole afternoon rewriting, really," adds Van Dyke. "Everybody got the chance to throw their two bits' worth in." At this stage of the weeklong rehearsal process, it was understood that nothing was carved in stone—a factor that many cast members found quite liberating. "The loosest part of the rehearsal was probably that first reading," notes writer and sometime *Van Dyke Show* performer Bill Idelson, "because nothing was at stake. You knew damn well none of the lines were gonna be there when you performed the show, so you'd kid around and have coffee and donuts."

While Persky allows that the peculiar form of creative democracy practiced at the *Van Dyke Show*'s weekly table reading was generally beneficial—"The show often got better," he says, "because everybody was pretty intelligent"—the story editor maintains that all that cross-table kibitzing had a downside as well. "There was always a tendency to fix and potchkeh around," he says. "It was like a disease. I used to call it rewrite-itis." It was a malady that the writer found particularly vexing, especially since it frequently resulted in more work for him and fellow story editor Denoff. "The flexibility to change anything was so ingrained in us," observes Persky, "that sometimes no one bothered to look at what was really there before they started looking to improve it."

By way of example, Persky describes one particularly maddening script session where the enthusiastic company spent the better part of an entire rehearsal struggling to improve a single joke line—only to discover that the setup already had a perfectly good rejoinder lurking on the following page. "Somebody read a line that happened to fall at the bottom of a page and said, 'Ooh, I'll bet we can find something funny to put here!'" In their enthusiasm to come up with a new punch line, says Persky, the company spent what seemed like forty-five minutes pitching brand-new jokes before somebody finally flipped the page and found the already-scripted comeback waiting for them at the top of the next page! "No one had even bothered to see that the end of the joke had already been written!"

For Persky and Denoff the ultimate nightmare was the prospect of taking part in a table reading so

The second episode filmed in the show's fourth production season saw the cast returning to *Twilight Zone* territory for the haunted house parody, "The Ghost of A. Chantz."

disastrous that an entire script would have to be scrapped. Fortunately, notes Van Dyke, that dreadful calamity occurred only once on *The Dick Van Dyke Show*.

"The script was called 'Art vs. Baloney,'" says Van Dyke, "and I cannot remember anything about it, except that it was unsalvageable. Ungodly! Just awful. We finished it in dead silence." As Van Dyke recalls, the script—which had been written by a freelancer whose name has long since faded from memory—was deemed so odious that he actually tossed it into the nearest wastebasket at the conclusion of its first and only reading. "I just took my script and threw it," says Van Dyke. "And everybody said, 'Yep, that's it. Out it goes.' That was the only time in five years that I ever threw a script."

THE *VAN DYKE SHOW* company's fluid approach to the written word was by no means limited to the show's early script conferences. "Our show was just one big rewrite," observes Van Dyke, who recalls that Reiner and his story editors thought nothing of fine-tuning a script right up to showtime. "We'd never stop," says Van Dyke. "We'd have a dress rehearsal, and then we'd go and have dinner while the audience came in. But, if Carl or someone had a brainstorm at the dress rehearsal, we'd spend that dinner hour rewriting while we were eating."

It was during these eleventh-hour rewrite sessions that the show's cast and crew came to truly appreciate the wizardry of their script supervisor, Marge Mullen, whose job it was to keep track of every single revision, addition, or deletion that the show's teleplay would undergo over the course of the average rehearsal week. According to no less an authority than Carl Reiner, Mullen was very, very good at her job. "You'd tell her, 'Change this, we'll do this. And, oh, yeah, let's change this line to this,'" recalls Reiner, "and she'd be writing." Then, while the company paused to take a break or have dinner, Mullen would take the latest changes and have them typed, mimeographed, collated, and back on the stage before rehearsal resumed. "And," adds Reiner, "the script would always come back exactly right."

One of Mullen's more formidable duties was to keep track of the show's rejects—all those stray jokes, unused sight gags, and spurned one-liners that, for one reason or another, failed to make it into the show's final shooting script. "Whenever we had to take out a joke," explains Denoff, "or a scene that was really terrific but didn't fit—for length or whatever—we would put it in a book so it could be used at a later time." Before long, all of these unused jokes and ill-fitting scenes would find their way into a loose-leaf folder that Mullen kept near the set, a compendium of rejected material that came to be known as Marge's S.O.S. file—S.O.S. being the writers' abbreviation for "some other show." "If we ever needed a joke someday," explains Reiner, "then Marge would be able to pull one from the back of her S.O.S. book."

At least that was the idea. But according to Denoff, in five years of production there was not one occasion where he or any of his colleagues ever drew even a single line of dialogue from their script supervisor's emergency inventory. "We never, ever used any of them!" the writer exclaims. The end result of Mullen's efforts, recalls Persky, was a notebook of unused *Van Dyke Show* material that was a full six inches thick by the time the show went out of production in 1966. "We always meant to use them," says Persky, who half-jokingly suggests one possible use for the *Van Dyke Show*'s cast-offs. "That file was so thick, you probably could have done another entire series using just the stuff in that book."

In addition to performing her duties as script supervisor, Mullen also served—in a strictly uncredited capacity—as the show's final arbiter of what was, and was not, funny. "Marge would watch the run-through," says Reiner, "and if she didn't react, we'd say, 'Oh, oh! Marge doesn't like it.' And we knew we were in trouble. She wasn't always right, but she was a very, very solid indicator."

ON THE EVENING of August 4, 1964, the company kicked off their fourth production year with the filming of the show's ninety-sixth episode, "My Mother Can Beat Up My Father," a flawless slapstick exercise in which Laura reveals a heretofore unknown talent for judo when she's called upon to defend her husband from the threat of an abusive drunk in a Manhattan bar. But though Laura succeeds in saving her husband's hide, her spontaneous act of gallantry threatens to cause even greater damage to Rob's fragile male pride. To restore his standing, the humiliated husband spends the better part of this classic episode engaged in a series of increasingly futile attempts to reestablish his manly preeminence over his surprisingly capable wife.

While Persky and Denoff's buoyant script provides another ideal showcase for Van Dyke's virtuoso physical prowess, Denoff insists that the real fun of this episode comes in watching the show's leading man fall apart, piece by piece, over the course of the show's half-hour running time, until, by the end of the episode, he's completely undone by his own stubborn pride. The theme of pride coming before a fall—illustrated quite literally in "My Mother Can Beat Up My Father"—was a favorite of writers Persky and Denoff. "Rob was always funniest when he was being a schmuck," says Denoff. "His humor came from a real man who at times is a very loving husband and father but can also be a schmuck, because he can't handle jealousy or whatever." And, adds Denoff, with his good looks and upstanding demeanor, Van Dyke made the perfect fall guy. "When you see the guy with the nice hair and the suit become a total schmuck, that's funny."

"When you see the guy with the nice hair and the suit become a total schmuck," says Sam Denoff, "that's funny." Pictured, Tracy Butler, Dick Van Dyke, and unidentified extras in a still from the show's 100th episode, "The Man from Emperor."

26

TEMPEST IN A BATHTUB

One of the unexpected advantages of Carl Reiner's decision to shift greater responsibility for the show's writing chores into the capable hands of Persky and Denoff is that it allowed the multitalented producer to spend more time in front of the camera in the show's final two seasons. It was a benefit that began to yield big dividends in the show's 104th episode, "Three Letters from One Wife," which featured Reiner's first full-frontal assault in the role of Alan Brady.

Of course, the actor had already logged a handful of appearances as Rob Petrie's blustery employer before he strode on-screen in "Three Letters from One Wife." But most of the character's earlier performances qualified as little more than cameos, since the actor's face was invariably blocked by a conveniently placed high-backed chair, or hidden from view behind a Santa Claus beard, or beneath a barber's steam towel—intentional visual dodges that were part of a carefully orchestrated, if rarely successful, campaign to keep the identity of the actor playing Alan Brady a secret from the audience. It was a conceit that Reiner insists was born out of his fear that viewers would refuse to accept a lowly character actor like him playing a star of Alan Brady's magnitude. "I said, 'They know who I am,'" recalls

Reiner. "I'm the second banana from *Your Show of Shows*. Nobody's gonna think I'm a big star.' So I used to turn myself around and hide."

Reiner insists that he briefly considered bringing in another actor to play the show's tyrannical boss, but he decided against it after it dawned on him that he wasn't going to find an actor of the stature he had in mind by going through central casting. "I wanted the audience to think of Milton Berle or Danny Thomas," he would later recall, "not some guy I hired for six hundred dollars."[1]

The producer's modest assessment of his own abilities aside, a more plausible explanation for Alan Brady's tangential presence in the show's first two or three years was that Reiner simply couldn't spare the time required to rehearse anything more complicated than a cameo appearance—at least not while he was also responsible for writing, producing, and story editing each episode of the show as well. But, with story editors Persky and Denoff available to man the rudder in season four, Alan Brady was finally allowed to step into the foreground and assume his rightful place among the show's primary cast of characters.

Reiner suggests that the blossoming of Alan Brady in the show's last two years was not part of a grand design, but rather a classic case of the tail wagging the dog. "We wrote a couple of shows where the character had to do more complicated things," he explains. "And I said, 'We're not being fair to the writer, because there's so much more you can do if you can see the character's face.' So we turned him around." As Denoff observes, it was a

Mary Tyler Moore's Laura awaits rescue from a most embarrassing predicament in "Never Bathe on Saturday," the *Van Dyke Show* classic that provided the backdrop for one of the series' most notorious backstage skirmishes.

long-overdue adjustment. "You couldn't make the conceit of never seeing Alan Brady last too long," notes the writer. "So we just said, 'Let's see Alan Brady—and let's make him a funny guy.'"

It's often assumed that Reiner based his characterization of *The Alan Brady Show*'s vain and hot-tempered headliner on Sid Caesar, the notoriously volatile star of *Your Show of Shows*. But according to Denoff, there were any number of equally tempestuous role models from television's golden age who fit the Alan Brady mold just as well—if not better—than Reiner's former employer. "Carl wasn't doing Sid, really," insists the writer. "The stars of *all* those early variety shows were crazy. And for legitimate reasons. They were on live every week. And it was terrifying. The stress made them crazy."

According to many firsthand observers, the most compelling aspect of Reiner's portrayal of the egomaniacal Alan Brady may have been how little the character actually had in common with the actor who played him. Despite the obvious delight Reiner took in bringing Rob Petrie's vain, abusive, and short-tempered employer to life, it's generally conceded that it would have been hard to find an actor who less resembled the show's hot-headed tyrant than he did. According to those who worked most closely with him on the *Van Dyke* set, in five years of production, the show's producer rarely so much as lost his temper.

Except once.

THE ONLY RECORDED instance of Carl Reiner blowing his stack on the set of the *Van Dyke Show* occurred on February 12, 1965, midway through rehearsals for the series' 121st episode, "Never Bathe on Saturday." No one who was present is likely to forget that day, if only because it also marked the first—and only—time that one of the show's actors stormed off the stage and out the studio's gates.

Ironically, the episode that provided the backdrop for the show's most notorious skirmish is today regarded as one of the series' most celebrated entries, if for no other reason than Reiner's provocative premise, which finds Laura Petrie trapped naked in a bathroom after she somehow manages to get her toe stuck in the bathtub's waterspout. In Reiner's faultless script, the hapless housewife announces her unlikely predicament from behind the locked bathroom door of a luxury hotel suite, where—until that moment—she and Rob had hoped to spend a romantic weekend. In fact, Rob has just donned his most debonair smoking jacket when his wife summons him to the bathroom door to explain that her toe has become stuck in what she erroneously describes as the bathtub faucet, or, you know, "the little pipe that the water comes out of."

"That's not the faucet, honey," Rob corrects. To which Laura replies, "I don't care what you call it, my big toe is stuck in it." When Rob asks how she managed such a feat, Laura spells it out for him in tones of mounting exasperation. "I was playing with a drip!"

Despite her husband's best intentions—he tries everything he can think of to break her out, including a valiant, if foolhardy, attempt to break the door down with his shoulder—there Laura stays, locked behind a thick wooden door for the better part of one of the show's funniest episodes. When the hotel detective finally offers to shoot the lock off, Rob insists on performing that task personally, because, he explains, "Only a husband can blow the lock off a bathroom with his wife in the bathtub with nothing on and her toe stuck in a pipe."

Like Persky and Denoff's treatment for the earlier "October Eve," Reiner's script for "Never Bathe on Saturday" is another masterpiece of sitcom sleight of hand—given the show's playful premise, what we *don't* see is naturally funnier than anything that the show's actors, producers, or set decorators could have concocted. Reiner understood this, of course, and he was justifiably proud to have created a situation so charged with comic potential that, for more than half the episode's running time, his leading lady would be able to command show-stopping laughs without even setting foot on stage. Which might explain why the writer got so upset when, halfway through rehearsals for the episode, that same leading lady stormed off the set, declaring that she had no intention of playing the role as written.

"Mary walked out in the middle of a rehearsal," recalled Bill Idelson, who played the hotel bellboy in the episode. "She didn't want to do that show, because she said the camera was never on her."

While Moore might have been physically out of sight throughout much of the episode, Denoff maintains that the actress was never out of mind—at least not so far as the show's many millions of male viewers were concerned. "Mary didn't get the idea," observes Denoff, "that during that whole episode, people in America were fantasizing seeing Laura Petrie naked in sudsy water in a bathtub! Whatta picture! But she didn't get that." Even so, it was an image whose potency was not lost on Reiner. "I remember in writing it," Reiner would later observe, "I fantasized a woman naked."[2]

Although Reiner might have been content to let his audience conjure the visual portion of his leading lady's performance, the actress explains that she had good reason to approach that particular episode with vastly different expectations. For that, the actress maintains, Reiner would have only himself to blame. "He kept talking about this show that was coming up that featured me," says the actress, recalling how the producer had unwittingly ratcheted her expectations unreasonably high in the weeks before he finally revealed his script for "Never Bathe on Saturday." "He kept talking about how it was gonna be all about me! So I had this show built up in my mind, and I was just waiting for it so excitedly."

The actress was forced to revise her expectations significantly once she finally read her producer's much-heralded script at the episode's first rehearsal. "When I read it," reports Moore, "I saw that I was off-camera the whole time! Everybody was talking about me—but the actress didn't have a thing to play!" And yet, as distressed as she was to discover that she would be playing her biggest scene of the entire season from five feet offstage, the actress insists that not even that dismaying news would have been enough to send her over the brink had it been *any* other week.

Bernard Fox played the suspicious house detective and Bill Idelson was the bellboy in "Never Bathe on Saturday," one of the show's most unforgettable episodes.

As fate would have it, the week Reiner brought in his script for "Never Bathe on Saturday" happened to be the same week that Moore had decided to quit smoking. Van Dyke suggests that the fallout from his costar's decision to kick her cigarette habit cold turkey may have been a greater contributor to her foul spirits than any reservations she had about the episode's shooting script. "I think it was more nicotine withdrawal than anything else," says Van Dyke, "because I never saw her complain before." As the actor recalls, the symptoms of his costar's withdrawal only seemed to grow worse over the course of the rehearsal week. "I watched her get a little paler each day," he observes, "and the circles under her eyes get a little deeper. The poor girl was beside herself."

By the end of the week, it had become clear to Van Dyke that Moore was nearing her breaking point. "She was a nervous wreck," he recalls. "Everything upset her."

"I was snapping and snarling at everyone all week," the actress concurs. "All because I was trying to quit smoking."

As Persky remembers, the actress first voiced her apprehensions about the script at one of the earliest rehearsals. "She couldn't understand how she could be funny in this part. And Carl said, 'Are you kidding? Everybody in the world wants to see you naked. And here's their chance.'"

But if, as Persky implies, it had been Reiner's intention to disarm his leading lady's anxiety with that flip observation, the producer obviously hadn't judged the depth of her unease. "I was terribly upset," she recalls, "and I guess I must have said so to Carl." Though no one remembers the exact words that Moore employed to express her dissatisfaction during those early rehearsals, her comments were—by her own admission—incendiary enough to cause a serious rift between her and the producer. "We ended up not speaking for a couple days," the actress admits, "which was rather impudent of a little twenty-something-year-old novice comedian."

"She was just being a brat," observes Denoff, who confesses that he too was perplexed by the actress's untoward behavior, since it was, as he recalls, "the first show of temperament we ever saw from Mary or any of them." Which might explain why Reiner maintained a tolerant attitude to the actress's emotional displays for as long as he did. But finally, after watching his leading lady sulk for the better part of the week, the normally mild-mannered producer had all but exhausted his reserves of patience.

"The blowup finally came on Friday night," remembers Persky. As Denoff makes clear, the producer's outburst did not exactly go unnoticed on the set. "Carl let her have it," recalls Denoff. "I don't remember many other times that he lost it. But Carl yelled at her that day."

"That was the only time I've ever seen Carl mad on stage," concurred the show's film editor, Bud Molin, who, decades later, still recalled the exact wording of the lecture that Reiner delivered to his recalcitrant leading lady that night. "Carl said, 'This show will work! I would never ask you to do a show that I didn't think would work! Do you think I'd send you out in a leaky crate? If I didn't think this show was good for you, I wouldn't do it!'" But despite the angry tone, it was obvious that Reiner still hoped to bring the actress around and continue the evening's rehearsal. Unfortunately, by that point, tempers had already flared past the point of no return. "Mary walked out of the rehearsal," recalls Persky. "The only time she ever did that. She walked out and went home."

The actress was barely outside the studio's gate before she began to regret her actions. By the time she arrived home to the Studio City house she shared with her young son and then-husband Grant Tinker, Moore was overcome with embarrassment and remorse for an action she had by then come to recognize as an ill-considered temper tantrum. That night, she began the process of mending her fences with an apologetic phone call to Reiner, whom she reached at home a few hours later.

"What bothered Mary most," recalls Reiner, "was that I'd blown my stack in full view of the sponsors and all the network people. When she called me she said, 'How can I come back to work? The sponsors know you never explode, so now I must look really terrible!'" Caught up in the spirit of the moment, the producer ended up tendering an apology of his own. "I told Mary, 'I've never blown up in five years, give me this one time.' And then she apologized to me a few days later when it turned out to be such a good show."

Sure enough, when "Never Bathe on Saturday" was finally committed to film the following Tuesday night, Mary Tyler Moore—in a far more compliant mood—turned in one of her most memorable performances, reading her lines, as written, from behind a bathroom door.

"*And*," the actress adds sardonically, "I was back smoking again."

27

PRACTICE MAKES PERFECT

For a series that had already logged upwards of 125 episodes, *The Dick Van Dyke Show* seemed exceptionally spry in the waning days of its fourth, and penultimate, year on the air—a fertile period that would see the creation of many of the show's most outstanding efforts. In addition to "Never Bathe on Saturday," other notable fourth-year entries in the *Van Dyke Show* canon include episode 119, "Your Home Sweet Home Is My Home Sweet Home," which reveals the comic details surrounding Rob and Laura's purchase of their house, the only suburban split-level in New Rochelle to come equipped with its own geological rock formation in the cellar; and "100 Terrible Hours," the show's 122nd episode, in which Rob describes the comical complications that resulted when he arranged his job interview with Alan Brady on the heels of an on-air radio promotion that required him to broadcast live for four straight days without sleep. Equally memorable was the show's 123rd episode, "A Show of Hands," a comedy of errors in which Rob and Laura accidentally dye their hands black on the very night that Rob is scheduled to accept a racial-tolerance award on behalf of *The Alan Brady Show*.

Of all the shows filmed during the closing weeks of the *Van Dyke Show*'s fourth year, the best of the lot may well be episode 124, "Baby Fat,"

Rob broadcasts live through "100 Terrible Hours," which is loosely based on a similar marathon radio shift that writers Persky and Denoff logged in their early days.

a searing parody of backstage life from writers Garry Marshall and Jerry Belson that chronicles Rob Petrie's brief, debilitating career as an uncredited script doctor for one of Alan Brady's rare forays onto the legitimate stage. Packed with in-jokes, clever literary illusions, and irresistible scenes of pure farce, "Baby Fat" ranks among the show's best—if most frequently overlooked—efforts.

"I had no recollection of that one at all," admits Dick Van Dyke, who insists that he rediscovered "Baby Fat" by chance, many decades after he filmed it, when he happened to catch the episode in reruns while he was flipping through the channels one night. "I was impressed by it," he says. "It was a bit of a farce, but it had a certain touch of sophistication that none of our other shows had." Oddly enough, in talking to Carl Reiner a few days later, the star discovered that his former producer had also stumbled across that same broadcast and had been no less impressed by his own reintroduction to their forgotten classic. "Neither of us had seen that one in at least twenty years," recalls Reiner, "and then we both just happened to see it that night. Dick told me he'd been laughing out loud, and I said, 'Me, too!'"

ON TUESDAY, MARCH 30, 1965, the *Van Dyke Show* company filmed "There's No Sale Like Wholesale," which would be broadcast as the final episode of the show's fourth season. But as in previous years, the company would cram one extra show into the season's production year—episode 127, "A Farewell to Writing"—which would be held for broadcast the following September. Of course, with the entire cast and crew anxious to get started on their long-awaited summer hiatus, no one was eager to linger on the lot any longer than they had to. As a result, "A Farewell to Writing" was filmed on a special accelerated rehearsal schedule of only three days from start to finish.

In the episode's storyline, Rob decides to sequester himself in the peaceful surroundings of a friend's remote cabin for a few days, hoping that the enforced solitude might inspire him to finally settle down and complete his long-gestating memoirs. The would-be author soon discovers that a little bit of peace and quiet goes a long way, and by the time he returns to civilization, Rob has logged more time playing with a pair of six-shooters and brushing up on his paddleball stroke than sitting behind the typewriter.

The spare production requirements of "A Farewell to Writing" made it an ideal episode to film on an abbreviated production schedule. If nothing else, the episode required minimal rehearsal, since much of its running time was devoted to Dick Van Dyke's extended monologue in the cabin. In fact, according to Van Dyke, his solo turn in "A Farewell to Writing" was filmed with almost no formal rehearsal at all.

"They had three cameras, and the place was full of props," says the actor, "so they just let me go—which I loved to do. I had an awfully good time with that one." Caught up in the spirit of improvisation, the star recalls that during the actual performance he ended up filming much more material than could be squeezed into the finished episode's running time. "I don't know how many pieces of shtick I did that were never in the show," he says, "'cause I just got going and kept going. We never worried about editing it, since it was on film, and could always be edited down to time later."

DESPITE VAN DYKE'S knack for on-camera spontaneity, the actor insists that he would usually begin visualizing sight gags and physical routines for any given episode at the very first reading. "That's when a lot of my physical pieces would come to me," he says. "Anytime I could find an opening for a piece of physical business, I'd put it in, because I loved to do it." Even so, the star acknowledges, he was usually at his most inventive during the show's second and third rehearsal days, when he could finally set his script aside and actually begin acting out all the physical gags and routines that he'd visualized earlier in the week. "My creative heat hit when we were on our feet actually rehearsing the movement," says Van Dyke. "That's when things would kind of instinctively happen to me. A lot of times those little flashes of inspiration would hit right in the middle of a scene, and then you'd just have to try it."

According to Rose Marie, on those rare occasions when Van Dyke lacked a suitable inspiration, the actor would simply substitute perspiration and hope for the best. She recalls many afternoons when she'd spot the star off in a quiet corner of the stage, diligently sweating out the choreography of a sight gag or bit of physical shtick until he'd polished it to his satisfaction. Of course, as Rose Marie confirms, the spectacle of Dick Van Dyke at work was a sight that rarely failed to attract a crowd—even in a busy rehearsal studio. And so, more often than not, by the time Van Dyke had perfected his latest flip, fall, or double take, he would often find himself surrounded by a small throng of delighted cast and crew members, many of them doubled over in laughter. "Then," recalls Rose Marie, "Dick would say, 'Is that funny?' I'd say, 'Funny? It's hysterical! Leave it in!'"

And if it didn't turn out to be so hysterical? Well, explains Van Dyke, that's what rehearsals were for. "Nobody was ever squelched for brainstorming an idea," the star explains. "We all felt free to do anything that came to us. That was the great part of it." "These people knew how to rehearse," insists John Rich, who helped instill that discipline during his early years as the show's director. "Our show was very, very carefully rehearsed."

That statement might have come as news to Guy Raymond. As Van Dyke's guest star on "A Farewell to Writing," it was the hapless actor's misfortune to arrive on the *Van Dyke* set during the one week when the show's normally dedicated cast seemed devoted to nothing more serious than getting through their final three days of work as painlessly as possible. "We were like kids getting ready for vacation," explains Ann Guilbert. "Who wants to study for exams? We just wanted to split. Guy came ready to bust his butt, and everybody else just wanted to play and get out of there."

"Nobody was paying much attention to anything," remembered Raymond, who recalled that he could barely get Van Dyke to rehearse their

Rob faces his most embarrassing speaking engagement ever in the show's 123rd episode, "A Show of Hands," costarring Joel Fluellen.

scenes together more than once or twice during the entire three days he was on the set. "Everyone was in such a hurry to get out of there that there wasn't time for rehearsal or anything."

After his first dispiriting morning on the *Van Dyke* set, Raymond remembered wandering into the Desilu commissary, where he was heartened to discover that costar Ann Guilbert had been thoughtful enough to save him a seat in the cramped lunchroom. "She was kind to me," recalled the actor, still thankful for the actress's gracious gesture. "She showed me compassion."

Such displays of courtesy were not uncommon for Guilbert, who admits that she frequently took it upon herself to make visiting performers feel at home on the *Van Dyke* set. "I always felt sorry for the people who were guest stars on the show," she explains. "When you go to a new set every time you do a show, you have to get reacquainted with all new people. You never know who to eat with." To Guilbert, who grew up as the nomadic daughter of a Veterans Administration doctor whose job required frequent reassignment, getting acquainted with strangers—and putting others at ease in strange surroundings—was practically second nature. "Having moved around all the time as a kid, I always felt compassion for whoever was a new kid on the block."

In a sweet—if largely coincidental—real-life postscript to the *Van Dyke Show*'s 127th episode, Guilbert and guest star Raymond would become reacquainted some years later in a friendship that blossomed into romance and, eventually, marriage. But despite the circumstances of their first meeting, Guilbert explains that their eventual union was hardly the result of an on-set infatuation. In fact, the actress admits that she and Raymond lost touch after his ill-fated *Van Dyke Show* appearance, only to meet again in the late sixties as members of a local theater group. By that time, both were single—though it was not a status they were destined to maintain for long.

"We struck up a friendship," says Guilbert, "which turned into matrimony."

ON SEPTEMBER 12, 1965, Carl Reiner continued what had by then become an annual tradition when he accepted, for the third year in a row, the Emmy Award for Outstanding Program Achievement in Entertainment on behalf on *The Dick Van Dyke Show*. Dick Van Dyke also made a return trip to the dais when he picked up the Television Academy's top acting award for the second year in a row. Reiner's script for "Never Bathe on Saturday" also earned an Emmy nomination that year, though the Academy's sole writing award that season went to dramatic writer David Karp for his work as author of an episode of *The Defenders*.

Even as the *Van Dyke Show* continued to make its impact felt at the industry's most important year-end awards ceremony, the series maintained an impressive showing on the popular front as well. When the A. C. Nielsen ratings service published the year-end averages for the 1964–1965 season, *The Dick Van Dyke Show* ranked as the seventh-highest-rated prime-time series for the year. The show's average audience rating of 27.1 for its fourth season put the series just a few points behind its all-time third-season peak, when *The Dick Van Dyke Show* ended the 1963–1964 season with an eye-popping year-end average rating of 33.3, making it the third-highest-rated prime-time program of that entire year.

By the end of the *Van Dyke Show*'s fourth season, it had been almost exactly seven years since Carl Reiner sat down in his Fire Island study to write the thirteen half-hour comedy scripts that would eventually change his life. In the years since, the writer had weathered his share of storms. But now,

Future director Rob Reiner dropped by to visit his father, Carl Reiner, the week the cast filmed their 125th episode, "Br-rooom, Br-rooom."

four seasons and untold man-hours later, Carl Reiner's acclaimed *Dick Van Dyke Show* seemed poised at the very pinnacle of its creative and commercial potential. Indeed, any other producer in Reiner's enviable position—with a critically lauded, and still relatively youthful, series firmly anchored in the Nielsen top ten—would no doubt have been working very hard to capitalize on his show's current critical and popular standing by trying to lock the series into a lucrative long-term production deal.

Instead, Carl Reiner was already planning his exit.

28

CURTAIN CALLS

Dick Van Dyke insists that Carl Reiner never intended *The Dick Van Dyke Show* to run forever. "He'd said at the outset," reports the actor, "that if the show went five years, that would be plenty." And though neither Van Dyke nor anyone else connected with the series seems to recall exactly when Reiner first declared his intention to end the show once its original five-year contract with CBS expired in 1966, the producer had been promising as much since at least the middle of season four.

"Carl says there is no possibility the show will go beyond its fifth year," noted the *Los Angeles Times*'s Cecil Smith in that paper's entertainment column on December 28, 1964. "Dick Van Dyke has a handsome movie career awaiting him, and Mary Tyler Moore is en route to movies."[1] As *Daily Variety*'s Dave Kaufman pointed out a few months later, Reiner himself was equally anxious to move beyond the confines of the small screen. "They're breaking up that gang," wrote Kaufman in late 1965, "because the series has done so well most everyone connected with it wants to go into other fields."[2]

Well, not quite everyone. It's worth noting that there was also a highly vocal contingent of the *Van Dyke Show*'s cast who made it clear that they were quite happy just where they were. "It was a shame we didn't go on for another couple years," says Rose Marie, who insists that she—along with Morey Amsterdam and Richard Deacon—lobbied long and loud on the show's behalf throughout the early months of 1965. "We told Dick and Carl, 'We think you're making a mistake,'" the actress recalls. "And they said, 'Naw, let's finish up on top.' They didn't want to go on—they figured that we had done the best show that we could, and they didn't want to fall down."

According to Amsterdam, the most fervent opponent to Reiner's plan to shut the series down was none other than the show's executive producer himself. "Sheldon was very, very upset," Amsterdam remembered. "He told Dick, 'Are you crazy? CBS would've taken us for another five years! You could have backed up the Brink's truck right here and had them unload as much money as you wanted!'"

"No question about it," acknowledged Sheldon Leonard, who confirmed that the CBS network made no secret of their desire to renew the show's contract well beyond the five-year mark. "We were offered a very fat deal for the three years to follow." And, as Leonard tried his best to explain to the show's principal players at the time, their own bargaining positions could not have been stronger. "Just tell them what you want!" the executive producer advised Moore, Reiner, and Van Dyke. "Tell them you want three times your present salary. Or four times—five, ten times! Whatever you want. If you're looking to solidify your future, you can write your own ticket!"

To illustrate his point, Leonard invoked the name of their Desilu Cahuenga neighbor Andy Griffith, who had successfully renegotiated the contract for his own Sheldon Leonard–produced series less than a year earlier. "Andy Griffith was faced with the same situation at the end of five years," Leonard explained to his stubborn stars and producer. "They came to him hat in hand. And Andy was amenable, and he wrote his own ticket—and it was a very rich ticket. And you people can do the same thing!" Eventually, the executive producer made his final pitch directly to the show's producer-creator. "If you go to color," Leonard told Reiner, "you could have five more years!"*

Despite the passion of his arguments on the show's behalf, Leonard knew he was pleading a lost cause. "The issue was settled before the

---

* Although Reiner chose not to heed his executive producer's advice to keep the series on the air, he insists that both he and Sheldon Leonard *had* given serious thought to filming *The Dick Van Dyke Show* in color as early as the show's third season. But, he says, the plan was quickly abandoned when it became evident that filming in the more expensive color process would've added about seven thousand dollars to the cost of each episode. "It didn't seem to make any sense at the time," explains the producer. "There was no big argument. It was like, 'What do we do? It'll cost us seven thousand dollars a week more to go to color.' 'Oh. Well, in that case, let's not.'"

question even arose," admitted Leonard. "The morale to go on with the show just wasn't there. Dick Van Dyke was being courted by everybody in the business. Carl Reiner was anxious to get out from behind his desk and become a director. And Mary Tyler Moore knew that there was a big contract waiting for her at Universal. They all felt that they were wasting their time in television—and here Universal and all of these people were throwing money at them in great, large gobs."*

Even if the offers tendered by the studios hadn't been quite so irresistible, Reiner maintains, the departure of Van Dyke and Moore for the big-screen arena was inevitable—if only because they were both still relatively young. "You have to remember," explains Reiner, "that in the days before our show, most of the big sitcoms were cast with people who had all had careers in movies—Andy Griffith, Lucille Ball, Danny Thomas—and most of them were perfectly happy to have found a niche in television and to just stay there." But here, notes Reiner, Van Dyke and Moore were being offered a chance to turn the tables—to become the first stars to make the transition from small screen to big, instead of the other way around. Who could blame them for wanting to give it a shot? "If we had been older folk, we probably would have let the show go on past the five years," he observes. "But Mary and Dick really wanted to move on. And so did I. We all wanted to do movies."

Notwithstanding Reiner's assertions to the contrary, Van Dyke insists he would have been delighted to continue in his series well beyond the term of his original five-year contract—as long as his producer agreed to stick around as well. "I don't think any of us wanted in the least to quit," says Van Dyke. "It really was the most pleasant way to make a living I've ever discovered. It was a real home." But, he observes, as far as he was concerned, the show's fate was sealed the day Reiner announced he would not be returning as the show's producer beyond season five. "No one would have dreamed of going on without Carl. It just wouldn't have been the same show without him."

---

* As Leonard suggested, neither of the show's two leading players would suffer financially in the years following the show's demise in 1966. Universal Pictures was the winner in the spirited bidding to lure the services of Mary Tyler Moore, who finally signed a seven-year, ten-picture contract with the studio at a reported fee of $100,000 per film. As for Dick Van Dyke—whose own per-picture fee had reportedly ballooned to five times that amount by 1966—the star would walk away from the series with a pair of multipicture deals in place, at Disney Studios and Columbia, that would keep him busy through the end of the decade. In 1965, Van Dyke had also negotiated an exclusive television contract with CBS that called for the star to headline a series of three annual specials for the network—the first to appear in 1967—all of which would be produced by the star's own Lotus Productions.

"Coast to Coast Big Mouth" provided Carl Reiner with one of his funniest Alan Brady turns, and earned writers Persky and Denoff their second Emmy for writing *The Dick Van Dyke Show.*

Sam Denoff also dismisses the commonly held view that Van Dyke's career ambitions—or anyone else's, for that matter—played a significant role in the show's demise. "It wasn't a matter of everyone wanting to go do movies or anything like that," Denoff maintains. "Dick already had a movie career!" The real reason the show left the air when it did, says Denoff, was Reiner's and Van Dyke's shared desire to end the series while the audience was still laughing. "Dick and Carl decided basically that they did not want to have the show go downhill. A lot of us felt that it could've gone on—I think we could have. But Dick and Carl wanted to bring it to an end, so they did."

IF NOTHING ELSE, Carl Reiner's decision to retire the series at the close of the season provided his staff with a renewed creative incentive as they gathered to start work on the show's fifth year in the last week of July 1965. "Everybody was aching to do the best fifth year we could possibly do," observes Reiner. And so, their creative edge honed by an awareness of the show's impending curtain call, the cast and crew of *The Dick Van Dyke Show* embarked on their fifth and final year together, determined to create their best season yet.

Rob and Laura take temporary custody of "The Ugliest Dog in the World" in the show's 130th episode.

It would be a tall order, of course. And if in the final analysis the show's creators fell short of their admittedly lofty goal, it wasn't for lack of trying. But, as Reiner himself acknowledges, after five seasons, it was perhaps inevitable that the series would begin to reveal a few signs of age. "We tried to do something new with every show," says Reiner, "but after a certain number of years it's very hard to come up with something different every single week."*

Despite the pressure of having to compete with the creative legacy of their own first four seasons, the cast and crew of *The Dick Van Dyke Show* still managed to craft a fifth season of thirty-one half hours that would include many of the series' most fondly remembered episodes, beginning with the season's very first entry, "Coast to Coast Big Mouth." Based on a script that would earn writers Bill Persky and Sam Denoff their second Emmy for the series, the episode details the hilarious complications that ensue after a glib quiz-show host tricks Laura into blurting out, on national television, the scandalous fact that her husband's boss wears a toupee. "That was Mary at her best," notes Denoff, who cites the scene where Laura finally tenders her

---

* Astute viewers will find plenty of evidence to back up Reiner's assertion in the striking number of fifth-season *Dick Van Dyke* episodes that borrow themes, settings, or—in some cases—entire plot elements from earlier shows. To name a few of the more notable examples: the dire straits in which Laura finds herself after she speaks out of turn on television in the fifth season's "Coast to Coast Big Mouth" recalls a similar plight that befell Rob after he found himself seated in Ray Murdock's hot seat for the show's forty-eighth episode, "Ray Murdock's X-Ray"; the plotline of season five's "The Ugliest Dog in the World," in which the Petries take a troublesome canine into their home, bears echoes of Rob and Laura's earlier frustrations with Buddy's German shepherd in the show's seventh episode, "The Unwelcome Houseguest"; and finally, the garish brooch that forms the centerpiece of season five's "The Curse of the Petrie People" bears a resemblance—thematically, at least—to the bauble that Rob presented his wife in the show's thirteenth episode, "Empress Carlotta's Necklace."

sheepish apology to a glowering Alan Brady as one of the best-performed set pieces of the entire series. As the scene begins, Laura shyly approaches Brady, who is seated behind his massive desk, surveying the line of wig stands that display his now obsolete toupee collection. "Fellas," he says, addressing the wigs, "there she is! There's the little lady who put you out of business."

"Alan," she protests, "it was an accident!"

"So was Custer's Last Stand!" Brady shouts, clutching one of the pathetic hairpieces in his hand. "Would you like a scalp for your belt?" When Laura tries to convince the star that he might actually be more attractive without a toupee, the quick-tempered egoist mocks her transparent insincerity by tossing the wigs onto his scalp, one atop the other. "*That*'s the receding hairline job," he exclaims, indicating a wig that's designed to make people think he's losing his hair slowly; next, he points out his crew-cut model, designed for summer wear; and, finally, Brady plunks an intentionally disheveled toupee on top of his head, explaining that it's his "Alan-you-need-a-haircut" model. "What, do you suggest I do with all of these now?" he asks her at last. "Well," Laura volunteers, ever helpful, "there must be *some* needy bald people."

Arriving in the very nick of time, Rob rushes in to rescue Laura just as his employer appears to undergo a sudden—and quite unexpected—change of heart. "I've decided to be adorable about this mess," Brady volunteers, suddenly turning philosophical about his baldness. "I'm not twenty-nine anymore. I'm an established genius," he admits. "Sooner or later it was bound to come out. And this way I'm getting a lot of sympathy—not to mention the publicity."

And so, all's well that ends well. Or so it seems, until Laura—giddy with relief—riles the tyrant all over again with her playful suggestion that she might garner even greater publicity for the star by revealing another of his best-kept secrets to the media. "Maybe I oughta go on television and tell them about your nose!" she blabs. At which point Rob wisely—and swiftly—entices her to beat a hasty retreat before the final fade-out.

WHEN "COAST TO COAST BIG MOUTH" was filmed as *The Dick Van Dyke Show*'s fifth-season opener on August 3, 1965, it's unlikely that any of the show's returning cast was as happy to be back at work as Dick Van Dyke, who'd just spent a less than stimulating summer shooting the undistinguished *Lt. Robinson Crusoe, USN* for Disney, the first feature in the star's four-film commitment to the studio. Despite the fact that the film had been directed by Van Dyke's friend and manager, Byron Paul, the star was hardly thrilled by the result—an opinion that he was only too happy to share with his trusted colleagues on the *Van Dyke Show* set as soon as he returned to work. "That was the year," recalls Rose Marie, "Dick came in and said, 'If you're a friend of mine, you won't go see the picture.'"

As the cast of the *Van Dyke Show* regrouped to begin their fifth year together, they would bid a fond farewell to the show's longtime film editor, Bud Molin, who left the show after four seasons to assume editing chores on *I Spy*, a lighthearted adventure series that was the latest brainchild of producer Sheldon Leonard. Although Molin viewed the transition as nothing more than a practical career choice—the *Van Dyke Show* was, after all, on its way out, while *I Spy* offered the promise of continued employment—

Dick Van Dyke stretches his range to play Rob's late Uncle Hezekiah in the fifth-season episode "The Great Petrie Fortune."

Carl Reiner viewed his long-established editor's departure as tantamount to treason.

"Carl got real annoyed," the editor recalled. "I didn't think it was such a bad thing. I just figured *Van Dyke* was gonna be folding, so I signed on to do *I Spy*. I just thought it would be fun to do another show. But Carl was a little hurt." Even so, there was little Reiner could do to prevent the defection, especially since it was his own executive producer who was responsible for luring the editor away. For the show's final season, Molin's longtime assistant editor, Beryl Gelfond, moved behind the *Van Dyke Show*'s editing table, leaving it to Reiner and Molin to patch up their differences at a later date—which they eventually did, with spectacular results. In 1970, Molin edited *Where's Poppa?*, the third feature film directed by Reiner. For the next twenty-three years, until Molin's 1993 retirement, he would edit every movie that carried the credit "directed by Carl Reiner."

In the show's final year of production, Sheldon Leonard became an increasingly shadowy presence on the set of *The Dick Van Dyke Show*. By 1965, the executive producer was spending much of his time out of the country, tending to the production demands of *I Spy*, a series that was frequently shot in far-flung locations around the globe. Even so, Leonard was hardly worried about the effect his absence would have on the *Van Dyke Show*. After five years of production, the executive producer recognized that his own guiding presence on the set was no longer the crucial factor it had once been. In fact, the show's well-oiled production machine was operating so smoothly by season five that the cast and crew managed to knock a full day off their previous five-day rehearsal schedule. "We got so good at it in the last year or so," observes Reiner, "that we could do the show in four days. We knew who we were by then."

It probably didn't hurt that by that time Reiner had in his employ a pair of story editors as talented, diligent, and tireless in their labors as Bill Persky and Sam Denoff, who had, in the space of two short years, risen from the status of freelance writers to become indispensable cogs in the show's weekly production apparatus. And the team's sterling capabilities were scarcely lost on Reiner. On the contrary, when the producer announced that he was taking a leave of absence a few weeks into the show's fifth year, he would pay his capable assistants the ultimate compliment of handing them the keys to the store.

29

SHENANIGANS

Given Carl Reiner's paternal attitude toward *The Dick Van Dyke Show*, his decision to take an out-of-town acting job at the height of the show's final production cycle could not have been easy to make. In fact, says Reiner, when director Norman Jewison called to offer him a choice role in *The Russians Are Coming, the Russians Are Coming*, his first impulse had been to turn him down flat.* "I said no to *The Russians Are Coming* five times!" recounts Reiner. "I told them, 'No, I can't leave the show, it's my baby. And we're almost at the end of the tunnel.' I wanted to go out big." Reiner finally relented—but only after he'd extracted an ironclad guarantee that he would be required to spend no more than twelve weeks on the film's Northern California location. "I told them," says Reiner, "'I'll do the movie, but only if I can get twelve *Van Dyke* shows down on paper before we start shooting.'"

And so it was that Reiner spent the better part of the summer of 1965 cramming with Persky and Denoff to get a dozen *Van Dyke Show* scripts in shape before his upcoming hiatus from the series. Finally, on September 11, 1965—a few days after the *Van Dyke Show* company wrapped their 133rd episode, "The Great Petrie Fortune"—Reiner flew to Fort Bragg, California,

---

* Although Reiner insists he was originally offered the part of the Russian sailor, Rozanov—the role eventually played by Alan Arkin—he opted instead to play the film's straight lead, Walt Whittaker, a Manhattan TV writer whose peaceful summer on a small resort island is disrupted by the unexpected arrival of an offshore Soviet submarine.

to begin principal photography on his most substantial acting role in five years. There, sequestered in what he would describe as "a charming town with one theater, a bowling alley, and a stoplight,"[1] he would spend the better part of the next twelve weeks in self-imposed exile from his beloved *Dick Van Dyke Show* for the first—and only—time in the show's five-year life span.

It would be no small consolation to Reiner that he'd left the show in the capable hands of Persky and Denoff, who had been promoted to the status of full-fledged producers for the duration of his absence. "I trusted that the guys knew my sensibilities," Reiner observes. "They knew what I hated." But, though Persky and Denoff were flattered by their mentor's confidence, they would soon discover that others were not so easily convinced. "The cast trusted us," explains Persky, "up to a point."

As Persky himself is quick to acknowledge, the challenge of stepping into Reiner's shoes—even as understudies—was no easy trick. "There never has been a guy as important to a show as Carl was on that show. *He* was the real star, and I think Dick would be the first one to acknowledge that. So, when Carl left, everybody in the cast felt betrayed. And the first show we did where Carl wasn't there, they were scared. We were like this loving family, and suddenly Daddy was gone and we were now on our own." Van Dyke is even more succinct in his appraisal of those first few rehearsals without Reiner. "We were lost," says the star.

It's unlikely Van Dyke would've gotten much argument from Persky and Denoff had he voiced that assessment at the first script meeting convened after their regular producer's departure—a tense gathering that the writing team approached with trepidation. But despite the sense of foreboding that hung over the stage as the fledgling producers passed that week's script around the table, the pair forged gamely ahead. "Page one!" announced Persky, doing his best to sound

"Morale was very important on that set," says Sheldon Leonard. "If you weren't happy when you came in, it would show up on the screen."

commanding despite the self-consciousness he felt repeating a phrase he'd heard Reiner intone at so many earlier script-reading sessions.

The panic bubbling beneath the surface seemed to ease for a moment as the actors flipped their scripts open and began to read their lines aloud. The novice producers were heartened by the laughter that greeted the show's opening scene, but their relief would be short lived. A few pages later, the actors hit a slight snag in the script, and suddenly the dark clouds were back overhead. "There was a problem in one scene, and a major problem in another scene," notes Persky, who emphasizes that coming upon a rough patch or two in an early draft of a *Dick Van Dyke Show* script was hardly unusual. "It needed the usual rewrites," says the writer, recalling the gathering anxiety he sensed rising in his company as it trudged on through the troubled script. "You could tell that they were worried."

That said, the actors were not entirely unsympathetic to their understudy producers' plight—as Persky discovered a few moments later, when his acting company dropped their guard long enough to share a moment of spontaneous comic relief, even if it was at his expense. As Persky recalls, the agonizing tension was finally broken when the studio phone rang in the middle of the reading.

"Yes?" answered Richard Deacon, after picking up the telephone handset. As Persky recalls, there was a short pause before the flamboyant actor turned and handed him the receiver with a grand flourish. "They want to talk to the *producer*," Deacon announced, putting a stinging emphasis on the final word.

"Richard Deacon was a particularly acerbic kind of guy," explains Persky, who could tell the actor was up to something by the wicked glint in his eye as he handed him the phone. Warily, the stand-in producer took the receiver, and—his nerves already frayed from the trial of the morning's reading—barked a gruff salutation into the phone.

"Yeah?" demanded Persky. At which point the person on the other end of the line chirped in a voice that was clearly audible to everyone around the table.

"Is this *Carl Reiner*?" the caller asked, somewhat confused.

"No, *it's not*!" snapped Persky, not missing a beat. "But I'm doing the best I can."

There was something so honest about Persky's response that the entire company burst into laughter, a welcome antidote to the glum spirits that had blanketed the room only moments before. When the reading resumed a few minutes later, the angst was gone, and the actors completed the reading in much better spirits. "They were insecure that first week," concludes Persky. "But they got over that as soon as they saw that we knew what we were doing."

IF ANYONE NEEDED evidence of Persky and Denoff's competence as producers, their capability would be immediately apparent in the very first show filmed under their auspices, "Odd but True." In the episode's deliriously offbeat storyline, Rob Petrie achieves a dubious notoriety when it's discovered that a constellation of freckles on his back forms a connect-the-dots facsimile of Philadelphia's Liberty Bell—a premise that Reiner insists could only have come from the twisted sensibilities of writers Garry Marshall and Jerry Belson. "That was Belson and Marshall," observes Reiner. "They always came up with crazy, wonderful things which stretched our show."

"I've always been obsessed with Ripley's *Believe It or Not*," confirmed cowriter Belson, who hastened to add that "Odd but True" was one of the few *Van Dyke* scripts that was most definitely *not* inspired by any real-life incident. "That never happened to any of us," says Belson.

Whatever their inspiration, Belson and Marshall's penchant for the bizarre served them well in the episode's climax, a surreal confrontation that takes place in the *Odd but True* waiting room. There, Rob and Laura unwittingly instigate a battle royal whose participants include a woman who swears that her pet dachshund has fasted for ten years, a man who brandishes a potato that bears an uncanny resemblance to a one-eyed duck, and an industrious hiker who claims he's just walked in from Buffalo—on his hands. "We had a lot of fun when we did that story," Belson recalled. "That was just me and Garry going nuts."

BUOYED BY THE audience's favorable response to "Odd but True"—which proved that it *was* possible to get through production of an entire episode of *The Dick Van Dyke Show* without Carl Reiner, if just barely—the cast approached rehearsals for their next episode with a more relaxed attitude. Maybe even a little too relaxed, as Van Dyke explains.

Rob prepares for a mock bullfight in "Viva Petrie," an episode that had a troubled rehearsal week.

"We got a little carried away on that one," the actor remembers, recalling the boisterous rehearsals that took place a few days before the cast shot episode 135, "Viva Petrie." "We were having so much fun that we got a little undisciplined, I'm afraid." Indeed, notes the star, things finally got so out of hand that the entire cast earned a scolding from Sheldon Leonard that Van Dyke still hasn't forgotten.

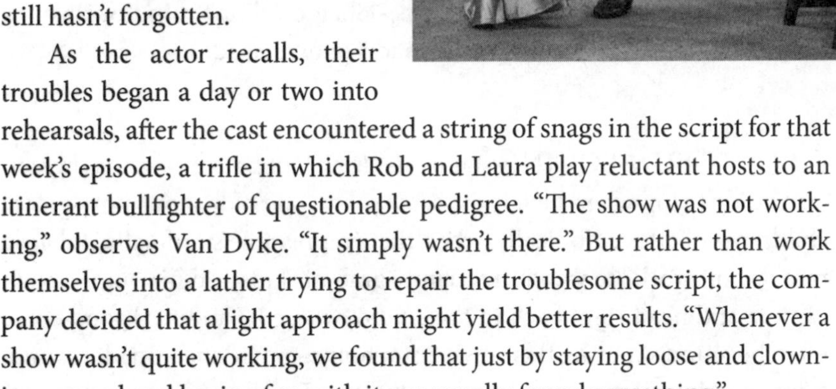

As the actor recalls, their troubles began a day or two into rehearsals, after the cast encountered a string of snags in the script for that week's episode, a trifle in which Rob and Laura play reluctant hosts to an itinerant bullfighter of questionable pedigree. "The show was not working," observes Van Dyke. "It simply wasn't there." But rather than work themselves into a lather trying to repair the troublesome script, the company decided that a light approach might yield better results. "Whenever a show wasn't quite working, we found that just by staying loose and clowning around and having fun with it, we usually found something."

Usually. But not always.

Finding little inspiration in the episode's thin storyline, the cast—led by Van Dyke and guest star Joby Baker—instead turned their attentions to the staging of a mock bullfight. The resulting antics struck most of those gathered on the set as wildly amusing, even if the horseplay had little to do with the episode as written. "We were having so much fun that we never did get around to putting the show together," confesses Van Dyke. It was a subtlety not lost on Sheldon Leonard, who—with his characteristically impeccable timing—happened to drop by the *Van Dyke* stage at the very height of the cast's rambunctious shenanigans.

"Sheldon walked in on us," confesses Van Dyke, "and we all had a bad case of the sillies. He looked at the show, and he saw that, obviously, it was not working, and we were doing nothing to repair it. And, for the first time I can recall, Sheldon lost his temper. He really screamed at us. It was two days before showtime, and he just couldn't believe that we were letting things fall apart the way we were." Suitably chastened, the actors retrieved their discarded scripts and tiptoed back to their starting positions. "Oh, boy," says Van Dyke, "you could've heard a pin drop! To get dressed down by Sheldon is an experience, I'll tell ya. He's worse than a high school principal."

Not surprisingly, the cast and their producers got the show into presentable shape by the time it went before the cameras the following Tuesday evening. "I don't know how good the show turned out to be," confesses the star, "but at least we made *something* out of it." The executive producer agreed, and, after watching the cast move effortlessly though their final dress rehearsal, Leonard made a point of going backstage to give them an approving nod—a gesture of benevolent acceptance that was greeted with audible sighs of relief from the actors. "Sheldon didn't mind our having fun," notes Van Dyke, "as long as we had a good episode."

FOR THE FUN-LOVING star of *The Dick Van Dyke Show*, the shenanigans didn't stop when he left the set—as any one of his four now-grown children will attest. Ironically, when the irrepressible star finally did get a rare day off work, he would frequently grab his kids and his home-movie camera and head right back to the studio, where he and his brood could often be found shooting their own 8mm home-movie epics on idle soundstages and back-lot streets. In one of the Van Dyke gang's more elaborate mini-epics—a Western spoof titled "Hide! It's Noon!"—Dad played a marshal named Shorty, while his two teenaged boys, Barry and Chris, donned black hats to play the film's outlaw gang.* An even more ambitious project was "The Beast that Ate Encino," a sci-fi parody set in and

---

* Perhaps inspired by his participation in the family's 8mm epics, Dick Van Dyke's son Barry would turn to acting full-time in the late seventies. After logging a string of one-shot roles on *Mork and Mindy*, *The Love Boat*, and *Remington Steele*, among others, Barry Van Dyke landed more prominent recurring roles on *Galactica 1980* and *Airwolf*, as well as costarring stints on his father's 1988 series *The Van Dyke Show* and, beginning in 1993, *Diagnosis: Murder*. The younger Van Dyke also made a cameo appearance on the original *Dick Van Dyke Show* in 1962, when he and his brother Chris appeared as child extras in the show's twenty-second episode, "The Talented Neighborhood."

around the rambling San Fernando Valley house at 4869 Encino Avenue that also served as home to the Van Dyke clan.

For a few memorable years in the mid-sixties, that Encino Avenue address was also the site of the San Fernando Valley's most spectacular Halloween attraction. It was there each October 31 that Dick Van Dyke—aided and abetted by a small army of the neighborhood's more industrious children—would transform his sprawling front yard and driveway into a homemade Halloween spook factory. "It was like a carnival," recalls Tony Paris, who was nine years old when his father, Jerry Paris, first took him to see the Van Dyke family's annual Halloween spectacular. "Dick had a mechanical Frankenstein coming out of the ground," remembers the younger Paris. "And a Dracula, and vampires, and mechanical men. It was the most impressive thing I'd ever seen one man do by himself." Nor was Tony Paris alone in his admiration of Van Dyke's Halloween handiwork. "It was the biggest thing in the Valley," he observes. "There was always a long line of cars waiting to get into his driveway on Halloween night."

"I'd get anywhere from three to five thousand people every year," boasts Van Dyke. "It finally got to the point where I had to hire two off-duty cops just to handle all the traffic." The star also took it as a point of pride that the vast majority of rubberneckers who drove through his driveway each year were unaware that the curator of the display also happened to be one of the country's top comedy stars. Which was just fine with Van Dyke, who insists that he created the neighborhood attraction purely for the fun of the undertaking.

"It all started out with a Frankenstein monster I built one year and stuck out in front. And it was such a big hit that the next year I made a Dracula. And then a mummy. And every year I'd add a few more. Finally I had a crew of teenage kids who helped me. Over the years, I built about thirty monsters out in the yard. Halloween used to be quite a big deal around my house."

THOUGH HIS CHERISHED *Dick Van Dyke Show* company performed their labors far from Carl Reiner's sight during the dozen weeks the producer spent filming *The Russians Are Coming, the Russians Are Coming* in Northern California in late 1965, they were by no means out of his mind. But, outside of a few short hops home—and, of course, the producer's daily phone calls to Persky and Denoff—Reiner's most significant contact with the *Van Dyke Show* for the better part of those three months came when he watched the program on television, along with the rest of America, each Wednesday night. Not surprisingly, the producer proved to be one of the show's biggest fans. "Some of the shows they did while I was gone were as good as any we did together," Reiner says. In fact, of all the episodes that were produced by Persky and Denoff during his leave of absence, Reiner recalls only one that gave him the slightest cause for worry: episode 141, "Who Stole My Watch?"

In the episode's storyline, Rob and Laura are stymied when Rob's expensive new watch comes up missing after a birthday party at their house. At his wit's end, Rob reluctantly considers the possibility that one of his friends may have taken the timepiece. And it was that somewhat shaky conjecture that made Reiner wince. "There's no chance on God's earth Rob would ever think that Buddy or Sally would steal from him!" exclaims Reiner, who insisted on judging his characters' behavior by the strict yardstick of his own personal code. "Would *I* ever think Mel Brooks took a watch from *my* house?" Reiner asks rhetorically. "Of course not!" After seeing the episode, the producer was outraged; and first thing the next morning, he called his understudy producers to share his umbrage. "Hey," he asked them, "how could you let that go?"

"We thought we dealt with that," explains Denoff. "We thought we covered that with a line where Rob says, 'This is impossible. None of my friends could have done that.' But these things are very subjective, and I guess Carl didn't agree." In any event, Reiner admits that his momentary disenchantment with his substitute producers was hardly significant in light of their far greater achievements during his leave of absence. "In all those shows they did, they missed that *one* little thing," Reiner reflects. "One little thing. But the rest of them were terrific."

A still from "Who Stole My Watch?," one of a handful of fifth-year *Dick Van Dyke* episodes produced in Carl Reiner's absence.

"Richard Deacon was a particularly acerbic kind of guy," says writer Bill Persky, who came by that knowledge firsthand when he found himself on the receiving end of one of the actor's well-timed jests.

Reiner finally wrapped his scenes in *The Russians Are Coming* in early December 1965, just in time to report back to the *Van Dyke Show* set to supervise production of the show's 145th episode, "The Curse of the Petrie People," which was filmed on December 14. Another fifth-season classic, "The Curse of the Petrie People" turns a comic lens on the mortification Laura suffers after Rob's mother presents her with a garish heirloom brooch in the shape of the continental United States, a family memento that's been passed down by generations of Petrie wives and mothers. Laura feigns gratitude for the monstrosity, but her in-laws are barely out the door before she accidentally mangles the irreplaceable heirloom in the garbage disposal—thus invoking an ancient family curse.

In desperation, Laura commissions a jeweler to cast a duplicate of the ruined brooch, but the fake is spotted by Rob's sharp-eyed mother. However, in the final twist, Clara Petrie announces that she finds Laura's attempt to replace the brooch more meaningful than the object itself, and then goes on to confess that she secretly detested the garish heirloom just as much as her daughter-in-law. By episode's end, mother and daughter-in-law have concluded that the only curse any Petrie suffered was having to wear the ugly brooch in the first place.

The episode's inventive script sprang from the typewriter of Carl Kleinschmitt and Dale McRaven, a pair of journeymen writers who'd been laboring as uncredited script doctors for *The Joey Bishop Show* before Persky and Denoff brought them over to *The Dick Van Dyke Show*, where they would write eight of the show's final thirty-one episodes. The team's impressive portfolio of fifth-season shows included "Uhny Uftz," a science-fiction–themed episode in which Rob has an apparent close encounter with a UFO; "Body and Sol," a flashback episode that explores Rob's brief

Rob experiences a surreal night in upstate New York during a convention of the Seals lodge in "Bad Reception in Albany," another offbeat premise from writers Garry Marshall and Jerry Belson.

career as "Pitter Patter" Petrie, middleweight champ of Company A; and, most memorably, the show's 153rd episode, "Obnoxious, Offensive, Egomaniac, Etc.," which describes a writer's nightmare in which the working draft of Rob, Buddy, and Sally's latest script accidentally finds its way into Alan Brady's hands before the writers have had a chance to delete a string of nasty comments they'd inserted for their own amusement.

"That actually happened to us," says Dale McRaven, who recalls that when he and Kleinschmitt were on *The Joey Bishop Show*, they frequently slipped blatantly unprintable stage directions into their first-draft scripts as a means of venting their frustrations about the show's star. "Joey Bishop was not a nice person to writers," says McRaven. To get back at him, the scribes would often describe their disrespectful boss in the unkindest terms imaginable in early drafts of the scripts they wrote for his show. But the writers got the fright of their lives the week they discovered they'd accidentally submitted their latest script to the studio typist before they'd had a chance to white out the expletives.

A sleepless night followed, but—unlike Rob, Buddy, and Sally—McRaven and Kleinschmitt were spared the indignity of having to climb through their boss's window to retrieve the incriminating script. The next morning, the writers were relieved to discover that their producer had caught their error and pulled the script from circulation before it could do any harm. "We came to work the next day and found out he'd saved our ass," says McRaven. "Otherwise it might've been a very interesting table reading—for *some* people."

30

THE LAST CHAPTER

As *The Dick Van Dyke Show's* final production season rolled to an end, the program's producers decided that a few curtain calls were in order. During their last thirteen weeks, Carl Reiner and story consultants Persky and Denoff contrived to spotlight each member of the show's supporting cast in at least one episode before the show's final curtain.

And so it was that Richard Deacon's Mel Cooley finally got to stand up to his domineering brother-in-law in the show's 146th episode, "The Bottom of Mel Cooley's Heart," which concludes with the optimistic suggestion that *The Alan Brady Show*'s beleaguered producer may have finally earned a small measure of respect from his tyrannical employer. Similarly, Sally Rogers's

For their final episode, the show's cast and writers indulged themselves with a trip to the Old West, Studio City–style, in "The Gunslinger."

oft-stalled search for romance reaches a tentative denouement in the show's 148th episode, "Dear Sally Rogers," when the gal writer's televised plea for a husband attracts a mountain of marriage proposals—including a poignant declaration from the pen of her long-suffering boyfriend, Herman Glimscher. And, though her character doesn't undergo any major transformation in the episode, Millie Helper gets a chance to share the spotlight with Laura in episode 150, "Long Night's Journey into Day," in which the two wives spend an eventful night protecting the Petrie house from all sorts of imagined disasters while their husbands are away on a fishing trip.

No one in the show's extended family would receive a more definitive send-off than Buddy Sorrell, whose character would undergo a literal rite of passage when he stands for his belated bar mitzvah at the close of the show's 149th episode, "Buddy Sorrell, Man and Boy," scripted by Ben Joelson and Art Baer. Morey Amsterdam insisted that the episode, one of his favorites, was inspired by a comment he made to Reiner one afternoon, after he overheard the producer swapping bar mitzvah stories with some of the other writers.

"Carl said to me, 'What happened at your bar mitzvah?'" Amsterdam recalled. "And I said, 'Nothing. I was never bar mitzvahed. We didn't have the money. In those days my folks couldn't afford to be Jewish.' And Carl started to laugh. He said, 'Well, you're gonna be bar mitzvahed now!'"

Art Baer, who was one of the episode's writers, recalled a slightly different origin of the show's bar mitzvah story, which he said was inspired by a comment his mother made on his fortieth birthday. Like Amsterdam, Baer had missed having a bar mitzvah when he was a youngster. But when he turned forty, his mother called to suggest it wasn't too late. Baer didn't take her up on the suggestion, though he did bring the idea to his next story meeting for the *Van Dyke Show*. "I mentioned it to Carl," the writer recalled, "and he thought it was funny, and that it would work for the show. And we worked it out on the spot."

In the episode, which was filmed on January 18, 1966, Rob and Sally suspect Buddy might be stepping out with a woman other than his wife, Pickles, after he repeatedly leaves work early to keep a string of mysterious appointments. When Rob finally confronts Buddy, the older writer comes clean: He hasn't been seeing another woman—he's been seeing a rabbi! After he reveals that he'd been too embarrassed to admit it sooner, he confesses that he's been cramming for the bar mitzvah he'd missed some thirty years earlier. By episode's end, surrounded by friends and well-wishers, Buddy Sorrell accepts the ancient rite of passage of his faith and declares to one and all, "Today I am a man."

In an effort to preserve a suitably pious atmosphere in the show's closing scene, the producers hired an actual cantor to sing the traditional prayers in the bar mitzvah sequence. But though cantor Arthur Ross-Jones was expected to lend gravity to the proceedings, Amsterdam recalled that the religious singer was hardly immune to the allure of the show's glamor.

According to the actor, the cantor was supposed to sing a brief passage of prayer, in Hebrew, at the top of the bar mitzvah scene. Although the cantor performed his task perfectly at the show's afternoon dress rehearsal, Amsterdam observed that by the evening show, the glow of the spotlight seemed to have gone to the singer's head. "When he saw there were about three hundred people in the audience," the actor recalled, "he got drunk with power." By the time the director shouted "Action!" that night, there was no stopping the starstruck cantor. "He just kept on singing and singing, for maybe five or ten minutes."

The impish comic decided to take the wind out of the cantor's sails. The next time the singer paused to take a breath, Amsterdam stepped forward and shouted, "One more time!" The audience howled, and another take was quickly arranged. This time, the cantor wisely chose to stick to the script.

AFTER THE UNCHARACTERISTIC reverence of "Buddy Sorrell, Man and Boy," the company moved back to more familiar ground for their 151st episode, "Talk to the Snail," a scathing show-business satire that offered solid evidence—as if any were needed—that *The Dick Van Dyke Show* was in no danger of losing its edge as it lurched toward its final fade-out. In the episode, written by Jerry Belson and Garry Marshall, Rob uncovers a secret network memo that suggests he's about to be fired. With the threat of unemployment looming, Rob secures a job interview with TV ventriloquist Claude Wilbur, a schizophrenic performer who allows a mean-spirited snail puppet named Jellybean to dominate the proceedings. "Don't talk to *him*," Jellybean instructs Rob, "*I'm* asking the questions."

The interview quickly disintegrates into a slapstick free-for-all, with the sadistic snail delivering a sharp smack to the side of Rob's head. "*I'll* decide what's funny," the arrogant puppet commands. After absorbing a few more well-placed blows, Rob stands up to the snail. "He better not hit me again," he informs the ventriloquist, even as the puppet continues to eye the writer with suspicion. "And I'm not kidding!"

Rob finally wins the stuffed snail's respect, as well as a job offer. Fortunately, Alan Brady intervenes in time for Rob to turn down the ventriloquist's contract. When the determined snail insists they've already shaken on the deal, Rob counters with a biological defense. "A shake with a snail is not binding," the writer declares, citing no less an authority on the subject than Walt Disney.

Like most of Jerry Belson and Garry Marshall's best work for the series, "Talk to the Snail" combines an off-kilter premise with gut-wrenchingly funny gags, sharply drawn characterizations, and an eye for the absurd. According to Belson—who counted this episode among his favorites—Garry Marshall's past experience as a writer for puppeteer Shari Lewis provided the episode's springboard, although, Belson hastened to add, the perky puppeteer was not a model for the episode's demented ventriloquist. "She wasn't mean like this guy was," he confirmed.

Nor did the show's actual guest star resemble the sadistic puppeteer he played in the episode. On the contrary, Paul Winchell demonstrated his own sense of humor by his willingness to spoof his well-established persona as America's preeminent television ventriloquist of the fifties and sixties. But, as the cast of the *Van Dyke Show* would discover, Winchell's talents were by no means limited to the field of children's entertainment.

By the mid-sixties, Winchell had for some time been pursuing his second passion as a self-taught medical researcher and scientific inventor—a field in which the ventriloquist had already earned some renown. In 1963, Winchell was awarded a patent for an artificial human heart he designed, a fact that stunned Van Dyke when he discovered that tidbit on the set of the *Van Dyke Show*. "I remember listening to Paul Winchell talk all that week," recalls Van Dyke. "I was fascinated to hear how this ventriloquist had come up with an artificial heart. It just floored me that he had been that creative."

IN FEBRUARY AND March of 1966, the *Van Dyke Show* company rounded out their final six weeks of production with a mixed bag of episodes that—regardless of their relative standing on the show's long and illustrious honor roll—would be forever remembered as the last batch of a very sweet vintage.

In the first of this final six, "A Day in the Life of Alan Brady," pandemonium erupts when narcissistic Alan Brady horns in on Millie and Jerry's anniversary party with a documentary camera crew in tow. Rob goes undercover in the show's 154th entry, "The Man from My Uncle," in which G-man Harry Bond, played by a deadpan Godfrey Cambridge, sets up a surveillance station in Ritchie's room. And Rob Petrie makes his feature-film debut—opposite a scorching Italian starlet—in the gritty underground film that plays a key role in the plot of the show's 155th episode, "You Ought to Be in Pictures," which was filmed on March 8, 1966. Finally, Jerry and Millie grow jealous when Rob and Laura develop a burgeoning friendship with a pair of exciting new neighbors in episode 156, "Love Thy Other Neighbor," which was filmed on March 15, 1966.

A few minutes after the cast finished shooting "Love Thy Other Neighbor," the company regrouped on the set to film the new scenes that would be used in the framing sequence of their 157th entry, "The Last Chapter," which would otherwise comprise classic clips from past shows. Despite the fact that the episode provides little more than a reprise of the show's "greatest hits," few fans of *The Dick Van Dyke Show* would be disappointed with the finished product when it aired—slightly out of order—on June 1, 1966, as the show's final installment.

As the title suggests, the episode, written by Carl Reiner, Bill Persky, and Sam Denoff, provides an affectionate denouement to the long-running saga of Rob and Laura Petrie and their extended family of friends, neighbors, and coworkers. In the storyline, Rob offers Laura an early peek at the just-completed manuscript of his long-awaited autobiography: *Untitled: A Series of Terribly Important Events in the Fairly Unimportant Life of Robert S. Petrie.*

As Laura flips excitedly through the pages of Rob's memoir—a comical look at the life and times of a TV writer and his loving wife—viewers are treated to flashbacks of key moments in the epic chronicle of Rob and Laura Petrie as it unfolded over the five years of *The Dick Van Dyke Show.* We watch Rob's stuttering marriage proposal in an open jeep at Camp Crowder, Missouri; and we witness his faltering stumble down the aisle on the day the pair are finally wed. We relive Laura's eventful trip to the maternity ward, and we laugh once again at the postnatal jitters that have

Rob convinced that their infant was switched at birth. But finally, the episode—and the series—ends as it began, when Carl Reiner's Alan Brady announces that he plans to produce and star in a TV series based on the real-life saga of a TV comedy writer.

Sound familiar?

"That was a very easy show to come up with," says Reiner, who recalls that he and his story editors knocked out the script for the episode's wraparound sequences in the space of a few hours. "We said, 'What are we gonna do for the last one?' And I said, 'Well, let's do this!' It seemed a very logical thing to do."

IRONICALLY, *THE DICK VAN DYKE SHOW*'S final episode had not even aired when the Academy of Television Arts and Sciences passed out their Emmy Awards for the 1965–1966 season on May 22, 1966. Even so, the Academy's members were impressed enough by what they'd already seen to reward the series with eight nominations and four awards. Dick Van Dyke and Mary Tyler Moore would each add another Emmy to their growing collections—it would be his third award in the leading actor category, her second. Two of Bill Persky and Sam Denoff's fifth-season scripts earned nominations in the Academy's writing category that year: "The Ugliest Dog in the World," and the show that would earn the writers their second Emmy, "Coast to Coast Big Mouth." And, in a presentation that must have surprised no one, Carl Reiner accepted his fourth consecutive Emmy in recognition of *The Dick Van Dyke Show*'s status as the year's Outstanding Comedy Series.

Shut out that evening was Jerry Paris, who was nominated for an Emmy in the director's category, which was awarded to William Asher, the director of *Bewitched*. And although he'd been nominated for an award for Outstanding Performance by an Actor in a Supporting Role, Morey Amsterdam would go home empty-handed when that trophy went to *The Andy Griffith Show*'s Don Knotts. For her third nomination in the supporting actress category, Rose Marie seemed the odds-on favorite to finally receive long-overdue recognition for her work on the series. In her two previous nominations, the actress had been aced out of the award by dramatic actresses who—perhaps unfairly—had shared the supporting category with comedic actresses. But, as the Academy had finally changed its nominating rules to give supporting comedy performers their own separate categories that year, Rose Marie looked to be a shoo-in to win the honor at last. Alas, it simply wasn't meant to be. In an ironic twist of fate, the supporting actress Emmy that year went to the one actress who had a stronger lock on Academy voters' sympathies than even Rose Marie: Alice Pearce—the original Mrs. Kravitz on *Bewitched*—who had died two months before the awards were handed out.

THE TITLE OF *THE DICK VAN DYKE SHOW*'S final episode was actually a misnomer. For though "The Last Chapter" would be aired as the show's swan song on June 1, 1966, it was not the last *Van Dyke Show* filmed.* That honor would go to "The Gunslinger," a whimsical spoof that imagines what life might have been like had Rob and Laura and their friends lived in the wild and woolly West. In Persky and Denoff's fanciful script for the episode, which was filmed on March 22, 1966, Rob plays a retired gunslinger turned small-town sheriff—or, more precisely, "a slinger-turned-singer-turned-dancer-turned-rancher-turned-parson-turned-sheriff"—who is forced to pick up his six-shooters one last time for a showdown with his archnemesis, Big Bad Brady, in the barroom of Miss Sally's saloon.

Sam Denoff admits that having the opportunity to make a real Western—even a parody Western—was, for most of the company, a dream come true. "Every guy fantasized about being a cowboy star—me, a Jewish guy from Brooklyn; Persky, a Jewish guy from Atlantic City; and Dick, a small-town boy from Danville, Illinois. So we decided we'd do a cowboy show."

As icing on the cake, Persky and Denoff even wrote themselves into the episode. The writers appear in a brief cameo as a pair of skeptical cowpokes who cast disapproving glances at Sheriff Rob near the top of the episode. Jerry Belson and Garry Marshall also got to don sideburns and six-shooters and join the show's star-studded cast of extras—Marshall plays the barkeep at Miss Sally's Saloon, and Belson is the unfortunate gambler who catches one of Sheriff Petrie's stray bullets during a card game. Not surprisingly, Denoff reports that he and his fellow writers had a smashingly good time

* Nor is "The Last Chapter" generally shown as the final episode in the show's syndicated rerun package, which follows the series' original production sequence.

playing Old West buckaroos. "We got to dress up as cowboys. What's more romantic than that?" asks the writer. "I still have the hat!"

WHEN THE CAST of *The Dick Van Dyke Show* lined up for their curtain call after filming their 158th and final episode, the ovation that greeted them was overwhelming. Although each of them understood that this would be their last appearance together as a company, no one wanted to prolong the bittersweet moment. And so, with the sound of applause still ringing in their ears, they joined hands for one final bow, and, as a group, gracefully exited the stage.

A few minutes later, the cast and crew regrouped on another part of the lot for the show's final official gathering—a huge luau-themed wrap party. A noisy and festive affair, *The Dick Van Dyke Show*'s closing-night bash was a celebration that would not soon be forgotten by anyone in attendance. "It was," in the words of writer Dale McRaven, "a very *up* party."

And yet, observes Carl Reiner, underneath the boisterous back-slapping and jubilant congratulations, there was a poignant undercurrent of sadness. "We'd gotten to really like each other," says Reiner, "and—in some cases—adore each other. And then, suddenly, we were splitting up. We all cried a lot that night."

"We were all a little in shock," observed Morey Amsterdam. "We knew we were breaking up a family."

"I don't think any of us realized how tough it was going to be to break it up," says Ann Guilbert, who acknowledges that when the end of *The Dick Van Dyke Show*

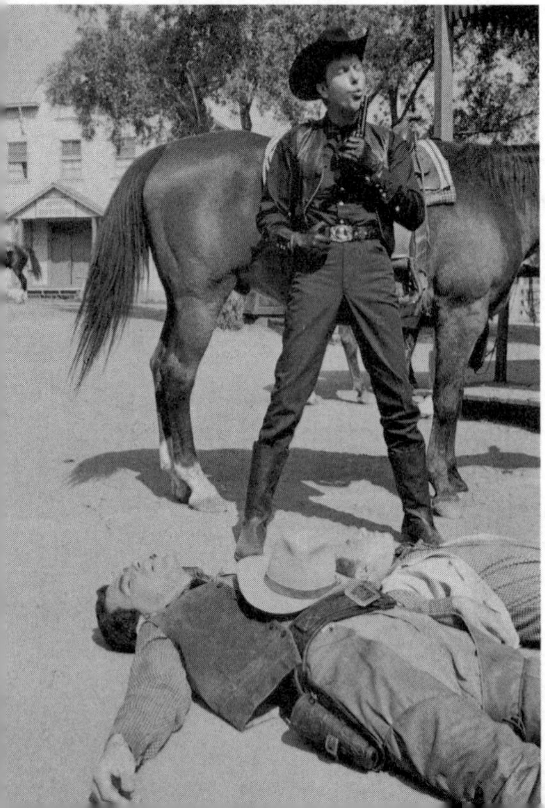

The vanquished desperadoes in this publicity shot were played by writers Persky and Denoff. "Every guy fantasized about being a cowboy," insists Denoff, "me, a Jewish kid from Brooklyn; Persky, a Jewish guy from Atlantic City; and Dick, a small-town boy from Danville, Illinois."

finally came, it took her—as it did most of the cast—completely by surprise. For Guilbert, the first real pangs of regret had surfaced suddenly, and quite unexpectedly, a few weeks earlier, during an informal lunch she shared with the rest of the show's cast at a local eatery near the studio. "Instead of going to the commissary for lunch," she reminisces, "we all went out to a restaurant that day." There, as the actress took in the easy laughter and casual chatter that surrounded her at the table, it struck her for the first time that the day was not far off when this remarkable group of people would no longer be together. "That was, for me, the beginning of really starting to miss the camaraderie. And, in little ways like that, it began to creep up on all of us that it really was ending."

And, says Guilbert, it was inevitable that the cast's sadness would peek through the soft glow of the Hawaiian lanterns that illuminated the show's closing-night party. "I think it sort of all came down that last night," she says. "Until that moment, I don't think any of us really realized that it really was, just . . . *over*."

Perhaps hoping to stave off the moment of final departure, many of the show's cast members lingered at the closing-night party well after the throng of well-wishers had thinned out to a hearty few. Although no one wanted to be first to leave, Frank Adamo recalls, it was Richard Deacon who finally broke the spell when—unable to face the unbearable task of voicing individual farewells to each of his beloved friends and colleagues—he simply slipped away from the party unannounced. "Richard Deacon couldn't handle it, God bless him," says Adamo. "So he just walked away. That was his way of dealing with it."

In the moments that followed Deacon's quiet, dignified exit, the rest of the cast soon followed suit, each in his or her own fashion. Some stole away, as Deacon had done, without saying a word, while others chose to make their departure in a hail of hugs and laughter. Either way, notes Adamo, it was not an easy exit for any of them. "Everybody had a very difficult time saying good-bye to each other," the actor recalls. "A *very* difficult time."

Perhaps more difficult for some than others, notes Bill Persky, who maintains that, although the end of *The Dick Van Dyke Show* was an emotional event for all concerned, the prevailing emotions as the final curtain rang down were relief and celebration rather than tears and regret. "I think everyone realized they'd been a part of something special," he observes, "but, in my mind, there was not a lot of sadness. We were looking to the future. Most of us—certainly Dick and Mary and Carl and Sam and myself—when we came off that show, had something big to go to. The feeling at the time was that the show had been wonderful. But now, whatever came next was gonna be wonderful, too."

And yet, as those most intimately involved in the show's creation and execution would soon discover—Persky among them—those five brilliant seasons of *The Dick Van Dyke Show* would be a very tough act to follow. "Only in retrospect," reflects Persky, "did we realize what a special time we had on the show. And that it was never gonna be recaptured."

For the last time,

Thank you, Academy

"THE DICK VAN DYKE SHOW"

Carl Reiner, Producer

OUTSTANDING COMEDY SERIES

1965-66

And thank you all,

SHELDON LEONARD
DANNY THOMAS
RONALD JACOBS, Associate Producer
BOB de GRASSE, A.S.C.
BERYL GELFOND
MARGE MULLEN
JOHN C. CHULAY
GLENN ROSS
JIMMY TREANOR

DICK VAN DYKE
MARY TYLER MOORE
ROSE MARIE
MOREY AMSTERDAM
RICHARD DEACON
ANN MORGAN GUILBERT
JERRY PARIS
LARRY MATHEWS

Writers

BILL PERSKY
SAM DENOFF
GARRY MARSHALL
JERRY BELSON
CARL KLEINSCHMITT
DALE McRAVEN
BEN JOELSON
ART BAER
JOE CAVELLA
JAY BURTON
ERNEST CHAMBERS
JOHN WHEDON
FRED FREEMAN
LAWRENCE J. COHEN
RICK MITTLEMAN
JOSEPH BONADUCE
RONALD AXE
JACK WINTER

Directors

JERRY PARIS
LEE PHILIPS
RICHARD ERDMAN

CALVADA PRODUCTIONS

Credit: Ronald Jacobs

Epilogue

On May 16, 1992, Morey Amsterdam, Rose Marie, Mary Tyler Moore, Dick Van Dyke, and Carl Reiner were reunited on the stage of Hollywood's Universal Amphitheatre for their first televised appearance together in twenty-six years. The occasion was *Comic Relief V*, the HBO cable network's fifth annual all-star comedy benefit to aid the homeless, and the cast of *The Dick Van Dyke Show* had been asked to appear as guests of honor. Although some of the biggest names in comedy were slated to appear on the Universal Amphitheatre's stage over the course of the four-hour event, the riotous ovation that greeted the entrance of television's Rob, Laura, Buddy, and Sally—along with their creator—left little doubt that they were indeed the evening's main event.

After the stunning spectacle of their entrance, the cast—perhaps wisely—remained low-key for the duration of their brief ceremonial appearance. Once the tumultuous applause finally died down, the company took center stage to volunteer a few sober remarks in support of the evening's worthy charitable cause. And then, with little more than a nod to the familiar characters with whom they'd become so closely identified, they were gone.

Although the cast's appearance on *Comic Relief V* would be the first and only time the show's four main players would appear together after the series wrapped in 1966, Carl Reiner would eventually reunite Dick Van Dyke, Mary Tyler Moore, and Rose Marie for *The Dick Van Dyke Show Revisited*, an hour-long CBS special that aired in May 2004, some six years after Morey Amsterdam's passing. But, although it was billed as the show's first official reunion, the special, which costarred Larry Mathews, Ann Guilbert, Jerry Van Dyke, and Carl Reiner, actually featured the *second* prime-time appearance of Rob and Laura Petrie since the show had gone off the air in 1966.

The idea of a *Dick Van Dyke Show* reunion was first broached as early as 1968, when Jerry Paris suggested it as a potential premise for Dick Van Dyke's second CBS special, which Paris directed. "At one point," Paris told

"We had so much fun," notes Dick Van Dyke, "that I knew even then that things would never get any better. And, as a matter of fact, they didn't."

a reporter in 1968, "some of us did think of doing an hour-long version of the old *Dick Van Dyke Show*. But Dick didn't want to do it this time."[1]

Despite Van Dyke's early resistance to the notion of a reunion, by the late seventies the actor's resolve had softened to the point where he agreed to revive Rob Petrie for a brief tongue-in-cheek send-up that he and Mary Tyler Moore performed as a sketch on the March 25, 1979, installment of *The Mary Tyler Moore Hour*. But other than that largely forgotten cameo, Rob and Laura Petrie remained happily in the wings until the 2004 special that reunited them for one last visit with each other—and the audience that grew up with them.

THOUGH MUCH HAS been made of the spectacular big-screen contracts that awaited Dick Van Dyke and Mary Tyler Moore after their series left the air in 1966, it's worth noting that life after *The Dick Van Dyke Show* was scarcely an ordeal for the other members of the show's acting ensemble, most of whom found no shortage of work waiting for them in the wake of the show's highly publicized demise.

Always popular with casting directors, Richard Deacon would continue to log an impressive array of credits in his post–*Van Dyke Show* career, including continuing roles on *The Pruitts of Southampton*, *The Beverly Hillbillies*, and *The Mothers-in-Law*. Though Deacon frequently played acid-tongued characters, the actor's offscreen kindnesses were legendary among members of Hollywood's acting community, many of whom openly mourned the beloved character actor's passing in 1984, when he died unexpectedly at the age of sixty-two.

The years since *The Dick Van Dyke Show* have been kind to Ann Guilbert, who racked up a substantial list of credits in the decades that followed, including memorable guest appearances on *Dragnet 1967*, *Barney Miller*, and *Newhart*, among dozens of other situation comedies, miniseries, and hour-long dramas. Guilbert also performed continuing roles on *Hey, Landlord!*—a 1966 series that was written and created by Jerry Belson and Garry Marshall—as well as on Andy Griffith's short-lived 1971 comeback series, *The New Andy Griffith Show*. She returned to the small screen in the early nineties in the cast of NBC's *The Fanelli Boys*, followed by a memorable run as Yetta Rosenberg on *The Nanny*. In 2010, the actress earned some of the best notices of her career playing an unlikable nonagenarian in the feature film *Please Give*.

Although Jerry Paris continued to accept occasional acting assignments until shortly before his death in 1986, his activities as a director kept him far busier behind the cameras than in front of them. Though Paris directed a handful of feature films in the late sixties—including the Jerry Lewis vehicle *Don't Raise the Bridge, Lower the River*; *How Sweet It Is*, which starred Debbie Reynolds; and *The Grasshopper*, from a script by Jerry Belson and Garry Marshall—he enjoyed his greatest success in television, where the director's credits included episodes of *The Mary Tyler Moore Show* and *The Odd Couple*, as well as a ten-and-a-half-year run as house director of *Happy Days*, which was created and produced by Garry Marshall. When *Happy Days* finally left the air in 1984, Jerry Paris returned to the feature-film arena. The director had just completed work on his eighth film, *Police Academy 3*, when he died at the relatively youthful age of sixty.

Unlike most of his *Dick Van Dyke Show* colleagues, child actor Larry Mathews chose to return to civilian life after the series folded in 1966. Upon resuming life as an ordinary Southern California kid, Larry Mazzeo reclaimed his given name and eventually graduated from UCLA with a degree in Theater Arts in 1976. Though he's spent the better part of his adult career working behind the scenes in television production, Mazzeo was briefly reunited with his TV dad when the former child star contributed a cameo to *The Chairman's Choice*, a 1993 cable TV special that Dick Van

Not long after *The Dick Van Dyke Show* wrapped, Rose Marie and Morey Amsterdam were reunited in *Don't Worry, We'll Think of a Title,* which costarred Richard Deacon.

Dyke hosted to promote reruns of *The Dick Van Dyke Show* on the Nick at Nite cable network.

In the years after the curtain fell on *The Dick Van Dyke Show*, Morey Amsterdam maintained a ubiquitous television presence as resident quipster on celebrity panel shows like *The Match Game* and *Hollywood Squares*. In 1966, the comic wrote and produced the film, *Don't Worry, We'll Think of a Title*, in which he costarred with Rose Marie and Richard Deacon. The trio would later reunite for a 1982 episode of *The Love Boat*; Amsterdam also performed opposite Rose Marie in a 1985 installment of Showtime's *Brothers*.* As fate would have it, the comedian was again paired with his old *Dick Van Dyke Show* costar in what would be his final prime-time appearance, when Rose Marie and Morey Amsterdam were cast as a married couple on an episode of *Caroline and the City* that aired a few months before the actor's death in 1996. In the wake of his passing, the legendary comic was eulogized by his show business peers in a loving—if irreverent—memorial service that Rose Marie insists was the funniest she ever attended. "Every comic in town was there," she recalls. "It was hilarious. And, you know, I'm pretty sure that's the way Morey would've wanted it."

After *The Dick Van Dyke Show* left the air in 1966, Rose Marie secured her reputation as one of TV's most reliable character actresses in a succession of comic and dramatic guest-starring roles on a wide array of episodic series, including *The Virginian*; *Hey, Landlord!*; *The Monkees*; *Kojak*; and *Cagney and Lacey*, to name only a few. Like her dear friend

* Ann Guilbert's youngest daughter, Hallie Todd, was one of the stars of *Brothers*. By coincidence, Guilbert was pregnant with the future actress when she filmed the first season of *The Dick Van Dyke Show* in 1961.

Morey Amsterdam, Rose Marie also found many years of profitable employment as one of the wisecracking stars of *The Hollywood Squares*, where she commanded her own cubicle from 1966 to 1981.

THE DICK VAN DYKE SHOW'S players were by no means the only members of the show's distinguished alumni to make good on the promise they demonstrated on the award-winning series. In the months after it was announced that *The Dick Van Dyke Show* would be shuttered, Bill Persky and Sam Denoff could probably have written for any half-hour comedy series on television. But after sizing up their options, the team decided that the time had come for them to create a show of their own. The result of their subsequent brainstorms was *Good Morning World*, which finally premiered—with Sheldon Leonard and Carl Reiner as executive producers—on CBS in the fall of 1967. Based very loosely on Persky and Denoff's own early days in radio, the series—which echoed *The Dick Van Dyke Show* in style, structure, and set design—featured Joby Baker and Ronnie Schell as a pair of early-morning Los Angeles disc jockeys.

Before the pair started work on *Good Morning World*, Persky and Denoff were approached by Danny Thomas, who wanted the talented writer-producers to work up a series for his daughter Marlo Thomas, who was at that time a largely untested actress with few substantial credits. It was an assignment, explains Sam Denoff, that the team undertook with some reluctance. "We weren't very familiar with Marlo's work," explains Denoff, "so when Danny said, 'Why don't you do a show for my daughter?,' we said, 'Uh. . . .' As very often happens, we thought that *Good Morning World* would be the big hit."

But that was not to be. As it turned out, Marlo Thomas proved to be an exceptionally capable comic actress, and *That Girl*—the series that Persky and Denoff created to showcase those talents—would enjoy a prosperous run of five seasons on ABC. *Good Morning World*, on the other hand, debuted the following year on CBS and lasted only a single season, despite the presence of an equally winning actress named Goldie Hawn in the supporting cast. After *That Girl* left the air in 1971, Persky and Denoff would collaborate on a handful of other original half-hour comedies—including *Big Eddie*, *Lotsa Luck*, and *The Montefuscos*—though none of these would capture the spark of their earliest collaborations. After Persky and Denoff amicably disbanded their durable partnership in the late seventies, Bill Persky resurfaced a few years later as executive producer of the popular and critically acclaimed CBS situation comedy *Kate and Allie*.

SHELDON LEONARD WAS already well into his first season as executive producer of *I Spy* by the time the *Van Dyke Show* wound to an end in 1966. After shepherding *I Spy* through three prime-time seasons, the veteran producer turned his energies back to situation comedy in 1969, when he executive-produced *My World and Welcome to It* for NBC. A half-hour situation comedy based on the life and works of James Thurber, the series would be widely hailed for its innovative premise—although low ratings would force it off the air after a single season. In 1975, the legendary producer returned once again to the half-hour form with *Big Eddie*, a situation comedy that reunited him with Bill Persky and Sam Denoff, who wrote, created, and produced the short-lived series, which brought Leonard back to prime time as an actor in the Runyonesque role of a reformed big-city gangster. When the show was cancelled after only three months on the air, Leonard scaled back his television commitments to devote more time to his family and his work with the Directors Guild. He died in 1997, having lived a long and wonderful life indeed.

The studio that Sheldon Leonard presided over during the glory days of *The Dick Van Dyke Show* is still in operation at 846 North Cahuenga Boulevard, although the lot has changed hands a number of times since then. After suffering through a lean period—during one extended production slump in the early seventies, the lot briefly functioned as a health club, its legendary soundstages reduced to light duty as indoor tennis and racquetball courts—the studio had regained much of its luster by the late eighties and nineties. During this second golden age, the lot would play host to a formidable list of prime-time comedies, including *Soap*, *The Golden Girls*, and *Empty Nest*, all of which originated from the creative brain trust behind the Witt/Thomas/Harris production company, one of whose principals just happened to be Tony Thomas, the son of Danny Thomas.

STILL ONE OF comedy's most prolific Renaissance men, Carl Reiner enjoyed his most consistent employment in the years after *The Dick Van*

Dyke Show as a director of big-screen comedies. After inaugurating his movie-directing career with *Enter Laughing* in 1967, Reiner moved on to create a distinguished list of directorial triumphs, including *The Comic*, *Where's Poppa?*, and *Oh, God!*, as well as most of Steve Martin's early film vehicles, including *The Jerk*, *The Man with Two Brains*, *Dead Men Don't Wear Plaid*, and *All of Me*. And yet, even with a resume that's thicker than some small-town phone directories, Reiner still points proudly to his five years as creator, writer, and producer of *The Dick Van Dyke Show* as the crowning achievement of a long and immensely rewarding career.

WHILE MOST OF the principal players in *The Dick Van Dyke Show* saga managed to forge long and successful careers after they left the series in 1966, few would go on to claim an accomplishment that rivaled the impact of the *Van Dyke Show*'s five esteemed seasons. Enter Mary Tyler Moore, whose own 1970 comeback series, *The Mary Tyler Moore Show*, burned a prime-time trail every bit as bright as that blazed by its illustrious predecessor.

And yet, as Sam Denoff points out, the groundbreaking achievement of *The Mary Tyler Moore Show* owed no small debt to its star's formative years in the cast of *The Dick Van Dyke Show*. "The success of Mary's own series came as a result of her doing the *Van Dyke Show* for five years," states Denoff, "and seeing how a well-run, homogeneous company should work." Grant Tinker, the former *Dick Van Dyke Show* advertising executive who would mastermind his then-wife's series, as well as the MTM empire that it

Mary Tyler Moore portrays Mary Richards in *The Mary Tyler Moore Show.*

would inspire, made no secret of the fact that he had the creative framework of *The Dick Van Dyke Show* in mind when he assembled the team of actors, writers, and directors who would eventually sustain *The Mary Tyler Moore Show* through seven critically acclaimed seasons.

As it happens, the magical chemistry that Moore shared with her former *Van Dyke Show* costar played an even more fundamental role in the actress's 1970 comeback. Indeed, there might never have been a *Mary Tyler Moore Show* had it not been for *Dick Van Dyke and the Other Woman*, the well-regarded 1969 CBS television special that reunited Van Dyke and his former TV wife for the first time since 1966. As the actress would no doubt be the first to admit, that providential reunion—and the creative rejuvenation that arose from their pairing—came not a moment too soon.

By 1969, Mary Tyler Moore's much-ballyhooed leap into feature films had proven to be a washout. In the space of only three short years, the actress's once-promising career had been stymied by a string of misfires that included *Thoroughly Modern Millie*, *What's So Bad About Feeling Good*, and—the absolute nadir of her big-screen career—*Change of Habit*, an Elvis Presley vehicle that featured the actress as a nun who's forced to choose between Elvis and the church. Nor had the actress fared much better when she ventured onto the Broadway stage in 1966, as the title character in *Breakfast at Tiffany's*, a little-remembered musical retelling of Truman Capote's novella. And so, when Dick Van Dyke called to invite the star to join him for a one-shot reunion on his 1969 variety-show special, the actress was primed to give the small screen another tumble.

It probably didn't hurt that *Dick Van Dyke and the Other Woman* also reunited the stars with writers Bill Persky and Sam Denoff, whose script for the special was perfectly tooled to show the multitalented actress to her best advantage. That opinion was obviously shared by the executives at CBS, who wasted little time signing the actress to the contract that led directly to *The Mary Tyler Moore Show* in 1970. Seven years and twenty-nine Emmy Awards later, *The Mary Tyler Moore Show* left the air voluntarily—like its predecessor—as one of the most honored television series of its time.

BY THE TIME Mary Tyler Moore engineered her spectacular television comeback in 1970, Dick Van Dyke had reached a creative impasse of his own. Like his former costar, the actor had been disillusioned by his own foray into the feature-film arena in the years following the *Van Dyke Show*. After a promising start, he soon found himself bogged down in a succession of undistinguished roles in films like *Fitzwilly*; *Lt. Robinson Crusoe, USN*; and *Some Kind of a Nut*—none of which delivered on the promise that Van Dyke had demonstrated so effortlessly week after week on his own series.

In 1969, the star was reunited with his TV mentor when Carl Reiner brought him *The Comic*, a feature film script about an aging silent-screen comedian that the writer—working with Van Dyke's old friend Aaron Ruben—had handcrafted for the actor. When the film failed to make a stir, its failure was enough to cause its star to eye the relative security of weekly television with renewed interest.

After watching Moore effect her graceful transition back to the small screen in 1970, Van Dyke was inspired to entertain offers for a comeback series of his own. The result was *The New Dick Van Dyke Show*, which reunited the star with Reiner, who signed on to create, write, and produce the new series, just as he had the original. When the show premiered on Saturday, September 18, 1971—fittingly, in the time slot immediately preceding Moore's own immensely popular half hour—television pundits predicted immediate and long-lasting success. However, it soon became obvious to all concerned that *The New Dick Van Dyke Show* was not likely to rekindle the magic of the old *Dick Van Dyke Show*, and the series quietly left the air at the end of its third season.

Although Van Dyke has remained a highly visible presence on our home screens over the years, with scores of appearances in specials, episodic series, and the occasional TV movie—including his return to prime time in 1993's *Diagnosis: Murder*, which would lead to a series of the same name—the star would have little luck in traditional comedy settings. In 1976, he headlined *Van Dyke and Company*, an Emmy-winning variety show that had a brief run on NBC. Five years later, he shot a pilot that failed to sell for a series titled *Harry's Battles*, a proposed ABC situation comedy that would have paired him with Connie Stevens. The star's luck wasn't much better when Grant Tinker teamed him with his son Barry for *The Van Dyke Show*, a troubled CBS situation comedy that ran for a few months in 1988. Ironically, none of the star's latter-day comeback attempts would finally generate the excitement that greeted the return of his original series to national prominence as part of cable TV's Nick at Nite lineup in 1992.

But if Dick Van Dyke has found it increasingly difficult to step out of Rob Petrie's shadow in recent years, the star would become cheerfully resigned to the fact that—whatever else he may do—he will always be identified, first and foremost, with the original series to bear his name. In fact, a few weeks after Nick at Nite added Van Dyke's vintage series to its schedule, the rerun network elevated the star to the status of elder statesman when they drafted him to portray the network's ceremonial "chairman of the board" in an entertaining series of on-air promotional spots. Almost immediately, the star's smiling countenance would once more become synonymous with quality television, as Van Dyke introduced the distinct charms of *The Dick Van Dyke Show* to a new generation of viewers, many of whom were not even born when the series premiered in the dark ages of the early 1960s.

WHEN *THE DICK VAN DYKE SHOW* voluntarily ceased production in 1966, the program was already being hailed as a modern television classic, a lone beacon of light in the vast wasteland of television. The show's unique blend of wit and warmth would prove beyond any argument that a situation comedy could be sophisticated and urbane—and still deliver a sizable audience. In the space of only five years, Carl Reiner and his company succeeded in creating a work of such consistent intelligence and invention that it would set a new standard for quality television—a standard that continues to serve as a benchmark for prime-time comedy to this day. As few TV shows had done before, and very few since, *The Dick Van Dyke Show* forever altered the way we watch television.

The Dick Van Dyke Show may be gone, but the magic shared by a loving company of friends on Desilu Cahuenga's stage 8 continues to cast its spell, if only in reruns. There, captured for all eternity in crisp images of black and white, the strange and wonderful world of *The Dick Van Dyke Show* will continue to delight audiences for as long as there are television sets on which to tune it—and people willing to share its gift of laughter.

Perhaps Morey Amsterdam summed it up best when he addressed a group of fans at a television seminar in Los Angeles some twenty years after the series ceased production. Toward the end of the evening, someone asked the character actor if working on *The Dick Van Dyke Show* had really been as much fun as it appeared. The aging performer shifted back in his chair, and said nothing for a moment, clearly savoring the memory. After a short pause, he leaned forward, smiling, with a twinkle in his eye. "It was," he answered, "like going to a lovely party that you never wanted to end."[2]

ACKNOWLEDGMENTS

I was fortunate in the writing of this book to enjoy the generous participation of every surviving cast member of *The Dick Van Dyke Show*, as well as a substantial number of the show's writers, producers, and crew members—and I remain indebted to each of them. So I'll open these acknowledgments by expressing thanks to those members of the show's acting ensemble whose anecdotes, insights, and perspectives enriched this book immeasurably: Dick Van Dyke, Mary Tyler Moore, Rose Marie, Morey Amsterdam, Ann Guilbert, and Larry Mathews. Thanks as well to the writers, directors, musicians, performers and other creative artists whose contributions made this show a classic, and whose generosity in sharing their stories brought these pages to life: Ronald Jacobs, John Rich, Bill Persky, Sam Denoff, Jay Sandrich, Frank Adamo, Art Baer, Jerry Belson, Harvey Bullock, Ruth Burch, Ross Elliott, Earle Hagen, Jerry Hausner, Bill Idelson, Harald Johnson, Sheldon Keller, Norm Liebmann, Dale McRaven, Garry Marshall, Rick Mittleman, Bud Molin, Marge Mullen, James Niver, Arnold Peyser, Lois Peyser, Al Rafkin, Guy Raymond, Ken Reid, Doris Singleton, Frank Tarloff, and Tom Tuttle.

For shedding light on the boardroom intrigues that once decided the show's fate, my thanks to Lee Rich, George Shapiro, Grant Tinker and Sol Leon; and for affording me fascinating glimpses into everyday life on *The Dick Van Dyke Show* set, I extend thanks to Rochelle Jacobs, Andy Paris, Julie Paris, Tony Paris, Michael Ross, and Tony Thomas. A tip o' the hat as well to Sylvia Miles for sharing her memories of making *Head of the Family*.

I'm also grateful for the help of Bess Scher in Carl Reiner's office, who provided invaluable support at every stage of this book's production; and I'm equally indebted to the late Ruth Engelhardt of the William Morris Agency, who was a good friend of *The Dick Van Dyke Show*, and of this book. I owe a large debt of gratitude as well to Paul Brownstein, the keeper of the Calvada flame, and an indispensable ally in preserving the show's legacy.

A big thanks to all the journalists, broadcasters, authors, and other professionals who helped me track down elusive images or unearth new information on the show and its players: Diane Albert, Lauri Allen, Caroline Ansell, Bart Andrews, Ashley Ayala at the Mark Moore Gallery, Jerry Beck at Cartoon Brew, Mark Bennett, Cheryl Blythe, David Bonner, Paul Buckley, Jim Clark, Kevin Cordero, Doug Denoff, Bill DiCicco at Research Video, Paul Dougherty, Andy Elkin, Mark Evanier, George Faber, Art Fein, Lynn Fero, Mary Schepis Johnson, Kate Light, Sal Maniaci, Suzanne Manlove, Shirley Mitchell, Catlin Moore of the Mark Moore Gallery, Bob Newhart, Bob Palmer, Annette Petelle, Wally Podrazik, Howard Prouty, Andrew Ramage, Paul Salerni, Steve Saunders, Mick Schott, Stu Shostak at Shostak Video, Terry Sims, Paul Surratt at Research Video, David Van Deusen, Betsy Vorce, Paul Ward, Ken Whittingham, Greg Williams, and Lewis S. Wechsler. Thanks as well to the researchers, curators, and staffs of the Margaret Herrick Library at the Academy of Motion Picture Arts and Sciences; the Paley Center for Media in New York and Beverly Hills; the UCLA Motion Picture and Television Archives; the UCLA Theatre Arts Library; New York's Lincoln Center Library for the Performing Arts; the Beverly Hills Public Library; and the Frances Howard Goldwyn branch of the Los Angeles Public Library.

For their generous support of this book in ways too numerous to mention, my warmest thanks to Amy Brooke Baker, Gordon Flagg, Jane Fujishige, David Goodman, Ian Maxtone-Graham, Katy Hickman, Rupert Kinnard, Richard Kulhman, Cynthia Berry Meyer, Peter Osterlund, Jill Kirchner Simpson, Amara Stapornkul, Montri Stapornkul, Elizabeth Waldron, Robert Waldron, and Chris Willman. And, for his early encouragement and support, I thank and acknowledge my teacher and friend, Michael Laurence.

Special recognition is due Dona Chernoff and Kim Witherspoon, who placed this work in the hands of its first editors, Mary Ann Naples and David Cashion. Thanks also to John Cerullo, Glenn Young, and Kay Radtke for keeping the flame burning. To Yuval Taylor and Lisa Reardon of A Cappella, a big round of applause for editing this revised and updated edition with unfailing patience and taste. Thanks as well to Drew Friedman for bringing the show's cast to life in his delightful drawing at the front of this book, and to Dan Castellaneta for contributing the eloquent foreword that follows it.

It seems only fitting that I close these acknowledgments by extending my thanks to Carl Reiner, Sheldon Leonard, and Dick Van Dyke, the founding fathers of *The Dick Van Dyke Show*: to Carl, for devoting five years to the creation and execution of a TV show that continues, more than a half century along, to delight, enlighten, and inspire; to Sheldon, for shaping Carl's vision and for being the show's most steadfast advocate and staunchest defender; and, finally, to Dick Van Dyke, for simply being Dick Van Dyke.

Vince Waldron
January 20, 2011
Los Angeles

A COMPLETE VIEWER'S GUIDE TO THE DICK VAN DYKE SHOW

REGULAR CAST AND CHARACTERS

Rob (Robert) Simpson Petrie	Dick Van Dyke
Laura Meeker/Meehan Petrie	Mary Tyler Moore
Ritchie (Richard) Rosebud Petrie	Larry Mathews
Sally Rogers	Rose Marie
Buddy (Maurice) B. Sorrell	Morey Amsterdam
Mel (Melvin) Cooley	Richard Deacon
Dr. Jerry (Gerald) Helper	Jerry Paris
Millie (Mildred) Krumbermacher Helper	Ann Morgan Guilbert
Alan Lester Brady	Carl Reiner

SUPPORTING CAST AND CHARACTERS

Stacey Petrie (Rob's brother)	Jerry Van Dyke
Herman Glimscher	Bill Idelson
Sol Pomeroy	Marty Ingels (1961–1962)
Sam Pomerantz (Sol in later episodes)	Henry Calvin (1963)
	Allan Melvin (1963–1966)
Pickles (Fiona) Conway Sorrell	Barbara Perry (1961–1962)
	Joan Shawlee (1963)
Edward Petrie (Rob's father)	Will Wright (1961)
Sam Petrie (Rob's father)	J. Pat O'Malley (1962, 1964)
	Tom Tully (1964, 1966)
Clara Petrie (Rob's mother)	Carol Veazie (1961)
	Isabel Randolph (1962, 1964, 1966)
Alan Meehan (Laura's father)	Carl Benton Reid
Mrs. Meehan (Laura's mother)	Geraldine Wall

Freddie William Helper	Peter Oliphant
Ellen Helper	Jennifer Gillespie (1961)
	Anne Marie Hediger (1962)

STOCK PLAYERS

Frank Adamo, Eleanor Audley, Arthur Batanides, Tiny Brauer, Jane Dulo, Ross Elliott, Jamie Farr, Herbie Faye, Bernard Fox, Dabbs Greer, Jerry Hausner, Peter Hobbs, Jackie Joseph, Ray Kellogg, Sandy Kenyon, Ken Lynch, Allan Melvin, Isabel Randolph, Patty Regan, Bert Remsen, Johnny Silver, Doris Singleton, Amzie Strickland, Herb Vigran, Geraldine Wall, Len Weinrib, Howard Wendell, Valerie Yerke

1958–1960 HEAD OF THE FAMILY

The pilot film for Carl Reiner's *Dick Van Dyke Show* prototype is filmed—with Reiner himself in the lead—a few weeks before Christmas 1958 at New York's Gold Medal Studios.

COMPLETE CREDITS

Written and Created by	Carl Reiner
Produced by	Stuart Rosenberg and Martin Poll
Directed by	Don Weis
Music Composed and Conducted by	Bernard Green
Director of Photography	Charles Harten
Film Editor	Angelo Ross
Sound by	Edward J. Johnstone
Art Director	Leo Kerz
Production Manager	Anthony LaMarca
Sound Editor	A. H. Pesetsky

(PILOT) HEAD OF THE FAMILY — Airdate: 7/19/60

Writer: Carl Reiner / Director: Don Weis

Cast: Robert Petrie—Carl Reiner, Laura Petrie—Barbara Britton, Ritchie—Gary Morgan, Sally Rogers—Sylvia Miles, Buddy Sorrell—Morty Gunty, Allan

Sturdy—Jack Wakefield, "Snappy," The Snappy Service Delivery Man—Milton Kamen, Mrs. Harley—Jean Sincere, Teacher—Nancy Kenyon, Roy—Joey Trent, Freddie—Mannie Sloan

Filmed in December 1958.

Television writer Robert Petrie is at his wit's end after he discovers that his six-year-old son is embarrassed to admit what his father does for a living.

Behind the scenes: The unsold *Head of the Family* pilot was originally aired at 9:30 P.M. on Tuesday, July 19, 1960, on *Comedy Spot*, a CBS anthology series that served as a clearinghouse for unsold TV pilots. . . . Director Don Weis would later distinguish himself as house director on some of TV's classiest comedies, including *The Andy Griffith Show* and *M*A*S*H*. . . . In the late 1980s, New York's Museum of Broadcasting—now the Paley Center for Media—added a copy of Carl Reiner's personal 16mm print of the *Head of the Family* pilot to its permanent collection. But, according to Reiner's longtime friend and manager George Shapiro, that print—which at the time was thought to be the only surviving copy of Reiner's historic telefilm—very nearly didn't make it to the museum at all. As Shapiro describes it, the night before he was set to drop off the film, he discovered that his car had been stolen, with Reiner's irreplaceable pilot in the trunk! "I can't tell you how upset I was," Shapiro recalls. "I didn't care about the car. I would have made a deal to leave the car stolen—plus my next *five* cars—just to get that film back!" The manager assumed his worst fears had been realized when the police called a few days later to report that they'd recovered his car—or what was left of it. "It was found abandoned and stripped," remembers Shapiro. "I never saw such a stripped car. They even stripped the bumpers off! I had old jackets and towels in the trunk. And they took the towels! They took everything in sight." Or almost everything, as Shapiro discovered once he finally gathered the courage to peek into the ravaged car's trunk. "But there, in the bottom of the trunk, was the film!" he says. "It was the *only* thing left in the whole car! They took my dirty towels—but they left that little 16mm film case!" After that scare, Shapiro refused to let the film out of his sight. "I slept with it next to me until they picked it up and took it to the Museum of Broadcasting. And only then did I tell Carl what had happened."

WINTER 1961 THE DICK VAN DYKE SHOW PILOT

"THE SICK BOY AND THE SITTER"

The pilot episode for the revamped *Dick Van Dyke Show* is filmed—with Dick Van Dyke in the role of Rob Petrie—at Hollywood's Desilu Cahuenga Studios.

COMPLETE CREDITS

Written, Created, and Produced by	Carl Reiner
Directed by	Sheldon Leonard
Associate Producer	Ronald Jacobs
Music Composed and Conducted by	Earle Hagen
Director of Photography	Robert De Grasse
Art Director	Kenneth A. Reid
Film Editor	Leon Selditz
Production Manager	Frank Meyers
Assistant Director	Jay Sandrich
Production Supervisor	W. Argyle Nelson
Prop Master	Stuart Stevenson
Camera Coordinator	James Niver
Casting	Ruth Burch
Script Continuity	Rosemary Dorsey
Set Decorator	Ken Swartz
Rerecording Editor	Edward Sandlin
Recorded by	Glen Glenn Sound Co.
Costumes	Harald Johnson
Makeup	Lee Greenway
Hairstylist	Irma Kusely
Sound Engineer	David Forrest
Music Coordinator	Walter Popp
Executive Producer	Sheldon Leonard in association with Danny Thomas

Mr. Van Dyke's wardrobe furnished by Botany 500.

1) THE SICK BOY AND THE SITTER Airdate: 10/3/61

Writer: Carl Reiner / Director: Sheldon Leonard

Supporting cast: Mel Cooley—Richard Deacon, Dotty—Barbara Eiler, Woman at Party—Eleanor Audley, Janie—Mary Lee Dearing, Sam—Michael Keith, Dr. Miller—Stacey Keach Sr., Man at Party—Fred Sherman

Filmed on January 20, 1961.

Songs: "The Sidewalks of New York" (Lawlor, Blake); "Hello, Hello" (Amsterdam); "I Wish I Could Sing Like Durante" (Wyle, Pola)

Rob talks Laura into going to a party at Alan Brady's penthouse, even though she'd sooner stay home and look after their ailing five-year-old.

1961–1962 THE DICK VAN DYKE SHOW

SEASON ONE

The triumphs and struggles of TV writer Rob Petrie and his wife Laura are chronicled in a first season of scripts written or story edited by Carl Reiner, who will shepherd the series through its first three seasons as the show's triple-threat head writer, story consultant, and producer. Sheldon Leonard serves as executive producer through each of the show's five seasons, and Ronald Jacobs is associate producer for the entire run. John Rich becomes the show's regular director as of the fourth episode.

FIRST-SEASON CREDITS

Created and Produced by	Carl Reiner
Associate Producer	Ronald Jacobs
Music	Earle Hagen
Director of Photography	Robert De Grasse, A.S.C.
Art Director	Kenneth A. Reid
Film Editor	Bud Molin, A.C.E.
Production Manager	Frank Myers
Assistant Director	(episodes #1–2) Jay Sandrich
	(episodes #3–30) John C. Chulay

Production Supervisor	W. Argyle Nelson
Prop Master	Glenn Ross
Camera Coordinator	James Niver
Casting	Ruth Burch
Script Continuity	Marjorie Mullen
Set Decorator	Ken Swartz
Rerecording Editor	Edward Sandlin
Recorded by	Glen Glenn Sound Co.
Story Consultant	Carl Reiner
Costumes	Harald Johnson
Makeup	Tom Tuttle
Hair	Elenore Edwards
Sound Engineer	Cam McCulloch
Music Coordinator	Walter Popp
Executive Producer	Sheldon Leonard in association with Danny Thomas

Dick Van Dyke's wardrobe furnished by Botany 500.

Women's fashions provided by Fabiola by David Barr, Lill-Ann, William Pearson, Ann Arnold of Beverly Hills, and Gino Paoli.

2) THE MEERSHATZ PIPE — Airdate: 11/28/61

Writer: Carl Reiner / Director: Sheldon Leonard

Supporting cast: Mel Cooley—Richard Deacon, Elevator Operator—Jon Silo, Alan Brady—Carl Reiner (uncredited voice-over)

Filmed on June 20, 1961.

Rob frets about his job security after Buddy and Sally prove themselves perfectly capable of polishing off an entire script in his absence.

Behind the scenes: Carl Reiner makes his first appearance as Alan Brady in an uncredited off-screen voice-over that can be heard near the end of this episode. . . . Sharp-eyed viewers will note that the building directory visible on the wall outside the writers' room includes such "tenants" as the show's property master, Glenn Ross, and its set decorator, who is listed as "Ken Swartz, M.D."

3) JEALOUSY! Airdate: 11/7/61

Writer: Carl Reiner / Director: Sheldon Leonard

Supporting cast: Mel—Richard Deacon, Jerry—Jerry Paris, Millie—Ann Morgan Guilbert, Valerie Blake—Joan Staley

Filmed on June 27, 1961. Songs "Say Goodbye for Charlie Jones" (Amsterdam)

Laura's jealousy gets the better of her when Rob starts working late hours with the gorgeous guest star of that week's *Alan Brady Show*.

Behind the scenes: This episode features the first appearance of Rob and Laura's next-door neighbors, dentist Jerry Helper and his wife Millie.

4) SALLY AND THE LAB TECHNICIAN Airdate: 10/17/61

Writer: Carl Reiner / Director: John Rich

Supporting cast: Thomas Edson—Eddie Firestone, Snappy Service Man—Jamie Farr

Filmed on July 5, 1961.

Laura plays matchmaker for Sally—with disastrous results—when she pairs the talkative comedy writer with her shy cousin, Thomas the pharmacist.

Behind the scenes: The first episode directed by John Rich, who would be a series mainstay for the better part of the show's first two years. . . . This episode also introduced *The Alan Brady Show*'s secretary, Marge—named after the show's script supervisor, Marge Mullen—who would remain an offstage presence throughout the show's run. . . . Jamie Farr makes the first of a handful of appearances in the bit role of *The Alan Brady Show*'s coffee man. The actor would achieve prominence a decade later, when a similar bit role he played on an early episode of *M*A*S*H* blossomed into eleven seasons as the cross-dressing Corporal Klinger on CBS's long-running antiwar comedy.

5) WASHINGTON VS. THE BUNNY Airdate: 10/24/61

Writer: Carl Reiner / Director: John Rich

Supporting cast: Mel—Richard Deacon, Man on Plane—Jesse White, Snappy Service Man—Jamie Farr

Episode 5, "Washington Versus the Bunny"

Filmed on July 11, 1961. Song: "You're the Top" (Porter)

Rob is plagued by parental guilt when he has to take a business trip on the night of Ritchie's debut as a bunny in a school play.

Behind the scenes: Carl Reiner admits that his only rationale for inserting a dream sequence in this episode—in which Rob imagines Laura, dressed in a bunny suit, haranguing him for parental malfeasance—was prurient interest. "I did that because I wanted to see Mary's legs in a bunny suit," he confesses. . . . Dick Van Dyke's on-set stand-in, Frank Adamo, is briefly visible as one of the passengers on Rob's airplane—it would be the first of many cameo appearances from the show's most frequently seen bit player.

6) OH HOW WE MET THE NIGHT THAT WE DANCED
Airdate: 10/31/61

Writer: Carl Reiner / Director: Robert Butler

Supporting cast: Sol—Marty Ingels, Mark Mullen—Glenn Turnbull, Marcia Rochelle—Chickee James, Ellen Helper—Jennifer Gillespie, Dancer—Pat Tribble (uncredited)

Filmed on July 18, 1961. Songs: "You, Wonderful You" (Warren, Brooks, Chaplin); "French-Fried Blues" (Hagen)

Rob recalls his frustrated attempts to date Laura when she was a USO showgirl and he was an overeager staff sergeant in the army's special services division.

Behind the scenes: The first of many flashback episodes that would trace the continuing saga of Rob and Laura's courtship, this was also one of the few *Van Dyke Show* episodes to be filmed without so much as a token appearance from Buddy and Sally. . . . Rob's wife-to-be is introduced as Laura Meeker, a behind-the-scenes reference to Mary Tyler Moore's then-husband Richard Meeker. . . . Rob's sidekick,

Sol, was based on Carl Reiner's real-life army chum, Sol Pomerantz, a name that would pop up—often with slight variation—throughout the series.

7) THE UNWELCOME HOUSEGUEST **Airdate: 11/21/61**

Writer: Carl Reiner / Director: Robert Butler

Filmed on July 25, 1961. Song: "Brahms' Lullaby" (arranged by Hagen)

Laura's plans for a quiet weekend in the country are spoiled when Buddy suckers Rob into looking after his German shepherd, Larry.

8) HARRISON B. HARDING OF CAMP CROWDER, MO. Airdate: 11/6/61

Writer: Carl Reiner / Director: John Rich

Supporting cast: Harrison B. Harding—Allan Melvin, Evelyn Harding—June Dayton, Police Officer #27809—Peter Leeds

Filmed on August 1, 1961.

Rob is too embarrassed to admit he doesn't remember the mysterious stranger who arrives at his doorstep claiming to be an old army pal.

Behind the scenes: Character actor Allan Melvin would also appear as Rob's army buddy Sol Pomerantz in numerous subsequent episodes. Melvin had previously held down a long-running role as one of Sergeant Bilko's recruits on *The Phil Silvers Show*, and would eventually log numerous appearances as one of Jim Nabors's barracks buddies on *Gomer Pyle, USMC*. The popular character actor would also play Sam the butcher on *The Brady Bunch*, as well as Archie Bunker's friend Barney Hefner on later seasons of *All in the Family* and its spin-off, *Archie Bunker's Place*. . . . Character actor Peter Leeds's unnamed police officer would return to the show for a second bit part, as Officer Jack Bain, in episode 18, "Punch Thy Neighbor."

9) MY BLONDE-HAIRED BRUNETTE **Airdate: 10/10/61**

Writer: Carl Reiner / Director: John Rich

Supporting cast: Millie—Ann Morgan Guilbert, Pharmacist—Benny Rubin

Filmed on August 15, 1961.

Convinced that the romance has faded from her marriage, Laura dyes her hair blonde to rekindle Rob's interest.

Behind the scenes: Though it was filmed as the series' ninth installment, the producers scheduled this episode to air as the second show to better spotlight the rapidly emerging talents of Mary Tyler Moore.

10) FORTY-FOUR TICKETS — Airdate: 12/5/61

Writer: Carl Reiner / Director: John Rich

Supporting cast: Mel—Richard Deacon, Jerry—Jerry Paris, Millie—Ann Morgan Guilbert, Mrs. Billings—Eleanor Audley, Cop—Paul Bryar, Scalper—Opal Euard, Man in Battered Hat—Joe Devlin, Usher—Frank Adamo (uncredited)

Filmed on August 22, 1961.

Rob is forced to deal with scalpers after he forgets to reserve forty-four *Alan Brady Show* tickets for a PTA group from Ritchie's school.

11) TO TELL OR NOT TO TELL — Airdate: 11/14/61

Writer: David Adler / Director: John Rich

Supporting cast: Mel—Richard Deacon, Snappy Service Man—Jamie Farr

Episode 11, "To Tell or Not to Tell"

Filmed on August 29, 1961. Songs: "You Gotta Start Off Each Day with a Smile" (Amsterdam); "Mambo Jambo" (Prado)

Rob worries that Laura might be tempted to return to show business full time after Mel offers the former USO performer an opportunity to fill in for an ailing *Alan Brady Show* dancer.

Behind the scenes: The first of three *Van Dyke Show* scripts written by the pseudonymous David Adler, the pen name of Frank Tarloff, a writer Carl Reiner first met in the Catskills in the early forties. Unable to find work after he defied the House Un-American Activities Committee in the early fifties, Tarloff managed to carve out a living writing—under his assumed name—for *The Danny Thomas Show* and other comedies produced by Sheldon Leonard on the Desilu lot. The writer recalled the difficulty he faced choosing a pen name after Leonard suggested he find a nom de plume that wouldn't attract undue attention to the blacklisted writer. "I struggled for a new name," Tarloff explained. "Not an easy thing really." According to the writer, Leonard rejected his first choice, Erik Shepard, on the grounds that it was insufficiently Jewish. "At that time almost all comedy writers were Jewish. So Sheldon told me to forget Erik Shepard, and to find a name that sounds like every other comedy writer—a Jewish name! So I came up with David Adler. And that one got through without a question." Though Tarloff would be one of the few *Van Dyke Show* freelancers to exhibit promise in the show's early days, the writer's tenure on the series was curtailed when he decided to move to England, where a blacklisted writer could more easily find work in the early sixties.

12) SALLY IS A GIRL — Airdate: 12/19/61

Writer: David Adler / Director: John Rich

Supporting cast: Mel—Richard Deacon, Ted Harris—Paul Tripp, Pickles—Barbara Perry, Snappy Service Man—Jamie Farr

Filmed on September 5, 1961.

Buddy and Mel jump to conclusions after Rob suddenly starts treating Sally like a lady.

Behind the scenes: This episode features a rare on-screen appearance by Buddy's wife, Pickles, who—despite the best efforts of two different actresses to breathe life into the character—would finally prove more durable as an off-screen presence. . . . Speaking in the pages of the December 1981 issue of *American Film* magazine, Carl Reiner recounted a salty anecdote involving Selma Diamond that may well have served as the inspiration for this episode. Recalling the outspoken actress and *Caesar's Hour* writer who would serve as his primary model for Sally Rogers, Reiner said, "Selma Diamond is the one who actually said one day in a writers' conference, 'Why don't we go out and find some girls and get laid?' She's not a lesbian. She just said it because she felt like one of the guys."[1]

13) EMPRESS CARLOTTA'S NECKLACE Airdate: 12/12/61

Writer: Carl Reiner / Director: James Komack

Supporting cast: Mel—Richard Deacon, Jerry—Jerry Paris, Millie—Ann Morgan Guilbert, Maxwell—Gavin MacLeod, Edward Petrie—Will Wright, Mrs. Petrie—Carol Veazie

Filmed on September 12, 1961.

Rob surprises Laura with an unexpected gift—a tasteless necklace that she's loath to wear in public.

Behind the scenes: This episode features the directorial debut of James Komack, who would enjoy success as producer of a string of popular TV comedies in the late sixties and seventies, including *The Courtship of Eddie's Father*; *Welcome Back, Kotter*; and *Chico and the Man*. . . . Guest star Gavin MacLeod would also discover fame in seventies television, when he would portray *The Mary Tyler Moore Show*'s quick-witted newswriter, Murray Slaughter, for seven seasons, followed by a nine-year stint as *The Love Boat*'s genial skipper, Captain Merrill Stubing.

14) BUDDY, CAN YOU SPARE A JOB? Airdate: 12/26/61

Writer: Walter Kempley / Director: James Komack

Supporting cast: Mel—Richard Deacon, Jackie Brewster—Len Weinrib

Filmed on September 19, 1961.

After Buddy's plan to desert *The Alan Brady Show* for greener pastures backfires, Rob and Sally face the difficult task of convincing Mel to let him return.

Behind the scenes: According to Carl Reiner, the part of insult-comic Jackie Brewster had originally been conceived for Don Rickles, who turned out to be unavailable the week the episode was filmed. The part was then offered to nightclub comic Shecky Greene, who rehearsed the role for three days before personal problems forced him to back out as well, just two days before the episode was to be shot. Finally, the producer called in Len Weinrib, a young comic actor Reiner had first spied in the company of *The Billy Barnes Revue*—a casting decision that proved most fortuitous. "We put Lennie on his marks, and he learned it overnight," recalls Reiner. "And he was sensational." In an ironic postscript, the producer remembers that after the episode aired, he got an angry phone call from the actor he'd replaced.

"I get a call from Shecky," recalls Reiner. "I'm sure he's going to say, 'Gee, you know, it turned out good anyway.' But he says, 'You stole some of my lines!'" According to Reiner, the lines in question had been an ad lib that Greene added during his three days of rehearsal on the show—a script improvement that Reiner naturally assumed was fair game after the actor voluntarily walked away from the part and left him hanging. "I couldn't believe it," notes Reiner. "I thought he was joking. I said, 'What?' And he says, 'You stole a line from me!'" . . . This episode would mark the final appearance of the original fanfare arrangement of the show's opening theme song. Beginning with the next episode, the more familiar "three-chord" arrangement of *The Dick Van Dyke Show* theme song—which had until then been heard exclusively under the show's end titles—would be moved to the top of the show as well.

15) WHO OWES WHO WHAT? **Airdate: 1/24/62**

Writer: Carl Reiner / Director: John Rich

Supporting cast: Mel—Richard Deacon, Jerry—Jerry Paris, Fight Announcer—Carl Reiner (uncredited voice-over)

Filmed on October 10, 1961.

Buddy remains oblivious to Rob's efforts to collect an old debt.

16) SOL AND THE SPONSOR **Airdate: 4/11/62**

Writer: Walter Kempley / Director: John Rich

Supporting cast: Sol Pomeroy—Marty Ingels, Henry Bermont—Roy Roberts, Mrs. Bermont—Isabel Randolph, Arlene—Patty Regan (as Patti Regan)

Filmed on October 17, 1961. Songs: "Frère Jacques" (traditional); "You, Wonderful You" (Warren, Brooks, Chaplin)

Rob can't bring himself to tell a boisterous old army buddy that he's not welcome at a fancy dinner party the Petries are hosting to impress one of Rob's sponsors.

Behind the scenes: This would be the second and final *Van Dyke Show* appearance of Marty Ingels, who departed the recurring role of Sol Pomeroy to costar with John Astin in *I'm Dickens, He's Fenster*, a short-lived ABC sitcom that premiered the following September. Allan Melvin would assume the role of Rob's army pal in later episodes.

17) THE CURIOUS THING ABOUT WOMEN **Airdate: 1/10/62**

Writer: David Adler / Director: John Rich

Supporting cast: Jerry—Jerry Paris, Millie—Ann Morgan Guilbert, Delivery Man—Frank Adamo, Alan Brady—Carl Reiner (uncredited voice-over)

Filmed on October 24, 1961.

Unable to control her curiosity, Laura can't resist opening a mysterious package that arrives addressed to Rob—unaware that it contains a large, self-inflating life raft.

Behind the scenes: Writing once again under the pen name of David Adler, Frank Tarloff based his script for this episode on a remarkably similar idea he and fellow writers Arthur Stander and Phil Sharp had concocted nine years earlier for the December 3, 1952, episode of the Joan Davis sitcom *I Married Joan*. . . . . Though no reference was made to it in the episode, actress Ann Guilbert was actually seven months pregnant when this show was filmed—a condition, she reports, that caused her no small amount of discomfort when she filmed the show's closing scene, in which Millie and Jerry are supposed to laugh uproariously after they discover Laura with the fully inflated life raft. "Jerry and I came in and didn't say anything," recalls Guilbert, "'cause we were just supposed to get into hysterical laughter. But it's very hard to laugh like that when you're seven months pregnant!"

18) PUNCH THY NEIGHBOR **Airdate: 1/17/62**

Writer: Carl Reiner / Director: John Rich

Supporting cast: Jerry—Jerry Paris, Millie—Ann Morgan Guilbert, Officer Jack Bain—Peter Leeds, Vinny the Milkman—Jerry Hausner, Freddie—Peter Oliphant, Singing Telegram Man—Frank Adamo

Filmed on November 1, 1961. Song: "Twinkle, Twinkle, Little Star" (traditional, arrangement by Hagen)

Rob is miffed when Jerry begins sharing his low opinion of *The Alan Brady Show* with anyone who'll listen.

Behind the scenes: When Rob deciphers the acronymical name of Alan Brady's production company, Jeffgregbarbloubenraypolly Productions, he reveals the following elusive, if utterly useless, data on his employer's personal life: Jeff and Greg are Alan Brady's kids; his wife's name is Barb; Ben is his lawyer; Ray is his brother; Lou, his manager; and Polly, it turns out, is the name of Alan Brady's parrot.

19) WHERE DID I COME FROM? Airdate: 1/3/62

Writer: Carl Reiner / Director: John Rich

Supporting cast: Mel—Richard Deacon, Millie—Ann Morgan Guilbert, Willie the Coffee Man—Herbie Faye, Charlie the Laundry Man—Jerry Hausner, Cabbie—Tiny Brauer, Dry Cleaning Man—Frank Adamo

Filmed on November 8, 1961.

Rob recalls the final frantic days of Laura's pregnancy—a tumultuous time that culminated with her arrival at the maternity ward in a laundry truck.

Behind the scenes: "Bedlam" is how Rose Marie describes the conditions that surrounded the shooting of the climactic scene where Rob convinces Buddy to surrender his trousers. "When Buddy took off his pants," she says, "the audience went crazy." As the actress recalls, the ovation was so sustained that her topper line—"Isn't anybody gonna ask me to turn around?"—was completely lost in the din. "I held it as long as I could," she says, "and then I finally just threw away the line." Director John Rich was forced to shoot the scene a second time just to get a clear take of Rose Marie's line—and it was this take that finally made it into the finished episode. In spite of the confusion that attended its shooting, Rich cites this episode as among the series' best. "That," says the director, "was my all-time favorite show."

20) THE BOARDER INCIDENT
Airdate: 2/14/62

Writers: Norm Liebmann and Ed Haas / Director: John Rich

Filmed on November 14, 1961.

Episode 20, "The Boarder Incident"

Rob invites Buddy to spend a few days at his house while Pickles is out of town.

Behind the scenes: Cowriter Norm Liebmann had been friendly with Dick Van Dyke since the late fifties, when the scribe served as a staff writer for *Flair*, a short radio program that Van Dyke recorded for daily broadcast during the late fifties and early sixties.

21) A WORD A DAY — Airdate: 2/7/62

Writer: Jack Raymond / Director: John Rich

Supporting cast: Mel—Richard Deacon, Rev. Kirk—William Schallert, Mrs. Kirk—Lia Waggner

Filmed on November 29, 1961.

Rob and Laura are disturbed to discover that Ritchie's vocabulary has suddenly expanded to include a small glossary of four-letter words.

Behind the scenes: Guest star William Schallert's on-screen spouse is played by his real-life wife, Lia Waggner. A ubiquitous character actor of the era, Schallert would soon land the role for which he's best known, Martin Lane, the paterfamilias of *The Patty Duke Show*, which premiered on ABC in September 1963.

22) THE TALENTED NEIGHBORHOOD — Airdate: 1/31/62

Writer: Carl Reiner / Director: John Rich

Supporting cast: Mel—Richard Deacon, Jerry—Jerry Paris, Mrs. Kendall—Doris Singleton, Mr. Mathias—Ken Lynch, Martin Mathias—Michael Davis, Kenneth Kendall—Jack Davis, Philip Mathias—Barry Livingston, Ellen Helper—Anne Marie Hediger, Cynthia—Liana Dowding, Annie Mathias—Kathleen Green, Frankie—Christian Van Dyke, Florian—Barry Van Dyke, Anya—Cornell Chulay (uncredited), Alan Brady—Carl Reiner (uncredited voice-over)

Filmed on December 6, 1961. Songs: "America, the Beautiful" (traditional); "Là ci darem la mano" (Mozart)

Rob is besieged by would-be child stars after Alan Brady announces a juvenile talent competition on his show.

Behind the scenes: Dick Van Dyke's two young sons, Barry and Chris, have bit parts as neighborhood children, as does assistant director John Chulay's daughter, Cornell. Also recognizable in the show's juvenile cast is young Barry Livingston, who would shortly land the long-running role of Ernie Douglas on *My Three Sons*.

23) FATHER OF THE WEEK **Airdate: 2/21/62**

Writers: Arnold and Lois Peyser / Director: John Rich

Supporting cast: Mel—Richard Deacon, Mrs. Given—Isabel Randolph, Allan—Allan Fielder, Floyd—Patrick Thompson, Candy—Cornell Chulay (uncredited)

Filmed on December 12, 1961.

Rob is crestfallen when he discovers that Ritchie is embarrassed to have him appear as Father of the Week at his school.

Behind the scenes: Although this episode reworks the basic storyline of Carl Reiner's *Head of the Family* pilot, Arnold Peyser, who cowrote the episode with his wife, Lois, insists that it was inspired by an incident that happened to him after he organized a Father of the Week tribute for his son's scout troop and noticed that one of the boys, Peter Nye—the son of comedian Louis Nye—seemed reluctant to have his dad participate. "He was always saying that his father had a cold," the writer recalled, "or that Louis was going out of town." Finally, after listening to excuses for three or four weeks, it dawned on the writer that the boy might simply be embarrassed. "He didn't know what his father might do. And he was afraid that everybody would laugh at him. And we thought that might make a good story." When the Peysers pitched the idea to Reiner as a potential *Van Dyke Show* premise, the producer snapped it up. It was Reiner's inspiration to meld the Peysers' storyline with his *Head of the Family* script, and to add the ending in which Rob offers the class an impromptu lesson in comedy, a slapstick sequence that would provide a showcase for Dick Van Dyke's trademark physical shtick. "It was the same story," says Reiner, comparing "Father of the Week" to his earlier *Head of the Family* pilot. "But Dick doing a show for the kids was so much better," he concludes, "because we knew Dick would add things to it, even if it wasn't in the script, and make it his."

Episode 24, "The Twizzle"

24) THE TWIZZLE
Airdate: 2/28/62

Writer: Carl Reiner / Director: John Rich

Supporting cast: Mel—Richard Deacon, Randy "Twizzle" Eisenbower—Jerry Lanning, Mr. Eisenbower—Jack Albertson, Counter boy—Tony Stag; Fred Blassie—himself

Filmed on January 9, 1962. Songs: "The Twizzle" (David, Livingston); "This Nearly Was Mine" (Rodgers, Hammerstein)

Sally drags Mel and the writing staff to a bowling alley to show off her latest discovery—a reluctant pop singer who's invented a new dance craze called "The Twizzle."

Behind the scenes: The song that inspires the episode's dance fad was composed by pop tunesmiths Mack David and Jerry Livingston. . . . Originally conceived as a showcase for Jerry Lanning, the son of pop vocalist Roberta Sherwood, the episode also provided a nice role for character actor Jack Albertson, who would go on to earn an Oscar as Best Supporting Actor for his performance in the 1968 film *The Subject Was Roses*. Albertson would also collect an Emmy for his role as junk man Ed Brown on prime time's *Chico and the Man*, which costarred the late Freddie Prinze. . . . According to Carl Reiner, "The Twizzle" bears the dubious distinction of being one of the cast's least-favorite episodes.

25) ONE ANGRY MAN **Airdate: 3/7/62**

Writers: Leo Solomon and Ben Gershman / Director: John Rich

Supporting cast: Marla Hendrix—Sue Ane Langdon, Juror—Patsy Kelly, Cab-driving Juror—Herbie Faye, District Attorney Mason—Lee Bergere, Defense Lawyer Burger—Dabbs Greer, Juror—Herb Vigran, Bailiff—Doodles Weaver, Honorable Judge George M. Tyler—Howard Wendell

Filmed on January 16, 1962.

Laura is convinced that a pretty face has tipped the scales of justice when Rob—on jury duty—sides with the attractive defendant.

Behind the scenes: An affectionate takeoff on *Twelve Angry Men*, the award-winning television drama written by Carl Reiner's old Fire Island neighbor, Reginald Rose, and brought to the big screen by director Sidney Lumet in 1957.

26) WHERE YOU BEEN, FASSBINDER? Airdate: 3/14/62

Writer: John Whedon / Director: John Rich

Supporting cast: Mel—Richard Deacon, Leo Fassbinder—George Neise, Pickles—Barbara Perry

Filmed on January 23, 1962.

Sally pins her romantic hopes on a mysterious suitor who bears the unlikely name of Leo Fassbinder, an old acquaintance whom she hopes will come to brighten an otherwise lonely birthday celebration.

Behind the scenes: Rose Marie recalls that director John Rich asked her to show up on the set an hour early on the first day of rehearsal for this episode, so he could help her find the proper frame of mind to play the show's moodier moments. "It was really fabulous," she recalls. "I walked through the apartment to see where I might do this line or that scene. John wanted me to do that just so I'd be more comfortable."

Episode 26, "Where You Been, Fassbinder?"; guest star: Barbara Perry

27) THE BAD OLD DAYS Airdate: 4/4/62

Writers: Norm Liebmann and Ed Haas / Director: John Rich

Supporting cast: Jerry—Jerry Paris

Filmed on January 30, 1962. Song: "A Bird in a Gilded Cage" (Lamb, Von Tilzer)

Rob rebels against what he perceives to be Laura's domestic tyranny after Buddy convinces him that he's become hopelessly henpecked.

Behind the scenes: Owing to the technical demands of shooting this episode's Gay Nineties costume fantasy, it would be one of the few *Dick Van Dyke* shows filmed without a live audience in attendance.

28) I AM MY BROTHER'S KEEPER Airdate: 3/21/62

Writer: Carl Reiner / Director: John Rich

Supporting cast: Mel—Richard Deacon, Stacey Petrie—Jerry Van Dyke

Filmed on February 6, 1962. Song: "Hello, Sunshine, Hello" (Tobias, Murray, Tobias)

Rob assumes something's wrong when Stacey Petire arrives telling jokes and singing songs—his shy, retiring brother only acts that lively when he's sleepwalking!

Behind the scenes: Though the spelling differs slightly, Stacey Petrie was named after Dick Van Dyke's then six-year-old daughter, Stacy. . . . The first half of the series' inaugural two-parter, the original broadcast of "I Am My Brother's Keeper" ended with a filmed teaser—which survives today on most of the prints currently in circulation—in which Dick Van Dyke addresses the camera in a direct appeal to the show's viewers. "I hope you'll be with us next week," the actor implores, "when my brother wrestles with the problem of auditioning for a television program while he's wide awake! Well, see ya next week!"

29) THE SLEEPING BROTHER Airdate: 3/28/62

Writer: Carl Reiner / Director: John Rich

Supporting cast: Mel—Richard Deacon, Stacey Petrie—Jerry Van Dyke, Jerry—Jerry Paris, Alan Brady—Carl Reiner (uncredited)

Filmed on February 13, 1962. Songs: "Hello, Sunshine, Hello" (Tobias, Murray, Tobias); "Bill Bailey" (traditional, arrangement by Hagen); "By the Light of the Silvery Moon" (Edwards, Madden); "Crying My Heart Out For You" (Johnson, Hopkins); "Mountain Greenery" (Rodgers, Hart); "Banjo Rock" (Jerry Van Dyke); "I Wish My Heart Would Keep Its Big Mouth Shut" (Amsterdam)

Rob's somnambulant brother lands an audition for *The Alan Brady Show*, and Rob wonders how Stacey will ever get through the tryout if he happens to be awake.

Behind the scenes: Although the part of Alan Brady is playfully credited to one "Alan Brady" in the show's closing credits, Carl Reiner contributes his first on-camera cameo in the role in this episode.

30) THE RETURN OF HAPPY SPANGLER **Airdate: 4/18/62**

Writer: Carl Reiner / Director: John Rich

Supporting cast: Mel—Richard Deacon, Happy Spangler—Jay C. Flippen, Customer—Frank Adamo (uncredited)

Filmed on February 20, 1962.

Rob runs into the old-timer who gave him his first break in show business, and then makes the mistake of trying to return the favor.

Behind the scenes: The monologue in which Rob describes why pain is funny is one of director John Rich's favorite sequences. "I was always looking for something that would cause Dick pain," the director confesses, "because pain can be funny, if it's done properly by a comic. So we used to look for what we called 'the pain take.' Dick would come in and inadvertently put his hand on the stove and dance around, saying,

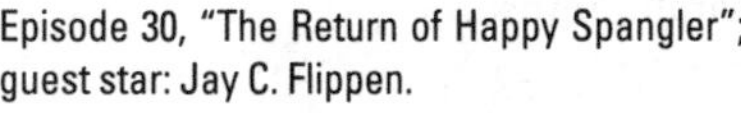

Episode 30, "The Return of Happy Spangler"; guest star: Jay C. Flippen.

'Why did I do that?' When he did a whole lecture on why pain was funny—where he was stabbing himself with prop scissors—he was really talking about what was true in his own comedy."

1962–1963 THE DICK VAN DYKE SHOW

SEASON TWO

Carl Reiner continues as the series' producer, story consultant, and chief writer in year two, contributing twenty-two of the thirty-two teleplays that would be produced in the show's longest production season. The producer gets a welcome assist from freelancers Sheldon Keller and Howard Merrill, who contribute four scripts over the course of the year. John Rich returns as the show's house director, and John C. Chulay continues as the show's assistant director—a position he would hold for the remainder of the show's run.

SECOND-SEASON CREDITS

Created and Produced by	Carl Reiner
Associate Producer	Ronald Jacobs
Music	Earle Hagen
Director of Photography	Robert De Grasse, A.S.C.
Art Director	Kenneth A. Reid
Film Editor	Bud Molin, A.C.E.
Production Manager	Frank E. Myers
Assistant Director	John C. Chulay
Prop Master	Glenn Ross
Camera Coordinator	James Niver
Casting	Ruth Burch
Script Continuity	Marjorie Mullen
Set Decorator	Ken Swartz
Rerecording Editor	Richard LeGrande
Story Consultant	Carl Reiner
Hair Stylist	Donna McDonough
Makeup	Tom Tuttle
Costumes	Harald Johnson
Sound Engineer	(episodes #32–45, 47–62) Cam McCulloch

	(episode #46)
	Frank Webster
Music Coordinator	Walter Popp
Recorded by	Glen Glenn Sound Co.
Executive Producer	Sheldon Leonard in association with Danny Thomas

Dick Van Dyke's wardrobe furnished by Botany 500.

Women's fashions provided by E.T. Jr., Los Angeles; William Pearson; Walter Bass of Beverly Hills; Peggy Hunt; Emerson's of Studio City; Arbe Originals; Mr. Mort; Gino Paoli Knits; Gibi Knits of Italy; Marjolaine Colberti Knits; Dee Dee Johnson; Lill-Ann of San Francisco; Dorothy O'Hara; White Stag Sportswear; Mr. Jules of California; Ann Arnold, Beverly Hills.

31) NEVER NAME A DUCK — Airdate: 9/26/62

Writer: Carl Reiner / Director: John Rich

Supporting cast: Mel—Richard Deacon, Mr. Fletcher—Jerry Hausner, Miss Singleton (poodle owner)—Jane Dulo, Miss Glasser (cat owner)—Geraldine Wall, Veterinarian's assistant—Frank Adamo

Filmed on August 7, 1962.

Rob tries to console Ritchie after he frees the boy's pet duck in a local pond.

Behind the scenes: This episode features the first on-air appearance of the show's classic opening-title sequence, in which Rob trips over his living room ottoman. The sequence was filmed on the night of August 14, 1962, following the filming of episode 32, "The Two Faces of Rob."

32) THE TWO FACES OF ROB — Airdate: 10/3/62

Writers: Sheldon Keller and Howard Merrill / Director: John Rich

Supporting cast: Millie—Ann Morgan Guilbert, Deli Man—Herbie Faye, Game Show Host—Carl Reiner (uncredited voice-over)

Filmed on August 14, 1962. Songs: "All of Me" (Simons, Marks); "Santa Lucia"(traditional, arrangement by Hagen)

Posing as a mysterious stranger, Rob calls Laura and asks for a date—a prank that backfires when she appears only too willing to be swept off her feet by the make-believe lothario.

Behind the scenes: The first *Dick Van Dyke Show* script written by Sheldon Keller and Howard Merrill, who would be frequent contributors in the show's middle years. Keller and Carl Reiner had spent time together in the writers' room on *Caesar's Hour* in the mid-fifties, and before that, at Camp Crowder, Missouri, where they both served in the armed forces during World War II. . . . "I used to love writing one-sided phone calls for Dick," says Reiner, who recalls that this episode was inspired by his star's uncanny ability to convincingly act out one half of a telephone conversation. "I would swear there was somebody on the other end of the line!" notes Reiner. "Every good actor can do it—Mary did it almost as well. But Dick did it better than everybody. He was the master."

33) BANK BOOK 6565696 — Airdate: 10/17/62

Writers: Ray Allen Saffian and Harvey Bullock / Director: John Rich

Supporting cast: Jerry—Jerry Paris

Filmed on August 21, 1962.

Episode 33, "Bank Book 6565696"

Rob's imagination runs wild when he discovers Laura has stashed a sizable sum of cash in a secret bank account.

34) THE ATTEMPTED MARRIAGE
Airdate: 10/10/62

Writer: Carl Reiner / Director: John Rich

Supporting cast: Doctor—Sandy Kenyon, Chaplain—Dabbs Greer, Corporal—Ray Kellogg

Filmed on August 28, 1962.

Rob recalls the disastrous circumstances that led up to his beleaguered arrival at his own wedding—battered, bruised, and three hours late.

35) HUSTLING THE HUSTLER Airdate: 10/24/62

Writer: Carl Reiner / Director: John Rich

Supporting cast: Mel—Richard Deacon, Blackie Sorrell—Phil Leeds

Filmed on September 4, 1962. Song: "Moonlight Bay" (Wenrich, Madden)

Buddy suspects his brother's motives when the supposedly reformed pool shark challenges Rob to a friendly game of eight-ball.

Behind the scenes: According to editor Bud Molin, the amazing pool shot that Mary Tyler Moore negotiates at the end of this episode—in which she sinks every ball on the table with a single flick of the cue—was actually a happy accident. Though the trick shot had been carefully laid out by a pool expert beforehand, no one actually expected the actress to make the shot in her first try—if at all. "We had it rigged," recalled the editor, "so that she just had to hit the balls in the right general direction." Of course, to get a filmed take of the difficult shot, director John Rich was prepared to reshoot the scene in close-up, with the pool expert standing in for the actress. But to the utter amazement of everyone in the studio, the actress managed to nail the shot in her first try. "It was just luck," said Molin. "She hit it, and she dropped every ball! And we were able to use the shot, because Dick and Mary didn't go to pieces after she finally got it."

36) WHAT'S IN A MIDDLE NAME? Airdate: 11/7/62

Writer: Carl Reiner / Director: John Rich

Supporting cast: Mel Cooley—Richard Deacon, Mr. Meehan—Carl Benton Reid, Mrs. Meehan—Geraldine Wall, Sam Petrie—J. Pat O'Malley, Mrs. Petrie—Isabel Randolph, Grandpa Petrie—Cyril Delevanti

Episode 36, "What's in a Middle Name?"

Filmed on September 11, 1962.

Rob reveals the mysterious story of how Ritchie wound up with the middle name "Rosebud."

Behind the scenes: Ritchie's middle name is revealed to be an acronym made up of the first letters of the names Robert, Oscar, Sam, Edward, Benjamin, Ulysses, and David.

37) MY HUSBAND IS NOT A DRUNK — Airdate: 10/31/62

Writer: Carl Reiner / Director: Al Rafkin

Supporting cast: Mel—Richard Deacon, Jerry—Jerry Paris, Millie—Ann Morgan Guilbert, Glen Jameson—Charles Aidman, Mr. Boland—Roy Roberts

Filmed on September 8, 1962.

Rob suffers from a posthypnotic suggestion that compels him to act inebriated every time he hears a bell ring.

38) LIKE A SISTER — Airdate: 11/14/62

Writer: Carl Reiner / Director: Hal Cooper

Supporting cast: Mel—Richard Deacon, Ric Vallone—Vic Damone

Filmed on October 2, 1962. Songs: "Santa Lucia" (traditional), "The Most Beautiful Girl in the World" (Rodgers, Hart)

Rob worries that Sally might fall prey to romantic delusions when she develops a crush on the show's guest star, the handsome singer Ric Vallone.

39) THE NIGHT THE ROOF FELL IN — Airdate: 11/21/62

Writer: John Whedon / Director: Hal Cooper

Supporting cast: Millie: Ann Morgan Guilbert

Filmed on October 9, 1962.

Rob and Laura recount vastly different accounts of a marital spat that sent Rob storming out of the house in a huff.

40) THE SECRET LIFE OF BUDDY AND SALLY Airdate: 11/28/62

Writer: Lee Erwin / Director: Coby Ruskin

Supporting cast: Mel—Richard Deacon, Waiter—Phil Arnold, Herbie "Hiawatha" Harris—Carl Reiner (uncredited voice-over)

Filmed on October 16, 1962. Songs: "Gilbert and Solomon" (Amsterdam); "Hungarian Folk Dance" (traditional); "Come Rain or Come Shine" (Mercer, Arlen); "Hello, Hello" (Amsterdam); "Harmony" (Burke, Van Heusen)

Rob suspects Buddy and Sally of extramarital hanky-panky after he discovers the pair have been secretly slipping away together every weekend.

41) A BIRD IN THE HEAD HURTS Airdate: 12/5/62

Writer: Carl Reiner / Director: John Rich

Supporting cast: Millie—Ann Morgan Guilbert, Game Warden—Cliff Norton

Filmed on October 23, 1962.

Rob and Laura worry that Ritchie may be suffering from a hyperactive imagination after he claims he's been attacked by a giant woodpecker.

Behind the scenes: Based on an idea contributed by Carl Reiner's friend and former New Rochelle neighbor Millie Schoenbaum, who was also the real-life model for the show's Millie Helper.

42) GESUNDHEIT, DARLING
Airdate: 12/12/62

Writer: Carl Reiner / Director: John Rich

Supporting cast: Jerry—Jerry Paris, Millie—Ann Morgan Guilbert, Allergist—Sandy Kenyon

Episode 42, "Gesundheit, Darling"

Filmed on October 30, 1962.

A sudden fit of uncontrollable sneezing has Rob worried that he may be allergic to Laura.

43) A MAN'S TEETH ARE NOT HIS OWN
Airdate: 12/19/62

Writer: Carl Reiner / Director: John Rich

Supporting cast: Mel—Richard Deacon, Jerry—Jerry Paris, Millie—Ann Morgan Guilbert

Filmed on November 6, 1962. Song: Hungarian Dance no. 5 (Brahms)

Rob is afraid Jerry will never forgive him after he lets another dentist perform emergency work on his teeth.

44) SOMEBODY HAS TO PLAY CLEOPATRA **Airdate: 12/26/62**

Writer: Martin A. Ragaway / Director: John Rich

Supporting cast: Jerry—Jerry Paris, Millie—Ann Morgan Guilbert, Harry Rogers—Bob Crane, Mrs. Billings—Eleanor Audley, Shirley Rogers—Shirley Mitchell, Cynthia Harding—Valerie Yerke

Filmed on November 13, 1962. Songs: "True, Man, True" (Amsterdam); "The Flowers That Bloom in the Spring" (Gilbert, Sullivan)

Episode 44, "Somebody Has to Play Cleopatra"; guest star: Bob Crane

Rob has his hands full directing the latest edition of his neighborhood's annual variety show, especially after he discovers that none of the husbands are keen on letting their wives play the show's romantic leading role.

Behind the scenes: Not long after his appearance here, guest star Bob Crane would move into a regular

Episode 45, "The Cat Burglar"

spot on *The Donna Reed Show* and, eventually, the lead role in CBS's wartime sitcom *Hogan's Heroes.*

45) THE CAT BURGLAR
Airdate: 1/2/63

Writer: Carl Reiner / Director: John Rich

Supporting cast: Jerry—Jerry Paris, Millie—Ann Morgan Guilbert, Police Lieutenant—Barney Phillips, Photographer—Johnny Silver

Filmed on November 20, 1962. Song: "Glow Worm" (Lincke, Robinson)

Rob and Laura are puzzled by the mystery of how a cat burglar stole their entire living room set without leaving a clue.

Behind the scenes: Dick Van Dyke recalls that this episode was inspired by a real-life incident that had happened to him and his wife a few years earlier. "I remember one night in Long Island," says the star, "my wife and I thought there was a burglar in the house. I had a little .25 automatic that I kept in the drawer. And I got it out, but it was empty. I said, 'Where are the bullets?' And my wife said, 'They're in my jewelry box!' So I opened the jewelry box—and it starts playing 'The Blue Danube Waltz.' It was so funny that we built a show on that."

46) THE FOUL WEATHER GIRL **Airdate: 1/9/63**

Writer: Carl Reiner / Director: John Rich

Supporting cast: Janie Layton—Joan O'Brien, Mel—Richard Deacon, Alan Brady—Carl Reiner (uncredited voice-over)

Filmed on November 27, 1962. Song: "Get Out in the Sun" (ad lib), "Just in Time" (Styne, Comden, Green)

The TV weather girl from Rob's hometown asks for his help in landing a role on *The Alan Brady Show*—a proposition that Laura eyes with suspicion.

Episode 47, "Will You Two Be My Wife?"; guest star: Barbara Bain

47) WILL YOU TWO BE MY WIFE?
Airdate: 1/16/63

Writer: Carl Reiner / Director: John Rich

Supporting cast: Millie—Ann Morgan Guilbert, Sam—Allan Melvin, Captain—Ray Kellogg, Dorothy—Barbara Bain

Filmed on December 4, 1962.

Rob faces the fury of a woman scorned in a flashback that recounts how he lowered the boom on his hometown sweetheart after he got engaged to Laura.

48) RAY MURDOCK'S X-RAY **Airdate: 1/23/63**

Writer: Carl Reiner / Director: Jerry Paris

Supporting cast: Ray Murdock—Gene Lyons, Stage Manager—Jerry Hausner, Assistant—Frank Adamo (uncredited), Announcer—Carl Reiner (uncredited voice-over)

Filmed on December 11, 1962.

Laura feels betrayed when Rob tells a talk-show host that she's the real-life inspiration for *The Alan Brady Show*'s zaniest domestic sketches.

Behind the scenes: Jerry Paris began his long tenure as the primary director of *The Dick Van Dyke Show* with this episode. . . . Carl Reiner confesses he never really liked the ending he came up with for this show, in which Laura is seduced by the notoriety that arises from her public identification as America's nuttiest wife. "For her to be proud of the fact that they called her a stupid idiot on the air is just kind of silly," Reiner insists. "But we had to finish the show, so that was the ending we did. Today, I don't know if I would've done the same thing."

49) I WAS A TEENAGE HEAD WRITER — Airdate: 1/30/63

Writers: Sheldon Keller and Howard Merrill / Director: Jerry Paris

Supporting cast: Mel—Richard Deacon

Filmed on December 18, 1962.

Rob recalls the trials of his early days as head writer of *The Alan Brady Show*.

50) MY HUSBAND IS A CHECK-GRABBER — Airdate: 2/13/63

Writer: Carl Reiner / Director: Al Rafkin

Supporting cast: Jerry—Jerry Paris, Pickles—Joan Shawlee, Herman Glimscher—Bill Idelson, Anatole—Phil Arnold

Filmed on January 8, 1963.

The Petries lock horns after Laura objects to Rob's habit of picking up the check every time they're out with friends.

Behind the scenes: "That one was on my desk for years," explains Carl Reiner, who recalls that this was the last episode to be adapted from the batch of scripts he composed for his proposed *Head of the Family* series in 1958. "I had it written as part of the original thirteen, but we couldn't figure out how to make it into a good three-camera show. It never went anywhere 'cause it was flawed." According to Reiner, it was Sheldon Leonard who finally diagnosed that the problem lay not in the story, but the theme. "Sheldon said, 'Money is a bad subject. People don't like shows about penuriousness or money.' And I said, 'Yeah, but this is an honest and true subject. I'll beat it!' And I had it on my desk for about two years. It was always there. Then one day I was upstairs, and I said, 'I got it! It's a flashback!'" Once he'd tackled the structural problem, the writer promptly retooled his script for this episode.

51) IT MAY LOOK LIKE A WALNUT! — Airdate: 2/6/63

Writer: Carl Reiner / Director: Jerry Paris

Supporting cast: Mel—Richard Deacon, Kolac—Danny Thomas (uncredited cameo), Horror Movie Victim—Carl Reiner (uncredited voice-over), Exercise Show Host—Jerry Paris (uncredited voice-over)

Filmed on January 15, 1963.

A late-show thriller gives Rob a nightmare in which he imagines the world being taken over by an alien who bears an uncanny resemblance to Danny Thomas.

Behind the scenes: The first show to feature the episode's title in the opening credits.

52) DON'T TRIP OVER THAT MOUNTAIN — Airdate: 2/20/63

Writer: Carl Reiner / Director: Coby Ruskin

Supporting cast: Jerry—Jerry Paris, Millie—Ann Morgan Guilbert, Nurse—Jean Allison, Doctor—Ray Kellogg

Filmed on January 22, 1963.

After she has a premonition of disaster, Laura pleads with Rob not to go on a weekend skiing trip.

53) GIVE ME YOUR WALLS! — Airdate: 2/27/63

Writer: Carl Reiner / Director: Jerry Paris

Supporting cast: Vito Giotto—Vito Scotti

Filmed on January 29, 1963.

Laura hires a flamboyant artist to paint the Petries' living room, only to have second thoughts when the enthusiastic painter begins to take over the entire household.

54) THE SAM POMERANTZ SCANDALS — Airdate: 3/6/63

Writer: Carl Reiner / Director: Claudio Guzman

Supporting cast: Sam Pomerantz—Henry Calvin, Mel—Richard Deacon, Pickles—Joan Shawlee, Danny Brewster—Len Weinrib

Filmed on February 5, 1963. Songs: "I Wanna Be Around "(Mercer, Vimmerstedt); "Carolina in the Morning" (Donaldson, Kahn); "The Nutty Song" (Livingston); "The Musicians" (Glazer, Grean)

Rob convinces Laura, Buddy, Sally, and Mel to take part in a variety show at an old pal's resort in the Catskills.

Behind the scenes: The show's bandleader finale, "The Musicians," would be memorably reprised a few months later on *The Dick Van Dyke Show*'s Christmas episode, "The Alan Brady Show Presents." . . . The extended Laurel and Hardy pantomime that Dick Van Dyke performs with Henry Calvin was an homage to the star's longtime idol, Stan Laurel. . . . Comic Len Weinrib reprises the role of comedian Jackie Brewster from the show's fourteenth episode, "Buddy, Can You Spare a Job?" although the character has been renamed Danny for this outing. . . . Weinrib's comic impression of then-president John Kennedy is one of the few instances where a topical joke found its way into a *Dick Van Dyke Show* script.

55) I'M NO HENRY WALDEN! Airdate: 3/27/63

Writer: Carl Reiner / Story by: Ray Brenner and Jack Guss / Director: Jerry Paris

Supporting cast: Henry Walden—Everett Sloane, Mel—Richard Deacon, Mrs. Huntington—Doris Packer, Yale Sampson—Carl Reiner, Mrs. Felicia Fellowes—Betty Lou Gerson, Dr. Torrance Hayworth—Howard Wendell, Miss Thomas Evelyn—Roxanne Berard, H. Fieldstone Thorley—Frank Adamo

Filmed on February 12, 1963.

Rob feels self-conscious after he discovers he's the only comedy writer at a literary gathering.

Behind the scenes: Carl Reiner logs his first guest-starring role on the show, playing Yale Sampson, an English philosopher prone to double-talk. . . . Guest star Everett Sloane had been a respected character actor dating back to his days with Orson Welles's *Mercury Theatre on the Air* in the thirties.

Episode 55, "I'm No Henry Walden!"

56) THE SQUARE TRIANGLE **Airdate: 3/20/63**

Writer: Bill Idelson / Director: Jerry Paris

Supporting cast: Jacques Savon—Jacques Bergerac, Mel—Richard Deacon, Millie—Ann Morgan Guilbert

Filmed on February 19, 1963. Song: "I Only Have Eyes for You" (Warren, Dubin)

Buddy and Sally are puzzled when they notice how Rob seems to vanish every time the show's handsome French guest star appears.

Behind the scenes: The first Van Dyke script from writer Bill Idelson, who frequently portrayed Sally's sad-sack boyfriend, Herman Glimscher. Idelson launched his career as a child star in radio, where he played Rush, the adopted son on the long-running family series *Vic and Sade*. In his later years, Idelson would forge a long and respected career as a teacher and comedy writer, contributing memorable scripts to *The Andy Griffith Show*, *Get Smart*, *M*A*S*H*, *The Bob Newhart Show*, *The Odd Couple*, and *Happy Days*, among others.

57) RACY TRACY RATTIGAN **Airdate: 4/3/63**

Writers: Ronald Alexander and Carl Reiner / Director: Sheldon Leonard

Supporting cast: Mel—Richard Deacon, Tracy Rattigan—Dick Dawson

Filmed on February 26, 1963.

Alan Brady's summer replacement star is Tracy Rattigan, a lecherous flirt who quickly sets his sights on the head writer's wife.

Behind the scenes: Although guest star Richard Dawson would find his greatest fame as emcee of the game show *Family Feud*, his acting work would include a memorable stint in the cast of *Hogan's Heroes*, as well as a brief run in the cast of *The New Dick Van Dyke Show* in 1973.

58) DIVORCE **Airdate: 4/10/63**

Writer: Carl Reiner / Director: Jerry Paris

Supporting cast: Pickles—Joan Shawlee, Steve Longfellow, the Bartender—Charles Cantor, Sheila—Marian Collier, Sheila's Date—Arthur Batanides, TV Defense Lawyer—Carl Reiner (uncredited voice-over), Mr. Thompson—Jerry

Episode 58, "Divorce"; guest star: Joan Shawlee

Paris (uncredited voice-over), Floyd B. Bariscale—Sheldon Leonard (uncredited voice-over)

Filmed on March 5, 1963.

Rob tries his hand at marriage counseling when Buddy threatens to divorce Pickles over a silly misunderstanding.

Behind the scenes: Executive producer Sheldon Leonard contributes an off-camera cameo as the blackmailer, Floyd B. Bariscale. . . . This episode would feature the final appearance of Buddy's wife Pickles, who would fade into off-screen limbo for the remainder of the show's run. According to director John Rich, the character was dropped to make more room for the show's already large supporting cast. "You can only write for so many characters on a continuing situation comedy," says Rich, who notes that the show's central cast—including Ritchie, Mel, Jerry, and Millie—already included eight continuing characters. "To service eight people effectively every week is a big chore," he says. "So you try very hard to not use everybody all the time. And Buddy's wife just wasn't an essential character for the comedy."

59) IT'S A SHAME SHE MARRIED ME — Airdate: 4/17/63

Writers: Sheldon Keller and Howard Merrill / Director: James Niver

Supporting cast: Mel—Richard Deacon, Jerry—Jerry Paris, Millie—Ann Morgan Guilbert, Jim Darling—Robert Vaughn, Edward—Frank Adamo (uncredited cameo)

Filmed on March 12, 1963.

Rob makes a fool of himself when he attempts to outshine one of Laura's dashing old flames.

Behind the scenes: Camera coordinator James Niver made his bow as a director with this episode, although he recalls that the week couldn't have gotten off to a worse start. "I broke my leg the first day," says Niver. "I was reaching up from the first

Episode 60, "A Surprise Surprise Is a Surprise"

row of the balcony down to the floor to get something, and my foot slipped off. I fell off the edge and cracked it. I remember Dick looked up from the stage and said, 'What was that sound?' And I said, 'I think it was my leg.' But I didn't go to the doctor until Monday. It was just a fracture."

60) A SURPRISE SURPRISE IS A SURPRISE Airdate: 4/24/63

Writer: Carl Reiner / Director: Jerry Paris

Supporting cast: Mel—Richard Deacon, Jerry—Jerry Paris, Millie—Ann Morgan Guilbert

Filmed on March 19, 1963. Song: "For He's a Jolly Good Fellow" (traditional)

Rob tries to second-guess Laura's plan to surprise him on his birthday.

Behind the scenes: In the episode, Sally teases Rob's amateur-detective activities by referring to him as "Sebastian"—a now-obscure reference to the actor Sebastian Cabot, who had recently starred as an ace criminologist on *Checkmate*, a popular early-sixties detective series.

61) JILTING THE JILTER Airdate: 5/1/63

Writer: Ronald Alexander / Director: Jerry Paris

Supporting cast: Freddy White—Guy Marks, Mel—Richard Deacon

Filmed on March 26, 1963.

Sally's latest heartthrob is a stand-up comic who's badly in need of a new writer, which is what Rob and Buddy suspect he's really after.

62) WHEN A BOWLING PIN TALKS, LISTEN — Airdate: 5/8/63

Writer: Martin A. Ragaway / Director: Jerry Paris

Supporting cast: Mel—Richard Deacon, Willie the Deli Man—Herbie Faye, Barber—Jon Silo, Alan Brady—Carl Reiner (uncredited), Uncle Spunky—Jerry Paris (uncredited voice-over)

Filmed on April 2, 1963. Song: "Beautiful Dreamer" (Foster)

Hoping to help his dad through a temporary bout of writer's block, Ritchie inadvertently inspires Rob to plagiarize a sketch idea from a TV kid's show.

63) ALL ABOUT EAVESDROPPING — Airdate: 10/23/63

Writers: Sheldon Keller and Howard Merrill / Director: Stanley Cherry

Supporting cast: Jerry—Jerry Paris, Millie—Ann Morgan Guilbert

Filmed on April 9, 1963. Song: "Go Tell Aunt Rhody" (traditional)

The Petries get an earful when they accidentally overhear Millie and Jerry on Ritchie's toy intercom.

Behind the scenes: Although filmed as the final entry in the show's second season, this episode would not be broadcast until the following October. . . . Interestingly, when this show first aired—as the fifth episode of the show's third season—it would sport the inaugural appearance of yet a third version of the show's familiar opening title sequence. In this seldom-seen variant, Rob avoids tripping over his troublesome ottoman, only to stumble in his tracks a few steps later. This alternate version of the opening credits would appear only sporadically in the show's final seasons.

1963–1964 THE DICK VAN DYKE SHOW

SEASON THREE

Carl Reiner's creative team expands in the show's third season with the addition of writers Bill Persky and Sam Denoff, who—along with *Van Dyke Show* stalwarts Martin A. Ragaway and the team of Jerry Belson and Garry Marshall—would make their first significant story contributions to the show. The new writers work under the close supervision of Reiner, who will continue to serve as the show's producer, story consultant, and head writer throughout the season. Jerry Paris succeeds John Rich as the series' regular director, a position that Paris will maintain through the show's final three years.

THIRD-SEASON CREDITS

Created and Produced by	Carl Reiner
Associate Producer	Ronald Jacobs
Music	Earle Hagen
Director of Photography	Robert De Grasse, A.S.C.
Art Director	Kenneth A. Reid
Film Editor	(episodes #64–69) Alan L. Jaggs (episode #70) James Ballas (episodes #71–95) Bud Molin, A.C.E.
Assistant Director	John C. Chulay
Prop Master	Glenn Ross
Camera Coordinator	James Niver
Casting	Ruth Burch
Script Continuity	Marjorie Mullen
Set Decorator	Ken Swartz
Rerecording Editor	(episode #65) Richard LeGrande (episodes #64, 66–95) Robert Reeve
Story Consultant	Carl Reiner
Hairstylist	Donna McDonough
Makeup	Tom Tuttle
Costumes	Harald Johnson
Sound Engineer	Cam McCulloch
Music Coordinator	Walter Popp
Recorded by	Glen Glenn Sound Co.
Executive Producer	Sheldon Leonard in association with Danny Thomas

Production Supervisor	Ronald Jacobs
Production Manager	Frank E. Myers

Mr. Van Dyke's wardrobe furnished by Botany 500.

Women's fashions by William Pearson; Gino Paoli; Ida K's, Wilshire; Helga; Laura Aponte of Rome; Ann Arnold; Mr. Mort; Nan Link, Beverly Hills; Sydney North; Peggy Hunt; Marjolaine Colberti; Norma Morgan; Walter Bass; Geno.

64) THAT'S MY BOY?? Airdate: 9/25/63

Writers: Bill Persky and Sam Denoff / Director: John Rich

Supporting cast: Jerry—Jerry Paris, Millie—Ann Morgan Guilbert, Maternity Ward Nurse—Amzie Strickland, Mr. Peters—Greg Morris, Mrs. Peters—Mimi Dillard, Mel—Richard Deacon

Filmed on August 6, 1963.

Rob recalls his early days of parenthood, including a complicated series of mix-ups that had him convinced he'd brought the wrong baby home from the hospital.

Behind the scenes: The first script from writers Bill Persky and Sam Denoff, who would eventually become—after Carl Reiner—the show's most prolific contributors. . . . Beginning with this episode, series regular Richard Deacon would receive a more prominent "single-card" credit in the show's closing titles.

65) THE MASTERPIECE Airdate: 10/2/63

Writers: Sam Denoff and Bill Persky / Director: John Rich

Supporting cast: Ernest Holdecker—Howard Morris, Auctioneer—Alan Reed, Competitive Bidder—Amzie Strickland, Competitive Bidder's Husband—Ray Kellogg

Filmed on August 13, 1963.

The Petries become instant art collectors after Rob inadvertently places the high bid on a painting at an auction.

Behind the scenes: This episode reunites Carl Reiner with his old friend Howard Morris, who plays art expert Ernest Holdecker. The pair launched their long personal and professional association as fellow GIs in Maurice Evans's special services unit during World War II. After the war, they shared the stage in the cast of Broadway's *Call Me Mister*. A few years later, the pair would be teamed again in the casts of *Your Show of Shows* and *Caesar's Hour*. In addition to his memorable guest role here, the actor would return to direct five episodes of *The Dick Van Dyke Show*. . . . Though it was supposedly the work of Frank Sinatra, the Artanis original that appears in this episode was actually painted by the show's art director, Ken Reid, who created most of the art props that appeared on the show over the years. The painting today resides in the collection of writer Sam Denoff, who remembers rescuing the prop from the studio trash bin shortly after the episode wrapped in 1963. . . . Guest star Alan Reed provided the voice of Stone Age breadwinner Fred Flintstone on TV's pioneering prime-time animated sitcom, *The Flintstones*.

66) LAURA'S LITTLE LIE — Airdate: 10/9/63

Writers: Carl Reiner and Howard Merrill / Director: John Rich

Supporting cast: Ed Rubin—Charles Aidman

Filmed on August 20, 1963.

The Petries discover that their marriage is not legally binding after it comes out that Laura lied about her age when she applied for her marriage license.

Behind the scenes: The first of two parts.

Episode 66, "Laura's Little Lie"

67) VERY OLD SHOES, VERY OLD RICE
Airdate: 10/16/63

Writer: Carl Reiner / Director: John Rich

Supporting cast: Millie—Ann Morgan Guilbert, Judge Krata—Russell Collins, Dodo Parker—Madge Blake, Donald Lucas Parker—Burt Mustin, Mel— Richard Deacon

Filmed on August 27, 1963. Song: "I Wonder What's Become of Sally" (Ager, Yellen)

Rob and Laura renew their marriage vows in a hastily arranged ceremony, despite the fact that they are barely on speaking terms.

Behind the scenes: After filming this episode, the cast staged a surprise farewell party for director John Rich, who would depart the series after this episode to direct feature films under contract to Hal Wallis at Paramount Pictures.

68) UNCLE GEORGE Airdate: 11/13/63

Writer: Bill Idelson / Director: Jerry Paris

Supporting cast: Uncle George Petrie—Denver Pyle, Mrs. Glimscher—Elvia Allman, Herman Glimscher—Bill Idelson, Mel—Richard Deacon

Filmed on September 3, 1963. Song: "Buffalo Gals" (traditional)

When Rob's exuberant Uncle George comes to New York looking for a wife, he quickly sets his sights on Sally Rogers.

Behind the scenes: "Dick hated that one," observes Carl Reiner, who recalls that his star felt underused in the episode. "When Dick had something really to do, he was a very giving guy. But everybody's still an actor. And when the fun thing you come to work for is not in there, you're not so crazy about the show. Now, in retrospect, every time we see one of these shows that we thought were terrible, we say, 'They're not so bad!' It almost always had something in it that you could point to with pride."

69) TOO MANY STARS Airdate: 10/30/63

Writers: Sheldon Keller and Howard Merrill / Director: Jerry Paris

Supporting cast: Jerry—Jerry Paris, Millie—Ann Morgan Guilbert, Anita Lebost— Sylvia Lewis, Mrs. Billings—Eleanor Audley, Howard Lebost—Eddie Ryder, Freddy, the Grocery Man—Jerry Hausner, Mel—Richard Deacon

Filmed on September 9, 1963. Songs: "My Heart" (Gelbart, Keller); "Blue Tail Fly" (traditional); "Cielito Lindo" (Fernandez, arranged by Hagen); "A Doodlin' Song" (Coleman, Leigh)

Rob debates whether to cast Laura or a beautiful neighbor in the lead role in the annual PTA revue.

Episode 69, "Too Many Stars"

Behind the scenes: English teacher Howard Lebost and his wife Anita were named in honor of Reiner's wife, the former Estelle Lebost. . . . Millie's audition piece, identified in the show as "A Sentimental Love Song, words and music by Mildred Helper," was actually a ditty called "My Heart" that Sheldon Keller and his occasional writing partner Larry Gelbart had composed sometime earlier. . . . According to Carl Reiner, the PTA variety show episodes that became a staple of the series were inspired by his friend Mel Brooks, who, along with his wife, Anne Bancroft, was constantly being drafted into appearing in benefit shows at their child's school. Reiner confesses that when it came to his own participation in his children's school shows, he was only slightly more enthusiastic than his on-screen alter ego Rob Petrie. "I was called upon very often to do benefits and things," notes Reiner, "and I was always turning them down. Or I'd do them, but they were always a pain in the A! I mean, I knew you had to turn things down."

70) WHO AND WHERE WAS ANTONIO STRADIVARIUS?
Airdate: 11/6/63

Writer: Carl Reiner / Director: Jerry Paris

Supporting cast: Mel—Richard Deacon, Graciella—Sallie Janes, Aunt Mildred— Amzie Strickland, Uncle Edward—Hal Peary, Red Hook Party Hostess—Betty Lou Gerson, Party Host—Chet Stratton

Filmed on September 17, 1963. Songs: "Caissons Go Rolling Along" (Gruber, arranged by Hagen); "Mambo Jambo" (Prado)

After suffering a bout of temporary amnesia, Rob finds himself the life of the party in Red Hook, New Jersey.

Behind the scenes: This episode's unlikely storyline was inspired by a real-life accident that befell Dick Van Dyke's father, Cookie Van Dyke, who once embarked on a mysterious sojourn not unlike Rob Petrie's after suffering a blow to the head during a family gathering. "It was Fourth of July," recalls Van Dyke. "He was about sixty-four at the time, and he'd been showing off for the grandkids and did a back flip off the diving board." "He dives in the pool," continues Carl Reiner, "and he hits his head on the way out. And he gets up. He's fine. Next thing you know, he gets dressed and he gets in his car and he leaves. And he ends up in Palm Springs!" And, as Reiner describes it, it was in this slightly discombobulated state that the senior Van Dyke eventually found himself entertaining a party of total strangers. "He parked the car, and he saw a backyard party," says Reiner. "And he's a friendly guy, Cookie Van Dyke, so he goes in and sits with these people. So now he's at a second party, only it's two hundred miles away, and he's got temporary amnesia!" Naturally, when the younger Van Dyke got to work the next day and relayed the strange tale of his father's amnesia, Reiner wasted little time seizing the story's possibilities. "I said, 'Boy, is that a show for us!'"

71) BIG MAX CALVADA — Airdate: 11/20/63

Writers: Bill Persky and Sam Denoff / Director: Jerry Paris

Supporting cast: Max Calvada—Sheldon Leonard, Bernard—Arthur Batanides, Kenny Dexter—Jack Larson, Mrs.Calvada—Sue Casey, Louie—Tiny Brauer, Waiter—Johnny Silver, Night Club Emcee—Carl Reiner (uncredited voice-over)

Filmed on October 8, 1963. Song: "I Love to Hear You Say 'Encore'" (Denoff, Persky)

Rob, Buddy, and Sally's latest assignment finds them under the gun—perhaps literally—when a mobster asks them to pen a comedy routine for his nephew.

Behind the scenes: Executive producer Sheldon Leonard was a natural for the role of Big Max, having played scores of similar Runyonesque tough guys in his years as a Hollywood character actor. The mobster's imposing vocabulary—at one point he describes Rob, Buddy, and Sally's work as "neither too esoteric nor too mundane; pragmatically speaking, it hits me right in the gut"—served double duty as a good-natured jibe at Leonard, whose own weakness for five- and ten-dollar words was legendary. Even the character's name was an in-joke—Calvada was, of course, the registered name of the corporate entity that produced *The Dick Van Dyke Show*.

72) THE BALLAD OF THE BETTY LOU Airdate: 11/27/63

Writer: Martin A. Ragaway / Director: Howard Morris

Supporting cast: Jerry—Jerry Paris, Millie—Ann Morgan Guilbert, Coast Guard Sailor—Danny Scholl

Filmed on October 15, 1963. Song: "Blow the Man Down" (traditional, arranged by Hagen)

Landlubber Rob is thrilled to go in on the purchase of a sailboat with his neighbor Jerry, until their petty squabbles threaten to run the operation aground.

Behind the scenes: According to his son Andy, this was one of actor/director Jerry Paris's favorite episodes. "That was my dad's biggest acting part on the show," observes the younger Paris, "the one that he really felt proudest of."

73) TURTLES, TIES, AND TOREADORS Airdate: 12/4/63

Writer: John Whedon / Director: Jerry Paris

Guest Stars: Maria—Miriam Colon, Immigration Officer—Alan Dexter, Cab Driver—Tiny Brauer

Filmed on October 22, 1963.

Laura's domestic frustrations mount after Rob hires a maid who proves to be utterly incompetent around the house.

Behind the scenes: At the end of the episode, Maria offers the Petries the gift of a box turtle with the family's caricature painted on its shell—a prop that was the handiwork of amateur cartoonist Dick Van Dyke.

74) THE SOUND OF THE TRUMPETS OF CONSCIENCE FALLS DEAFLY ON A BRAIN THAT HOLDS ITS EARS . . . Airdate: 12/11/63

Writers: Bill Persky and Sam Denoff / Director: Jerry Paris

Supporting cast: Officer Nelson—Bernie Hamilton, Lt. Yarnell—Ken Lynch, Witness—Edward Holmes, Intimidating Hoodlum—Alan Dexter, Police Officer— Ray Kellogg, Nervous Witness—Frank Adamo

Filmed on October 29, 1963.

Rob is reluctant to testify after he discovers he's the lone witness to a jewelry store robbery.

75) THE THIRD ONE FROM THE LEFT Airdate: 1/1/64

Writer: John Whedon / Director: Jerry Paris

Supporting cast: Mel—Richard Deacon, Ernie Murphy—Jimmy Murphy, Joan Delroy—Cheryl Holdridge

Filmed on November 5, 1963.

Rob seeks Laura's advice after he discovers he's the object of an enthusiastic young dancer's affections.

76) THE ALAN BRADY SHOW PRESENTS Airdate: 12/18/63

Writers: Sam Denoff and Bill Persky / Director: Jerry Paris

Original Songs: Denoff and Persky

Supporting cast: Mel—Richard Deacon, Little Girl—Cornell Chulay (uncredited), Little Boy— Brendan Freeman (uncredited), Alan Brady—Carl Reiner (uncredited), Announcer—Jerry Paris (uncredited voice-over)

Filmed on November 12, 1963. Songs: "Anthem to Alan Brady" (Persky, Denoff); "Deck the Halls" (traditional, arranged by Hagen); "Santa, Send a Fella" (Persky, Denoff); "Jingle Bells" (traditional, arranged by Hagen); "I Have Everything but You" (Persky, Denoff); "Little Drummer Boy" (Davis, Onorati, Simeone); "The Musicians" (Grean, Glazer)

Alan Brady revamps his Christmas show into a yuletide extravaganza starring Rob, Laura, and the rest of his show's talented writing staff.

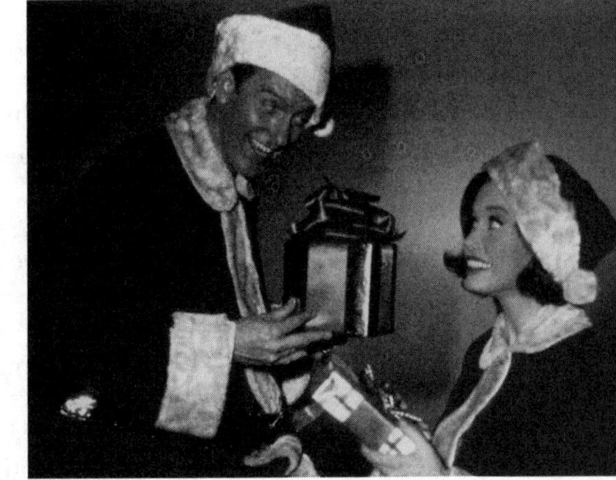

Episode 76, "The Alan Brady Show Presents"

Behind the scenes: When Persky and Denoff first pitched the idea of a holiday episode, Carl Reiner says he was initially cool to the notion, worrying that the episode would have little value as a summer rerun. However, he recalls, he reconsidered when it dawned on him that he could rerun the holiday episode once each year for the remainder of the show's run. "Okay," he remembers telling Persky and Denoff, "we'll do one Christmas show for the whole five years." . . . Owing to the large number of costume and set changes, the show would be filmed over the course of two days, without a studio audience in attendance. . . . The episode's format was inspired by Persky and Denoff's days as writers on *The Andy Williams Show*, whose star frequently invited his own staff and their families to join him on stage for his annual holiday installment.

77) MY HUSBAND IS THE BEST ONE — Airdate: 1/8/64

Writer: Martin A. Ragaway / Director: Jerry Paris

Supporting cast: Mel—Richard Deacon, Diane Mosby—Valerie Yerke, Waiter—Frank Adamo, Alan Brady—Carl Reiner (uncredited)

Filmed on November 19, 1963.

Rob faces a frigid reception from his coworkers after Laura convinces a visiting journalist that her husband is, in fact, the primary creative force behind *The Alan Brady Show*.

Behind the scenes: Writer Martin A. Ragaway's fourth script for the series would earn the scribe a Writers Guild of America Award for Episodic Comedy.

78) HAPPY BIRTHDAY AND TOO MANY MORE — Airdate: 2/5/64

Writers: Bill Persky and Sam Denoff / Director: Jerry Paris

Supporting cast: Pony delivery man—Johnny Silver, Ritchie's Party Guests—Brendan Freeman, Cornell Chulay, Michael Chulay, Tony Paris

Filmed on November 26,1963. Songs: "Old Macdonald's Farm" (traditional); "The Circus Comes to Town" (Andrew, Denoff)

After Rob scotches Laura's elaborate plans for Ritchie's birthday party, he faces the challenge of entertaining sixty-three screaming kids in the Petrie living room.

Behind the scenes: Due to circumstances beyond their control—the episode was filmed a mere four days after the assassination of President John F. Kennedy—the producers opted to shoot this episode without a live audience.... Included among the large cast of extras at Ritchie's birthday party are assistant director John C. Chulay's real-life son and daughter, Michael and Cornell Chulay, as well as director Jerry Paris's seven-year-old son, Tony Paris.

79) THE LADY AND THE TIGER AND THE LAWYER Airdate: 1/15/64

Writers: Garry Marshall and Jerry Belson / Director: Jerry Paris

Supporting cast: Arthur Stanwyck—Anthony Eisley, Donna Palmer—Lyla Graham

Filmed on December 3, 1963.

The Petries vie in a matchmaking competition to determine whether a new bachelor in the neighborhood prefers Sally or Laura's cousin Donna.

Behind the scenes: The first *Dick Van Dyke Show* episode written by Garry Marshall and Jerry Belson.

80) THE LIFE AND LOVE OF JOE COOGAN Airdate: 1/22/64

Writer: Carl Reiner / Director: Jerry Paris

Supporting cast: Mel—Richard Deacon, Millie—Ann Morgan Guilbert, Joe Coogan—Michael Forest, Country Club Waiter—Johnny Silver

Filmed on December 10, 1963.

Rob is overcome with jealousy when he meets one of Laura's old beaus at a country club.

Behind the scenes: Carl Reiner named this episode's title character after one of his old army buddies.

81) A NICE, FRIENDLY GAME OF CARDS Airdate: 1/29/64

Writer: Ernest Chambers / Director: Howard Morris

Guest Stars: Jerry—Jerry Paris, Millie—Ann Morgan Guilbert, Lou Gregory—Edward C. Platt, Beth—Shirley Mitchell

Filmed on December 17, 1963.

Episode 82, "The Brave and the Backache"

A friendly game of cards threatens to turn ugly when it's discovered that Rob's been dealing from a marked deck.

Behind the scenes: Howard Morris would later direct the pilot episode of the 1965 sitcom *Get Smart*, in which Don Adams would find able support from Edward C. Platt, this episode's memorable guest player.

82) THE BRAVE AND THE BACKACHE
Airdate: 2/12/64

Writers: Sheldon Keller and Howard Merrill / Director: Jerry Paris

Supporting cast: Millie—Ann Morgan Guilbert, Dr. Phil Nevins—Ross Elliott, Tony Daniels—Ken Berry

Filmed on December 31, 1963.

Laura is convinced that Rob's mysterious backache is the result of his subconscious desire to avoid spending a weekend alone with her.

Behind the scenes: Ken Berry's choreographer character would return for a second appearance in the show's ninety-sixth episode, "My Mother Can Beat Up My Father." A few years later, Berry would assume a central role in the cast of *The Andy Griffith Show* and its spin-off series, *Mayberry RFD*.

83) THE PEN IS MIGHTIER THAN THE MOUTH — Airdate: 2/19/64

Writers: Bill Persky and Sam Denoff / Director: Jerry Paris

Supporting cast: Mel—Richard Deacon, Stevie Parsons—Dick Patterson, Bernie Quinn—Herb Vigran, Dave—Johnny Silver, Announcer—Carl Reiner (uncredited voice-over), Announcer—Jerry Paris (uncredited voice-over)

Filmed on January 7, 1964.

Sally considers leaving her job on *The Alan Brady Show* after she makes a splash on a late-night talk show.

Behind the scenes: The first of two parts.

84) MY PART-TIME WIFE — Airdate: 2/26/64

Writers: Bill Persky and Sam Denoff / Director: Jerry Paris

Guest Stars: Mel—Richard Deacon, Millie—Ann Morgan Guilbert, Jackie—Jackie Joseph

Filmed on January 14, 1964.

Rob reluctantly agrees to hire Laura as interim secretary during Sally's unexpected absence.

Behind the scenes: This episode was inspired by writer Bill Persky's memories of casting his then-wife as an actress on a show he'd written. "My wife wanted to be an actress," he recalls, "and we actually put her on a show. And it was a nightmare for me. It was just the worst—like having your mother around."

85) HONEYMOONS ARE FOR THE LUCKY — Airdate: 3/4/64

Writer: Carl Reiner / Director: Jerry Paris

Supporting cast: Millie—Ann Morgan Guilbert, Sam—Allan Melvin, Capt. E. Lebost—Peter Hobbs, Mrs. Campbell—Kathleen Freeman, Alfred Campbell—Johnny Silver, Soldier—Frank Adamo

Filmed on January 21, 1964.

Rob recalls how he went AWOL from Camp Crowder in order to spend his honeymoon with Laura.

Behind the scenes: Captain Lebost was named after Carl Reiner's wife, the former Estelle Lebost.

86) HOW TO SPANK A STAR — Airdate: 3/11/64

Writers: Nathaniel Curtis and Bill Idelson / Director: Jerry Paris

Supporting cast: Paula Marshall—Lola Albright, Mel—Richard Deacon, Alan Brady—Carl Reiner (uncredited voice-over)

Filmed on January 21, 1964.

Laura grows jealous after Rob is promoted to producer at the behest of *The Alan Brady Show*'s beautiful guest star.

87) THE PLOTS THICKEN — Airdate: 3/18/64

Writer: Carl Reiner, Bill Persky, and Sam Denoff / Director: Jerry Paris

Guests Stars: Sam Petrie—J. Pat O'Malley, Clara Petrie—Isabel Randolph, Alan Meehan—Carl Benton Reid, Mrs. Meehan—Geraldine Wall

Filmed on February 4, 1964.

Rob and Laura are caught in the middle when their in-laws wage a battle of wills to determine where the young couple will take their eternal rest.

Behind the scenes: Though this episode's three writers would leave their collective fingerprints on most of the scripts written in the show's final three years, this was one of only five episodes on which Persky and Denoff shared a joint scriptwriting credit with their producer. "I think it was just for a change of pace," recalls Bill Persky. "We actually sat in a room and said, 'Well, let's write this one together.'" . . . Sam Petrie's penchant for grand toasts was a character trait borrowed from writer Persky's own real-life father. "My father," says Persky, "if you gave him any form of liquid, he would make a toast. I mean, if he took a tablespoon of medicine, he would use it as an opportunity to make a toast. He'd hold up the spoon and say, 'May none of you ever be sick!' I called him Harry Persky, the automatic toaster. You put a glass in his hand and he pops up. So we incorporated that into the show."

88) SCRATCH MY CAR AND DIE — Airdate: 3/25/64

Writer: John Whedon / Director: Howard Morris

Guest Stars: Mel—Richard Deacon, Millie—Ann Morgan Guilbert

Filmed on February 11, 1964. Songs: "On the Sunny Side of the Street" (McHugh, Fields)

Laura frets over how to break it to Rob that she's put a scratch in the new sports car that is his pride and joy.

Behind the scenes: This episode was inspired by Dick Van Dyke's own weakness for fancy sports cars; shortly after he signed to star in his own series, the actor indulged himself with the purchase of an expensive British import. "I'd had Corvettes back in the fifties in New York," he recalls, "but at the time the Jaguar E-Type had just come out—I think it was about '60 or '61. And I ordered one, and it came in off the boat down in San Pedro. I think I had one of the first ones in L.A.—and I protected that car with my life."

89) THE RETURN OF EDWIN CARP — Airdate: 4/1/64

Writer: Carl Reiner / Director: Howard Morris

Supporting Cast: Edwin Carp—Richard Haydn, Mel—Richard Deacon, Arlene Harris—Herself, Bert Gordon—Himself, Mrs. Carp—Amzie Strickland, Announcer—Carl Reiner (uncredited voice-over)

Filmed on February 18, 1964. Song: "You Need Feet" (R. Irnin, arranged by Sid Colin)

Rob attempts to coax a legendary radio star out of retirement.

Behind the scenes: The show's storyline echoes Carl Reiner's own desire to stage an affectionate tribute to the golden days of radio featuring three stars from the medium's heyday: Bert Gordon, Arlene Harris, and Richard Haydn.

90) OCTOBER EVE — Airdate: 4/8/64

Writers: Bill Persky and Sam Denoff / Director: Jerry Paris

Supporting cast: Serge Carpetna—Carl Reiner, Mel—Richard Deacon, Henry—Howard Wendell, Henry's Wife—Genevieve Griffin, Sketch Artist—Frank Adamo

Filmed on March 3, 1964.

Laura encounters a long-forgotten skeleton in her closet when a nude oil portrait bearing her distinct resemblance surfaces at a prominent New York gallery.

Behind the scenes: Dick Van Dyke's priceless reaction after hearing Laura explain the origin of the controversial painting resulted in one of the show's funniest moments. Privately fuming, Rob waits until Laura leaves the kitchen, and then, in pent-up anger, accidentally clenches the rings on the oven range with such force that he can't let them go, even after he realizes how hot they are. "Whenever I talk about Dick's genius," says Bill Persky, "I point out that stove take. There's no way you can write that, you know? It just happened." And though most *Van Dyke Show* staffers cite the ovation that greeted Greg Morris's entrance in "That's My Boy??" as the show's longest single laugh, film editor Bud Molin awarded that distinction to Van Dyke's classic stove take in this episode. "*That*," insisted the editor, "was a bigger laugh."

91) DEAR MRS. PETRIE, YOUR HUSBAND IS IN JAIL
Airdate: 4/15/64

Writers: Jerry Belson and Garry Marshall / Director: Jerry Paris

Supporting cast: Benny Joey—Herkie Styles, Maureen Core—Barbara Stuart, Alberta Schweitzer—Jackie Joseph, Arnold—Art Batanides, Nick—Johnny Silver, Policeman—Henry Scott, TV Car Salesman—Carl Reiner (uncredited voice-over)

Filmed on March 10, 1964.

Rob ventures into a steamy honky-tonk to catch an old friend's nightclub act and winds up spending the night in jail.

Behind the scenes: According to Sam Denoff, this episode's opening scene—an extended monologue in which Rob does little more than mutter to himself in his living room—was devised to capitalize on one of the actor's lesser-known talents. "Dick was the best mumbler in the business," observes Denoff. "We used to love to put Dick alone in a room, just to hear him mumble to himself."

92) MY NEIGHBOR'S HUSBAND'S OTHER LIFE **Airdate: 4/22/64**

Writers: Carl Reiner, Bill Persky, and Sam Denoff / Director: Jerry Paris

Supporting cast: Jerry—Jerry Paris, Millie—Ann Morgan Guilbert, Waiter—Johnny Silver

Filmed on March 17, 1964.

Rob and Laura suspect the worst when they spot Jerry having dinner at a fancy restaurant with a beautiful blonde.

93) I'D RATHER BE BALD THAN HAVE NO HEAD AT ALL
Airdate: 4/29/64

Writers: Bill Persky and Sam Denoff / Director: Jerry Paris

Episode 93, "I'd Rather Be Bald Than Have No Head at All"; guest star: Ned Glass

Supporting cast: Mel—Richard Deacon, Irwin—Ned Glass

Filmed on March 24, 1964.

Worried that he might be going prematurely bald, Rob consults a quack whose miracle hair restoration formula bears a peculiar resemblance to salad dressing.

Behind the scenes: Cowriter Sam Denoff insists that the springboard for this episode came from a conversation he and Bill Persky had with the show's star one morning before a reading. "Dick," recalls the writer, "who has this marvelous head of hair, came in one day and said, 'I think I'm losing my hair.' And I said, 'Get out of here.' And he said, 'No, no. I'm serious. I think I'm losing my hair.'" Naturally, the writers wasted little time translating the actor's insecurities into the premise of this memorable episode. . . . The sight gag that arrives at the episode's climax—where Rob wakes up to discover that his scalp has been transformed into an actual head of lettuce—was a special effect that makeup man Tom Tuttle achieved by ingenious means, employing a standard theatrical bald cap and an item he picked up at his local grocery store. "I found an old cabbage," explained Tuttle, "and then I took a needle and thread and just sewed it through. Leaf by leaf."

94) TEACHER'S PETRIE **Airdate: 5/13/64**

Writers: Jerry Belson and Garry Marshall / Director: Jerry Paris

Supporting cast: Mr. Caldwell—Bernard Fox, Millie—Ann Morgan Guilbert, Miss Prinder—Cheerio Meredith

Filmed on March 31, 1964. Song: "Blue Danube" (Strauss)

Rob is unable to share Laura's enthusiasm for her creative-writing course after he begins to suspect her attentive instructor's motives.

95) MY TWO SHOW-OFFS AND ME **Airdate: 12/16/64**

Writers: Sheldon Keller and Howard Merrill / Director: Jerry Paris

Episode 95, "My Two Show-Offs and Me"; guest star: Doris Singleton

Supporting cast: Mel—Richard Deacon, Lorraine Gilman—Doris Singleton

Filmed on April 3, 1964.

The attentions of a visiting reporter transform Alan Brady's writing staff into a trio of bickering grandstanders.

Behind the scenes: This would be the final *Van Dyke Show* script from writers Sheldon Keller and Howard Merrill. . . . Although produced at the end of the show's third year, this episode would not be broadcast until the following December, when it would be aired as the thirteenth episode of the show's fourth season.

1964–1965 THE DICK VAN DYKE SHOW

SEASON FOUR

The series enters a fourth year of popular and critical acclaim with Carl Reiner continuing as the show's producer. Reiner and his newly appointed story consultants, Bill Persky and Sam Denoff, write the majority of the season's scripts, with notable contributions from Joseph C. Cavella and the team of Garry Marshall and Jerry Belson, among others. Once again, Jerry Paris would direct the majority of the season's episodes.

FOURTH-SEASON CREDITS

Created and Produced by	Carl Reiner
Associate Producer	Ronald Jacobs
Music	Earle Hagen
Director of Photography	Robert De Grasse, A.S.C.

Art Director	Kenneth A. Reid
Film Editor	(episodes #107–108)
	Beryl Gelfond
	(episodes #96–106, 109–127)
	Bud Molin, A.C.E.
Assistant Director	(episode #105)
	Edward M. Hillie
	(episodes #96–104, 106–127)
	John C. Chulay
Prop Master	Glenn Ross
Camera Coordinator	Robert Sousa
Casting	Ruth Burch
Script Continuity	(episode #127)
	Gloria Morgan
	(episodes #96–126)
	Marjorie Mullen
Set Decorator	Ken Swartz
Rerecording Editor	(episodes #96, 98–103, 105, 107, 109–118, 120–26)
	Dick Maier
	(episodes #97, 104, 119)
	John Hall
	(episodes #106, 108)
	Robert Reeve
	(episode #127)
	Sid Lubow
Story Consultants	Bill Persky and Sam Denoff
Hairstylist	Donna McDonough
Makeup	Tom Tuttle
Costumes	Harald Johnson
Sound Engineer	Cam McCulloch
Music Coordinator	Walter Popp
Recorded by	Glen Glenn Sound Co.
Executive Producer	Sheldon Leonard in association with Danny Thomas
Production Supervisor	Ronald Jacobs
Production Manager	Frank E. Meyers

Mr. Van Dyke's wardrobe furnished by Botany 500.

Women's fashions by Ann Arnold; Mancini; Catalina, Inc. Swimwear; Nardis; House of Gold; Suivante; Michael Anthony; Dorothea Beatty; Gibi Knits; Mannis of Hollywood.

96) MY MOTHER CAN BEAT UP MY FATHER **Airdate: 9/23/64**

Writers: Bill Persky and Sam Denoff / Director: Jerry Paris

Supporting cast: Cavendish, the Drunk—Paul Gilbert, Tony Daniels—Ken Berry, Miss Taylor—Imelda de Martin, Ed Wilson—Tom Avera, Vinnie—Lou Cutell

Filmed on August 4, 1964.

Laura reveals a hitherto unknown talent for self-defense when she defends Rob against an unruly drunk in a bar.

Behind the scenes: Effective with this episode, the show's closing titles list each character's name along with the actor's credit. . . . Guest star Tom Avera was a member of the original cast of *Your Shows of Shows* in the early 1950s. . . . According to cowriter Sam Denoff, the script for this episode was inspired by little more than the availability of an actor who could pull off a convincing judo flip. "Somebody said, 'Paul Gilbert can do a great flip,'" recalls Denoff. "So we said, 'Gee, it would be fun to have him do it on the show.' And that was the start of that—the fact that we knew an actor who could do a funny fall."

97) THE GHOST OF A. CHANTZ **Airdate: 9/30/64**

Writers: Bill Persky and Sam Denoff / Director: Jerry Paris

Supporting cast: Mel—Richard Deacon, Mr. Little—Maurice Brenner, Caretaker— Milton Parsons

Filmed on August 11, 1964.

Rob and Laura share an unsettling night in a haunted cabin with Buddy and Sally.

Episode 97, "The Ghost of A. Chantz"

Episode 98, "The Lady and the Babysitter"; guest star: Eddie Hodges

98) THE LADY AND THE BABYSITTER
Airdate: 10/7/64

Writers: Bill Persky and Sam Denoff / Director: Jerry Paris

Supporting cast: Roger McChesney—Eddie Hodges, Man in Library—Frank Adamo (uncredited)

Filmed on August 18, 1964. Song: "The Thing" (Grean)

The Petries' teenage babysitter develops an adolescent crush on Laura.

Behind the scenes: This episode was designed to showcase the talents of former child star Eddie Hodges, who'd made his first splash some seven years earlier as the lisping juvenile lead in the original cast of Broadway's *The Music Man*. . . . Never a fan of this particular episode, cowriter Bill Persky nevertheless cites the scene where Rob playfully chides Laura for having the temerity to offer him a slice of chocolate cake—*without* a companion glass of milk!—as one of the most fondly remembered moments of the entire series. "That was really a kind of lame show," confesses Persky. "But people still come up to me and say, 'I love the milk cake show!' Only it wasn't about milk and cake at all. But it had that two-page exchange that people always remember." "When Rob says, 'Chocolate cake is *milk* cake,'" observes Sam Denoff, "the audience howled. Because they recognized that as a true moment. And it became a very human moment, all because we were willing to leave the story for a few minutes so they could talk about cake."

99) A VIGILANTE RIPPED MY SPORTS COAT **Airdate: 10/14/64**

Writer: Carl Reiner / Director: Peter Baldwin

Supporting cast: Mel—Richard Deacon, Jerry—Jerry Paris, Millie—Ann Morgan Guilbert

Filmed on August 25, 1964.

Rob and Jerry lock horns after Rob refuses to join a vigilante group that's been formed to protest a neighbor's unruly crabgrass.

100) THE MAN FROM EMPEROR — Airdate: 10/21/64

Writers: Carl Reiner, Bill Persky, and Sam Denoff / Director: Jerry Paris

Supporting cast: Drew Patton—Lee Philips, Coffee Girl—Nadia Sanders, Laura #2—Gloria Neil, Florence—Sally Carter, Miss Finland—Tracy Butler, Sam, the Secretary—Mary Tyler Moore (uncredited voice-over)

Filmed on September 1, 1964.

Rob is tempted by an offer to join the editorial staff of a glossy men's magazine, although Laura has other ideas.

Behind the scenes: Mary Tyler Moore contributes an uncredited voice-over as Drew Patton's sultry off-screen secretary, Sam—a sly reference to the actress's early role as the unseen receptionist of the same name on the *Richard Diamond* series in the late fifties.

101) ROMANCE, ROSES, AND RYE BREAD
Airdate: 10/28/64

Writers: Garry Marshall and Jerry Belson / Director: Jerry Paris

Supporting cast: Mel—Richard Deacon, Bert Monker—Sid Melton, Usherette—Jeri Lou James, Actor—Frank Adamo

Filmed on September 8, 1964.

Sally becomes aware she's got an unlikely admirer when the deli man starts delivering flowers along with her pastrami sandwiches.

Episode 101, "Romances, Roses, and Rye Bread"; guest star: Sid Melton

102) 4 1/2 **Airdate: 11/4/64**

Writers: Garry Marshall and Jerry Belson / Director: Jerry Paris

Supporting cast: Lyle Delp—Don Rickles, Mel—Richard Deacon

Filmed on September 15, 1964.

Rob recalls the story of Lyle Delp—an inept stick-up artist who once tried to rob the Petries in a stalled elevator.

Behind the scenes: The first of two parts. . . . Story editors Persky and Denoff had contributed material to guest star Don Rickles's nightclub act during their early days in New York.

103) THE ALAN BRADY SHOW GOES TO JAIL **Airdate: 11/11/64**

Writers: Bill Persky and Sam Denoff / Director: Jerry Paris

Supporting cast: Lyle Delp—Don Rickles, Boxer Morrison—Robert Strauss, Warden Jackson—Ken Lynch, Harry Tinker—Arthur Batanides, Guard Jenkins— Allan Melvin, Convict—Vincent Barbi, Guard—Alfred Ward

Filmed on September 22, 1964. Songs: "Vienna, Vienna" (Amsterdam); "Camptown Races" (Foster); "Cotton Fields" (Ledbetter); "I've Got Your Number" (Coleman, Leigh)

Rob and the gang are preparing to perform a prison benefit show when Rob gets mistaken for one of the inmates.

Behind the scenes: Alan Brady's name was inadvertently misspelled—with two *l*'s—in this episode's opening titles.

104) THREE LETTERS FROM ONE WIFE **Airdate: 11/18/64**

Writers: Bill Persky and Sam Denoff / Director: Jerry Paris

Supporting cast: Mel—Richard Deacon, Millie—Ann Morgan Guilbert, Alan Brady—Carl Reiner, Miss Thomas—Valerie Yerke, Jack Sullivan—Jerry Paris (uncredited voice-over)

Filmed on September 29, 1964.

Episode 104, "Three Letters from One Wife"

Against Laura's better judgment, Millie wages an ill-fated write-in campaign to bolster Rob's professional standing with his boss, Alan Brady.

Behind the scenes: This episode marks Carl Reiner's first full-fledged appearance as Alan Brady—as well as the first time the producer would receive an on-screen credit for playing the role in the show's closing titles.

105) IT WOULDN'T HURT THEM TO GIVE US A RAISE
Airdate: 12/2/64

Writer: Jay Burton and Ernest Chambers / Director: Peter Baldwin

Supporting cast: Mel—Richard Deacon, Doug Wesley—Roger C. Carmel

Filmed on October 6, 1964.

Rob enters a labyrinth of corporate finance when he tries to squeeze a raise for Buddy and Sally from Alan Brady's tight-fisted accountant.

106) PINK PILLS AND PURPLE PARENTS **Airdate: 11/25/64**

Writers: Jerry Belson and Garry Marshall / Director: Al Rafkin

Supporting cast: Millie—Ann Morgan Guilbert, Sam Petrie—Tom Tully, Clara Petrie—Isabel Randolph

Filmed on October 20, 1964. Songs: "Jeanie With the Light Brown Hair" (Foster); "Monkey Doodle Polka" (Bagley, Horton)

Episode 107, "The Death of the Party"

Rob recalls the disaster that transpired when Laura attempted to host a dinner party for his parents after accidentally taking an overdose of Millie's prescription pills.

Behind the scenes: Mary Tyler Moore's "drunk" scene in this episode recalls Dick Van Dyke's comical inebriation in the show's thirty-seventh episode, "My Husband Is Not a Drunk," which was—by odd coincidence—one of only three other *Dick Van Dyke Show* episodes also directed by Al Rafkin.

107) THE DEATH OF THE PARTY **Airdate: 12/9/64**

Writers: Bill Persky and Sam Denoff / Director: Al Rafkin

Supporting cast: Millie—Ann Morgan Guilbert, Uncle Harold—Willard Waterman, Cousin Margaret—Jane Dulo, Cousin Grace—Patty Regan, Paul—Pitt Herbert, Frank—Frank Adamo (uncredited)

Filmed on October 27, 1964.

Despite a raging fever and a bad case of the chills, Rob is determined to get through Laura's family gathering without anyone suspecting he's sick.

108) STRETCH PETRIE VS. KID SCHENK **Airdate: 12/30/64**

Writers: Garry Marshall and Jerry Belson / Director: Jerry Paris

Supporting cast: Neil Schenk—Jack Carter, Bill Sampson—Peter Hobbs, Headwaiter—Albert Carrier, Second Model—Lynn Borden, First Model—Judy Taylor, Girl—Sally Carter

Filmed on November 3, 1964.

Rob finds it almost impossible to stand up to Neil Schenk, an opportunistic old friend who comes around fishing for a job in return for an ancient favor.

109) THE IMPRACTICAL JOKE Airdate: 1/13/65

Writers: Bill Persky and Sam Denoff / Director: Jerry Paris

Supporting cast: Mel—Richard Deacon, Phil Franklin— Lennie Weinrib, William Handlebuck—Alvy Moore, Guest #1—Johnny Silver

Filmed on November 10, 1964. Song: "Battle Hymn of the Republic" (Steffe, Howe)

Wary of being taken in by a practical joke, Buddy refuses to heed a visit from an agent of the Internal Revenue Service.

110) BROTHER, CAN YOU SPARE $2,500? Airdate: 1/6/65

Writers: Garry Marshall and Jerry Belson / Director: Jerry Paris

Supporting cast: Mel—Richard Deacon, Main Hobo—Gene Baylos, Harry Keen—Herbie Faye, Hobo #3—Jimmy Cross, Hobo #2—Tiny Brauer, Woman—Sheila Rogers, Cop—Larry Blake, Warren—Brian Nash

Filmed on November 17, 1964.

A lost *Alan Brady Show* script is recovered by a vagrant who demands $2,500 in exchange for its safe return.

111) STACEY PETRIE—PART I Airdate: 1/20/65

Writer: Carl Reiner / Director: Jerry Paris

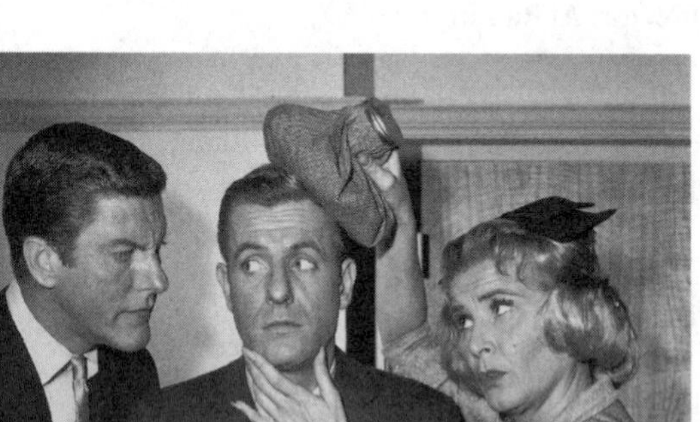

Episode 111, "Stacey Petrie"; guest star: Jerry Van Dyke

Supporting cast: Stacey Petrie—Jerry Van Dyke, Herman Glimscher—Bill Idelson, Dr. Lemler—Howard Wendell

Filmed on November 24, 1964.

Rob talks Sally into coaching his withdrawn brother Stacey through a practice date at her apartment.

Behind the scenes: The first of two parts.

112) STACEY PETRIE—PART II Airdate: 1/27/65

Writers: Carl Reiner, Bill Persky, and Sam Denoff / Director: Jerry Paris

Supporting cast: Stacey Petrie—Jerry Van Dyke, Millie—Ann Morgan Guilbert, Julie Kincaid—Jane Wald, Lou Temple—Herbie Faye, Tinker, the Butler—Kendrick Huxham, Willie Cook—Carl Reiner

Filmed on December 1, 1964. Songs: "Jeanie with the Light Brown Hair" (Foster); "Hello Dolly" (Herman)

Rob and Laura help Stacey recover after he's rejected by the woman of his dreams.

Behind the scenes: Listen closely and you'll hear Julie Kincaid's butler referred to as Tinker, a joshing reference to Grant Tinker, who was at that time married to Mary Tyler Moore. . . . The comic high point of this two-parter arrives in the slapstick altercation that ensues after a jealous Herman Glimscher confronts Stacey in Sally's apartment. But despite the apparent mayhem that follows, guest star Idelson insists that director Jerry Paris made certain that conditions on the set were anything but chaotic when the sequence was filmed. "Jerry Paris choreographed that entire fight," Idelson recalled. "It's a wild bit. But if you watch it, you'll see that that thing is choreographed down to a gnat's eyelash. We went over that, and over that, and over that. Jerry Paris loved doing that kind of physical comedy. That was fun." . . . Cowriter Bill Persky insists that he'd completely forgotten this episode until he stumbled upon it one night on television. "One morning I got up around four-fifteen or something like that," he recalls, "and I couldn't fall back to sleep. So I flipped on Nickelodeon and the *Van Dyke Show* was on. It was the one with Dick's brother, with the Cyrano de Bergerac plot. It was so great. I said, 'Jesus, this is so brilliant!' I couldn't remember who'd done that one. And then when I saw the credits, I saw that *we* had written it!"

Episode 113, "The Redcoats Are Coming"; guest stars: Chad Stuart and Jeremy Clyde

113) THE REDCOATS ARE COMING
Airdate: 2/10/65

Writers: Bill Persky and Sam Denoff / Director: Jerry Paris

Supporting cast: Mel—Richard Deacon, Millie—Ann Morgan Guilbert, Ernie—Chad Stuart, Freddie—Jeremy Clyde, Richard Karp—William Beckley, Marge—Trudi Ames, Estelle—Ellie Sommers, Phoebe—Mollie Howerton, Janie—Wendy Wilson, Girl #1—Shelley Cochran, Girl #2—Linda Cochran

Filmed on December 8, 1964. Songs: "No Other Baby" (Bishop, Watson); "My How the Time Goes By" (Stuart, Alquist)

The Petrie residence becomes a mob scene after Rob opens his home to a pair of English teen idols called the Redcoats.

Behind the scenes: The Redcoats were played by the real-life British folk-rock duo Chad & Jeremy, who must have had very good agents—just a few weeks after they filmed this *Van Dyke Show* episode, the pair would repeat their performance, almost beat for beat, on ABC's *Patty Duke Show*. The singers also logged an appearance on the Western series *Laredo* during that same period, and on an episode of ABC's *Batman*, in which they played themselves.

114) BOY #1, BOY #2 — Airdate: 2/3/65

Writer: Martin A. Ragaway / Director: Jerry Paris

Supporting cast: Mel—Richard Deacon, Jerry—Jerry Paris, Millie—Ann Morgan Guilbert, Freddie Helper—Peter Oliphant

Filmed on December 15, 1964.

Episode 115, "The Case of the Pillow"

Millie and Laura turn into stage mothers when Ritchie and Freddie are chosen to play small parts in a TV commercial.

115) THE CASE OF THE PILLOW

Airdate: 2/17/64

Writers: Bill Persky and Sam Denoff / Director: Howard Morris

Supporting cast: Judge—Ed Begley, Jerry—Jerry Paris, Millie—Ann Morgan Guilbert, Wiley—Alvy Moore, May—Amzie Strickland, Bailiff—Joel Fluellen, Man #1—Johnny Silver

Filmed on December 22, 1964.

Rob fancies himself an amateur Clarence Darrow when he takes an unscrupulous pillow salesman to small claims court.

Behind the scenes: Another eccentric *Van Dyke Show* storyline inspired by real life. "That happened to me," swears coauthor Bill Persky, describing a scenario that's almost a carbon copy of Rob Petrie's plight. "I bought these pillows from this guy who came to my apartment when I first got married. And I said they smelled like ducks. He said, 'No they don't!' Then my wife said, 'Yes, they do. It's two against one.' So then he went down to his car and got *his* wife. And she said, no, they didn't. So, I went next door and knocked on my neighbor's door—people I'd never met before. They said, 'Hi, welcome! Come on in, have a drink.' I said, 'No. Come into our apartment.' And I said, 'Smell this. Don't these smell like ducks to you?' It was hysterical, and we put it all in the show."

116) YOUNG MAN WITH A SHOEHORN **Airdate: 2/24/65**

Writers: Jerry Belson and Garry Marshall / Director: Jerry Paris

Supporting cast: Mel—Richard Deacon, Millie—Ann Morgan Guilbert, Lou Sorrell—Lou Jacobi, Sid Feldman—Milton Frome, Laughing Woman—Amzie

Strickland, Woman Customer #1—Jane Dulo; Sexy Girl—LaRue Farlow, Male Customer—Irving Bacon

Filmed on January 12, 1965.

Rob and Buddy sign on as not-so-silent partners in a discount shoe store operation.

117) GIRLS WILL BE BOYS — Airdate: 3/3/65

Writers: Jerry Belson and Garry Marshall / Director: Jerry Paris

Supporting cast: Millie—Ann Morgan Guilbert, Ogden Darwell—Bernard Fox, Doris "Dolly" Darwell—Doris Singleton, Priscilla Darwell—Tracy Stratford

Filmed on January 19, 1965.

Laura is understandably concerned when Ritchie arrives home with a bruise inflicted by a bully named Priscilla.

118) BUPKIS — Airdate: 3/10/65

Writers: Bill Persky and Sam Denoff / Director: Lee Philips

Supporting cast: Frank "Sticks" Mandalay—Greg Morris, Buzzy Potter—Robert Ball, Sheila, the Secretary—Patty Regan, Songwriter—Tim Herbert, Mr. Doldan—Charles Dugdale, Traffic Announcer—Carl Reiner (uncredited voice-over)

Filmed on January 26, 1965. Songs: "Weather Jingle" (Persky, Denoff); "Bupkis" (Persky, Denoff) (sung by Dick and Dee Dee); "Sergeant Foley" (Persky, Denoff); "Attila the Hun" (Persky, Denoff); "The Only Girl I Ever Loved" (Persky, Denoff)

Rob is delighted to hear a novelty song he penned with an old army buddy pop up on the radio, until he discovers that his former partner has taken all the credit.

Behind the scenes: Persky and Denoff's "Bupkis" is sung by Dick and Dee Dee—Dick St. John Gosting and Dee Dee Sperling—a pop singing duo whose modest string of hits in the early 1960s included "The Mountain's High" and "Thou Shalt Not Steal". . . . Coauthor Sam Denoff recalls that he borrowed his fictitious pop song's title from an old Yiddish expression he picked up from his mother, which he'd always been told meant "nothing." He didn't discover that the word had more subtle shades of meaning until the night the episode was filmed. "My mother and father came to see the show," recalls Denoff, "as they very often did on Tuesday night. And my mother laughed like everybody else. But afterward, she says, 'Sammy, you can't put that on the air!' And I said, 'Why not?' And she said, 'Don't you know what bupkis means?' And I said, 'Sure, it means "nothing." 'And she says, 'No. "Nothing" is the loose translation. The literal translation for *bupkis* in Yiddish is "goat shit." Goat shit is worth nothing, so *bupkis* is goat shit.' We decided to leave it in anyway—but we didn't tell the guy from network standards and practices." . . . Coauthor Bill Persky recalls the episode with less fondness than his former partner. "The worst show we ever did was 'Bupkis,'" he insists. "Oh, I hated it. Just hated it."

119) YOUR HOME SWEET HOME IS MY HOME SWEET HOME
Airdate: 3/17/65

Writers: Howard Ostroff and Joan Darling / Director: Lee Philips

Supporting cast: Jerry—Jerry Paris, Millie—Ann Morgan Guilbert, Mr. Parkly— Stanley Adams, Mr. Steele—Eddie Ryder

Filmed on February 2, 1965.

Rob recalls the day he and Laura decided to buy their dream house, even after they discovered it came fully equipped with a massive rock jutting out of the basement floor.

Behind the scenes: In the episode it's revealed that Rob and Laura's dream castle carried an asking price of of $27,990. . . . The script also establishes that before they moved to New Rochelle, the Petries and the Helpers lived in a city identified as Willetown.

120) ANTHONY STONE **Airdate: 3/24/65**

Writer: Joseph C. Cavella / Director: Jerry Paris

Supporting cast: Anthony Stone—Richard Angarola, Delivery Boy—Frank Adamo, Waiter—Bob Hoffman

Filmed on February 9, 1965.

Rob and Buddy make the startling discovery that Sally's mysterious new boyfriend is a mortician—and a married one, at that.

121) NEVER BATHE ON SATURDAY **Airdate: 3/31/65**

Writer: Carl Reiner / Director: Jerry Paris

Supporting cast: Millie—Ann Morgan Guilbert, The Detective—Bernard Fox, Bruce, the Bellboy—Bill Idelson, Maid—Kathleen Freeman, Engineer—Arthur Malet, Waiter—Johnny Silver

Filmed on February 16, 1965.

Laura finds herself in an embarrassing fix when she gets her toe stuck in the water spout of a fancy hotel bathtub—with the door locked from the inside.

Behind the scenes: According to story editor Bill Persky, Dick Van Dyke's decision to switch shoulders in midrun during his assault on the bathroom door was the result of an inspiration that hit the actor the night of the performance. "That was another great move that Dick did spontaneously while he was filming." . . . Although it did not win, Carl Reiner's script for "Never Bathe on Saturday" would earn the writer his fourth consecutive nomination for an Emmy Award in the writing category.

122) 100 TERRIBLE HOURS **Airdate: 5/5/65**

Writers: Bill Persky and Sam Denoff / Director: Theodore J. Flicker

Episode 122, "100 Terrible Hours"

Supporting cast: Mel—Richard Deacon, Mr. Van Buren—Fred Clark, Alan Brady—Carl Reiner, Mr. Waring—Dabbs Greer, Mr. Chambers—Howard Wendell, Dr. Gage—Harry Stanton, Photographer—Johnny Silver, Dr. Adamo—Frank Adamo

Filmed on March 2, 1965.

Rob recalls the time he attempted to broadcast a

radio show nonstop for one hundred hours just before he was scheduled to meet Alan Brady for the very first time.

Behind the scenes: Like his on-screen persona, Dick Van Dyke was also raised in Danville, Illinois. . . . Though Van Dyke had also held down an early job as a disc jockey, writers Persky and Denoff drew most of their inspiration for this episode's script from their own experience as reluctant deejays at New York's WNEW-AM in the late fifties. "I was the assistant program director," recounts Persky, "and Sam was the head of the commercial continuity department. And there was a strike. Because we were management, Sam and I had to go on the air for eight hours a day until it was settled. So we did the Sam and Bill show in the afternoon. Then we had like an hour off before we had to come back, when we'd do the Bill and Sam show at night. We were exhausted, but we just kept it up, doing our regular jobs and doing these eight hours a day of broadcasting, too. By the end of that week, we were pretty punchy." . . . Supporting actor Frank Adamo retains his own name in his cameo as Dr. Adamo.

123) A SHOW OF HANDS — Airdate: 4/14/65

Writer: Joseph C. Cavella / Director: Theodore J. Flicker

Supporting cast: Mel—Richard Deacon, Millie—Ann Morgan Guilbert, Chairman Roger Johnson—Joel Fluellen, Vice-Chairman Joe Clark—Henry Scott, Delivery Man—Herkie Styles

Filmed on March 9, 1965.

Rob and Laura are forced to wear gloves to a prestigious awards banquet after they accidentally dye their hands an indelible shade of black.

Behind the scenes: Yet another episode inspired by a real-life incident, as Carl Reiner explained at a 1988 public appearance. "When we'd get together with new writers," said Reiner, "we'd always ask the question, what happened to you lately at your house? Don't give us any fantasy

Episode 123, "A Show of Hands"

ideas. But if you've got anything that really happened, we'll build a show around it. And the guy was fussing around all day—it was Joe Cavella—and he said, 'The only thing that happened, my wife was dying some clothing in black dye, and her hands got black and she couldn't get it off.' We said, 'That's it!' So he wrote it."[2]

124) BABY FAT — Airdate: 4/21/65

Writers: Garry Marshall and Jerry Belson / Director: Jerry Paris

Supporting cast: Mel—Richard Deacon, Buck Brown—Richard Erdman, Lionel Dann—Sandy Kenyon, Harper Worthington Yates—Strother Martin, Alan Brady—Carl Reiner

Filmed on March 16, 1965.

Rob agrees to doctor the script for Alan Brady's Broadway debut, only to have second thoughts about performing the thankless task without recognition.

Behind the scenes: "That was a story out of Garry's life," recalled cowriter Jerry Belson. "He was brought in to ghostwrite a play like that—I think it was summer theater with Jack Carter. I don't know if they made him hide in a closet, but I think he did have to hide in the next room." . . . Strother Martin's flamboyant playwright Harper Worthington Yates is clearly modeled after Tennessee Williams; the script doctor who finally ends up ghosting Brady's play is identified as Dave Murrows, an obvious reference to the real-life Pulitzer Prize–winner and well-known Broadway fixer Abe Burrows. . . . Carl Reiner would be particularly proud of his work as an actor in this episode, one of his favorite *Van Dyke Shows*. Says Reiner, "I'd put that in my bank as one of the best things I ever did."

125) BR-ROOOM, BR-ROOOM — Airdate: 5/12/65

Writers: Dale McRaven and Carl Kleinschmitt / Director: Jerry Paris

Supporting cast: Policeman—Sandy Kenyon, Jolly—Jimmy Murphy, Mouse—Bob Random, Gus—Carl Reindel, Doris—Linda Marshall, Counter Man—Johnny Silver

Filmed on March 23, 1965.

Rob takes his new motorcycle out for a spin and unwittingly falls in with a gang of unruly bikers.

Behind the scenes: The first *Van Dyke Show* script from newcomers Carl Kleinschmitt and Dale McRaven, the teleplay would go on to win a Writers Guild of America Award. . . . Van Dyke reportedly improvised much of his own dialogue in the solo scene that takes place in Rob's garage—a circumstance that, according to his friend and stand-in, Frank Adamo, was not at all unusual in the show's later days. "A lot of that stuff," recalls Adamo, "they would never even rehearse. They'd say, 'Dick does X number of minutes here. And then they'd block the area where they thought he'd be, and they'd just let him loose to do what he wanted." . . . A prop billboard used in this episode advertises the fictional soft drink Calvada, an in-joke reference to Calvada Productions, the legal name of the partnership that produced *The Dick Van Dyke Show*.

126) THERE'S NO SALE LIKE WHOLESALE — Airdate: 5/26/65

Writers: Garry Marshall and Jerry Belson / Director: Jerry Paris

Supporting cast: Millie—Ann Morgan Guilbert, Nunzio Vallani—Lou Krugman, Opal Levinger—Jane Dulo, Emil—Peter Brocco, Mr. Garnett—A. G. Vitanza

Filmed on March 30, 1965.

Rob decides to save a few bucks on a new fur coat for Laura by letting Buddy order it wholesale.

127) A FAREWELL TO WRITING — Airdate: 9/22/65

Writers: Fred Freeman and Lawrence J. Cohen / Director: Jerry Paris

Supporting cast: Millie—Ann Morgan Guilbert, Horace—Guy Raymond

Filmed on April 2, 1965. Song: "The Caissons Go Rolling Along" (Gruber)

Rob hopes a few days of seclusion in a mountain cabin will motivate him to complete his book—instead, it nearly drives him stir-crazy.

Behind the scenes: The final show in the series' fourth production season, this episode was filmed on a Friday—four days earlier than the show's customary Tuesday-night performance—after a mere three days of rehearsal. As in the show's two previous seasons, this final episode of the year would be held back for broadcast until the following season. . . . Ann Guilbert first met her future husband Guy Raymond on the set during the filming of this episode.

1965–1966 THE DICK VAN DYKE SHOW

SEASON FIVE

In *The Dick Van Dyke Show*'s fifth and final year on the air, Carl Reiner trades off producing chores with Persky and Denoff, who also continue as the show's story consultants throughout the season. Other memorable fifth-year scripts are contributed by a wide array of freelancers, including the teams of Garry Marshall and Jerry Belson; Dale McRaven and Carl Kleinschmitt; Jay Burton and Ernest Chambers; Fred Freeman and Lawrence J. Cohen; and Art Baer and Ben Joelson; as well as Joseph C. Cavella, John Whedon, Rick Mittleman, and Joseph Bonaduce. Jerry Paris would once again serve as the show's primary director.

FIFTH-SEASON CREDITS

Created by	Carl Reiner
Produced by	(episodes #128–133, 145–158) Carl Reiner (episodes #134–144) Bill Persky and Sam Denoff
Music	Earle Hagen
Associate Producer	Ronald Jacobs
Story Consultants	Bill Persky and Sam Denoff
Production Assistant	Joel Swanson
Director of Photography	Robert De Grasse, A.S.C.
Art Director	Kenneth A. Reid
Film Editor	Beryl Gelfond
Assistant Director	(episodes #128–154) John C. Chulay (episodes #155–158) Stanley J. Brooks
Prop Master	Glenn Ross
Camera Coordinator	Robert Sousa
Casting	Ruth Burch
Script Continuity	Marjorie Mullen
Set Decorator	Ken Swartz
Rerecording Editor	(episodes #128–129, 131, 133, 157–158) Dick Maier

	(episodes #130, 132)
	Sid Lubow
	(episodes #134–156)
	Reg Browne
Hairstylist	Donna McDonough
Makeup	Tom Tuttle
Costumes	(episodes #128–149)
	Harald Johnson
	(episodes #150–158)
	Margaret Makau
Sound Engineer	Cam McCulloch
Music Coordinator	Walter Popp
Recorded by	Glen Glenn Sound Co.
Executive Producer	Sheldon Leonard in association with Danny Thomas
Production Supervisor	Ronald Jacobs
Production Manager	Frank E. Meyers

Mr. Van Dyke's wardrobe furnished by Botany 500.

Women's fashions by Suivante; Nardis of California; Nardis of Dallas; Gibi Knits; California Girl; Michael Anthony, Inc.; Bridallure, Inc.; Torino Imports; Glenhaven, Ltd.; House of Gold.

128) COAST TO COAST BIG MOUTH — Airdate: 9/15/65

Writers: Bill Persky and Sam Denoff / Director: Jerry Paris

Supporting cast: Mel—Richard Deacon, Millie—Ann Morgan Guilbert, Johnny Patrick—Dick Curtis, Alan Brady—Carl Reiner

Filmed on August 3, 1965.

Laura faces Alan Brady's wrath after a fast-talking game-show host goads her into admitting that the star wears a toupee.

Behind the scenes: This script would earn Persky and Denoff their second Emmy Award for Outstanding Writing Achievement in Comedy. . . . According to Bill Persky, he and partner Sam Denoff were inspired to write the show

Episod. 129, "Uhny Uftz"; guest stars: Karl Lukas and John Mylong

one morning after watching Carl Reiner fret over having to buy a new hairpiece. "The toupee was a pain in the ass for him," says Persky. "So we decided to do an episode about it."

129) UHNY UFTZ Airdate: 9/29/65

Writers: Carl Kleinschmitt and Dale McRaven / Director: Jerry Paris

Supporting cast: Mel—Richard Deacon, Dr. Phil Ridley—Ross Elliott, Lady-Madge Blake, Karl—John Mylong; Hugo—Karl Lukas; Sound Effects—Carl Reiner (uncredited voice-over)

Filmed on August 10, 1965.

No one seems to believe Rob's claim that he spotted a flying saucer hovering outside the office window.

Behind the scenes: The versatile Carl Reiner provided the sound effects for the show's gurgling water cooler, as well as most of the other miscellaneous vocal effects heard on the soundtrack. . . . Writers Kleinschmitt and McRaven wrote this episode's script in response to the UFO-sighting fad of the early sixties. "Everybody was seeing flying saucers at the time," notes McRaven, "but it was usually a guy somewhere in Indiana. We thought it would be funny for an urban writer living in New York to see a flying saucer."

130) THE UGLIEST DOG IN THE WORLD Airdate: 10/6/65

Writers: Bill Persky and Sam Denoff / Director: Lee Philips

Supporting cast: Mel—Richard Deacon, Rexford Spaulding—Billy De Wolfe, Mrs. Rocky Spaulding—Florence Halop, Mr. Mack—Michael Conrad, Berkowitz—George Tyne, Customer—Barbara Dodd

Filmed on August 17, 1965.

A homely mongrel becomes the temporary ward of the Petries after he's cut from a scheduled appearance on *The Alan Brady Show*.

Behind the scenes: Persky and Denoff's script for this episode would earn the writers their second Emmy nomination of the year, though the award would go to their script for the show's 128th episode, "Coast to Coast Big Mouth". . . . Dog groomer Rexford Spaulding was named after a pair of prominent streets in Beverly Hills.

131) NO RICE AT MY WEDDING Airdate: 10/13/65

Writers: Jerry Belson and Garry Marshall / Director: Lee Philips

Supporting cast: Millie—Ann Morgan Guilbert, Clark Rice—Van Williams, Sam Pomerantz—Allan Melvin, Heckler—Bert Remsen, Humphrey Dundee—Johnny Silver

Filmed on August 24, 1965.

Rob recalls his only serious competition for Laura's hand, a charming army corporal who won a date with her in a USO charity raffle.

Behind the scenes: Guest star Van Williams would return to prime time the following season in the title role on ABC's *The Green Hornet*.

132) DRAW ME A PEAR Airdate: 10/20/65

Writers: Art Baer and Ben Joelson / Director: Jerry Paris

Supporting cast: Millie—Ann Morgan Guilbert, Valerie Ware—Ina Balin, Missy—Jackie Joseph, Agnes—Jody Gilbert, Doris—Dorothy Neumann, Sebastian—Frank Adamo

Filmed on August 31, 1965.

Episode 132, "Draw Me a Pear"; guest star: Ina Balin

Laura suspects Rob's comely drawing instructor may be interested in something other than her husband's artistic abilities.

Behind the scenes: Dick Van Dyke contributed the caricature of Mary Tyler Moore that figures prominently in this episode.

133) THE GREAT PETRIE FORTUNE — Airdate: 10/27/65

Writers: Ernest Chambers and Jay Burton / Director: Jerry Paris

Supporting cast: Leland Ferguson—Dan Tobin, Mr. Harlow—Forrest Lewis, Luthuella Detweiller—Elvia Allman, Alfred Reinback—Herb Vigran, Rebecca—Amzie Strickland, Ezra—Howard Wendell, Ike Ballinger—Tiny Brauer

Filmed on September 9, 1965. Songs: "Me and My Shadow" (Dreyer, Jolson, Rose); "Dixie" (traditional)

Rob discovers he's heir to a mysterious fortune hidden somewhere in his Uncle Hezekiah's rolltop desk.

134) ODD BUT TRUE — Airdate: 11/3/65

Writers: Garry Marshall and Jerry Belson / Director: Jerry Paris

Supporting cast: Mel—Richard Deacon, Millie—Ann Morgan Guilbert, Tetlow—James Millhollin, Lady with Dog—Hope Summers, Potato Man—David Fresco, Freddie Helper—Peter Oliphant, Upside Down Man—Bert May, Receptionist—Rhoda Williams, Stagehand—Ray Kellogg

Filmed on September 21, 1965.

Rob becomes a reluctant candidate for the *Odd but True* newspaper column after Ritchie plays connect-the-dots with the freckles on his father's back and discovers a reasonable facsimile of the Liberty Bell.

Behind the scenes: The first of eleven consecutive *Van Dyke Show* episodes produced by Bill Persky and Sam Denoff, who stepped in while Carl Reiner was out of town to play a leading role in *The Russians Are Coming, the Russians Are Coming.*

135) VIVA PETRIE — Airdate: 11/10/65

Writer: John Whedon / Director: Jerry Paris

Supporting cast: Manuel Luis Rodriguez—Joby Baker, Doctor—Jack Bernardi

Filmed on September 28, 1965. Song: "La Virgen de la Macarena" (Monterde, Ortiz, Calero)

Rob and Laura attempt to find work for a newly landed immigrant whose only occupational skill is bullfighting.

Behind the scenes: This show is a sequel to episode 73, "Turtles, Ties, and Toreadors". . . . Joby Baker would also appear—as a different character—in the show's 156th episode, "Love Thy Other Neighbor." The light-comic actor would later play a starring role in Persky and Denoff's 1967 series *Good Morning World*.

136) GO TELL THE BIRDS AND BEES — Airdate: 11/17/65

Writer: Rick Mittleman / Director: Jerry Paris

Supporting cast: Dr. Gormsley—Peter Hobbs, Miss Reshovsky—Alberta Nelson

Filmed on October 5, 1965.

Ritchie regales his schoolmates with tall tales about where babies come from.

137) BODY AND SOL — Airdate: 11/24/65

Writers: Carl Kleinschmitt and Dale McRaven / Director: Jerry Paris

Supporting cast: Sol Pomerantz—Allan Melvin, Capt. Worwick—Ed Peck, Bernie Stern—Michael Conrad, Referee—Garry Marshall, Norma—Barbara Dodd, 1st Soldier—Burt Taylor, Boom Boom Bailey—Paul Stader

Filmed on October 12, 1965.

Rob recalls his short-lived career as "Pitter Patter" Petrie—middleweight champ of the US Army special services division.

Episode 137, "Body and Sol"

Behind the scenes: Writer Garry Marshall has a cameo as the boxing referee.

138) SEE ROB WRITE, WRITE ROB, WRITE Airdate: 12/8/65

Writers: Lawrence J. Cohen and Fred Freeman / Director: Jerry Paris

Supporting cast: Ollie Wheelright—John McGiver

Filmed on October 19, 1965.

The Petries find themselves competing in a literary rivalry after Rob volunteers to help Laura write a children's book.

139) YOU'RE UNDER ARREST Airdate: 12/15/65

Writer: Joseph C. Cavella / Director: Jerry Paris

Supporting cast: Millie—Ann Morgan Guilbert, Detective Norton—Phillip Pine, Detective Cox—Sandy Kenyon, Joe, the Bartender—Lee Krieger, Mrs. Fieldhouse—Bella Bruck, Policeman—Ed McCready, Taxey—Johnny Silver, Man in Line-up—Tiny Brauer (uncredited), Off-screen Voice—Jerry Paris (uncredited voice-over)

Filmed on October 26, 1965.

Rob has difficulty coming up with a plausible alibi after the police accuse him of taking part in a barroom brawl.

140) FIFTY-TWO, FORTY-FIVE OR WORK Airdate: 12/29/65

Writer: Rick Mittleman / Director: Jerry Paris

Supporting cast: Mel—Richard Deacon, Dawn McCracken—Reta Shaw, Joe Galardi—James Frawley, Herbie Finkel—Jerry Hausner, Johnson—Alfred Ward, Truck Driver—John Chulay, Mr. Brumley—Dabbs Greer

Filmed on November 2, 1965.

Rob recalls the financial stresses that forced him to take a job writing copy for an electronics catalog during his first summer hiatus from *The Alan Brady Show*.

Behind the scenes: Among the tidbits that Rob reveals in his unemployment interview are his middle name—Simpson—as well as his home phone number,

NE 6-9970. The show's assistant director, John C. Chulay, makes a cameo appearance as a truck driver in this episode.

141) WHO STOLE MY WATCH? Airdate: 1/5/66

Writer: Joseph Bonaduce / Director: Jerry Paris

Supporting cast: Mel—Richard Deacon, Mr. Evans—Milton Frome, Jerry—Jerry Paris, Millie—Ann Morgan Guilbert

Filmed on November 9, 1965.

When Rob's brand-new watch turns up missing at his birthday party, he's forced to confront the possibility that it may have been stolen by one of his closest friends.

142) BAD RECEPTION IN ALBANY Airdate: 3/9/66

Writers: Garry Marshall and Jerry Belson / Director: Jerry Paris

Supporting cast: Forrest Gilly—Tom D'Andrea, Wendell—Robert Nichols, Sugar—Chanin Hale, Sam—John Haymer, Fred—Joseph Mell, Bartender—Bert Remsen, Chambermaid—Bella Bruck, Edabeth—Lorraine Bendix, Newlywed Man—Ed Rice, Newlywed Girl—Candace Howard, Lou—Tiny Brauer, Organist—Joyce Wellington (uncredited)

Filmed on November 23, 1965. Songs: "Who Cares "(Gershwin, Gershwin); "All or Nothing at All" (Altman); "I'll Remember April " (Raye, de Paul, Johnston)

Rob encounters difficulty trying to find a functioning television set in an Albany hotel during the annual Seals lodge convention.

Episode 142, "Bad Reception in Albany"

143) I DO NOT CHOOSE TO RUN **Airdate: 1/19/65**

Writers: Dale McRaven and Carl Kleinschmitt / Director: Jerry Paris

Supporting cast: Mr. Howard—Philip Ober, Doug—George Tyne, Bill Schermerhorn—Arte Johnson, John Gerber—Howard Wendell, Man—Peter Brocco, Woman—Helen Spring

Filmed on November 30, 1965.

Rob is drafted to run for an open seat on the New Rochelle City Council.

Behind the scenes: The first of two parts. . . . The episode was inspired by writer Carl Kleinschmitt's real-life bid for local office in Los Angeles. . . . Arte Johnson, one of the future stars of NBC's *Laugh-In*, has a featured role as Rob's high-powered media coordinator.

144) THE MAKING OF A COUNCILMAN **Airdate: 1/26/66**

Writers: Carl Kleinschmitt and Dale McRaven / Director: Jerry Paris

Supporting cast: Millie—Ann Morgan Guilbert, Lincoln Goodheart—Wally Cox, Doug Miller—George Tyne, Mrs. Birdwell—Margaret Muse, Martha Goodheart—Lia Waggner, 1st Lady— Kay Stewart, 2nd Lady—Holly Harris, 3rd Lady—Marilyn Hare, Herb—Arthur Adams, Samantha—Lorna Thayer, Duke—Remo Pisani, Booth Mitchell—James Henaghan Jr., Election Night Announcer—Bert Remsen (uncredited voice-over)

Filmed on December 7, 1965.

Rob has second thoughts about his bid for a city-council seat after he meets his more qualified opponent.

Behind the scenes: Rob's well-versed competitor is portrayed by Wally Cox, who played the title role in the early-fifties TV classic *Mr. Peepers*.

145) THE CURSE OF THE PETRIE PEOPLE **Airdate: 2/2/66**

Writers: Dale McRaven and Carl Kleinschmitt / Director: Jerry Paris

Supporting cast: Sam Petrie—Tom Tully, Millie—Ann Morgan Guilbert, Clara Petrie—Isabel Randolph, Mr. Mark, the Jeweler—Leon Belasco

Filmed on December 14, 1965.

Laura threatens to end a generations-old Petrie family tradition when she accidentally crushes a ghastly heirloom brooch in the garbage disposal.

Behind the scenes: Carl Reiner returns to his post as the show's producer with this episode.

146) THE BOTTOM OF MEL COOLEY'S HEART Airdate: 2/9/66

Writer: John Whedon / Director: Jerry Paris

Supporting cast: Mel—Richard Deacon, Alan Brady—Carl Reiner

Filmed on December 21, 1965.

Mel loses his job after Rob convinces him to stand up to Alan Brady's bullying.

147) REMEMBER THE ALIMONY Airdate: 2/16/66

Writers: Dale McRaven and Carl Kleinschmitt / Director: Jerry Paris

Supporting cast: Sol Pomerantz—Allan Melvin, Bernie—Lee Krieger, Gonzales— Don Diamond, Juan—Bernie Kopell, Maxine—Shelah Hackett, Mariachio— Jose Nieto, Mariachio—Guillermo DeAnda

Filmed on January 4, 1966. Songs: "Novillero" (M. T. Lara); "Alia en el Rancho Grande" (Ramos, Del Moral)

Rob and Laura recall a hectic trip to Mexico that almost spelled the end of their marriage.

148) DEAR SALLY ROGERS Airdate: 2/23/66

Writer: Ronald Axe / Director: Richard Erdman

Supporting cast: Mel—Richard Deacon, Stevie Parsons—Dick Schaal, Herman Glimscher—Bill Idelson, Announcer—Bert Remsen (uncredited voice-over)

Filmed on January 11, 1966. Song: "Swanee River" (Foster, arranged by Hagen)

Sally's televised plea for a husband on a late-night talk show yields unexpected results—including a letter from a suitor who could be Mr. Right.

Behind the scenes: A sequel to the third-season episode "The Pen Is Mightier Than the Mouth," in which Dick Patterson essayed the role of talk-show host Stevie Parsons. Interestingly, the character of Stevie Parsons in his earlier appearance seemed to be modeled after then-reigning talk-show champ Jack Paar; however, as played by Dick Schaal in this installment, the talk-show host appears to be patterned after Johnny Carson, who had by then risen to prominence as the host of NBC's *Tonight Show*.

149) BUDDY SORRELL, MAN AND BOY — Airdate: 3/2/66

Writers: Ben Joelson and Art Baer / Director: Richard Erdman

Supporting cast: Mel—Richard Deacon, Dorothy—Pippa Scott, Leon—Ed Peck, David Feldman—Sheldon Golomb, Cantor—Arthur Ross-Jones, Mrs. Sorrell—Maria Sokolov

Filmed on January 18, 1966. Song: "Sheyibone Beis Hamikdosh" (Schorr, arranged by A. Ellenstein, English lyrics: S. L. Lefkowitch)

Buddy's odd behavior has Rob and Sally puzzled until they discover he's been secretly preparing for his belated bar mitzvah.

150) LONG NIGHT'S JOURNEY INTO DAY — Airdate: 5/11/66

Writers: Jerry Belson and Garry Marshall / Director: Jerry Paris

Supporting cast: Jerry—Jerry Paris, Millie—Ann Morgan Guilbert, Artie, the Delivery Boy—Ogden Talbot, Herschel, the Mynah Bird—Carl Reiner (uncredited voice-over)

Filmed on January 25, 1966.

Laura and Millie spend a terrifying night with only a mynah bird to keep them company after Rob and Jerry go off on a weekend fishing trip.

Behind the scenes: Though Millie stands shoulder to shoulder with neighbor Laura throughout most of this episode, actress Ann Guilbert remembers that her character hardly figured at all in the script's earliest draft, which was apparently conceived as a solo piece for Mary Tyler Moore. "Originally the script had Mary talking to this bird," says Guilbert. But, notes the actress, it was the star herself who scotched that plan. "Mary said, 'I can't just do that. That doesn't make any sense.' So they brought me in to be the bird. But it was fun for me, because I really had something to do in that one." Not surprisingly, this episode remains one of Guilbert's personal favorites.

151) TALK TO THE SNAIL — Airdate: 3/23/66

Writers: Jerry Belson and Garry Marshall / Director: Jerry Paris

Supporting cast: Mel—Richard Deacon, Alan Brady—Carl Reiner, Claude Wilbur—Paul Winchell, Doug Bedlork—Henry Gibson

Filmed on February 1, 1966.

Fearing that network budget cuts might cost him his job, Rob interviews for a position as staff writer for a talking snail puppet.

Behind the scenes: As Sally's forlorn date, Douglas Bedlork, Henry Gibson recites "Keep a-Goin'," the poem that would be his trademark on NBC's *Laugh-In* and would eventually provide the basis for the actor's showcase song in director Robert Altman's 1975 feature film *Nashville*. . . . Jellybean the Snail is brought to life by real-life ventriloquist Paul Winchell.

152) A DAY IN THE LIFE OF ALAN BRADY — Airdate: 4/6/66

Writer: Joseph Bonaduce / Director: Jerry Paris

Supporting cast: Mel—Richard Deacon, Millie—Ann Morgan Guilbert, Jerry—Jerry Paris, Hi—Lou Wills, Girl—Kim Ford, Cameraman—John Chulay, Blanche—Joyce Jameson, Alan Brady—Carl Reiner

Filmed on February 8, 1966. Song: "Some of These Days" (Brooks)

Pandemonium follows Alan Brady when he arrives at Millie and Jerry's anniversary party with a documentary film crew in tow.

Behind the scenes: The show's assistant director, John C. Chulay, has a cameo as the director of Alan Brady's documentary crew.

153) OBNOXIOUS, OFFENSIVE, EGOMANIAC, ETC. — Airdate: 4/13/66

Writers: Carl Kleinschmitt and Dale McRaven / Director: Jerry Paris

Supporting cast: Mel—Richard Deacon, Mac—Forrest Lewis, Alan Brady—Carl Reiner

Filmed on February 22, 1966. Song: "How Dry I Am" (traditional)

Rob, Buddy, and Sally try to retrieve a script that contains less-than-flattering descriptions of their arrogant boss before he has a chance to see it.

Behind the scenes: Late in the episode, Mel establishes that Alan Brady's wife's name is Margaret, despite the fact that her off-screen character had been identified as Barbara in one of the show's earliest episodes.

154) THE MAN FROM MY UNCLE — Airdate: 4/20/66

Writers: Garry Marshall and Jerry Belson / Director: Jerry Paris

Supporting cast: Harry Bond—Godfrey Cambridge, Wendall P. Gerard—Steve Geray, Mr. Phillips—Biff Elliott

Filmed on March 1, 1966.

A dull weekend in the Petrie home is enlivened by the arrival of a deadpan secret agent who wants to conduct a stakeout from Ritchie's bedroom.

155) YOU OUGHT TO BE IN PICTURES — Airdate: 4/27/66

Writer: Jack Winter / Director: Jerry Paris

Supporting cast: Leslie Merkle—Michael Constantine, Lucianna Mazetta—Jayne Massey, Headwaiter—Frank Adamo

Filmed on March 8, 1966.

When Rob is cast opposite a voluptuous Italian starlet in an underground film, Laura keeps a close eye on their chemistry.

Behind the scenes: Writer Jack Winter won a Writers Guild of America Award for this script. . . . The episode's fictional Italian actress, Lucianna Mazetta, was named after Rose Marie, who was born Rose Marie Mazetta.

156) LOVE THY OTHER NEIGHBOR — Airdate: 5/4/66

Writers: Dale McRaven and Carl Kleinschmitt / Director: Jerry Paris

Supporting cast: Jerry—Jerry Paris, Millie—Ann Morgan Guilbert, Mary Jane Staggs—Sue Taylor, Fred Staggs—Joby Baker, Actor—Carl Reiner (uncredited voice-over)

Filmed on March 15, 1966.

Jerry and Millie grow jealous when Rob and Laura begin spending much of their spare time with a new couple on the block.

157) THE LAST CHAPTER Airdate: 6/1/66

Writers: Carl Reiner, Bill Persky, and Sam Denoff / Directors: Jerry Paris and John Rich

Supporting cast: Mel—Richard Deacon, Jerry—Jerry Paris, Millie—Ann Morgan Guilbert, Chaplain—Dabbs Greer, Vendor—Herbie Faye, Delivery Boy— Frank Adamo, Cabbie—Tiny Brauer, Mr. Peters—Greg Morris, Mrs. Peters—Mimi Dillard, Alan Brady—Carl Reiner

Filmed on March 15, 1966.

Laura excitedly reads the completed manuscript of Rob's book, an autobiography that affords a comical look at the life and times of a TV comedy writer and his loving wife.

Behind the scenes: Broadcast out of order as the series' final episode, "The Last Chapter" was largely comprised of choice clips from three classic *Dick Van Dyke Show* episodes: "The Attempted Marriage," "Where Did I Come From?" and "That's My Boy??," bookended by new footage that was shot on March 15, a few minutes after the cast completed filming the show's 156th episode, "Love Thy Other Neighbor." In the episode's final scene, Alan Brady announces that he's retained Leonard Bershad to executive produce the series he plans to film from Rob's memoir—a teasing reference to *The Dick Van Dyke Show*'s real-life executive producer, Sheldon Leonard, who was born Sheldon Leonard Bershad.

158) THE GUNSLINGER Airdate: 5/25/66

Writers: Bill Persky and Sam Denoff / Director: Jerry Paris

Supporting cast: Mel—Richard Deacon, Jerry—Jerry Paris, Millie—Ann Morgan Guilbert, Gun Drummer—Allan Melvin, Big Bad Brady—Carl Reiner

Filmed on March 22, 1966. Songs: "I Don't Care" (Sutton, Lennox); "Every Little Movement" (Hoschna, Harbach); "Oh, Susannah" (Foster)

Episode 158, "The Gunslinger"

Under Jerry's anesthetic, Rob dreams he's a sheriff in the Old West—the only man who can save the town from the threat of Big Bad Brady.

Behind the scenes: The last episode of *The Dick Van Dyke Show* ever filmed, "The Gunslinger" features unbilled cameos from most of the show's writing staff, including Garry Marshall and Jerry Belson—who are featured prominently in the show's barroom sequence—and Bill Persky and Sam Denoff, who are instantly recognizable as the two cowpokes who glance disapprovingly at Sheriff Rob's stoic entrance, where the hapless lawman dismounts his horse, only to discover he's left his boot in the stirrup. That particular scene also marked the only occasion where the show's crew moved outside for an exterior shot. It was filmed on standing Western sets at the CBS lot in Studio City, on the same street that provided the backdrop for countless episodes of *Gunsmoke* and other horse operas of the era. By coincidence, that same lot would later serve as home to Mary Tyler Moore's MTM Enterprises throughout most of the seventies and eighties. The remainder of the episode was filmed on soundstages at Desilu Cahuenga, where the cast would later gather for their well-earned closing night celebration.

SPRING 2004 THE DICK VAN DYKE SHOW REUNION SPECIAL

"*THE DICK VAN DYKE SHOW* REVISITED"

The show's official reunion special was filmed at CBS Studio Center in Studio City, California.

COMPLETE CREDITS

Written by	Carl Reiner
Directed by	Ken Whittingham
Executive Producer	Carl Reiner
Produced by	Sal Maniaci, Michael Petok
Creative Consultants	Bill Persky, Sam Denoff
Executive Consultants	George Shapiro, Howard West
Associate Producers	Marshall Boone, Jay O'Connell
Talent Producer	Barry M. Greenberg
Original Music	Paul Buckley
Cinematography	Victor Nelli Jr.
Film Editor	Michael Karlich
Clip Sequences Produced by	Paul Brownstein
Set Decoration	Claudette Didul
Set Dresser	Brock Helfer
Art Department Coordinator	Ari Jacobs
Assistant Property Master	Jim Landis
On-Set Dresser	Jeffry C. Voorhees
Makeup	Blake Shepard
Post-production Supervisor	Robert Boles
Sound Re-recording Mixer	John W. Cook II
On-line Editor	Bill Admans
Production Accountant	Peter Barnett
In Loving Memory	Morey Amsterdam, Richard Deacon, Jerry Paris, Sheldon Leonard, Danny Thomas

"*THE DICK VAN DYKE SHOW* REVISITED" **Airdate: 5/11/2004**

Writer: Carl Reiner / Director: Ken Whittingham

Cast: Host—Ray Romano, Rob Petrie—Dick Van Dyke, Laura Petrie—Mary Tyler Moore, Ritchie Petrie—Larry Mathews, Millie—Ann Guilbert, Sally Rogers—Rose Marie, Stacey Petrie—Jerry Van Dyke, Alan Brady—Carl Reiner, Herman Glimscher—Bill Idelson, Livia Petrie—Jeanne Allen, Frank—Sandy Kenyon, Terry—Terry Sims, Jerri—Lana Whittingham

Filmed on March 11 and 12, 2004.

Songs: "Ballet Etude" (Buckley); "Rob's Soft Shoe" (Buckley); "You, Wonderful You" (Warren, Brooks, Chaplin); "Carolina in the Morning" (Kahn, Donaldson); "Cotton Fields" (Ledbetter); Mountain Greenery (Rodgers, Hart); "Bill Bailey" (traditional, arrangement by Hagen); "Anthem to Alan Brady" (Persky, Denoff); "Dick and Mary Waltz" (Buckley)

Rob receives an unexpected call from his old boss, Alan Brady, who wants Rob and Sally to compose a flattering eulogy for him—while he's still alive.

Behind the scenes: When he finally saw the newly reconstructed set of the Petrie living room, which was painstakingly recreated from color photographs of the original, Carl Reiner admits that he and his cast were taken aback. "I let out a little gulp," he recalls. "And, of course, we all teared up a little bit." . . . A new addition to the Petrie family tree is introduced when Rob and Laura's granddaughter, Livia, performs a short pas de deux with Laura early in the show. The youngest Petrie was named after one of Carl Reiner's own grandchildren. . . . The animated dance sequence that Rob shows off on his computer was the work of Dick Van Dyke, who'd taken up computer animation as a late-life hobby. . . . Reiner wrote the part of Alan Brady's butler, Frank, to provide a cameo role for frequent *Van Dyke Show* bit player Frank Adamo. As it turned out, Sandy Kenyon wound up playing the part after Adamo begged off, citing an unusual prior commitment: he was booked to perform a puppet show. "Frank comes from a family of puppeteers going way back," notes Reiner. . . . The special included extended clips from five *Van Dyke Show* classics: "Coast to Coast Big Mouth," "Don't Trip Over That Mountain," "That's My Boy??," "October Eve," and "The Ghost of A. Chantz." . . . Laura's piano player was portrayed by Mary Tyler Moore's longtime assistant, Terry Sims. . . . Although Rob, Laura, and Sally had been largely absent from prime time since 1966, Alan Brady had already staged a pair of high-profile comebacks by the time this special aired in 2004. Reiner first revived the egomaniacal showman for a 1995 guest appearance on NBC's *Mad About You*. Eight years later, the veteran actor reprised his favorite character on *The Alan Brady Show*, an animated half-hour special that debuted on the TV Land network in August 2003, with Reiner voicing the title role.

THE DICK VAN DYKE SHOW THEME SONG

MUSIC BY EARLE HAGEN, LYRICS BY MOREY AMSTERDAM

So you think that you've got trouble?
Well, trouble's a bubble,
So tell old Mister Trouble to "Get lost!"

Why not hold your head up high and
Stop cryin', start tryin',
And don't forget to keep your fingers crossed.

When you find the joy of livin'
Is lovin' and givin'
You'll be there when the winning dice are tossed.

A smile is just a frown that's turned upside down,
So smile and that frown will defrost.
And don't forget to keep your fingers crossed!

NOTES

The reader may assume that any direct quote in this book that's not otherwise cited was drawn from an interview conducted by the author. Sources for previously published quotes—including quotes drawn from public seminars and panel discussions involving the show's principals—are identified below.

The author welcomes corrections or comments, which may be sent via the e-mail link on the book's official website: www.dickvandykeshowbook.com.

CHAPTER 1: ONE MAN'S REALITY

1. "I was what we called . . ." Carl Reiner. 1959 MGM studio biography.
2. "I was never comfortable . . ." Carl Reiner. "Let's Put Another Laugh Here." *Travel and Leisure*, March 1974.
3. "I fell right into the work . . ." Ibid.
4 "He used to call that . . ." Ibid.
5. "I took her to dinner . . ." Sidney Skolsky. "Hollywood Is My Beat." Syndicated newspaper column, November 28, 1959.
6. "I created my own theater . . ." Carl Reiner. "Let's Put Another Laugh Here." *Travel and Leisure*. March 1974.
7. "Even though I acted . . ." Carl Reiner interview: "Dialogue with Carl Reiner." *American Film*, December 1981.
8. "David Kokolovitz is a fictitious character . . ." Carl Reiner. From the author's introduction to *Enter Laughing*. New York: Simon & Schuster, 1958.
9. "I intended to record . . ." Patterson Greene. "Comical Versatility." *Los Angeles Herald Examiner*, March 29, 1964.
10. ". . . decided it was time . . ." Ibid.
11. ". . . as an actor and a writer and a husband . . ." Ibid.

CHAPTER 2: SIFTING THROUGH SAND

1. "My wife, in her infinite wisdom . . ." Carl Reiner, quoted at a symposium on *The Dick Van Dyke Show* convened by the Academy of Television Arts and Sciences at the Directors Guild of America, November 1986.
2. "Sally was a combination . . ." Ibid.
3. "It was an easy way to make a good living . . ." Dan Jenkins. "He Puts Words in His Own Mouth." *TV Guide*, May 14, 1960.

CHAPTER 3: HEAD OF THE FAMILY

1. "Carl Reiner has written eight of the first thirteen . . ." Burt Boyar. News item. *TV Guide*, September 20, 1958.
2. "This was the first situation comedy where . . ." Carl Reiner, quoted at a panel seminar convened by New York's Museum of Broadcasting—now the Paley Center for Media—at the Los Angeles County Museum of Art, March 12, 1988.

CHAPTER 4: A BASKET FULL OF SCRIPTS

1. "I thought that basketful of scripts . . ." Sheldon Leonard, quoted at a panel discussion on *The Dick Van Dyke Show* convened by the Academy of Television Arts and Sciences at the Directors Guild of America, November 1986.
2. "How do you tell an actor . . ." Jerry D. Lewis. "Carl Reiner: Laughs for Stage, Screen and Dick Van Dyke." *TV Guide*, January 4, 1964.
3. "He showed me the expensive shoes . . ." Joe Hyams. "Just a Hyphenated Cut-up." *New York Herald Tribune*, March 25, 1962.
4. "Where are you going as an actor?" Ibid.
5. "While I was sitting there . . ." Ibid.
6. "I never saw anybody take that kind of blow . . ." Jerry D. Lewis. "Carl Reiner: Laughs for Stage, Screen and Dick Van Dyke." *TV Guide*, January 4, 1964.
7. "I'll always be grateful to Sheldon . . ." Carl Reiner, quoted at a symposium on *The Dick Van Dyke Show* convened by the Academy of Television Arts and Sciences at the Directors Guild of America, November 1986.

CHAPTER 5: FALL GUY

1. "I've reworked the scripts to fit . . ." Dan Jenkins. "He Puts Words in His Own Mouth." *TV Guide*, May 14, 1960.
2. "He did a bit that fractured me . . ." Uncredited. "What's a Dick Van Dyke?" *TV Guide*, December 9, 1961.
3. "I did a monologue and sketches . . ." Uncredited. "Fall Guy." *TV Guide*, May 29, 1965.
4. "In which . . . I fell a lot, too . . ." Ibid.
5. "He had a natural stage presence . . ." Uncredited. "What's a Dick Van Dyke?" *TV Guide*, December 9, 1961.
6. "They bought us the ring . . ." Uncredited. "*Redbook* Readers Talk with Dick Van Dyke." *Redbook Magazine*, November 1966.
7. "I had finally achieved what I figured was my ultimate success . . ." Ibid.
8. "Byron Paul brought me to New York . . ." Ibid.

CHAPTER 7: THE GIRL WITH THREE NAMES

1. "We knew she would be too strong for Dick . . ." Carl Reiner, quoted at a symposium on *The Dick Van Dyke Show* convened by the Academy of Television Arts and Sciences at the Directors Guild of America, November 1986.
2. "I gave up college to learn to become a star . . ." "Who Is That Cutie Playing His Wife?" *TV Guide*, June 2, 1962.
3. "I was getting scale . . ." Leslie Raddatz. "They've Got No Kick Coming." *TV Guide*, March 27, 1965.
4. "Other shows seemed to want to use the girl who played Sam . . ." Ibid.
5. "She had the wrong nose . . ." Danny Thomas, quoted by Carl Reiner in a September 26, 1992, interview with the author.
6. "Honey . . . people just won't be able to believe . . ." Uncredited. "Who Is That Cutie Playing His Wife?" *TV Guide*, June 2, 1962.
7. "I'll have it fixed . . ." Ibid.
8. "If I were a dirty old man . . ." Jane Mosely. "Carl Reiner Does Just Everything," *Hollywood Citizen-News*, October 16, 1967.

CHAPTER 8: NERVOUS WRECKS

1. "I woke up the next morning and knew I was in love . . ." Richard Gehman. "Mary Tyler Moore Is Laura Petrie—or Is She ?" *TV Guide*, May 23, 1964.

CHAPTER 10: SOFT SOAP

1. "But then I noticed that he made a little 'okay' sign . . ." Carl Reiner, quoted at a symposium on *The Dick Van Dyke Show* convened by the Academy of Television Arts and Sciences at the Directors Guild of America, November 1986.
2. "After six or eight months . . ." Hedda Hopper. "Hedda Hopper's Hollywood." Syndicated newspaper column, February 10, 1962.
3. "With TV . . . there's a new script each week . . ." Ibid.

CHAPTER 13: COURTSHIP

1. "Producers all over town . . ." Uncredited. "Who Is That Cutie Playing His Wife?" *TV Guide*, June 2, 1962.
2. "With Dick and Rose Marie and Morey Amsterdam . . ." Ibid.

CHAPTER 14: CAPRI PANTS

1. ". . . highly strung worrier . . ." Uncredited. "What's a Dick Van Dyke?" *TV Guide*, December 9, 1961.
2. "When [Rob] was about sixteen . . ." Carl Reiner, quoted in "Playboy Chat: Carl Reiner—A Nice Talk About Rob's Problems with His Dad" (Sidebar to "A Candid Conversation with Rob Reiner"), *Playboy*, July 1985.

CHAPTER 15: WEDNESDAY NIGHTS

1. "How d'ya like that . . ." Cecil Smith. "Van Dyke: Oz Wasn't Like This." *Los Angeles Times TV Times Magazine*, December 10, 1961.
2. "He apparently didn't mind . . ." Uncredited. "So This Is Who Ann Morgan Guilbert Is." *TV Guide*, December 4, 1965.
3. "Before I started it . . ." Hedda Hopper. "Hedda Hopper's Hollywood." Syndicated newspaper column, April 15, 1965.

4. "Joan's husband forbids her . . ." Program listing for December 3, 1952, episode *I Married Joan*. *TV Guide* (New England edition), November 30, 1952.

CHAPTER 17: ON THE BANKS OF THE OHIO

1. "I went back East . . ." Sheldon Leonard, quoted at a symposium on *The Dick Van Dyke Show* convened by the Academy of Television Arts and Sciences at the Directors Guild of America, November 1986.
2. "One of the few freshman shows to be renewed . . ." Uncredited. "Van Dyke Show Renewed." *Daily Variety*, March 21, 1962.
3. "Procter & Gamble . . . will have Lorillard . . ." Ibid.

CHAPTER 18: NEVER NAME A DUCK

1. "I've found movies the hardest . . ." Hedda Hopper. "Hedda Hopper's Hollywood." Syndicated newspaper column, February 10, 1962.
2. "I seemed so stiff . . ." Louella O. Parsons. "A Rubber Faced Comic." Syndicated newspaper column, October 14, 1962.

CHAPTER 21: NUTS

1. "I was 100 percent wrong . . ." Jerry D. Lewis. "Carl Reiner: Laughs for Stage, Screen and Dick Van Dyke." *TV Guide*, January 4, 1964.
2. "I called him as soon as the show went off . . ." Bob Thomas. "Laurel and Hardy Special to Be Emceed by Van Dyke." Associated Press wire story, August 16, 1965.
3. "25 minutes of notes . . ." Ibid.
4. "I did everything I could to get a flat brim . . ." Ibid.

CHAPTER 24: PLAYING TO AN EMPTY HOUSE

1. "Carl encouraged us to take incidents . . ." Garry Marshall with Lori Marshall. *Wake Me When It's Funny: How to Break into Show Business and Stay There*. Paperback edition, pg. 71. New York: Newmarket Press, 1997.
2. "We would relate the most horrifying . . ." Ibid.
3. "Our pitching sessions . . ." Ibid.

CHAPTER 25: PICTURING MARY NAKED

1. "Every other Friday night I tape two shows . . ." Hank Grant. "On the Air with Hank Grant." *Hollywood Reporter*, April 9, 1964.
2. "Sometimes when I'm home at night . . ." Leslie Raddatz. "They've Got No Kick Coming." *TV Guide*, March 27, 1965.

CHAPTER 26: TEMPEST IN A BATHTUB

1. "I wanted the audience to think of Milton Berle . . ." Carl Reiner, quoted at a symposium on *The Dick Van Dyke Show* convened by the Academy of Television Arts and Sciences at the Directors Guild of America, November 1986.
2. "I remember in writing it . . ." Carl Reiner, quoted at a panel seminar convened by New York's Museum of Broadcasting—now the Paley Center for Media—at the Los Angeles County Museum of Art, March 12, 1988.

CHAPTER 28: CURTAIN CALLS

1. "Carl says there is no possibility . . ." Cecil Smith. "The TV Scene." *Los Angeles Times*, December 28, 1964.
2. "They're breaking up that gang . . ." Dave Kaufman. "On All Channels—Analyzing the Van Dyke Click." *Daily Variety*, December 28, 1965.

CHAPTER 29: SHENANIGANS

1. ". . . a charming town with one theater . . ." Hedda Hopper. "Hedda Hopper's Hollywood. Syndicated newspaper c1olumn, December 11, 1965.

EPILOGUE

1. "At one point . . . some of us did think . . ." Uncredited. "The Van Dyke Signature Is Unmistakable." *Los Angeles Times TV Week*, April 1, 1968.
2. "It was . . . like going to a lovely party . . ." Morey Amsterdam, quoted at a symposium on *The Dick Van Dyke Show* convened by the Academy of Television Arts and Sciences at the Directors Guild of America, November 1986.

A COMPLETE VIEWER'S GUIDE TO *THE DICK VAN DYKE SHOW*

1. "Selma Diamond is the one . . ." Carl Reiner interview. "Dialogue with Carl Reiner," *American Film*, December 1981.
2. "When we'd get together with new writers . . ." Carl Reiner, quoted at a panel seminar convened by New York's Museum of Broadcasting—now the Paley Center for Media—at the Los Angeles County Museum of Art, March 12, 1988.

SELECTED BIBLIOGRAPHY

Andrews, Bart. *The "I Love Lucy" Book*. Garden City, NY: Dolphin/Doubleday, 1985.

Bennett, Mark. *TV Sets: Fantasy Blueprints of Classic TV Homes*. New York: TV Books, Inc., 1996.

Brooks, Tim. *The Complete Directory to Prime Time TV Stars: 1946–Present*. New York: Ballantine Books, 1987.

Brooks, Tim, and Earle Marsh. *The Complete Directory to Prime Time TV Network Shows: 1946–Present*. 5th ed. New York: Ballantine Books, 1992.

Brown, Les. *Les Brown's Encyclopedia of Television*. 3rd ed. Detroit: Visible Ink Press, 1992.

Dick Van Dyke: In Rare Form, DVD. Orland Park, IL: MPI Home Video, 2007.

Dick Van Dyke Show, The: The Complete Series, DVD. Chatsworth, CA: Image Entertainment, 2005.

Eisner, Joel, and David Krinsky. *Television Comedy Series: An Episode Guide to 153 TV Sitcoms in Syndication*. Jefferson, NC: McFarland & Company, 1984.

Halliwell, Leslie, with Philip Purser. *Halliwell's Television Companion*. 2nd ed. London: Granada Books, 1982.

Inman, David. *The TV Encyclopedia*. New York: Perigee Books, 1991.

Katz, Ephraim. *The Film Encyclopedia*. New York: Perigee Books, 1979.

Marshall, Garry, with Lori Marshall. *Wake Me When It's Funny: How to Break into Show Business and Stay There*. Paperback ed. New York: Newmarket Press, 1997.

McNeil, Alex. *Total Television: A Comprehensive Guide to Programming from 1948 to the Present*. 3rd ed. New York: Penguin Books, 1991.

Mitz, Rick. *The Great TV Sitcom Book*. Expanded ed. New York: Perigee Books, 1983.

Sanders, Coyne Steven, and Tom Gilbert. *Desilu: The Story of Lucille Ball and Desi Arnaz*. New York: William Morrow, 1993.

Salerni, Paul. *The Life and Love of Joe Coogan: A One-Act Opera in Seven Scenes.* Libretto by Kate Light. King of Prussia, PA: Theodore Presser Company, 2011.

Terrace, Vincent. *Encyclopedia of Television Series, Pilots, and Specials.* New York: Zoetrope, 1985.

Waldron, Vince. *Classic Sitcoms: A Celebration of the Best in Prime-Time Comedy.* 2nd revised expanded ed. Los Angeles: Silman-James Press, 1998.

Weissman, Ginny, and Coyne Steven Sanders. *The Dick Van Dyke Show: Anatomy of a Classic.* New York: St. Martin's Press, 1983.

INDEX

ABOUT THE AUTHOR

Vince Waldron is an Emmy-winning writer, and author of *Classic Sitcoms: A Celebration of the Best in Prime-Time Comedy*, which has been hailed as the definitive study of the genre. With pop legend Ronnie Spector, he coauthored *Be My Baby: Miniskirts, Mascara, and Madness, or My Life as a Fabulous Ronette*, which *Blitz* magazine called "one of the three greatest rock' n' roll memoirs." An alumnus of Chicago's Second City and Paul Sills' Story Theatre, Vince is the creator and director of *Totally Looped*, the hit stage show in which comedians provide new dialogue to old movie clips. He lives in Los Angeles.

Photo by: Alan Shaffer